10/94

Albuquerque Academy
Library
6400 Wyoming Blvd. N.E.
Albuquerque, N.M. 87109

ALSO BY JOHN FEINSTEIN

Hard Courts

Forever's Team

A Season Inside

A Season on the Brink

Running Mates
(A MYSTERY)

PLAY BALL

P·L·A·Y
B·A·L·L

THE LIFE AND TROUBLED TIMES OF MAJOR LEAGUE BASEBALL

John Feinstein

Villard Books
New York
1993

Copyright © 1993 by John Feinstein

All rights reserved under International and Pan-American
Copyright Conventions. Published in the United States by
Villard Books, a division of Random House, Inc., New York,
and simultaneously in Canada by Random House of Canada
Limited, Toronto.

Villard Books is a registered trademark of Random House, Inc.

Library of Congress Cataloging-in-Publication Data

Feinstein, John.
    Play ball: the life and hard times of major league
baseball/John Feinstein.
        p. cm.
    ISBN 0-679-41618-8
    1. Baseball—United States. 2. Major League Baseball
(Organization)   I. Title.
GV863.A1F45 1993
796.357′64′0973—dc20   92-53820

        9 8 7 6 5 4 3 2

                    First Edition

            Book design by Richard Oriolo

796.35764
FEI

This is for Keith and Barbie Drum . . .
Who have always been there—even when
Keith didn't want to be.

ACKNOWLEDGMENTS

Before I started this book, my wife made one request of me: "Try to make your acknowledgments less than an entire night's reading."

I am going to try. To begin at the beginning, there are literally hundreds of people in baseball who need to be thanked. Owners, general managers, managers, and players who were generous with their time. Public relations people who did their best to make it possible for me to get my research done. Reporters who welcomed an outsider and went out of their way to be helpful during the course of a long season.

Some must be singled out: It would be impossible to live through a book like this one without a remarkably patient travel agent. I have one: Lynda Hart. Rick Vaughn of the Orioles and Phyllis Merhige of the American League were friends and supporters almost from day one and I could not have survived my rather rough beginnings without them. Other public relations people who went out of their way to help were Rich Levin and Jim Small of the commissioner's office, Bob DiBiaso in Cleveland, Doug Abel in Chicago, Greg Shea in Detroit,

Tom Skibosh in Milwaukee, Bob Miller in Baltimore, Jeff Idelson in New York, Jim Schultz in Atlanta, Jay Alves in Oakland, Jon Braude in Cincinnati, Rich Griffin in Montreal, and Rick Cerrone and Jim Trdinich in Pittsburgh.

I am also thankful for help I received from Jeff Porter of the Braves and Phil Itzoe of the Orioles. But I owe a special debt of gratitude to Bill Acree of the Braves, one of those rare people who when asked if something can be done always says, "Why not?" My friendship with him is one of the major bonuses I take away from this experience.

Lots of reporters must be mentioned and the list will be far too short: Bill Zack, Mark Maske, Peter Schmuck, Ken Rosenthal, John Delcos, Tim Kurkijian, Mel Antonen, Rod Beaton, Larry Whiteside, Alan Solomon, Jerome Holtzman (my hero), Bob Verdi, Paul Hoynes, John Lowe, Tom Verducci, Kit Stier, Pedro Gomez, Frank Blackman, Joe Strauss, Barry Rozner, Rob Parker, Gordon Edes, Bill Plaschke, Terry Johnson, Steve Adamek, Marty Noble, Dan Castellano, Joe Sexton, Jack Curry, Jack Lang, Rick Hummel, Barry Bloom, and Larry Stone. Special thanks go to the Baltimore crowd, which had to put up with me more than the others. And thank you also to Brad Snyder, who was a huge help when I went through my crippled (torn Achilles) stage.

A number of broadcasters also went out of their way to be helpful: John Rooney and Jon Miller, both of whom were very generous with their time and advice right from the start; Joe Angel; Sean McDonough; Tom Hamilton; Bob Rathbun and Rick Rizzs (both of whom lived to tell about it); Fred White, Ted Robinson, and Marty Brennaman (all of whom opened key doors for me in their home cities); Michael Kay; Harry Caray I (a.k.a. Harry), Harry Caray II (a.k.a. Skip), and Harry Caray III (a.k.a. Chip); Thom Brennaman; Tim McCarver; Jim Kaat; Vin Scully; Bob Murphy, Ernie Harwell, and Gary Cohen; Andy Musser and Hank Greenwald. Everyone mentioned here gave me time and, in many cases, advice and guidance.

Special thanks to John Rawlings of *The Sporting News* whose occasional assignments and early support made my life a lot easier. Thanks also to Kelly Wolf for the hours she labored transcribing tapes.

Last and never least, my family and friends. I am lucky enough to have not one but two families—mine and Mary's—who are patient and supportive throughout what is often a trying process. The same is true of my friends. I thank them as a group since I am under orders not to list them all here.

A few must be separated out: My agent, Esther Newberg, makes me laugh when I need to and work when I have to; my editor, Peter Gethers, is an author's dream—someone who asks for nothing more than a book everyone involved can feel good about. The people who work with them—Amanda Beesley, Stephanie Long, Jackie Deval, and Mary Hahn Hendon, make all our lives much easier.

And then there are the usual suspects: Dave Kindred; Terry Hanson; Ken Denlinger; Steve and Lexie Barr; Tom Kenworthy; Tim Maloney; David Maraniss; Bob and Anne DeStefano; Bill Sulahian; Tom Mickle; Bill Brill; Doug Doughty; Jill Mixon; Mike Cragg; Warren Miller; Norbert Doyle (who should be secretary of the treasury); Mary Carillo; Sally Jenkins; Bud Collins; Larry King; Roy Firestone; John Hewig; Sandy (still Flailin') Genelius; Dick (Hoops) Weiss; Tony Kornheiser (who has two children); Juan Williams; Neil Amdur; Bill Brink; Mark Schramm; Tom Goldman and yes, even the Colonel—Bob Edwards; Pete Alfano; Lisa Dillman and Mike Penner; Larry Siddons; Ray Ratto; Luiz and Claire Simmons; and, of course, Jacquece Moss and little Jacquece.

I tried, I really did. This is as brief as I can be. If truth be told, I could write a book about all these people and what they mean to me. Fortunately for the world, I'll settle for saying thank you one more time.

—JOHN FEINSTEIN
Bethesda, Md.
December 1992

CONTENTS

INTRODUCTION

O n the night of October 18, 1992, a baseball fan named Francis T. Vincent, Jr., sat down in his Greenwich, Connecticut, home to watch Game Two of the World Series. He had missed Game One the previous evening because he had been at a wedding reception and, like a lot of fans, was curious to see whether the Toronto Blue Jays could bounce back after having lost the opener to the Atlanta Braves.

Vincent watched for four innings. Then he turned off his TV and went to bed. "I tried to watch the game and just see the players and what they were doing," he said. "But I couldn't. Everything seemed to remind me of the owners. After a while, I just couldn't take it anymore."

In a sense, Fay Vincent spoke for all baseball fans. The fact that he had been the game's commissioner for three years before being hounded out of office in September explains the animosity he felt toward his former employers. But even for someone who has never run baseball or, for that matter, worked in or known anyone connected to the game, it has become increasingly difficult to turn on the television or go to the ballpark and enjoy the simple pleasure of the national pastime.

Like Vincent, fans do not just see Cal Ripken or Kirby Puckett; they see men making six million dollars a year. You pay for your ticket—at higher and higher prices—and realize what you are doing is handing your money over to a group of men who, for the most part, could not care less about anyone involved in the sport except themselves. You want to get excited about your team's prospects for 1993, but with all the free-agent signings and switches, you don't even know who the hell is *on* your team, Or whether your team will even be playing at all.

"Owning a baseball team makes you a part of the most exclusive club in the country," says Don Fehr, who has run the Major League Player's Association for almost ten years. "It's more exclusive than the U.S. Senate and it's like no other club of sports owners because baseball is exempt from antitrust laws. Because of that, these are people who honestly believe that the rules of the world do not apply to them. These are people who extort millions of dollars from cities to build them stadiums and then are voted Citizen of the Year. When someone *does* call them on something, they are shocked and angry."

Fay Vincent was fired because he called the owners on something. In no uncertain terms, he told them that they were fools if they went to war with the player's union again. Their chief negotiator, Richard Ravitch, the new $750,000-a-year kid on the block, told the owners not to listen to Vincent, that there was nothing wrong with war. He told them they could *win* a war. But, he added, Vincent had to be removed from the picture.

And so Vincent was fired. "Only once in history has one nation bombed another into submission," Vincent says. "And that was in 1945 when the weaponry was unique. The owners can't win this war, but they want to fight it anyway."

The owners, led by their newly appointed mouthpiece, Milwaukee Brewers owner Bud Selig, vehemently deny wanting anything but peace with the players. And yet, on December 7—a fitting date— they announced that they would reopen the union contract a year early. It should be noted that the last *seven* negotiations between these two groups have resulted in a work stoppage. In other words: war.

"Cheap billionaires fighting with whiny millionaires is how the public will see this," Vincent says. "It will be a disaster if it occurs." Fehr, who had hoped until the last minute that the owners would reconsider their hard-line position, agrees with Vincent. "If you take away the thrill and expectation of baseball games for an extended period of time—*again*—you will hurt the game greatly," he says. "Because I think at this point in time there are people who won't come back."

Fehr knows that has been said before. And he believes that, ultimately, baseball will survive. Baseball always survives. As Tony LaRussa, the manager of the Oakland Athletics, says, "The game is better than all of us."

No doubt it is. But these are ugly times if you love baseball. If you aren't reading about Marge Schott and her racist, bigoted comments, you're reading about a possible lockout. Or about franchise shifts. Or player shifts (during one three-day period in December no fewer than thirty-five free agents signed with new teams). Or the dire problems teams will face in 1994 when the TV golden egg becomes a lot less golden.

If you live in New York, you wonder what will happen when George Steinbrenner regains control of the Yankees on March 1. Will Buck Showalter, the bright young manager, still be around in July? If you live in Seattle, you wonder if you will ever see a contender. In San Francisco you wonder if there will ever be a new ballpark. In St. Petersburg you are almost convinced you won't live to see a major-league team arrive, no matter how many times you're told it will happen. In Baltimore, after going through a joyous eighty-nine-victory season in a gorgeous new ballpark, you wonder why owner Eli Jacobs refuses to spend a nickel to improve the team. The answer to that one is easy: Jacobs's other businesses are going bankrupt and he is loath to touch the $20-million profit he made with the Orioles. In all likelihood, he will be forced to sell the team.

And yet, amid all the predictions that baseball will kill itself off, you know better. Twenty-five years ago, following the 1968 Year of the Pitcher, when no one could score a run, the doomsayers said baseball was done for, that football had replaced it as the national pastime, that baseball would sink into gradual oblivion. Now, games take much too long, pitchers can't throw strikes, postseason games start so late that no baseball-crazed kid (the next generation of ticket buyers) can possibly stay up to watch, and owners refuse to police themselves, so the doomsayers are rampant again. This time, it is basketball that is replacing baseball and the impending oblivion will befall us quickly rather than gradually.

Oblivion won't happen, though, because as usual, LaRussa is right.

Is Barry Bonds's $43.75-million contract the ceiling that salaries inevitably must reach? Perhaps, perhaps not. But skyrocketing salaries are not the real problem in the game (the Boston Red Sox, New York Mets, and Lost Angeles Dodgers warmed the hearts of purists in 1992 by spending over $40 million apiece to win seventy-three, seventy-two, and sixty-three games respectively). The problem is the lack of a level playing field. Over the long haul, teams in Seattle and Cleveland and Milwaukee simply cannot compete with teams in New York, Los Angeles, Chicago, and Atlanta until and unless there is revenue sharing.

In 1991, according to an economic study commissioned by the owners, the twenty-six major-league teams showed a net profit of approximately $98 million. That was down from 1990 and *way* down from 1989, but it was still a substantial profit. If the teams had divided the money equally, each team would have walked away with a profit of just under $4 million. That is far more equitable and, in the end, makes the game far more competitive than having one team net $20 million while another loses $15 million.

"It is a simple fact that every team cannot make money every year," says Fehr, a forty-four-year-old midwesterner who once worked for George McGovern when he was young and idealistic. "But there is an assumption that clubs are troubled now because of labor relations. That is wrong. Clubs are troubled because their revenue-sharing methods are forty years out of date."

The sad thing about writing a book about baseball in the 1990s is that it is impossible to do so without getting into the financial and structural issues addressed above, issues that are far too complex to explain in a few pages and far too tedious to explain completely.

Baseball is a big, often brutal business. The days when players stayed with one team for their entire careers are as far gone as the days of the twenty-five-cent hot dog. But baseball is worth saving and it is worth caring about, even with its myriad problems.

When I started this project, I was warned by friends who cover the sport to be prepared to deal with a group of selfish, spoiled, arrogant athletes. I met some players who fit that description to a T. Barry Bonds, he of the aforementioned $43.75-million contract, told me he wouldn't talk to me unless he was paid for the interview. When I told him that reporters don't pay to talk to news sources, he said, "I'm not talking and if you use my name in the book, I'll sue you."

See you in court, Barry.

But most of the players and managers I came into contact with—about two hundred in all—were patient, reasonable, and generous with their time. A number of people with whom I spent a good deal of time ended up not fitting into the narrative. I apologize to them, but the problem posed by dealing with the scope of an entire season is that it is impossible to predict in March who will make the best stories when you sit down to write in October.

Three examples of this stand out in my mind:

Doug Melvin, the very bright assistant general manager of the Orioles, pointed out to me early in my travels how the upcoming expansion draft would affect baseball people during 1992. "You can't

even talk to other scouts about any of your own players," he said. "You never know what might get back to an expansion team, and none of us wants to lose a key player."

Melvin is forty, a rarity in baseball in that he was born and raised in Canada but loved baseball rather than hockey. He pitched briefly in the minor leagues, then worked his way up through the Yankee organization, starting as a batting practice pitcher. In 1985, when he asked George Steinbrenner for a raise so he could move his family closer to Yankee Stadium (he was making a 152-mile round-trip commute every day at the time), Steinbrenner told him to take what he had been offered or be out of the office by five o'clock that day.

"Well George, I guess I'll be out of here by five o'clock then," Melvin said.

He has been with the Orioles ever since and is one of the bright young minds in the game. Some day soon, he will be a general manager.

Then, there is Dave Righetti, a true class act. Once, he was the premier closer in the game. But last year, with the Giants, it all fell apart for Righetti. He ended up the season as the mop-up man on a bad team, wondering, at thirty-three, how much of a future he still had left in the sport. Righetti is a rare athlete: He never blames anyone else for his own failures. "I just haven't pitched very well," he said late in the season. "I've made some mistakes [like trying to become a starter again] and I've had some bad luck. But it all comes back to me in the end. I just hope I can turn it around next season."

I hope so, too.

And finally, there is Skeeter Barnes. For fifteen years, Skeeter went to spring training camps, hoping to make a major league roster. For fifteen years, he was sent down to the minors before his team went north. In 1992, Skeeter Barnes made a big league team at the end of spring training, going north with the Detroit Tigers.

When I asked Skeeter Barnes if he had lost sleep toward the end of spring training, wondering if he was going to finally make a major league team to start a season, he smiled and said: "I've been losing sleep now for sixteen years."

Doug Melvin, Dave Righetti, and Skeeter Barnes deserve more attention than this book gives them. So do people like Mark Leiter and Dan Plesac and Danny Tartabull and Tony Peña and Craig Biggio and Jay Bell and Terry Mulholland. And a host of others.

Jeff Innis, too. Innis is the very intelligent, funny middle-relief pitcher for the Mets who has managed to keep being a baseball player in perspective in an era when it is very easy to think a major league uniform makes you something special.

"I used to think that being a big league player was a really big deal," Innis said one morning with a smile on his face. "But when I look around at some of the guys who are big leaguers, I realize it really isn't that big a deal."

Of course, we all have dreamed of coming up with the bases loaded in the World Series. Only a very tiny percentage get to live that dream and be a member of the elite seven hundred (as of 1993). If it takes sixteen years or lasts only a few days, it *is* a big deal to reach the major leagues.

Will Clark, one of the best hitters in baseball, may have explained it best when he described one at-bat in his career. It was very early one morning during spring training as he talked about the 1989 playoffs, Game Five, his San Francisco Giants against the Chicago Cubs. The game was tied 1–1 in the bottom of the eighth; the Giants needed one more victory to reach the World Series. The bases were loaded for Clark as the Cubs brought in their relief ace, Mitch Williams.

"I can remember everything that happened during that at-bat," Clark said. "I knew they were going to bring Mitch in, so I went back to [hitting coach] Dusty Baker and said, 'What should I look for?' He said, 'Fastball in.' That's what I had been thinking, too. First pitch he threw was a fastball away. Good pitch. Strike one. Then he threw a slider and I fouled it off. Now I'm down oh-two and I just want to get a piece of the ball. He throws two more sliders, I foul them off. Then he comes in with a really good, high fastball and I just barely nicked it. I guessed he would try the same pitch because he just about had me out on the one before. He did, but this one was a little closer to the plate—fastball inside—I swung and hit it up the middle for the hit."

The hit that won the game and the pennant.

Clark smiled when he finished the retelling, as if he had just lived through the entire experience again. "When I got home that night, I thought about that at-bat and it hit me all of a sudden that for twenty years I had waited for that. It wasn't the World Series, but it was damn close. The point was, it was the other guy at his absolute best in a situation that really mattered and I still beat him.

"I just sat there for a minute and thought, 'Yeah, that was it, that's what all of this is about.' "

Whether it's Clark against Mitch Williams in 1989 or Francisco Cabrera against Stan Belinda in 1992, those are the moments when baseball is special. They happen not just in the glare of postseason but in the less powerful lighting of April and June and even September, when a pennant may not be on the line but the game still means something to those involved.

Because if baseball is Marge Schott and Richard Ravitch and Barry Bonds, it is also Nolan Ryan and Carlton Fisk and Cal Ripken and Kirby Puckett. And Dave Stewart and Dennis Eckersley and Mike

Bordick. And lots of other people who love being part of the game, guys who would play if the top salary were seven *thousand* dollars a year instead of seven million.

At its very best, baseball is Rich Donnelly, the third-base coach of the Pittsburgh Pirates. Last March, Donnelly found out that his seventeen-year-old daughter, Amy, had brain cancer. All season, as Amy went through chemotherapy and radiation treatments, Donnelly recounted how much he was learning from his daughter—about courage and about dealing with real adversity every single day.

But never once did Rich Donnelly say, "This puts it all in perspective," the cliché that rolls off everyone's tongue whenever tragedy strikes in sports. "I'm forty-six years old," he said. "If I haven't got it in perspective by now, it isn't likely that I ever will."

Amy Donnelly slowly got stronger as the summer progressed. By September she was bored, so she found a part-time job. She went to work answering phones at a cancer hotline, helping others with the disease deal with the traumas that come with it.

When the Pirates lost Game Seven of the National League playoffs to the Braves, on Cabrera's two-out, two-run single in the bottom of the ninth, Rich Donnelly was as devastated as anyone in the Pirate clubhouse. He sat for a long time after the game, doing little but staring at the ceiling. Finally, he straightened up and looked around him.

"That's almost as tough as it can get," he said softly. Then he paused and managed a weak smile. "Almost. But not quite."

If everyone in baseball understood winning and losing the way Rich Donnelly does, the game would be a lot different. And a lot better off. But, as Rich and Amy Donnelly can tell you, baseball, like life, has a lot of flaws. And like life, baseball has a lot going for it.

Still.

PROLOGUE:
OCTOBER 25, 1992 . . .
12:35 A.M.

Baseball has always been a waiting game.

Once, everyone waited for the day pitchers and catchers reported to spring training. They waited for Opening Day and the World Series, for Fourth of July doubleheaders and the Saturday *Game of the Week*. Waiting—*anticipating*—was half the fun.

These days, waiting isn't nearly as much fun. Now, everyone waits for television to give the command for the games to begin. Or for the commercials to end. They wait for nervous pitchers who step off the rubber ceaselessly while equally nervous hitters step out of the batter's box just to let the tension—or lack of tension—mount.

Everyone still waits for spring training and for Opening Day but now they wait until almost nine o'clock at night for the season's best games to begin. Kids almost never get to wait up to find out who wins those games. And when the season is over, everyone waits to find out which of their team's free agents won't be back the next year.

In the long history of baseball, it might be fair to say that no one had waited longer than Dave Winfield. For twenty seasons, he waited for the chance to be accepted as a star without an asterisk, for the chance, as he would put it later, "to finally get to celebrate after the very last game."

Beyond that, Winfield had waited eleven years to wipe out the memory of his first World Series, a 1-for-22 humiliation in 1981, when the Los Angeles Dodgers had beaten his New York Yankees in six games. It was not long after that World Series that Yankee owner George Steinbrenner, Winfield's longtime antagonist, labeled him "Mr. May."

On Saturday, October 24, 1992, a surprisingly warm, clear fall night, Winfield had waited almost four hours for this particular at-bat. It wasn't as if he had not had chances. In fact, he had already been up three times in the game with a teammate in scoring position. Each time, though, he had failed to get a hit. So, as he walked to the plate in the top of the eleventh inning with his Toronto Blue Jays tied 2–2 with the Atlanta Braves, Winfield carried not only the memory of that 1-for-22, but the burden of a 1992 World Series in which he had gone 4-for-21. Not humiliating, but not exactly brilliant either.

"I hadn't done much," he said later that night. "It was time."

Time to end the waiting, not only for himself but for a franchise that had done everything that could be done in baseball *except* win the World Series. That was why Toronto general manager Pat Gillick had signed Winfield the previous winter at the age of forty. He knew his team had the talent to win a world championship, but he wondered if they had the maturity. So he added 1991 World Series hero Jack Morris to his pitching staff and 1981 World Series washout Winfield to his lineup. Needless to say, the Morris acquisition was considered far more important.

But Morris had been the washout this time, failing to win in four postseason starts. Even so, the Blue Jays had built a 3–1 lead in the Series before Morris bombed out one more time in Game Five, bringing the two teams back to Atlanta–Fulton County Stadium for one final baseball weekend.

In spite of Winfield's failures at the plate that night, the Blue Jays had carried a 2–1 lead to within one out—one *strike* even—of the title. But Tom Henke, the Jays' bullpen closer, who had held every lead handed to him since July 24, couldn't hold this lead, and now it was the top of the eleventh inning, the score was tied, and two men were out. Devon White, Toronto's center fielder, stood on second base and Roberto Alomar, the All-Star second baseman, stood on first. Joe Carter had just popped to center field, leaving the two runners frozen. And so Dave Winfield stepped into the batter's box and waited for Charles Leibrandt to pitch to him.

•

Charles Louis Leibrandt, Jr., had World Series memories of his own. In 1985, as a member of the Kansas City Royals, he had pitched superbly as a starter in Games Two and Six and although he hadn't been the winning pitcher in either game, the Royals had come back to win Game Six and then become world champions the next night.

More vivid, though, both to Leibrandt and everyone in the ballpark, was 1991—another Game Six, another eleventh inning. With the Braves leading the World Series 3–2, Leibrandt, a starter all season, had come in to pitch to the Minnesota Twins in the eleventh. He faced one batter, Kirby Puckett, who hit Leibrandt's fourth pitch into the bleachers to win the game. Twenty-four hours later, the Twins won Game Seven 1–0 in ten innings. Puckett and Jack Morris, who pitched ten shutout innings that night, were the heroes. Leibrandt and Lonnie Smith, whose baserunning blunder cost the Braves what would have been the winning run, were the goats.

Leibrandt, as personable and patient as anyone who plays baseball, just couldn't deal with questions after the pitch to Puckett. "Not tonight, fellas," he announced softly to the media hordes who approached his locker.

"I probably should have talked about it then," he said many months later. "It might have been cathartic, but I just couldn't face up to it that night. As it was, it seemed like every day of spring training someone showed up and wanted to ask me about Kirby. I couldn't seem to escape it. Then, when the season started, I couldn't get anybody out and I began to second-guess myself. I started thinking, 'Is this still bothering me? Am I haunted by it?' It was only when I started to get people out that I put it behind me."

Now Leibrandt was faced with it again. The situation was different: The Braves were *behind* 3–2 in the Series and were playing at home. Leibrandt came into the game in the tenth and retired the Blue Jays. In the eleventh, with one out, he hit White with a pitch. Then Alomar singled.

That brought up Carter and, behind him, Winfield, both right-handed power hitters. Logic dictated that Atlanta manager Bobby Cox hobble to the mound on his surgical knees and wave in a right-hander to face them. But Cox wasn't moving from the dugout. Down the right-field line, in the Braves' bullpen, Jeff Reardon had been warming up. As Carter stepped to the plate, though, Reardon stood with his arms folded, knowing, just as everyone else did, that there wasn't a chance in hell Cox was going to bring him in.

Reardon has saved more baseball games than any relief pitcher in history. But, at thirty-seven, the days when he would stalk to the mound and blow hitters away were a fading memory. He was with the Braves only because they had been unable to swing a late-August deal for John Franco of the New York Mets. Desperate to strengthen a bullpen that had been their one weakness all season, the Braves acquired Reardon hours before the trading deadline on August 31, not because they were convinced he was the answer, but because he was the best they could find—a question mark with experience.

Reardon pitched well in September and in the National League Championship Series. But a high fastball to backup catcher Ed Sprague in the ninth inning of Game Two had turned a 4–3 Braves lead into a 5–4 Blue Jays victory. Two nights later, brought into a game-tied, bases-loaded, one-out situation in the bottom of the ninth, Reardon had let an 0-2 breaking pitch wander too close to the plate and Candy Maldonado had smacked it to deep center field to end that game, too.

That was the Reardon Cox saw from the dugout as Carter dug in, not the Reardon who had saved 357 games in his major league career. That Reardon would most surely have trotted in from the bullpen to face Carter and Winfield. Instead, like everyone else, he watched. And waited.

•

Leibrandt had not pitched since Game Six of the Braves' remarkable National League Championship Series against the Pittsburgh Pirates. He had hoped that Cox would go back to a four-man rotation for the World Series and name him the starter for Game Four, but after Tom Glavine pitched superbly in the opening game, Cox decided to stick with his three-man rotation of Glavine, John Smoltz, and Steve Avery.

Leibrandt understood Cox's thinking, but it was tough for him to take. Glavine, Smoltz, and Avery were three of the game's brightest young pitching stars. Leibrandt had turned thirty-six on the final day of the regular season and was a classic example of someone who made himself into a solid major league pitcher through hard work, brains, and guts.

Nine years earlier, when he had been traded by the Cincinnati Reds to the Royals for another left-handed pitcher named Bob Tufts, it had been a deal that swapped—in Leibrandt's words—"two journeyman left-handers going nowhere."

Actually, Tufts did go somewhere, to law school, shortly after the trade. Leibrandt, with a career record of 16-17, spent the rest of 1983 in the minor leagues. By then, he had realized that his career wasn't going anywhere with an eighty-five-mile-an-hour fastball and an eminently hittable curveball. A year earlier, he had learned a new pitch, a change-up, from the Reds' Mario Soto, who threw one of the best change-ups in baseball. It took Leibrandt a while to get comfortable with the grip and the idea of counting on location and changing speeds rather than power, but by 1984 he had it figured out.

He was called up to the Royals in May and got his first start against the Twins in the Metrodome. He pitched well but was still insecure about his place on the roster. The next night, as he shagged balls during batting practice, Leibrandt looked up and saw the late Dick Howser, then the Kansas City manager, approaching him.

"I thought, 'Uh-oh, I'm going back down,' " he said, smiling at the memory. "Instead, Dick walks up and says, 'When we get back to Kansas City, find yourself an apartment. You're in the rotation.' "

Leibrandt justified Howser's faith in him by going 11-7 that year and was 17-9 the next year, finishing fifth in the Cy Young Award voting. "I think I amazed everyone," he said. "I know I amazed myself."

He had been traded to the Braves after the 1989 season and missed part of the 1990 season with a rotator-cuff problem in his shoulder. But he had come back from the injury to win fifteen games in 1991 and another fifteen in 1992. That made him the second-winningest pitcher on the club—behind Glavine—for those two seasons, but it was clear he was the fourth man in a four-man rotation. There was no doubt that if the Braves decided to use only three starters, Leibrandt would be the odd man out. Once, Leibrandt had dreamed only of lasting four years in the majors so he could qualify for a pension. Now, after eleven years and 131 victories, his competitive juices wouldn't let him settle—at least, not happily—for being nothing more than a spectator during postseason.

During the final week of the regular season, even as he was pitching his best baseball of the year, Leibrandt had wondered about his status for the playoffs. He had thrown back-to-back shutouts; one of them to clinch the Western Division title for the Braves. That was a euphoric evening for him, one that helped purge any demons left over from '91.

"I was amazed at the number of people who told me how happy they were that I had been the one to pitch the clincher," he said. "I guess what had happened to me last year was still on a lot of people's minds."

That wasn't what was on the mind of Cox or pitching coach Leo Mazzone when they called Leibrandt in on the last day of the regular season—his birthday.

"I could tell by the look on their faces that it wasn't good news for me," Leibrandt said. "They both said it was a tough decision and they weren't even sure it was right. It wasn't easy for me to swallow, but I did. My attitude was, 'Whatever will help the club win.' "

Leibrandt believed, in his heart of hearts, that the club's chances of winning would be enhanced by sticking with the four-man rotation that had worked so well for two years. But the decision wasn't his, so he sat in the bullpen and waited his turn—a turn he almost hoped wouldn't come. "If the guys do well, I don't get in," he said. "I want them to do well."

They had, for much of the Series, but when Game Six pushed into extra innings, Cox had used up most of his bullpen. The only pitchers left other than Leibrandt and Reardon were Marvin Freeman, who'd been little more than the club's mop-up man, and David Nied, a rookie who had spent only one month of the season in the majors.

As Leibrandt jogged in, one could hear the murmur running through the crowd. The Blue Jays' lineup was loaded with right-handed hitters who could hit the ball out of any park, and Leibrandt, who doesn't blow away people at his sharpest, was coming in to pitch for the first time in twelve days.

He survived the tenth and, when he got Carter for the second out of the eleventh, it appeared possible he might get out of the inning. He pitched carefully to Winfield, not wanting to give him anything good to hit, hoping he could make him swing at a bad pitch for the third out. On 2-2, he came inside with a breaking pitch. Winfield took a step forward as if to swing, then held back. Umpire John Shulock shook his head.

Ball three. The count was 3-2. Leibrandt stepped off the rubber for a moment, while Winfield stepped out of the box and took a deep breath. Winfield was looking for a change-up, which was exactly what Leibrandt intended to throw. But he had no intention of throwing it over the plate.

"I would rather have walked him and taken my chances with Candy [Maldonado]," he said. "I wanted him to swing at a bad pitch or take ball four."

Leibrandt stepped back onto the rubber and looked to catcher Damon Berryhill for the sign. Winfield cocked the bat.

Once again, everyone waited.

•

In his seat behind home plate, Pat Gillick watched impassively as Winfield dueled with Leibrandt. A few minutes earlier, when Henke had come within one strike of ending the game, Gillick had let himself think for a split second that his sixteen-year quest to make the Blue Jays world champions was finally over.

Now he tried not to think of *anything*. His wife, Doris, who had grown up in Germany with no knowledge of baseball, squirmed in the seat next to him. "She gets much more nervous than I do," Gillick said. "I'm usually pretty good. During the play-offs, I sleep, she tosses and turns."

At fifty-five, Gillick rarely betrays emotion. He has been in base-ball all his adult life: five years as a minor league pitcher, ten years with the Houston Astros front office, then three with the New York Yankees before being offered, in July 1976, the chance to put together the expansion Blue Jays.

Leaving the Yankees, as it turned out, wasn't that easy. The day after Gillick informed then–general manager Gabe Paul that he was planning to work for Toronto, Paul came to him with some bad news: George Steinbrenner wasn't willing to release him from his contract. "It was kind of silly," Gillick said. "I only had three months left anyway. But George is a funny guy. He doesn't like anyone telling him ·that they're walking away. He likes to be the one who says, 'You're done.' I guess he wasn't quite done with me."

Blue Jays president Peter Bavasi, Gillick, and Paul spent a couple of weeks trying to get Steinbrenner to change his mind. He wouldn't budge. Finally, exasperated, Gillick told Paul, "Tell George if he doesn't let me go, I'll tell *The New York Times* what's going on."

The ploy worked. Paul called Gillick the next morning to tell him that Steinbrenner was releasing him—as long as Gillick agreed to send a telegram promising not to tamper with any Yankee personnel in his new capacity. Fine, Gillick said, and sent the telegram.

Paul called again the next day to say, "George says this isn't good enough. He wants more details."

Gillick sighed. "Look, Gabe, you dictate it and I'll send it." Paul dictated, Gillick sent it, but Paul was back on the phone the next day. "Still not good enough," he said. "We have to try again."

Gillick hit the wall. "Okay, Gabe," he said. "I'll send him one more telegram. Here's what it'll say: 'George: Go fuck yourself. Pat.' "

Paul got the message. "I'll take care of it," he told Gillick. "You go to Toronto."

And Gillick did exactly that, using the Dodgers, who had moved to Los Angeles just as Gillick was graduating from the University of Southern California, as a model for building his team. The Blue Jays have the most extensive and experienced scouting system in baseball as well as the deepest farm system. They have always emphasized developing young pitchers. And, when they began to be a competitive team in 1983, their owners were willing to spend money on the free-agent market to fill any holes that remained.

It was during that 1983 season that one of the more extraordinary flukes in baseball history began the process that would eventually lead to Winfield's presence in Atlanta. On the night of August 4, the Yankees were playing the Jays in Exhibition Stadium, the crumbling edifice that was the Blue Jays' home park until the space-age SkyDome opened in 1989. The ballpark was visited often by sea gulls, who glided in from adjacent Lake Ontario and made themselves at home. On this particular evening, Winfield, warming up in the outfield, conked one of the gulls with a baseball. The ball wasn't thrown hard, in fact it was just tossed, but it hit the gull in just the right (or wrong) place and the bird fell to the ground, dead.

Animal-protection laws in Canada are stricter than in the United States. A couple of animal protectionists who'd witnessed the incident from the stands were outraged and went to file charges with the authorities. By the time the game was over, Gillick found himself confronted by local police with a warrant for Winfield's arrest.

"It was about as weird and awful a situation as you could ever find yourself in," Gillick said, able to laugh now at the memory. "I had to go into the Yankee clubhouse and tell Billy Martin, who was the manager, that Winfield couldn't go to the airport with the team because of what had happened. You can imagine how happy he was about that. Then I had to tell Dave."

Much to Gillick's relief, Winfield stayed calm throughout the rest of the night. Gillick volunteered to go with him to the police station, did everything he could to expedite the process, and then drove Winfield to the airport in Hamilton—about forty minutes away—where the rest of the Yankees were waiting.

"I was really impressed with Dave through the whole ordeal," Gillick said. "A lot of people would have gone off, but he just dealt with it and got it over with. I actually enjoyed talking to him—we were together for several hours—so that winter, I invited him to come up here for a banquet. He came and we sort of fell into a friendship."

Gillick and Winfield kept in touch, and when Winfield was let go by the California Angels at the end of the 1991 season, Gillick remembered that night in 1983. He remembered Winfield's calmness in a tough situation and his maturity. And so, when a lot of people thought Winfield was finished as an impact player, Gillick signed him for $2.3 million. The contract raised a few eyebrows but, coming just twenty-four hours after the Jack Morris signing, it was treated in Toronto as little more than an addendum to the big news of the week.

Winfield justified Gillick's faith in him by becoming the oldest man in baseball history to drive in 100 runs during the regular season (he wound up with 108). Perhaps more importantly, he and Morris were the leaders in the clubhouse from the very first day of spring training. Occasionally, manager Cito Gaston liked to play Winfield in the outfield, but most of the time he used him as the designated hitter. "He can still play the field," Gaston said. "But I like him on the bench. We've got a lot of quiet guys on this team, including me. I like Dave on the bench because he makes noise."

•

There was no dearth of noise now, as Winfield waited for Leibrandt's 3-2 pitch. The stadium was on its collective feet, urging Leibrandt to get Winfield one more time.

Leibrandt's change-up darted toward the outside corner. But it wasn't as far outside as he wanted it. At six feet six, Winfield has as long a reach as anyone in baseball. He extended his arms, turned on the ball, and slammed a hard ground ball down the third-base line.

If there hadn't been a man on second, third baseman Terry Pendleton would have been guarding the line with two out. But with the potential season-ending run on second in the person of White, he had to play toward the bigger hole, the one between third and shortstop. So his lunge was too late. The ball skittered past third into foul territory, bounced off the bullpen mound, and caromed wildly off the lower-box railing. By the time left fielder Ron Gant could corral it, White and Alomar were across the plate and Winfield stood on second.

His moment had finally come. The Blue Jays led 4–2. On the mound, Leibrandt's shoulders sagged. Berryhill would defend him later, saying, "It wasn't a bad pitch."

Leibrandt's response to that was succinct: "It wasn't good enough."

In the stands, surrounded suddenly by silence, the Blue Jay contingent celebrated. Advance scout Don Wehle turned around and saw tears running down Tonya Winfield's face. Gillick was the calmest of the group, remembering the ninth. "I still didn't feel like we had it won," he said. "Three outs can be a lot to get."

His fears almost proved justified. The Braves actually got the tying run to third base in the bottom of the inning before Mike Timlin, who had spent part of the season in the minor leagues, came in to face Otis Nixon—the same Otis Nixon who had already tied the game once with his ninth-inning single. Nixon tried a surprise drag bunt, but Timlin, fighting off nerves, fielded the ball cleanly and got the ball to first baseman Joe Carter a step before Nixon arrived.

The Blue Jays had won. Their wait was over. So was Winfield's. The joy in their clubhouse was overwhelming. If you walked into the room, someone was going to hug you before you got out whether you were a member of the team or not.

Down the hall, in the Braves' clubhouse, Leibrandt stood in front of his locker and faced up to every question. Around him, his teammates dressed in virtual silence. Stan Kasten, the team president, having circled the room to quietly thank each of his players, made his way down to the Toronto clubhouse. There, he fought his way through the throngs to find his counterpart, Paul Beeston, and offer him congratulations.

Kasten is a man who does not take losing terribly well. Unlike

Gillick, he cannot sit still during a ball game. During the eighth inning of the seventh game of the National League Championship Series, Kasten paced back and forth in the back of the press box, reading a *New York Times* review of the new collected letters of James Joyce. The only reason he was watching in the bottom of the ninth when the Braves staged their miraculous rally was that he had given up.

"By then there was nothing to be nervous about," he said. "We had lost."

They didn't lose that night, but now they had. "How bad can I feel?" Kasten said as he walked back into the Braves' clubhouse. "In two years we've been part of the greatest World Series ever and the greatest comeback in play-off history. That's really not too bad when you think about it."

He stopped and looked around at the almost empty room. "The only hard part is that now we have to start back on square one. We have to wait all winter and then go back to spring training and try to do all this over again so we can have another chance."

For the Blue Jays, the winter would feel about fifteen minutes long. For the Braves, and for everyone else in the game, the wait would no doubt seem interminable.

It always does.

PART I

HOPE SPRINGS ETERNAL

"IN CHICAGO IT'S TWENTY-TWO DEGREES— AND SNOWING"

Shortly after ten o'clock in the morning, on an early-breathtak-ingly clear and gorgeous March day, Al Harazin, the general manager of the New York Mets, sat in his team's dugout in Port St. Lucie, Florida, a huge smile of contentment on his face.

"When they write all about the romance and poetry that goes with spring training," he said, sweeping his hand to indicate the scene in front of him, "I think this is what they had in mind."

Everywhere Harazin looked, he could see baseball players going through their morning drills. A few yards to his right, Jeff Torborg, the manager Harazin had hired in the first major act of his tenure, sat surrounded by reporters, telling the world how happy he was with the way the Mets were accepting his managing philosophy. Every time a player's name came up, Torborg smiled and talked about how pleased he was with the attitude and approach the guy had brought to camp.

In March, even Vince Coleman has a good attitude.

There is no doubting the idealized notions that are attached to spring training. It begins in late winter, when most of the country is shivering or digging out from underneath snowstorms. Suddenly, the eleven o'clock news is rife with taped reports from the camps, complete with pictures of palm trees and ballplayers doing stretching exercises under a warm sun. If the Boys of Summer are in Florida or Arizona, then spring can't be that far away. It is no coincidence that in recent years, when several clubs have started sending out satellite feeds from their daily workouts, television stations have snapped them up.

"If we miss a day for some reason, we get phone calls from all over," said Rick Vaughn, the Baltimore Orioles' public relations director. "People want their fix."

The people watching up north are no different from those participating down south. Baseball is the only sport where the players actually look forward to training camp. In other sports, camp is a grind; veterans often hold out just to avoid the workouts. In baseball, the workouts aren't very taxing; before the exhibition games begin, most teams finish their work by early afternoon, leaving plenty of time for golf or fishing.

"There just isn't very much pressure down here," Joe Torre, the manager of the St. Louis Cardinals, said one morning as he watched his catchers go through a pop-up drill. "Sure, there are a few guys fighting for jobs, but most people know their roles when they get here. And now, with off-season conditioning, everyone comes to camp in shape. There aren't too many guys who show up needing to lose thirty or forty pounds anymore."

As a player, Torre often held out early in spring training, but it wasn't because he was afraid of the work. "I never liked taking batting practice in the morning," he said. "I remember Stan Musial telling me how hard it is to see early in the day, and he was right. You get in there against some kid throwing ninety inside to try to prove he can get Joe Torre out and you can't even see the damn ball. I didn't need that."

Nowadays, with all the funky sunglasses that players wear, that isn't a problem. And with all the rules regarding contracts, very few players show up at camp late. In fact, most arrive early. "Let's face it," said Greg Olson, the Atlanta Braves catcher, "this is The Life."

The Life has changed quite a bit over the years. Once, spring training was the time when fans could mingle with the players, casually chat with them while getting autographs. The little ballparks were throwbacks, tiny and creaky, but usually full of corners where fans and players could find a spot to relax and get some sun.

Most of those parks are gone, and so is the laid-back ambience. The shiny new facilities that have sprung up in recent years, built with public funds to lure teams to a particular community, are set up specifically to keep the fans at a distance from the players. The Mets' facility, which is considered the prototype for a modern spring camp, has a fenced-in players' parking lot that leads directly to the club-house. At no time can a fan approach a player; the fence ensures that.

Autographs have become such big business that some players won't sign except at card shows, where they are paid to appear. Players who do enjoy stopping to sign are frequently put off by the knowledge that even the kids they sign for may be using their signature to make a buck for themselves.

"When a ten-year-old hands you five cards and asks you to sign with a special pen, there isn't much doubt what he's up to," Tom Glavine, the Braves' 1991 Cy Young Award winner, said as he stood by the dugout signing one day. "Sometimes you look up and you see a guy with a card portfolio sending some little kid to get you to sign. It's discouraging."

It is also, to some degree, a no-win situation for players. If they sign for 100 people, person number 101 is bound to be upset. Olson, who may spend more time signing autographs and talking to fans than any player alive, learned firsthand how easy it is to become a bad guy one afternoon when a workout ran long and he came racing out of the clubhouse, late for a charity golf tournament.

"I stopped and said to all the people, 'Look, I'm really sorry—I can't sign today because I'm way late, but if you're here tomorrow, I promise I'll sign for everyone then.' I felt bad, but everyone seemed to understand."

Almost everyone. As Olson unlocked his car, a man approached with his son. "Greg, you can sign just one for my son, can't you?"

Olson looked up and saw a number of other hopefuls who had followed him into the parking lot. "Sir, I really can't," he said. "If I sign for you, I'd have to sign for all those other people."

"Come on," the man persisted. "Just one."

"Sorry," Olson said. "Tomorrow, I promise."

He opened his car door and got in. The last thing he heard before he shut the door was, "What an asshole! Can you believe these guys! One autograph and this asshole can't sign."

Olson was actually shaken by the incident. "I'm not an asshole," he said a couple of days later. "I know there are a lot of guys who are, who won't sign—ever. To get ripped like that, it hurt."

Incidents like that one are still the exception, even in the newly pressurized world of spring training. There are still places—like Dodgertown in Vero Beach—where the players mingle with the fans as they work their way across the little bridge (on Vin Scully Way) that leads from their clubhouse to Holman Stadium. Fans can still gather right outside the clubhouse door at Tigertown in Lakeland and in the parking lot (as Olson can attest) at West Palm Beach, where the Braves and Expos train.

Spring training has become big business, but it is still worlds away from the atmosphere of the regular season. Everyone is happy to be where the weather is warm; friendships are renewed; the workday begins and ends early—of the 383 exhibition games played in Florida and Arizona in 1992, only 36 were night games—and everything feels fresh and alive.

What is most important, though, is the won-lost record: Everyone is undefeated and believes they have a chance. That has always been part of the charm of spring training and it became even more true after both the Minnesota Twins and the Atlanta Braves went from last place in 1990 to the World Series a year later.

The cliché about hope springing eternal is accurate. Especially in an atmosphere where, after the lineups have been introduced, the public address announcer gives the game-time weather report: "The temperature here is seventy-four degrees," he will say. "In Chicago it's twenty-two degrees—and snowing."

•

On the morning of March 5, Jim Leyland drove his car through the parking-lot gate at Ed Smith Stadium, waved at the guard, and pulled into a spot a few yards away from the right-field fence.

Since most spring ballparks have tiny visiting clubhouses, Leyland had put on his gray uniform with *Pittsburgh* in script across the chest before making the twenty-minute trip from the Pirates' camp in Bradenton to the almost-new White Sox facility in Sarasota. This was the first of 199 games Leyland would manage in 1992, and it meant nothing. Yet, as he and his coaches walked through the fence in right field and down the first-base line toward the third-base dugout, Leyland still felt chills running down his spine.

"I'm forty-seven years old and I've been in this game all my life, been a major league manager seven years, and I still get a big kick out of the whole deal," he said, smiling under his mustache. "I never played above Double-A, never even got close to the big leagues. How can it not be a thrill to walk into a ballpark in September knowing there's fifty thousand people gonna be in the place and I'm the manager of one of the teams playing?

"I mean, how great is that? I like to think I know a little more about the game than most people, with all due respect, but the bottom line is, in the end, I'm just a fan with a lineup card."

With all due respect—a favorite Leyland phrase—he is far more than a fan with a lineup card. Ask any manager to list the three best managers in the game today and Leyland will make every list; ask them to go one step further and pick one name and Leyland will be that name on an awful lot of ballots.

Like many people who are good at something, Leyland is uncomfortable with the praise that has been heaped on him. During the winter of '92, with rumors flying that the expansion Florida Marlins were about to offer him a blank check to be their first manager, he surprised most of baseball by signing a five-year extension with the Pirates.

Even though the club had won back-to-back Eastern Division titles, it was slowly being broken up by the game's economy. During that winter, star right fielder Bobby Bonilla defected to New York for $29 million. Barry Bonds would surely be gone after the 1992 season, and, as spring training began, Leyland's two best pitchers, Doug Drabek and John Smiley, were also only a year from free agency. Additionally, Leyland had been told by top management that before spring training was over, the team would have to jettison "a salary"— in other words, a key player making big money.

And yet Leyland had signed on for five more years. "I've always said, 'Don't fix what ain't broke,'" he said in explanation. "I've had six great years with this club. They've given me good players to work with, and I like the town. I like my players. If you look around, how many teams are there that *aren't* in our situation financially? Six? Seven? Almost no one can go out and buy any player they want.

"What's more, the money I was offered by the Pirates was more than I'll ever need. Hell, I've been poor and didn't mind it. Now I've got enough money to know that no matter what happens, my wife and my son will be taken care of for life. I walked out of the stadium the day I signed that contract, got in my car, and burst out laughing. I just couldn't believe anybody would pay me that kind of money to manage a baseball team. I'd do the job for nothing and they're paying me like a king. Unbelievable."

Leyland's first job of the exhibition season was to patiently pose for pictures with new White Sox manager Gene Lamont, who had been his third-base coach for the last six years. Both men smiled for the cameras over and over again. And why not? The weather was perfect and the first game that either man had to worry about was still more than a month away.

Trouble was a lot closer than that, however, Lamont, the rookie manager, already suspected as much. Leyland, the veteran, had no clue.

•

Lamont, a Christmas baby born in 1946, had walked into the exact opposite situation of what Leyland had faced in Pittsburgh in 1986. Leyland took over a team that had lost 100 games the previous year and traded most of its experienced players. He would lose 98 games that first season but knew he would be given time to improve.

The team Lamont took over had finished second for two straight years, winning 94 games in 1990 and 87 in '91. There were some in Chicago who had been stunned by the willingness of the White Sox to let Jeff Torborg leave for the Mets. Lamont was about to stun them even more by being as different from Torborg as anyone could be.

Torborg is the kind of person you expect to find on those positive-thinking commercials that show up on late-night TV. If one of his players goes 0-for-5, Torborg will insist that he saw a couple of good cuts in that last at-bat. If his team loses six straight, Torborg will shake his head and say, "How can you criticize them when they're fighting their guts out?" He constantly preaches the concept of family to his players; during his tenure with the White Sox, the clubhouse was often overrun with children and relatives. Torborg married his high school sweetheart and has a clause in his contract that guarantees his wife a seat on the team charter at all times.

One of Lamont's first moves when he became the White Sox manager was to ban all children from the clubhouse before games. He announced that there would be no team captain, because "I'm this team's captain." He got off to a very bad start with his most famous player, Carlton Fisk, when he told him during their initial phone conversation that he would have to earn the catching job in spring training.

Like Leyland, Lamont answers questions directly. If a player goes 0-for-5 that usually means he had a rotten day. If his team drops six in a row, Lamont will tell you it is probably because it is playing lousy baseball. He is as quiet as Torborg is gregarious. He is the kind of man who grows on people: The more they know him, the more people respect him. But two weeks into spring training, Lamont and his new players were still feeling one another out.

As he posed with Leyland, Lamont already had two major crises to deal with—one short term, the other long.

The short-term crisis was named Vincent Edward Jackson, better known to the world as Bo, as in "Bo knows" . . . baseball, football, sneakers, and, most of all, money. At twenty-nine, Jackson was a corporate phenomenon, having marketed his ability to play both professional baseball and football into the most popular and best-known sneaker commercials of all time. At his tender age, he'd even had a best-selling autobiography. In surveys in which high school students were asked to list their sports heroes, Jackson was consistently the highest-ranked baseball player, finishing ahead of perennial hero Nolan Ryan.

Fay Vincent, then commissioner of baseball, saw this as a bad sign for his sport: "Bo is not a hero because he plays baseball," he said. "He's a hero because he makes commercials about playing two sports. We don't have a single *baseball* player ranked among the top ten. That's a problem for the game."

It was not, however, a problem for Jackson. What was a problem was the hip injury he had suffered fourteen months earlier while being tackled in a football play-off game. That play had ended his football career and, most doctors thought, would surely end his baseball career too. The Kansas City Royals were so certain he was through that they released him before spring training was over in 1991.

The White Sox decided to take a chance and signed him to a free-agent contract. If nothing else, signing with the team allowed Jackson to make another classic commercial in which he appeared in his new white socks and was identified as "Shoeless Bo." That turned out to be his major contribution to the team that season, although he did manage to defy the doctors by making it back to the majors in September. He played in twenty-three games as a designated hitter and even hit three home runs.

But he was running with a limp and, over the winter, the hip deteriorated even more. The White Sox had to decide by March 15 whether to pick up his contract for 1992. The early word was that Jackson had no chance to play, even as a DH.

The word proved to be accurate from the very first time Jackson came to bat in the spring-training opener. As always, he received a bigger ovation than anyone, and as he settled into the batter's box, the buzz of chatter and small talk that usually pervades a park during exhibition games disappeared. Everyone was paying attention.

The count ran to 1-2 before Pirate left-hander John Smiley got a fastball up. Jackson, as strong as ever, crushed the ball on a line directly over Andy Van Slyke's head in center field. Even playing deep, Van Slyke had no chance to get back to the fence before the ball slammed into it. For a moment, the crowd roared in appreciation. But the roar turned quickly into a collective gasp as Jackson began to run. His limp was so pronounced it was painful to watch. Once, he would have easily turned the hit into a triple. Now he limped painfully into second, looking like a thoroughbred that has broken down in the stretch. Clearly this man could not play baseball. The legs that had made him rich and famous simply couldn't carry the burden of the torn-up hip.

Jackson came up twice more, walking in the third—the limp looked even worse when he wasn't running—and then singling in the fourth. He came out at that juncture to a warm round of applause, the kind you give to someone you feel sorry for. The last thing Bo Jackson wanted was sympathy.

He walked very slowly to the White Sox clubhouse with the media in hot pursuit. During spring training, clubhouses are open during games so that reporters can go in and talk to starters, since, unlike during the regular season, starters often leave the park before the game is over. As soon as Jackson emerged from the training room, he was surrounded by cameras and notebooks.

Jackson always speaks slowly because he stutters if he tries to talk too fast. Now, though, each word sounded pained as he spoke. There were tears in his eyes. For a split second, it appeared that he might announce his retirement.

"I'm very disappointed in myself right now," he said softly. "I'm not giving the White Sox their money's worth and if I decide I can't do better, I won't play anymore. I'm not ready to turn my back on baseball, though. The pain isn't excruciating, but it is very uncomfortable to run right now."

Then, when someone asked Jackson if he was thinking of retiring, he looked up defiantly. The mention of the word seemed to anger him. "Retire? That's a joke. If you had this injury, you'd be on crutches right now. If the sun comes up tomorrow, I'll play."

The sun came up the next day and Jackson did play. And the day after that. But four days after the exhibition season began, Jackson had to stop. There was too much pain. Ultimately, he would need hip-replacement surgery. He vowed to come back in 1993. In the meantime, the White Sox were without someone they had hoped could take them that extra step from second place to first.

"To see Bo now makes me want to cry," said Frank Thomas, the prodigious young first baseman who had followed Jackson to Auburn as both a football and a baseball player. "I've never seen an athlete like him—never. He used to hit routine ground balls and beat them out. Now he can barely make it to first at all. It hurts him just to walk. It hurts to watch him try to walk."

All of Jackson's teammates felt for him because they respected him. But his departure did remove one large question mark from the team. Now there were no more Bo questions.

There were, however, plenty of others.

2

THE ICONS

The stickiest question facing Gene Lamont as spring training moved along was Carlton Fisk. The question was simple: How do you handle a forty-four-year-old future Hall of Famer who holds just about every catching record in existence but isn't very happy with his team or his situation?

The question, as it turned out, would not be answered until late July. In the meantime, Fisk and his manager, who were only a year and a day apart in age, continued to be miles apart as people. Like Torborg, Lamont was an ex-catcher. Unlike Torborg, Lamont didn't think Fisk was necessarily entitled to special treatment because of his age or his status as a superstar.

Fisk was angry when the White Sox refused to exercise their option to renew his contract for $2.8 million and instead forced him to sign a new deal worth closer to $1 million.

"It's not the idea that I'm going to go hungry at this salary," he said, sitting in an empty clubhouse on a rainy March morning while the rest of the team was taking batting practice. Fisk was indoors because he had been ordered not to play or even work out for at least four days because of tendinitis in his right foot.

"What upset me was that they acted as if I hadn't done anything to deserve the money. Look at my numbers last year. Forget how old I am. I was third on this team in every statistical category. I made the All-Star team.

"Right after Gene got the job he called me and started talking about how he likes to start from square one in camp but I *am* getting along in age and let's see what kind of shape I'm in. He sounded like a tape recording of [owner] Jerry Reinsdorf and [general manager] Ron Schueler. Then he says something stupid like 'You know Kark wants to be the number one catcher.'

"Well, no shit. Of course he does. So did Joel Skinner, so did Ron Hassey. Hell, once they tried to make me a goddamn left fielder." The look on his face was fierce. "I've played a long time. I deserve better than that. I've come to camp in shape for twenty-six straight years. Did he think that was going to change? What they did and what they said was disappointing. I was hurt. I deserved better."

What Fisk deserved was the same kind of treatment Nolan Ryan was accorded with the Texas Rangers. Fisk and Ryan are baseball's two active icons, guaranteed first-ballot Hall of Famers because of the numbers they have put together as well as role models for anyone who puts on a baseball uniform.

Both were physical wonders. At forty-five, Ryan still threw a baseball as hard as anyone. Fisk, a year younger, continued to play the most grueling position in the game and, as he pointed out, had played extremely well in 1991—hitting eighteen home runs and driving in seventy-four runs. Although he joked often about towels being smaller than they were when he first arrived in the major leagues twenty years earlier—"they used to go all the way around me"—he still looked like a bodybuilder after countless hours in the weight room. The same was true of Ryan.

In Texas, where the Rangers have never made the play-offs in their twenty-year history, Ryan was treated like the franchise. He was being paid $4.7 million in 1992 and the club had made it clear it would pay him just as much in 1993 as long as he wanted to come back and pitch. During spring training, Ryan had his own workout routine, almost never made road trips with the rest of the team, and, if he needed to fly home to Texas for a day to be at a board-of-directors meeting at a bank he owned, that was fine with the Rangers. Clearly, they understood what Ryan meant to them.

Ryan and Fisk were similar in work ethic and in their respect for the game. Both loved to compete. But their personalities could not have been more different: Fisk, who was supposed to be the austere New Englander, was mercurial, capable of huge mood swings. He could be cuttingly, brutally funny one minute, explosively angry the next, quietly reflective soon after.

Ryan's temperament never seemed to change. He was unfailingly polite, patient, and sincere. He was, by his own admission, *never* reflective, and, after twenty-five years in the major leagues, wasn't all that different from the drawling Texas teenager who had first shown up in New York with an eye-popping fastball and almost no idea where any pitch he threw was going to end up.

Growing up, Ryan and Fisk both thought of themselves as basketball players first, baseball players second. In Fisk's case, baseball was an afterthought.

"I played baseball when it was baseball season, because that's what was there," he said, shaking his head. "Basketball was what I really loved. I still thought of myself as a basketball player the first couple of years I was in the major leagues. Every winter, I'd go home and play basketball in the gym every day. It seemed like a natural progression, baseball to basketball and then back to baseball again. If I'd been big enough, I guarantee you I would have ended up playing basketball."

Size was never a problem for Fisk. He was a huge baby—twelve pounds at birth, thirty-five pounds when he was eighteen months old—and was tagged with the nickname Pudge before he could walk. No one who plays with Fisk ever calls him Carlton. It was Pudge then, Pudge now.

He was always an athlete, the second of six kids and, like a lot of younger brothers, he tested himself competing with his older brother's friends. "It was always a struggle when I was young because they were bigger and stronger than I was," he said. "But then, when I was fifteen, it seemed as if I woke up one morning and *boom!* I was there, right with them."

It was about that time that Fisk began to understand that his skills as an athlete might go beyond the borders of small-town life in Charlestown, New Hampshire. During his sophomore year, Charlestown traveled to the Boston Garden to play before a Celtics game against a school from Winooski, Vermont. "They were Goliath, we were David," Fisk said. "We only had sixty-eight boys in the whole school."

Late in the first half, Charlestown's leading scorer, Paul McCallister, went down with an ankle injury. No one said anything to Fisk, but he remembers looking around the locker room at halftime and thinking, "This must be me." He scored eighteen points in the second half and had ten rebounds. Charlestown won the game. Almost thirty years later, Fisk remembers the night and the feeling vividly.

"It's a feeling that's never changed for me. It has to do with responsibility." He smiled. "Maybe that's the New Englander in me, but I've always felt that if you're an athlete, people are looking at you. You have a responsibility not to act like an idiot. Maybe that's why I always liked catching. So much falls on your shoulders. Not just calling the game, but dealing with the pitchers. You have game responsibility, but people responsibility too."

Fisk has always felt that way. And acted accordingly. Take August 1985, for example. It was a muggy afternoon in Yankee Stadium, the day Tom Seaver was trying to win his three hundredth game. Leading 5–3, Seaver was tiring in the eighth. The tying runs were on, two men were out, and Dave Winfield was coming up. Fisk noticed Seaver walking around in circles on the mound as if he expected then White Sox manager Tony LaRussa to come and get him. So Fisk strolled out to talk to Seaver.

"I looked him in the eye and said, 'Tom, don't even think of someone else coming in here. *You* are responsible for this.' I could tell he was tired. He had pitched a lot in his past five or six starts, it was midsummer, and he was sagging just a little bit. I put my hand on his shoulder and said, 'Hey, this is yours, this is your time, your moment.' He just looked at me and said something like 'You're right.' Then he got Winfield out and finished the game, just like he should have."

After that game, Seaver spoke emotionally about what he called "the kick in the pants Pudge gave me." In all likelihood, if another catcher had thought to speak to Seaver that way, he would have been ignored or told to get the hell back behind the plate. But when the words came from Fisk, they meant something.

It wasn't always that way. Fisk remembers walking to the mound as a Red Sox rookie to give veteran lefty Gary Peters a pep talk. As Fisk approached, Peters turned his back on him, walked off the back of the mound, and stood rubbing the baseball for what seemed like forever.

"I'm just standing there like an idiot, the helmet pushed back on my head, waiting," Fisk said. "Finally, Gary turns around, looks at me, and says, 'What the *fuck* are you doing out here?' I just shrugged and said, 'Heck if I know,' and got the hell out of there."

The most famous Fisk story—not counting *the* home run in the 1975 World Series—is from 1989, during Deion Sanders's initial stint with the Yankees. Sanders popped a ball up, took a few languid steps toward first base, then started to turn back to the dugout. He was intercepted by Fisk—the opposing catcher.

"I'm still not exactly sure what happened to me that night," Fisk said. "All I know is, I snapped. To be fair to Deion, it wasn't just him. The game stunk, everyone was playing lousy, and it just seemed to me that it had been that way for a while. I know how hard I've worked at baseball and I know how much the game has given me and sometimes I just get *offended* by how superficial it's all become. Everything now seems to be so individual. Guys talk team but they don't *play* team. There's just so much bullshit and when Deion didn't run the ball out, it all crashed on me."

Fisk shook his head. "Maybe it was playing in Yankee Stadium. Maybe I felt the presence of all those ghosts. But something inside me said, 'Someone in pinstripes should not be taking advantage of the game this way.' I started screaming at him about how wrong he was, how there was no excuse for not running *every* ball out.

"The next time he came to bat, he said something to me about what I said being racist. I took the mask off, looked at him, and said, 'Deion, fuck you. There's a right way to play and a wrong way to play and the way you're playing offends the hell out of me. Sooner or later, this game is going to stick that bat right up your ass.' That was when the benches emptied."

The next time the teams met, in Chicago, Sanders made three running catches on balls hit by Fisk. "Robbed me of three doubles," Fisk said. "I called him a motherfucker and then I clapped for him. Hell, that's the way the game is supposed to be played. If you've got the kind of physical talent he has, why waste it being an idiot?"

Fisk was surprised by the general reaction to his outburst at Sanders. He wondered if he wouldn't be looked at as "some cynical old guy who sits in the corner and just spits and chews and doesn't understand today's ballplayers." Instead, almost everyone in the game applauded what he had done.

"I defended the game, I guess," Fisk said. "It wasn't as if I thought about it or planned it, but that's the way it came out. The game shouldn't be abused—by *anyone*. I thought it was being defaced, *raped*. So I reacted."

Fisk's reactions are never mild, regardless of the subject. When he talks about his famous home run, it is with great emotion. He doesn't downplay its significance in his life, although he says he has seen the hallowed tape only about half a dozen times.

"I have no memory of waving the ball fair or running around the bases," he said. "There are certain things about that night I remember vividly, like looking for my wife in the stands when the game was over. But to understand what that night meant to me, you have to go back to the year before, when I thought my career was over. Knowing how hard I had worked to come back was what made the whole thing so special for me."

The previous July, in Cleveland, Fisk had been run over by Leron Lee on a play at the plate and had torn up his right knee. The doctors told him that if the reconstructive surgery was a success, he might come back in eighteen months. They also told him it was possible he would limp for the rest of his life and perhaps have chronic back problems.

"Remember, this was before knee surgery got sophisticated," Fisk said, rubbing one of the scars that dot both his legs. "I was naïve enough to think that if I worked hard I would come back and that hard work would be rewarded.''

Fisk paused and his eyes widened. ''And the thing is, I *was* rewarded. All the work, all the hours of rehab were for that. The home run was my reward. That was the moment in my life that we all dream about having. I was lucky. A lot of people have moments like that but mine was *visible.*

''That game, moments like that, they symbolize how good base-ball can be. I still remember Pete Rose coming up in the twelfth inning and saying to me, 'This is the best fucking game I've ever been in in my life.' I remember watching Bernie Carbo in the eighth inning take the single worst swing I've ever seen a major leaguer take and then watching him hit a three-run homer on the next pitch to tie the game.

''And I remember standing in the on-deck circle in the bottom of the twelfth and saying to Freddy Lynn, 'I'm gonna hit one off the wall, then you drive me in.' Then, when I hit the ball I thought to myself, 'That's up there, if it just stays fair . . .' ''

The rest, he said, is a blur. A blur, until he walked out of the ballpark at 2 A.M. and realized he had a long way to travel before he slept. Game Six of the '75 World Series had been postponed for three straight days because of rain in Boston. The day that they finally played again, the lease on the apartment that Fisk and his family had rented for the season ran out. A new tenant was moving in that same day. There wasn't a hotel room to be found in the entire city because, of course, the World Series was in town.

And so, on the night that he hit what may be the most remem-bered home run in World Series history, Carlton Fisk had no place to sleep. He packed his family into the car and drove home, a little more than two hours, to New Hampshire. Then, after sleeping—for about fifteen minutes—he drove back to Boston the next afternoon for Game Seven.

What does Fisk think now when he does see the tape? ''I think, 'Who is that guy?' '' he said. '' 'He's so skinny, so *young.*' ''

In that sense at least, Carlton Fisk will always be young.

•

Nolan Ryan doesn't get nearly as emotional when he talks about his past. In fact, he would just as soon not talk about it at all.

''I never reminisce,'' he says. ''I don't like to look back and I don't like to look ahead. I just figure I've got enough to think about right now and the rest will take care of itself.''

Perhaps the most amazing thing about Lynn Nolan Ryan is how unamazed he is by what he has accomplished: the strikeouts (5,701); the wins (319); the no-hitters (seven—*seven!!!*) in twenty-five (yes, twenty-five) seasons in the major leagues. He is the most unassuming of star athletes, someone who has heard every question there is, yet patiently answers them all over and over again.

"I understand that reporters have a job to do just like I do," he said, pouring a diet Coke after an afternoon workout in the weight room. The Rangers were playing down the road in Sarasota, so Ryan had their Port Charlotte training complex almost to himself. "If you're polite to me, what right do I have to not be polite to you? That's just the way I was raised."

There's little doubt that the way Ryan was raised, on a farm in Alvin, Texas, has a lot to do with the kind of man he is today. He came from a close-knit family. The main reason he signed as a free agent with the Houston Astros in 1980 was so he could live back on the farm in Alvin. In 1989, before he agreed to sign with the Rangers, he sat down with his wife, Ruth, and their children, Reid, Reese, and Wendy, and asked them how they felt about his pitching on the other side of the state.

"They were the ones who talked me into it," he said. "I really wasn't sure. To tell you the truth, when I signed with the Astros, I figured I'd play four years with them and that would be it. I'd be thirty-six in 1983 and ready to go on." He smiled. " 'Course, it hasn't quite worked out that way."

If he *had* retired at thirty-six, he would have left the game with 219 victories—100 shy of his current total—and 3,677 strikeouts—almost 2,000 shy of his strikeout record.

If he had retired then, baseball would have been denied one of its most extraordinary figures. Because what has set Ryan apart from other power/strikeout pitchers has been his durability. No one in the game's history has done what he has after the age of forty. Even during 1992, a frustrating, injury-plagued season for Ryan, there were still nights when the magic and the fastball were there. That's why Ryan decided to come back in 1993: The arm still has it if he can just get the rest of his body to the mound in one piece.

And he still enjoys it. He likes the work, the competition, the pressure of pitching. More than anything, though, like many elder statesmen, Ryan still loves the camaraderie of the clubhouse.

Ask any former ballplayer what he misses most about playing and the answer will always be the same: "the guys." A baseball clubhouse is like no other locker room in sports. It is not by accident that in baseball the term "locker room" is never used. It is always the *club*house and there is no doubting the fact that those who change clothes there are part of a very exclusive club, one that includes no one except those in uniform.

"Baseball players have a natural distrust of anyone who doesn't wear a uniform," Jeff Torborg says. "That includes everyone: front-office people, scouts, friends, family, and certainly reporters. It isn't that they don't like those people, or in some cases love them. They do. But they just aren't a *part* of it."

Ryan takes that a step further. "The only thing worse than not being here is being here when you're hurt," he said. "To hang around the clubhouse when you're on the disabled list is an awful feeling. You're invisible. It's like being a ghost."

In the Rangers' clubhouse, Ryan is anything but a ghost. He is always the center of attention, whether he's pitching or not. Some-times that embarrasses him. What helps is the way his teammates harass him about the constant glare of his personal spotlight.

Early in the '92 season, Ryan started a game in Baltimore on a drizzly afternoon. He was hit hard in the first inning and was lucky to escape down 3–0. He got the side without trouble in the second inning, then it really began to rain. After the delay, Ryan came out of the game. There was no point risking his arm or having him pitch on a wet mound.

The Rangers came back and won the game 5–3, and the winning pitcher was Jeff Robinson, an ex-Oriole. Robinson was surrounded by reporters after the game, until Ryan emerged from the shower and walked to his locker. Suddenly Robinson was sitting all alone.

The other Ranger pitchers started in.

"End of interview for you, Jeff," Kevin Brown yelled.

"Hey, Nolie, tell them who the winning pitcher was," added Scott Chiamparino.

"Tell 'em about all forty-eight pitches in detail" was the contribu-tion from Kenny Rogers—pitcher, not singer.

Ryan smiled through it all, knowing that when the day comes that his teammates don't tease him about all the attention, it will be be-cause he isn't one of them anymore.

He came to New York as part of the pitching staff that turned the Mets from jokes to champions. He was the kid on the staff behind Tom Seaver, Jerry Koosman, and Gary Gentry. Military duty, wildness, and blisters on his pitching hand limited him during the New York years. It was only after he was traded to California in 1972 that his career took off.

"A lot of people have said I couldn't handle New York because I was just a good ol' boy from Texas," he said. "That really wasn't it at all. We liked New York. I just never really got the chance to throw a lot of innings there."

During his first three years in California, Ryan threw 943 innings. His first year there he started weight-training. It was unheard of then. Now everyone does it. Ryan is one of those rare pitchers who has gotten better with age. He throws about as hard as he ever has but his control has steadily improved over the years.

What also makes Ryan unique is the way other players view him. Occasionally someone will whine that Ryan doctors the baseball (does doctoring make a pitch go ninety-six miles per hour?), and there's no doubt that Ryan *will* throw inside when he thinks it necessary. He admits that, like Fisk, he gets angry at younger players who showboat, especially those who stand at the plate and watch their home runs leave the ballpark. "I've yelled at a few guys for that," he said. "I've always believed the one thing you don't do is show up the other guy."

But 99 percent of those who have played with him or against him will tell you that he never changes in victory or defeat, before or after no-hitters.

On the night he pitched his last (or is that most recent?) no-hitter in 1991, Ryan completed his interviews and headed, as always, to the weight room for his postgame workout. He was about halfway through his routine when someone came in and asked if he could come outside long enough to do one more standup with ESPN. Ryan got off the stationary bicycle, went out and did the interview, then came back and finished.

Skeptics might argue that an athlete's giving time to ESPN hardly makes him unusual. But consider a scene during spring training of that same year as described by Peter Gammons, the baseball guru for ESPN and *The Boston Globe.*

"Nolan had finished all the interviews they had scheduled for him that day and went off to finish his workout," Gammons said. "Some kid from a college newspaper somewhere had just shown up hoping he might somehow get some time with Nolan Ryan. He was, of course, told no, that Nolan just didn't have time and that to talk to him you had to have an appointment.

"The kid hung around. Finally, Nolan came off the field and the kid walked up, explained what he was doing, and asked if he could somehow have five minutes. Nolan sat down with him in the dugout and they started to talk. I left half an hour later. They were still talking."

Ryan will always talk, even though he doesn't really enjoy it. He has been asked to consider running for commissioner of agriculture in Texas but has politely declined—he doesn't think a political campaign would be comfortable for him.

Baseball still is, though. The aches and pains and the days on the disabled list are a little tougher to take each year and Ryan doesn't want to overstay his welcome, but it's still fun.

"I always figure every year that this may be the last go-round," he

ALBUQUERQUE ACADEMY
LIBRARY

said. "Then, when the season's over, if I still feel like I can pitch, I think about doing it again. I hope when the day comes that I've had it, I'll be the one to know first."

Whenever that day comes, baseball will be a little less fun. Even for those who have to try to hit him.

3

WHEELING AND DEALING

Spring-training camps are divided into four different regions: the east coast of Florida, central Florida, the west coast of Florida, and Arizona. Five teams—the Yankees, Mets, Braves, Expos, and Dodgers—train on the I-95 corridor on the east coast. Eleven teams—the Rangers, Twins, White Sox, Pirates, Orioles, Cardinals, Tigers, Red Sox, Blue Jays, Phillies, and Reds—train on or near the west coast. Two teams—the Royals and Astros—are hybrids, staking out central Florida. They are near almost no one but not too far from either coast.

Exhibition games in Florida are all about bus trips. They can range from twenty minutes to three hours. Nowadays, teams bus across state only occasionally and never more than once a spring. Stars usually pick their trips. Often as not, the big-name players will play most of their spring-training games at home.

Arizona is an entirely different story. Six of the eight teams that train in the desert have camps in the Phoenix area for most of February and March. The Giants, Athletics, Cubs, Mariners, Brewers, and Angels (until the last two weeks of March, when the Angels move to Palm Springs) all train within a twenty-mile radius of one another.

Although all six teams draw well, there is no doubting the fact that the "home" team in Phoenix is the Cubs. They are the only team whose games are broadcast on a regular basis by one of the local radio stations, and, during the six weeks that the teams are in town, there may be more Cub fans around than there are fans of the other five teams combined.

One of the reasons for this is clearly the weather. The only other Phoenix-area team that comes from a true cold-weather city is the Brewers, and, after only twenty-three years in existence, they just can't compete with the Cubs when it come to tradition. Not only are there bunches of Chicago-area retirees in the area, but many fans plan their vacation around spring training out west as both a respite from the weather and a chance to get an early look at their beloved baby bears.

The other factor in Cubs mania there, as well as in other parts of the country, is cable television. The Cubs, Braves, Mets, and White Sox all have TV contracts with superstations, outlets that are available on cable systems throughout most of the country. But the White Sox have been on WGN for only two years and they take a backseat on the station to the Cubs—not surprising, since both the Cubs and the station are owned by the Tribune Company. The Mets are not seen as many places as the Cubs, and, although the Braves are seen in more places than anyone, on WTBS, they have been worth watching only for the past two years.

What's more, the Cubs have Harry Caray. No doubt there have been better broadcasters down through the years than Caray. No doubt he is a huge homer—although, unlike his son Skip on WTBS, he almost never calls the Cubs "us." But there's no one quite like Harry Caray.

He admits to being seventy-four, although some people will tell you he is closer to seventy-nine. "How old is Dad?" Skip Caray asks rhetorically. "Last time I checked, he was sixty-one. I'm fifty-three now. The way I've got it figured, in five years I'll be older than he is. I guess that'll be a broadcasting first."

Harry Caray has been in the business forty-eight years, working for the St. Louis Cardinals, the Oakland A's, the White Sox, and, for the last twelve years, the Cubs. He has made his share of enemies through the years, but he has also made as many friends as anyone. Thom Brennaman, one of his broadcast partners, turned twenty-nine late in the 1992 season. He doesn't know how old Harry is either. But he does know one thing for sure: "I can't keep up with him at night."

Everyone who knows Caray has a Harry-on-the-town story. Bob Verdi, the longtime *Chicago Tribune* columnist, tells one about an evening in Phoenix several years ago. "We met at a restaurant about seven o'clock," Verdi said. "Harry said, 'Let's have a couple of drinks here.' So we did. Harry then suggested we go to another place. I said fine. We arrived, sat down, and Harry said, 'Let's have a couple of drinks.' So we did. He looked at his watch and said, 'The night is young, Bobby—I've got another place.' Off we went. At the third place he said, 'Let's have a couple of drinks.'

"By now I had given up on surviving the evening. We had a few more rounds there and Harry said, 'I know a great place just down the street.' Off we went. Of course every place we went, Harry was treated like a king. They were thrilled just to have him there. We pulled into the fourth place and Harry said, 'You know what would be nice? A couple of drinks.'

"So we started again. Finally, about one o'clock in the morning, I couldn't see, I couldn't talk, I was fairly certain I couldn't walk. So I said, 'Harry, I've had it, I'm done.'

"And Harry looked at me and said, 'You're absolutely right, Bob. Waiter! Bring us some menus!' "

And so it goes every spring. Cub fans pour into Phoenix full of hope and in search of Harry. They line up to get into the overcrowded parking lot at HoHoKam Park in suburban Mesa and tell one another that this will be The Year. Given the Cubs' futility over the years it is somehow ironic that HoHoKam (named after a local Indian tribe) sits directly across the street from a cemetery. On one side of the street, life begins again every spring. On the other . . .

•

The Cleveland Indians trained in Tucson for forty-six years until the spring of 1993, when they moved to Florida. They were replaced in Tucson by the expansion Colorado Rockies. The only other Arizona team that does not headquarter in the Phoenix area is the San Diego Padres. Ever since the team came into existence in 1969, the Padres have trained in Yuma. Where is Yuma? No one is quite sure. But it isn't close to anything.

"Except cactus," general manager Joe McIlvaine jokes. "I tell people to get here, drive to the first cactus and turn left. Or right."

McIlvaine came to the Padres in 1990 after eleven years with the Mets. General managers usually come in two categories: ex-player or ex-scout. There are exceptions to this rule, of course. The Mets' Al Harazin and the Athletics' Sandy Alderson are both onetime corporate lawyers who came to baseball relatively late in life.

McIlvaine is an ex-player *and* an ex-scout. He played in the Detroit Tigers' farm system for five years before becoming a scout at age twenty-five. He is also one thing that no other general manager has ever been: an ex-seminarian.

The oldest of three boys, McIlvaine grew up outside of Philadelphia. His first love was baseball, but as a senior in high school he was a six-foot-one 130-pound pitcher. "Needless to say, I didn't blow anyone away with my fastball," he said. "I had some savvy, though, and I threw a decent curveball, so I wasn't bad."

Not a pro prospect, however. Even if he had been, McIlvaine's interest lay elsewhere when he graduated from high school. Fascinated by the Catholic religion, he entered St. Charles Seminary, planning to become a priest. He spent four years there, studying Greek and Latin, philosophy, and the classics.

"The work is very hard," he said on a spectacular Arizona morning en route to Tucson to watch his team play the Indians. "I can talk about abstract thinking now and understand it, but what I learned in the seminary was that I'm more of a concrete guy: numbers, facts and figures. In philosophy you have to get to the abstract rather than the concrete. I was never very good at it."

By the end of his fourth year in the seminary, McIlvaine was fairly certain he didn't want to be a priest. "I just didn't feel as if I was being called to do that," he said. "I liked the idea of teaching, but I didn't think I wanted the Church to be my entire life's work."

By that point McIlvaine also had another alternative—baseball. During the previous two summers, he had been given permission by his teachers at the seminary to pitch in a semipro league in southern New Jersey. Late in the second summer, the summer of 1968, McIlvaine's team played in a tournament that drew a number of pro scouts. By then McIlvaine had grown and filled out. He was six-five, weighed 170 pounds, and could throw hard. The scouts were interested and told him he might be drafted. He told them he wasn't sure what he was going to do with his life but there was a good chance he would leave the seminary before he became a priest.

The following January, the Detroit Tigers drafted McIlvaine. Six months later, he signed a contract, left the seminary, and flew to Florida to join the Tigers for extended spring training.

"I didn't leave the seminary because of baseball," McIlvaine said. "I would have left regardless. But it did offer me a chance to do something right away. The only thing was, I had never been anywhere that was more than a couple of miles from my house. The seminary was less than two miles from where I had grown up. When I flew to Florida, it was the first time I had ever been on an airplane.

"I mean, I was different from the other guys, really different. It didn't take them long to figure that out. I had been isolated from the world for almost four years. Naturally, the first question I got almost every morning was, 'So, Mac, did you get laid last night?' "

McIlvaine spent parts of five years in the minor leagues, making it to major league camp once, in 1972. The first person he faced in batting practice was Al Kaline. "All I could think was, 'If you hit this guy, you're done.' Then I threw him a really good pitch and he swung and missed. I was amazed. But it taught me a lesson—if you throw anyone a good pitch, even a Hall of Famer, they aren't going to hit it."

After five years, McIlvaine realized he wasn't going to make the major leagues. He wanted to get married and start a family, which meant finding a job that would pay him more than $6,000 a year. He knew he wanted to stay in baseball, so he wrote to fifteen major league ball clubs. One responded: the Orioles. He was invited in for an interview and hired as a scout.

"I got lucky," McIlvaine said. "They had three scouts retiring that year and they had decided to hire some young people. Scouting was generally considered an older man's game at that point, but things were starting to change. I was in the right place at the right time."

McIlvaine worked for the Orioles, Angels, and Brewers as a scout before moving to the Mets in 1980 as director of scouting. The next six years were baseball nirvana for McIlvaine. The Mets were a team that had been mismanaged into the ground in the late 1970s. When Nelson Doubleday and Fred Wilpon bought the franchise in 1980, they hired Frank Cashen, who had been McIlvaine's first boss in Baltimore, to put the team back on its feet.

Cashen did exactly that. In 1984, the Mets won 90 games. The following year they won 98 and lost a stirring pennant race to the Cardinals. In 1986, there was no pennant race. The Mets won 108 games, virtually wrapped up the division title by the All-Star break, then won two remarkable postseason play-offs, first beating the Houston Astros in six games for the National League pennant, then taking the World Series from the Red Sox in seven games—after winning Game Six in the tenth inning with what may be the most famous two-out rally in history.

That period, when the Mets were being built from jokes to contenders to champions, was a joyride for McIlvaine and everyone associated with the building process. Over the years, Cashen gave McIlvaine more and more authority on the player-personnel side while gradually turning over much of the business side to Al Harazin.

But even though the Mets continued to contend after their championship season, things changed. There was now pressure to *win* every year, which was a lot different from the pressure to improve. When McIlvaine, at the urging of manager Davey Johnson, put together a 1989 trade that sent Lenny Dykstra and Roger McDowell to Philadelphia for Juan Samuel just before the All-Star break, the deal wasn't considered that important. The Mets had traded an unhappy, platooned center fielder and a relief pitcher whose sinkerball had lost some of its sink for a converted outfielder who had put up some great numbers in the past.

The trade turned out to be a disaster. Samuel left New York after the '89 season while Dykstra, given the chance to play every day, blossomed into an All-Star. Throughout 1990, McIlvaine was lambasted for the trade. One columnist, in a particularly cruel piece deriding McIlvaine's abilities as a baseball man, kept referring to him as "Father Joe."

McIlvaine understood the vagaries of baseball dealing. But he was stung by some of the comments he heard on the radio and read in the newspaper. Once, he never would have thought seriously about leaving New York, where it was a given that he and Harazin would run the club when Cashen retired. But by the end of 1990, when the Padres contacted him about their vacancy in the general manager's office, McIlvaine was willing to listen.

"Some of the things that people said and wrote were vicious," Harazin remembers. "The Father Joe thing was just unconscionable. I know Joe was stung by those things, but I don't think that's why he left New York. I think San Diego looked like Shangri-la to him. It's a great place to raise your kids and it was a chance for him to put his personal stamp on something. Even so, I think we were shocked when he came in and told Frank he was seriously thinking of leaving."

Cashen was both shocked and hurt. He pleaded with McIlvaine to reconsider.

McIlvaine *was* torn, more by loyalty to Cashen—who had been his mentor for eleven years—than anything else. But in the end he realized that he had to decide what was best for him and for his family.

"You're talking about moving to one of the country's most livable cities," McIlvaine said. "You're also talking about having a chance to really shape something, to mold it. And there were still some questions about just how the front office would be structured when Frank left. I like to think of myself as an architect. This was my chance to design and build my own house. In the end, I couldn't resist that."

McIlvaine was aggressive from day one on the job. The Padres had been 75-87 in 1990 and had changed managers in midseason, giving the job to third-base coach Greg Riddoch. McIlvaine decided the team needed an overhaul and he accomplished that in one fell swoop— trading his number one run producer, Joe Carter, and his star second baseman, Roberto Alomar, to the Toronto Blue Jays for shortstop Tony Fernández and first baseman Fred McGriff. The trade was announced during the winter meetings.

"You announce a trade like that to the media at the winter meetings, you are doing so in a room full of cynics," McIlvaine said. "I still remember that as each name was announced, you could hear a little gasp. When the whole thing had been laid out, there were actually guys applauding—*reporters!*" McIlvaine grinned. "Boy, was that fun.

"I enjoyed making that deal because it was a *baseball* deal, nothing else. People don't make pure baseball deals anymore. These days, deals are made based on who is going to be a free agent, who is trying to dump a salary, who has arbitration coming up. It almost never had to do with baseball. That trade was talent for talent, value for value. We each thought we were making our club better—period." Sadly, two years later, Fernández would be traded to the Mets for one reason: McIlvaine had been ordered to dump salaries.

The Padres were better in 1991, winning eighty-four games. Still, McIlvaine thought more changes were needed. In truth, he wanted to change managers. He was never comfortable with Riddoch, a onetime psychology teacher who liked to post inspirational messages all over his office. Privately, McIlvaine nicknamed Riddoch "The Music Man," in honor of the con man made famous on Broadway and in the movies by Robert Preston.

But he decided firing Riddoch would be unfair. "I just thought with the club he had he did as good a job as anyone could have," he said. "I had said I would give him a fair chance. Firing him then would not have been fair."

McIlvaine thought there were other ways to make the Padres better. A priority for him was finding a third baseman who could provide some offense to go along with perennial batting champion Tony Gwynn and the Fernández-McGriff duo, both of whom had played well after the big trade. McIlvaine was willing to listen to any name put before him by other general managers. There was one player he really wanted, though, someone he honestly thought he could get: Gary Sheffield.

•

The name Gary Sheffield was well known to everyone in baseball. By the spring of 1992, he was considered by most a problem child, a potential star gone wrong. He had been hurt for most of 1991 and had hit only .194 when he did play. He had fought with almost everyone in Milwaukee—management, teammates, the media, fans. Most general managers would shake their head when his name came up and say one word: poison.

There is no worse label for a baseball player. Its meaning is simple: Put this guy in your clubhouse and he is capable of killing the entire club. Vince Coleman carried that reputation with him from St. Louis when he signed with the Mets in 1991 and proved himself more than worthy of it. Kevin Mitchell, one of the game's best power hitters, has been traded four times in the last six years—because he has the same monkey on his back. Other active players who have worn the "poison" tag at one time or another: Reds reliever Rob Dibble, ex–Red Sox now Yankee third baseman Wade Boggs, and Rangers second baseman Julio Franco.

Only a player with talent can be considered poison. If a second-line player is a problem in the clubhouse, he doesn't last very long. Talent is forgiven; mediocrity is released.

There was no doubting Sheffield's talent. "I first saw him play when he was still in high school," McIlvaine said. "I loved him then. And the word around was that the Brewers were going to move him one way or the other."

The Brewers had made Sheffield the sixth pick in the nation in 1986 after he graduated from Hillsborough High School in Tampa. Growing up, Sheffield had followed closely in the footsteps of his uncle—Dwight Gooden. Although Sheffield was the son of Gooden's older brother, he was only four years younger than Dwight.

"Dwight and I were like brothers growing up," Sheffield says. "We were together all the time. Everything he did, I wanted to do. I threw just as hard as he did in high school, maybe a little harder. When he made it to the major leagues at nineteen, I just figured I would do the same thing."

As a senior, Sheffield had a 1.31 ERA as a pitcher. But he also hit .500 and showed some power. The Brewers drafted him as a shortstop even though Sheffield assumed he was going to be a pitcher. When he reported to his rookie-league team in Helena, Montana, he put on his pitcher's toe plate, asked for a jacket, and headed for the bullpen. When he arrived there, he was told he was in the wrong place.

"I pinch-hit that day and struck out," he says, laughing. "After the game I called home and said, 'Guess what—I'm an infielder.' "

Sheffield liked playing every day and he hit .365 during his fifty-seven-game stint at Helena that year. It was the next year in Class-A ball at Stockton that he began to develop his reputation.

"I was very immature," he says. "I was only seventeen when I was drafted and I'd never really dealt with authority. I think there was a tendency to think of me as older because physically I was. But I couldn't deal with being picked on—at all. I always wanted to challenge people. That wasn't the right way to go about doing things. But I didn't know that then."

Immature or not, Sheffield was in the major leagues before he was twenty, called up at the tail end of 1988. He was the Brewers' Opening Day shortstop in 1989, though injuries and problems in the clubhouse landed him back in the minors. A year later, he stayed healthy the whole season and hit .294, driving in sixty-seven runs while batting second. He was twenty-one. It seemed that he had arrived.

But the next season was a nightmare from start to finish. By the time it was over, the poison label was plastered all over Sheffield.

"There's no question I did some things wrong in Milwaukee," he says. "I became a mean person. I look back on that now and I feel like it wasn't even me, it was someone else. I did and said things I regret. But I also think I was misunderstood some of the time.

"Look, I tend to talk in street slang a lot, especially when I'm excited or angry. Sometimes people see you as more threatening when you talk that way. I hate to look at it this way, but let's face it—there are people who are uncomfortable with an outspoken young black player. People want to write you off quicker. They want to see you fail because it might shut you up. I think there were people in Milwaukee who wanted to see me fail and I almost let them have their way."

When Sal Bando replaced Harry Dalton as general manager at the end of the '91 season, Sheffield asked him to try to trade him. He didn't feel comfortable in the clubhouse. Tom Trebelhorn, the manager, who Sheffield felt supported him, had been fired.

McIlvaine had been making overtures to Dalton about Sheffield throughout 1991. Shortly after taking the San Diego job, McIlvaine began writing down the gist of each and every conversation he had with another general manager in a spiral notebook.

General managers talk to one another constantly. Frequently, they contact one another just to make what is known as a "maintenance" call—maintaining contact. They will toss names around, each man listening for a clue that might tell him someone he wants can be had or, conversely, looking to drop a name to see if it will stir any interest on the other end.

McIlvaine was never coy about his interest in Sheffield. The first page of the Brewers' section of his notebook says, "Harry Dalton is looking for starting pitching. I've asked him to come back to me with a concrete offer for Gary Sheffield." This was in April 1991.

When McIlvaine didn't hear back from Dalton, he called him and asked again about Sheffield. This was on May 10, when Sheffield's troubles with the Brewers were just beginning to get serious. Dalton wanted the Padres' number one pitching prospect, Andy Benes, plus another young player. That price was too steep for McIlvaine.

The two men continued to talk. Dalton called in early June to let McIlvaine know he was entertaining offers from a number of other teams for Sheffield. McIlvaine repeated that the asking price was too high. A month later, Dalton called again and asked McIlvaine if he'd be interested in a three-way deal that would bring Charlie Hayes, then with the Phillies, to the Padres. McIlvaine, who had been anticipating a call from Dalton, quickly turned the subject back to Sheffield.

McIlvaine wrote in his notebook: "I told him that I was scrawling

names on a piece of paper and I thought I might be interested in
[pitcher] Chuck Crim and Sheffield for [pitcher] Dennis Rasmussen and
[outfielder] Bip Roberts."

Actually, he had planned all along to throw those names at Dalton
but he wanted the offer to sound casual. Dalton didn't bite.

Several more months passed. Sheffield's season fell apart; Dalton
was fired. Shortly after the season ended, McIlvaine called Dalton's
replacement, Bando, and brought up Sheffield's name again. Bando
told him the Brewers were reluctant to trade Sheffield because, since
Sheffield had been hurt most of the season, they were dealing from
weakness. Two weeks before the winter meetings began, Bando's
assistant, Al Goldis, called McIlvaine to tell him things had changed:
The Brewers *were* willing to deal Sheffield.

McIlvaine and Bando spoke nine different times in December and
January. They kept throwing names at each other. Twice, Bando
brought up possible three-way deals. One would have put Dick Scho-
field on the Padres; another would have brought them Scott Cooper
from the Red Sox. McIlvaine wasn't interested. The two men had three
different conversations on January 28. Bando kept steering away from
Sheffield; McIlvaine kept coming back to him. They were still far apart,
but agreed to talk again in Arizona.

On the morning of March 14, with the teams scheduled to play
that afternoon at the Brewers' base in Chandler, McIlvaine and Bando
met in Bando's office. Sheffield had again criticized the club publicly.
Bando said he would trade Sheffield if McIlvaine would give up Ricky
Bones, a young pitcher, and two other players he would name later.

Three days later, Bando's other assistant, Bruce Manno, called
McIlvaine early in the morning and named the other two players, both
young prospects: José Valentin and Mark Mieske. McIlvaine called
Bando later that day and said the price was too steep. He asked Bando
to add outfielder Darryl Hamilton to the deal.

According to McIlvaine's notes, Bando was adamant: "He was
insistent on Bones-Valentin-Mieske," McIlvaine wrote. "I told him no
and asked again about Hamilton. He said Hamilton had just signed a
two-year deal and was going to be their starting right fielder. At that
point he suggested we table the deal since we weren't going to meet
his price, and we began to talk about other players." McIlvaine's final
note from that day is simple: "The Sheffield deal is dead."

Five days later, with Bando and McIlvaine face-to-face again, this
time in Yuma, McIlvaine tried to resurrect the trade one more time. He
threw several other names at Bando, telling him Mieske would not be
part of the deal. Bando kept shaking his head as McIlvaine mentioned
other names. No—it had to be Mieske.

Two days later, the men spoke again. McIlvaine ran the list of

names and Bando held firm. Finally, reluctantly, McIlvaine threw out
the name of Jeremy Hernandez, a raw but talented right-handed
pitcher. That piqued Bando's interest. He said he would caucus with
manager Phil Garner and get back to McIlvaine. Soon.

The next day, Garner said that Hernandez was a no-go. It still had
to be Bones, Valentin, and Mieske. He offered to add another player on
his end, perhaps left-handed pitcher Kevin Brown, if McIlvaine would
consider adding another player too. McIlvaine brushed off Brown and
asked again about Hamilton. "I'm not giving you two starters in this
deal," Bando said. In his notes, McIlvaine described Bando's position
as "stolid." So was his: "We won't make the three-for-one," he told
Bando, ending the conversation.

McIlvaine didn't mean what he had said, though. He still held out
hope of finding a way to replace Mieske in the package but he'd
decided the trade had to be made, even if it meant giving up Mieske.
The next day, McIlvaine spent the entire morning meeting with his
staff, all his scouts, Riddoch, and his coaches to talk about the deal.
The consensus was in favor of it. Finally, McIlvaine called in Ed Lynch,
who, as farm director, ran the Padres' minor league system.

"The farm director is the guy who knows your prospects best,"
McIlvaine said. "I wanted to know his gut feeling." Lynch's gut feeling was the same as McIlvaine's: "Joe," he said, "you should make
this deal."

McIlvaine called Bando that afternoon and told him he would
make the swap if Bando would throw in a minor league pitcher. Bando
told him that his owner, Bud Selig, was arriving in town that afternoon.
He would talk to him and call back the next day.

At nine o'clock the next morning, Bando called back. The Brewers
would make the deal. Each club would call a press conference for 1
P.M.—just as their exhibition games were starting that day—to make
the announcement. That phone call was the twenty-sixth time McIlvaine had talked to the Brewers about a Sheffield deal over the span of
eleven months.

When McIlvaine hung up with Bando, it suddenly dawned on him
what day it was: March 27. Five years earlier, McIlvaine had completed a trade for the Mets on March 27. In that deal, he had sent a
catcher named Ed Hearn to the Kansas City Royals for a young pitcher
named David Cone. That had been, without any doubt, the best trade
McIlvaine had made in his life. Little did he know that he had quite
possibly just topped himself.

Shortly after McIlvaine and Bando finished talking, as the Brewers
were taking batting practice before their game with the San Francisco
Giants, Bando and Garner called Sheffield in and told him about the

trade. Sheffield thanked them both, shook hands, and walked into the empty clubhouse.

"As soon as I was alone, I just hit my knees and started to cry," he said months later. "I said, 'Thank you, Lord. This is my gift.' I just knew I was going to do well in San Diego."

How well, neither Sheffield nor anyone in baseball could possibly have imagined.

HELL-RAISING

Joe McIlvaine and Sal Bando were not the only general managers at work during March. There are, generally speaking, three times each year when teams are eager to make trades:

- Late August, when contenders are looking to pick up one or two key players who can put them over the top, and also-rans are looking to unload older, higher-paid players to those contenders in return for prospects.
- The winter meetings, held in early December when all of baseball is in one place at one time, each club hoping to strengthen itself for next season while making some winter headlines that will stir season-ticket sales.
- Spring training. There is an old saying in baseball that all players improve from October to February. Each winter, almost every team convinces itself that several players on the roster are better than they had appeared to be in the past. Then, spring training begins and September's bust who had become December's prospect is clearly a bust again. General managers scurry for the phones, hoping to fill holes before the season begins.

Ted Simmons, the new general manager of the Pittsburgh Pirates, wasn't looking to fill any holes. In fact, he was looking to create one—on his ledger sheet. Simmons had been hired by the Pirates two weeks before spring training began to replace Larry Doughty. Doughty had been fired suddenly the previous month, apparently because he had angered top management by re-signing thirty-five-year-old Bob Walk to a two-year contract considered much too generous.

Simmons's marching orders were clear when he was hired: Reduce the payroll before the season starts. Not a great way to start a new job, but Simmons was pragmatic about it. "There are only twenty-eight general managers' jobs available," he said. "When the chance came up, I didn't think I was in a position to sit around and wait for the Dodgers or Blue Jays or one of the other big-money clubs to call. This was a chance, so I took it."

At forty-two, Simmons had been retired for only three years after spending almost twenty years in the major leagues. Like Jim Leyland, his new manager, he had been a catcher. Like Leyland, he almost always had a cigarette in his hand. The similarities ended there. Simmons had been a natural as a ballplayer, an excellent hitter who played on the All-Star team eight times. Simmons was smooth, Leyland rough. Simmons tried always to be diplomatic; Leyland was blunt and straightforward.

And when Simmons announced on March 17 that he had made his first major trade by sending twenty-game winner John Smiley to the Minnesota Twins for two prospects, pitcher Denny Neagle and Class-A outfielder Midre Cummings, Leyland went crazy.

He had known some kind of move was coming but he had never figured it would be as drastic as Smiley, who, along with Doug Drabek, anchored his pitching staff. This trade would be damaging, not only on the field, but in the clubhouse. The message to the players would be clear: Money means more than winning. Smiley was being paid $3.44 million in 1992 and was eligible for free agency at the end of the season. Everyone knew that Smiley, Barry Bonds, and Drabek were likely to leave at the end of the season. But three weeks *before* the season started?

On the day the trade was announced, Simmons made things worse by claiming that money had nothing to do with the move. "I would have made this trade regardless of salaries," he said. "I think we helped ourselves in the long run."

Not a single person believed it.

"It's bad enough they did it," catcher Mike LaValliere said a few days later. "But to come in and try to tell us it had nothing to do with money is unbelievable. I mean, *come on.* Don't treat us like a bunch of idiots. We aren't *that* stupid."

Leyland was at least as angry as his players and he said so publicly. Under any circumstances, the trade and Simmons's handling of the announcement would have upset Leyland. But circumstances that had nothing to do with baseball conspired to make the situation even tougher for him.

One week before the trade, Leyland's third-base coach, Rich Donnelly, had learned that his seventeen-year-old daughter, Amy, had a brain tumor. Leyland sent Donnelly to Texas to be with her. He talked to Donnelly daily, getting progress reports on Amy, who had come through surgery okay but was still weak and, as might be expected, scared.

Amy Donnelly's illness shook Leyland for a number of reasons. He is very close to his coaches, seeing them all as good friends and managers-in-training. Often he'll have them sit with him when he talks to the press so they can get an idea of what it will be like when they're the ones behind the desk.

Donnelly had been one of Leyland's first hires when he got the job in Pittsburgh and, with Gene Lamont gone to Chicago, had moved not only into Lamont's job as third-base coach but also into the unofficial job of confidant/shoulder-to-cry-on. Leyland had played this role for Tony LaRussa in Chicago, then Lamont had played it for him. Now, it was Donnelly's turn.

Only now Donnelly had things to worry about that were far more important than John Smiley or Denny Neagle. Leyland wanted desperately to help him, but was, of course, helpless. He *hated* feeling helpless, but, on completely different levels, both Amy Donnelly's illness and the trade of John Smiley left him with no other option.

On the day of the trade, Donnelly could hear the hurt in his boss's voice. "I'm coming back in a couple of days," he told Leyland.

"No you're not—you stay there."

"It's okay, Jim. If I stay, it'll only make Amy think she's worse off than she is."

"Only come if you really think you're ready."

"I'm ready, Jim."

Leyland felt guilty and relieved. It was only mid-March and already he was drained.

•

Across the state, the Era of Good Feeling that had existed in the Mets' camp in February was already a fading memory.

It was not by accident that the cover of the Mets' media guide had four men on it who had not been associated with the team in 1991: the new manager, Jeff Torborg; free-agent signees Bobby Bonilla and Eddie Murray; and pitcher Bret Saberhagen, acquired in the biggest

trade of the offseason. The message was clear: The 77-84 record of
1991 and all the sourness that had invaded the clubhouse were in the
past. Everything was new: the general manager, the manager, the key
players. Even before the Pirates made the Smiley trade, most people
were picking the Mets to win the National League East.

"Right now everything is wonderful," Al Harazin said a week into
camp. "The new players are fitting in and I think everyone is excited
about playing for Jeff. The atmosphere really couldn't be better."

Atmosphere was a key word to Harazin. He had been named to
succeed Frank Cashen as general manager during the final week of the
disastrous 1991 season. There was little doubt that Cashen had been
the key man in rebuilding the Mets during the 1980s. There was also
little doubt that he had played a key role in the team's dismantling at
the start of the '90s.

It was Cashen who had fired manager Davey Johnson in May 1990
and replaced him with Bud Harrelson, a sensitive, gentle man who
was badly overmatched trying to manage in New York. At the end of
1990, after a public feud, Cashen allowed Darryl Strawberry to leave for
Los Angeles. Strawberry often got himself into trouble with his outspo-
kenness and, at times, could be both overbearing and immature. But
compared to Vince Coleman, Strawberry was Winston Churchill.
Cashen loved Coleman's speed and gave him a four-year contract for
just under $12 million, even though Coleman carried the poison label.
In 1991 Coleman proved to be as sulky as advertised. He also managed
to play in only seventy-two games, spending large chunks of the season on the disabled list. So did Hubie Brooks, as good a person in the
clubhouse as Coleman was bad, but at thirty-five clearly not a replacement for Strawberry. Darryl, after a slow start with the Dodgers, finished the season with twenty-eight home runs and ninety-nine RBIs,
a legitimate MVP candidate.

The Mets stayed in the '91 race until late July, then fell completely
apart. They bickered with one another, took anonymous potshots at
Harrelson in the newspapers, and, on most nights, simply didn't play
hard. They were dogs, symbolized by three men: the oft-injured, always unhappy Coleman; silent, get-me-out-of-the-clubhouse Kevin
Reynolds (whom Cashen *had* re-signed while letting Strawberry flee);
and Gregg Jefferies, once billed as the team's star of the future. There
was no questioning Jefferies's ability to hit, but he was a dreadful
infielder who became estranged from his teammates, partly because
management coddled him, partly because he had the maturity of a
fourteen-year-old. An immature fourteen-year-old.

The two men who had co-owned the Mets since 1980, Nelson
Doubleday and Fred Wilpon, remained quietly in the background,
watching as their team fell into a state of near-total disarray, and
reached a conclusion: It was time to go back to square one. Cashen's

retirement as general manager was pushed forward a year, Harrelson was fired, and Harazin was put in Cashen's seat with a mandate to make major changes.

"This team needs an overhaul," Harazin said on the day he was introduced as Cashen's successor. Those words directly contradicted what his mentor Cashen had been saying—that the team needed only some retooling.

The promotion to general manager thrilled Harazin. It was a chance to finally prove he wasn't simply an ex–corporate lawyer who knew how to draw up contracts—although Harazin *was* an ex–corporate lawyer who did know how to draw up contracts. He had grown up as a Cubs fan in suburban Chicago, the son of a chemical engineer who gave him one piece of professional advice: "Don't do what I'm doing."

Harazin listened. After graduating from law school, he went to work for a conservative Cincinnati law firm as a management-labor lawyer. Most of his work involved arbitration cases. In 1971, Harazin was twenty-nine and a couple of years from partnership. He was also bored. Still fascinated by baseball, he managed to get himself an interview with Dick Wagner, then the general manager of the Reds. "He just about threw me out of his office," Harazin said, laughing. "He said, 'Are you crazy? Leave a prestigious law firm to get into baseball?' "

Sage as that advice may have been, Harazin ignored it. He and his wife spent their vacation that spring touring minor league cities. And when Harazin heard that the Washington Senators were moving to Dallas–Fort Worth, he thought he saw an opening.

"By then I had studied the minor leagues enough to know that the Orioles had a Double-A team in that area that would have to move. That meant they would need new ownership and new management."

Harazin called the Orioles cold and was politely told, "Don't call us, we'll call you." But a few weeks later, an arbitration case sent Harazin the lawyer to Columbia, Maryland. He called the Orioles again, saying he'd like to swing by since he was going to be less than thirty minutes away. Farm director Jim McLaughlin told him he would try to find five minutes to see him.

Five minutes became four hours and included a meeting with Cashen. Two weeks later McLaughlin called: The Orioles had narrowed their choices to Macon, Georgia, and Asheville, North Carolina. Was Harazin interested in running the team?

Absolutely. Harazin and his wife flew to Macon. The temperature when they arrived was 110 degrees and the ballpark was falling apart. "We almost went home from there," he said. "But we figured, we'd come this far, so we might as well go to Asheville."

Asheville was as perfect as Macon was horrid. The only problem was there was no local financing. Harazin agreed to put up $10,000 to become majority owner—51 percent—of the new franchise. "I paid myself eight thousand the first year and my wife four thousand. We were the whole staff. Cal Ripken, Sr., was my manager; Cal Junior was the batboy, and Billy [Ripken] was the visiting clubhouse kid. We had a ball."

After two years in Asheville, Cashen asked Harazin to come to Baltimore. Six years later he followed Cashen to the Mets. Now he was the man in charge.

His new status raised some eyebrows in the baseball world. When Joe McIlvaine had left the Mets a year earlier, most people thought the club would bring in a "baseball person" to run the team. Harazin thought that notion was silly.

"You always hear 'But he never played' from people in the game. That's just the way it is. One columnist called me Wally Peepers. Fine, I can live with that. But my assumption was I'd be given the job with the understanding that I would put my stamp on the team. Otherwise, why bother?"

Harazin's stamp was an emphatic one. After hiring Torborg in October—a move greeted with great enthusiasm by the New York media—he dove headlong into the free-agent market. Thirty-five-year-old Eddie Murray received $7.5 million for two years, then Harazin won a bidding war for Bobby Bonilla, paying him a then-record $29 million for five years.

"We had become an uninteresting ball club," Harazin said. "Looking at it from a business standpoint, we simply couldn't afford to come back with the same cast. We'd spent years creating a very valuable asset, then we took this dive. In New York, everything is larger than life. If you're a good guy, you're a *great* guy. If you're a little bit of a pain in the ass, you're a *cancer.* We had to stir some interest or we were going to face a lot of empty seats. The free-agent signings, in my mind, took care of some of that."

They did not, however, take care of two other problems: the atmosphere in the clubhouse and the pitching staff. For years, the Mets had had the best starting pitching in baseball, anchored by Dwight Gooden, David Cone, Ron Darling, Bob Ojeda, Sid Fernandez, and Frank Viola. Now, though, Darling and Ojeda had both been traded; Viola was leaving via free agency, Fernandez was coming off surgery and an offseason weight-loss program, and, most significant, Gooden had undergone elbow surgery the previous summer. Once, Gooden had been the game's wunderkind. At age twenty, in 1985, he went 24-4 with an ERA of 1.53. Since then, he had been a good, though sometimes troubled pitcher. He had gone through drug rehabilitation in 1987, had missed almost half the season in 1989 with shoulder problems, and then had this elbow surgery in 1991. His ERA during the past two seasons had been 3.75—*before* the surgery.

Harazin felt he needed another top starting pitcher. He talked to Seattle about Randy Johnson, to the White Sox about Jack McDowell, to the Angels about Chuck Finley, and, finally, to the Royals about Bret Saberhagen. The general manager most willing to talk about a trade was Kansas City's Herk Robinson, who, like Harazin, felt he needed to substantially alter the makeup of his team.

"I first talked to Herk at the World Series," Harazin remembered. "I told him I wasn't looking for a number-four or -five starter, I wanted a number one. That meant Saberhagen. He was very interested in Jefferies, but he kept trying to put me onto other pitchers."

One of the pitchers Robinson kept trying to push toward Harazin was Kevin Appier. When Appier's name hit the grapevine, it was greeted with yawns (which proved to be ironic since Appier emerged as one of the best pitchers in the American League in '92).

Early in November, Harazin and his assistant Gerry Hunsicker were in St. Louis for business meetings. At the airport, Harazin called his office to check messages. One was from Robinson, whom he called back immediately.

"I just wanted to tell you that I'm willing to talk about any pitcher on our staff," Robinson told Harazin.

Harazin took a deep breath. "That includes Saberhagen?"

"Any pitcher on our staff," the K.C. GM repeated. He would not actually *say* the name *Saberhagen,* Harazin assumed, because he wanted to be able to honestly tell the Kansas City media that he had not specifically discussed the pitcher in any trade talks. Saberhagen, a two-time Cy Young Award winner and a World Series hero in 1985, was player 1-A in the Royals franchise, right behind George Brett. In terms of trade value, at twenty-seven, he was *it.*

Harazin thanked Robinson for the call, hung up, and turned to Hunsicker. "You aren't going to believe this," he said, "but I think we have a chance to get Saberhagen."

Rarely in baseball does trade talk remain a secret. Every front office has leaks. But both Harazin and Robinson kept their circles narrow enough that there was no rumor of the trade, even as the winter meetings in Miami Beach began to wind down. Appier's name kept popping up, but once the Angels had re-signed Finley, it looked as if the Mets would not pick up a pitcher.

Shortly after a press conference called on December 10 to announce that Hubie Brooks had been traded to California for Dave Gallagher, Harazin shook his head when someone asked if anything major was still pending. "No door is ever totally closed," he said. "But there sure isn't much ajar right now."

He wasn't lying. The deal with Kansas City looked dead. Robinson wanted Jefferies, McReynolds, and Keith Miller. Harazin had no problem giving up McReynolds and he understood that he would have to give up Jefferies to get Saberhagen. But he thought adding Miller, a versatile, hardworking player, was too much. At Torborg's urging, he had asked Robinson to add Bill Pecota, a thirty-one-year-old utility infielder coming off a career (.282) year, to the package. Robinson didn't like that idea at all.

"The funny thing was, we both knew the trade was about Saberhagen and Jefferies and we were both reluctant about it," Harazin said. "So we kept raising other issues that held things up."

On the morning of December 11, Harazin and Robinson talked once more. The deal on the table was three-for-two: Jefferies-McReynolds-Miller for Saberhagen-Pecota. They agreed to consult with their staffs and talk again before dinner. At one o'clock that afternoon, Harazin convened a meeting of his entire baseball staff: Cashen, Torborg, Hunsicker, scouts, and coaches, and laid out the trade. He went around the room, asking each person for an opinion. Most of the argument against the trade centered around Jefferies, who, for all his troubles, had played only three full seasons in the big leagues and was just twenty-four.

"We were talking about trading away a potential batting champion," Harazin said. "Of course, we'd be *getting* a two-time Cy Young winner. That was the main thrust of the argument."

After ninety minutes, nothing had been decided, so Harazin ended the meeting. He wanted some time alone.

He was still wrestling with his thoughts when Cashen knocked on his door. During the staff meeting, Harazin had felt that Cashen, while not dead set against the trade, was more against it than for it.

After almost twenty years of working for Cashen, Harazin still valued his opinion. "Al, if you can make this trade, make it," Cashen said now. "You've got to have a number one pitcher. What's more, I think your gut tells you this is a good deal. Go with that."

Harazin felt better. "If Frank had really been against the trade, I don't think I could have gone through with it," he said. "As it was, I was swallowing hard."

An hour later, the conversation seemed moot. Harazin was giving the New York media its daily briefing when the team's longtime public relations director, Jay Horwitz, came in. "Your aunt's on the phone in the other room," he told Harazin. The reporters snickered, knowing it had to be another general manager.

It was Robinson. "My people don't like the deal," he announced. "They don't want to give up Pecota unless you'll add Anthony Young or Pete Schourek . . ."

"Absolutely not. I'm already gagging as it is."

That was it. The deal was off. Harazin went out to the suite's balcony to tell Torborg and his staff there would be no trade. They left for dinner; he then went back to the media and told them there was no news from his aunt. Everyone went in different directions.

The winter meetings were ending the next day. Harazin figured he would have to wait until spring training to try again. He was getting ready to pack for the flight home when his phone rang. It was now seven-thirty. Robinson wanted to talk one more time. Harazin went down to see him in person.

If Harazin still had Jefferies-McReynolds-Miller on the table, Robinson said, he was willing to move Saberhagen and Pecota. He had tried to bluff Harazin, hoping that Harazin was so desperate to deal he'd cave in and give up too much. This is common practice. But Harazin had called Robinson's bluff—so now Robinson was back.

By nine o'clock, the deal was agreed upon. Still, there was much left to do. Before an announcement could be made, the five players had to be contacted. Even before that, each team's doctor had to certify the health of the players involved. This was usually routine, but Royals team doctor Steve Joyce was in surgery, operating on a woman who had been in an automobile accident. He finally came out of the operating room and told the Mets' new team doctor, David Altchek, that, yes, both Saberhagen and Pecota were healthy.

Saberhagen was rummaging through a closet in the new house he and his wife, Janeane, had just moved into in Thousand Oaks, California, when the phone rang. "I was organizing all the CDs," he said. "Janeane came in and said, 'Herk Robinson's on the phone.' I said, 'Uh-oh, we must have been traded.' Soon as I said that, Janeane burst into tears."

The tears flowed for a while after Robinson gave him the news, complete with the obligatory speech about how much he'd meant to the Royals. Saberhagen had never been anything *but* a Royal. Now, suddenly, he was a Met.

Back in Florida, Harazin couldn't find his manager. Torborg was still at dinner and no one could track him down. A press conference had been scheduled for eleven-thirty. The media, tired and grumpy after being shut inside for five days, wanted to know what the hell was going on. Was this another trade like Brooks for Gallagher or was it a headline-maker? Harazin was about to go into the press conference when he spotted Torborg walking in the front door of the hotel. He grabbed him, pushed him into a corner, and told him what had happened.

"What the . . . ?" were the only words Torborg was able to get out in response before Harazin dragged him into the media workroom to make the announcement.

The trade was a stunner. The Royals felt they had acquired three starters. "We were a sixth-place team last year," manager Hal McRae said. "If we didn't make a change, we'd still be a sixth-place team."

In New York, Harazin was hailed as a conquering hero. He had acquired one of the best arms in baseball for a whiny brat and an aging outfielder who had the personality of a doorknob. Miller for Pecota was seen as a straight swap of utility men.

Harazin had clearly put his own stamp on the club. The Mets would be new and different in 1992. When Willie Randolph, the classy ex-Yankee second baseman, was signed the next week, the picture seemed complete. Ten weeks later, Harazin was still basking in what he had created.

"I warned my wife, though, that this could all change," he said, smiling. "Let's face it, the deal made people happy, not only because we got Saberhagen but because neither Jefferies nor McReynolds was very popular. There was no sentimental attachment in New York to either one of them.

"Right now, everyone says I'm a genius. I'm enjoying that. But I know that if we finish *third* or something, and Jefferies wins the batting title, I could be the village idiot before the season's over. It's very easy to go from genius to dunce in this game."

At the time, such a fall seemed impossible to imagine.

•

The unraveling of Harazin's carefully laid plans began on the morning of March 3. On that day, excerpts of the new book *Darryl* began showing up in New York newspapers. Not surprisingly, Strawberry was tough on his old team. He accused the Mets' management of being racist in its dealings with him. At one point he wrote that in New York he had felt like "Dred Scott in Johannesburg."

As soon as he read that phrase, Marty Noble, the longtime Mets beat writer for *Newsday,* got in his car and made the thirty-mile trip up I-95 to Vero Beach. He arrived in the Dodger locker room at eight-thirty in the morning and went directly to Strawberry. According to Noble, the following conversation took place:

NOBLE: Who is Dred Scott?
STRAWBERRY: I don't know.
NOBLE: Where is Johannesburg?
STRAWBERRY: Africa.

Noble was convinced that Strawberry's ghostwriter, Art Rust, Jr., had put words in Strawberry's mouth. Later that day, the two men— beat writer and superstar—would again confront each other, this time in a press conference.

The Mets weren't the least bit concerned with Strawberry's knowledge of history or geography. But they were extremely concerned by Strawberry's assertion in his book that his good pal Gooden might have been using cocaine during the 1986 World Series.

This was not, by any means, a brand-new theory. During that World Series, there had been much speculation about what was wrong with Gooden—and drug use had been mentioned. This is not uncommon in sports: Star athlete tails off for reasons no one can explain; speculation begins that he's using drugs. Often that speculation is correct. Often it is not.

The Gooden rumors had started in part because he clearly wasn't the same pitcher in '86 that he'd been in '85 (but then, what human being could have been?). Also, *everything* looked so much more difficult for him. Throughout Game Five of the World Series, a game the Mets lost 4–2, Gooden sweated profusely, even though it was a cool night in Boston.

The evidence at that time was circumstantial and fairly weak. The next spring, however, when Gooden tested positive, the evidence was absolute. He spent a month in the Smithers Alcoholism Treatment Center in New York (the same place Strawberry would go three years later for treatment of a drinking problem).

Now Strawberry was stirring up the '86 World Series controversy again. When Gooden arrived for work that morning, several writers met him at his locker to ask about the Strawberry book. Diplomatically, Gooden said he hadn't seen or read it and thus wasn't going to say anything about it. But when he trotted to the outfield a few moments later, David Cone could see he was upset.

"Darryl says in his book that I was on the stuff in 'eighty-six," Gooden told Cone. "The writers just told me."

Like everyone else on the Mets, Cone was extremely sensitive to Gooden's state of mind. Since his first day in New York, Gooden has been as popular as any player in the clubhouse. Unlike Strawberry, the pitcher has always been forgiven for his mistakes. It's easy to forgive Dwight Gooden—he's easygoing, funny, and he has never taken himself or his celebrity too seriously.

When the morning workout was over, a worried Cone strode into the clubhouse and got a hold of the excerpt, which had been faxed from the Mets' executive offices in New York. When Cone got to the crucial line, he became furious. Strawberry had *not* said that Gooden had been using cocaine. The actual line in the book was, "Given all the pressure we were all under, it wouldn't have surprised me to learn that [Dwight] was using cocaine" during the '86 Series.

"Not surprised" isn't *radically* different from "he was" but it was enough to set Cone off. Still holding the fax in his hands, he went looking for the press. The first person he found was Bob Klapisch of the New York *Daily News*.

"Klap, what is this shit?" Cone asked, waving the fax in the air.

"You guys are asking Doc [Gooden's nickname: short for Doctor K] to respond to something Darryl didn't say! What the hell is with you guys?!"

Cone's tirade brought other reporters running and quieted the normally raucous postpractice clubhouse. On every team there are moments during the season when a player and a reporter will get into a shouting match. The media has more access to the athletes in baseball than in any other professional sport. Often, familiarity breeds contempt (not to mention suspicion, anger, and frustration) on both sides, especially when things aren't going well for a team.

But Cone was not one to go around blaming the media for most of the world's ills. He was just the opposite. He often socialized with writers; occasionally he showed up at their pickup basketball games. He was *always* accessible. Cone was that rarest of athletes—he was willing to share feelings rather than just words.

That was why his anger drew a crowd. Klapisch and Cone were friends. But Cone and Gooden were teammates. That was far more important.

"Look, Dave, we were just trying to get him to react to what Darryl said."

"But he didn't say *that,*" Cone challenged. "Don't get me wrong—I think what he did say is bullshit and unfair. That's another issue, though. You guys were reckless, man, really reckless. All of you—Harp [John Harper of the *New York Post*], Joe [Sexton of *The New York Times*]—what you did sucks. It really does."

"Hang on, Dave, that's not fair," Sexton insisted. "I haven't talked to Doc all day."

That seemed to bring Cone up short. "In that case, I'm sorry. The rest of you guys, though, wow. Reckless stuff."

He turned and walked to his locker. Klapisch followed. Cone never stays angry long; a few minutes later he and the reporter shook hands. Cone then went and found Sexton to apologize again for including him in his tirade. Cone was mature; he wouldn't hold a grudge. But other Mets would.

There was more to come. Much more.

Ten days later, a New York woman filed a complaint in Port St. Lucie alleging that three Mets—Gooden, Coleman, and outfielder Daryl Boston—had sexually assaulted her the previous spring.

From that moment on, the Mets clubhouse was like an armed camp. It wasn't just players against media; it was also media against media. The beat writers resented the arrival of the newswriters on their turf. Not only were a lot of them printing vicious gossip, but their presence eliminated any possibility of talking quietly with players to find out what was *really* going on. Everyone was looking over his shoulder, waiting for the next bombshell.

The New York tabloid media went nuts. Rumors ran rampant. Every day there was a new headline. Things really turned ugly when *New York Post* columnist Andrea Peyser wrote about seeing Cone, Saberhagen, and Kevin Elster in a local bar on St. Patrick's Day. According to the column, each of the three had left with a different woman. Saberhagen and Elster said they had left together—and with no one else—and had several witnesses to prove it. Exactly why Cone leaving a bar with a woman—he was single—was newsworthy, no one was quite sure.

Once again, the old fax machine set the clubhouse abuzz. When Saberhagen saw the column the following day, he quietly walked up to Peyzer and said, "You got your facts wrong. If you're going to spy on us, at least get it right. I left with Kevin."

Cone wasn't as calm. He was angry and said so. When Jay Horwitz, who was suddenly looking down the barrel at another nightmare season in the Mets PR office, tried to get in between Cone and Peyzer, she accused Horwitz of trying to hustle her out of the clubhouse. Yet another crisis.

That afternoon, the Mets made an announcement: For the duration of the spring, only *sports*writers would be granted access to the clubhouse. But the damage had already been done. Even the always-upbeat Torborg was beginning to betray signs of tension. During the manager's daily press briefing, Steve Levy, the beat reporter for the team's flagship radio station, WFAN, asked Torborg if he would think twice about leaving Gooden (who was being moved along very slowly, due to his operation) in Florida for extended spring training, "because of the off-field problems."

"Don't ask me about off-field problems!" Torborg snapped angrily. "Ask me about *on*-field things. I'm not interested in talking about anything that's not on-field."

Only Harazin seemed able to keep his sense of humor: "We fooled you guys," he said. "You all thought Darryl's book was going to be the big crisis of the spring. Not even close."

There was one more crisis still to come. The following week, a lawsuit was filed by two women against Cone. It alleged, among other things, that he had once called them into the bullpen during a game, exposed himself, then masturbated. Cone didn't even get a chance to tell his side of things after the suit was filed—amid more screaming tabloid headlines—because by then the team had voted to stop speaking to the media entirely.

Although the players claimed to be unanimous in reaching this decision, that was far from true. Three players—newcomers Bonilla and Murray and relief pitcher John Franco—were at the heart of the boycott.

Bonilla, who was having a miserable spring, was delighted to have a few days off from answering questions about his contract. Murray had virtually no use for anyone in the media under any circumstances, and Franco, although generally cordial, saw the media as unwanted and uninvited guests in the clubhouse.

So for ten days, while he was the subject of every bad joke ever told, Cone had to suffer in silence. Then, after a clubhouse meeting in Baltimore on April 3, Dave Magadan convinced his teammates enough was enough: "We've made our point, we've proven that we'll stick together," Magadan said. "The season starts Monday. Why not start out with a clean slate?"

Cone, relief pitcher Jeff Innis, and Willie Randolph backed Magadan up. The boycott was lifted and the Mets headed for St. Louis to start the season. On opening night, Cone pitched well and Bonilla hit two home runs.

"Boy, did I get fooled," Harazin said, months later. "I figured we were going to go a hundred and sixty-two and oh and Bobby was going to hit three hundred home runs."

Three days later, the St. Lucie police concluded their twenty-six-day investigation into the alleged '91 sexual assault, announcing that Gooden, Coleman, and Boston would not be charged. That was a huge relief to the Mets. The 450-page report that the police released was not. There was not enough evidence to bring charges, but there was plenty in the report to embarrass the players involved. Their behavior may not have been criminal, but it was hardly exemplary.

That night, the Mets returned home from St. Louis. They were 2-2. As they arrived at Shea Stadium, a number of news reporters and TV cameramen were waiting, hoping to get a response to the news from St. Lucie. When one cameraman got a little too aggressive—at least as far as they were concerned—Bonilla and Murray got into a shoving match with him. Horwitz tried to intervene. For his trouble, he had the pleasure of seeing himself on the back page of one of the tabloids the next morning.

The Mets were home. Opening Day at Shea Stadium was gorgeous, a perfect spring day. No one seemed to notice.

STRAW, LASORDA, AND DODGER BLUE

If there was anyone in baseball entitled to giggle at the Mets' troubles it was Darryl Strawberry.

During his eight years in New York, Strawberry had been canonized and crucified, and, at varying times, had deserved a little of each. One fact stood out above everything else: The Mets *needed* Strawberry. They needed his bat, which could carry the team when he was hot; they needed his charisma and flair; they even needed his personality.

Sure, Strawberry could act childish at times. More often, he was a lightning rod, especially after Keith Hernandez, Ray Knight, and Gary Carter, each a leader in his own way, were either dumped (Knight) or ceased being major factors on the team (Hernandez, Carter).

The sniping between Strawberry and Frank Cashen boiled down to one thing: Strawberry's craving to feel wanted and loved. The Mets didn't satisfy that craving—but the Dodgers did. So the youngest player ever to reach two hundred home runs went back to his roots and signed with the Dodgers.

He had talked for years about ending up in Los Angeles, perhaps even being reunited with his childhood pal Eric Davis, who was then playing in Cincinnati. In 1991 the Dodgers paid Strawberry $4.7 million (the first year of a five-year contract) and welcomed him with the open arms Strawberry had been begging for in New York. A year later, they went a step further, trading one of their best pitchers, Tim Belcher, to the Reds to acquire Davis. Strawberry thought he had found baseball nirvana.

"This is, without question, the best spring I've ever had," he said one day, sitting in front of his locker while Davis, his neighbor, bummed a cigarette. "I've just turned thirty and I feel strong and healthy. I'm with a beautiful organization. I'm content."

There was little doubt that Strawberry was pleased with the Dodgers, even if they hadn't followed his other offseason suggestion—jettisoning oft-injured outfielder Kal Daniels. Manager Tommy Lasorda also wanted Daniels gone, but general manager Fred Claire insisted on holding on to him in the hope that a switch to first base would keep him in the lineup and allow him to be the productive offensive player he had been in Cincinnati.

After Strawberry had publicly called for Daniels's exit, Daniels was quoted as saying that Strawberry was mentally ill, and the relationship between the two was still frosty. They would stand right next to each other waiting their turn in the batting cage without exchanging a word. That sort of quiet was rare for Strawberry.

"That's you, Bugsy!" he yelled one afternoon during batting practice as Brett Butler slapped one of his trademark hits to the opposite field. Butler walked out of the cage, shot a look at Strawberry, and whispered something to utility infielder Lenny Harris.

"Straw, you've hurt Bugsy's feelings," Harris said, arm around Butler. "He thinks you're making fun of him for hitting singles instead of home runs. I think you owe him an apology."

Strawberry flung his bat down, dropped to his knees, and screamed, "Bugsy, forgive me, please forgive me!"

Butler again whispered in Harris's ear. "Bugsy says you should kiss his feet," Harris reported.

Strawberry crawled forward to where his two teammates stood and kissed each of Butler's feet. "Never again, Bugsy," he wailed. "Never again!"

Butler whispered in Harris's ear again. "You are forgiven," Harris said, then, like everyone else watching, he was convulsed with laughter as Strawberry continued to kiss Butler's feet.

When it was Strawberry's turn in the cage, he didn't bother with any opposite-field singles. One after another he sent balls soaring into the palm trees beyond the chain-link fence in the outfield. The crowd of four hundred sitting in the blue-and-orange seats oohed and aahed.

Dodgertown is a spring-training throwback, an immaculate complex that also includes golf courses and tennis courts. But it is more open and accessible than any training camp around. Only in the last four years have the Dodgers even bothered to put up a fence in the outfield. Before then, umpires ruled that balls hit into the trees were either doubles or home runs—usually depending on which would get the game over with faster. One of the more famous stories dates back to 1971, when Richie Allen, having just been acquired by the Dodgers, ran smack into a palm tree chasing a fly ball and knocked himself out.

When the players finished their workout in the stadium, they walked back along Vin Scully Way to reach the clubhouse. Most stopped to sign autographs. No one seemed to enjoy it more than Strawberry.

There is still a lot of kid in Darryl Strawberry, even though at six feet six, with arms that Paul Bunyan might have envied, he is one of the most impressive physical specimens in the game.

"There's a part of me that never wanted to leave New York," Strawberry said, relaxing in the clubhouse. "We had something very special there. I learned a lot from guys like [Keith] Hernandez and [Ray] Knight even if I had my battles with them. They both taught me about winning and competing. I would like to have stayed in New York and won more titles. We *should* have won more than we did.

"I just felt at the end that it was all too much. Frank said I wasn't worth the kind of money I was asking for—now he's paying Bobby Bonilla considerably more than that. Does that make sense? Maybe it does. Bobby's a great player.

"I had regrets about leaving—that's why I sounded so confused. One minute I was thrilled to come home, the next I wanted to be back in New York. Now I'm not confused anymore. I really think when I look back at what I accomplished in New York with all the distractions and the pressures and the problems I had, that I have the ability to have great years out here. Now I'm happy, I'm relaxed. I feel good about myself and my life."

That Strawberry still hadn't figured out how he felt about the Mets and his years in New York was obvious. In one breath, he talked about having no hard feelings and only good memories. In the next, he railed angrily at the team for giving Bret Saberhagen his old number, 18. "Just like that they gave someone my number," he said. "What if I end up going to the Hall of Fame? I've hit two hundred and eighty home runs and I just turned thirty—isn't it possible I'll hit five hundred? If I do, what will they say to me if they want to retire the number *then*?

"I'll tell you what *I'll* say. I'll say, 'Forget it. Don't even ask me back—I'm not coming!' "

He smiled. "Actually, I should thank them. They've just given me that much more incentive to make it to the Hall of Fame."

Not everyone in Dodgertown was as sanguine as Strawberry. While he was thrilled with Eric Davis's arrival, others were not so certain the trade was a wise idea. Fred Claire and manager Tommy Lasorda had spent a good deal of the offseason disagreeing on personnel.

By the time the Dodgers reported to camp, a lot of people were convinced that Lasorda's sixteenth season as manager would be his last. He would turn sixty-five in September, his contract was up at the end of the season, and Bill Russell, considered the manager-in-waiting, had been moved from a coaching slot with the major league club to the manager's job in Albuquerque, presumably to prepare for the next step up.

Lasorda was cranky as camp opened, a mood not unfamiliar to those around the club. Perhaps no other personality in sports is the subject of more divergent opinions than Lasorda.

To most fans, Lasorda is Everyman in a uniform. He was never quite good enough to make it in the big leagues—parts of three seasons with the Dodgers and Kansas City produced a career record of 0-4 and an ERA of 6.48—but Lasorda never gave up the dream. After years of toiling in the Dodger farm system, he was rewarded with the managing job in 1977 when, after twenty-three years at the helm, Walter Alston retired. Lasorda promptly won back-to-back pennants, singing the praises of Dodger Blue everywhere he went, and became a celebrity in a town that lives for celebrities.

Lasorda was warm and cuddly and fans loved him. Put a TV camera in a room and Lasorda would light up. Tell him that a national columnist was heading his way and he would crank up the machine and tell all his wonderful anecdotes. But catch Lasorda at the wrong moment, or ask him a question he didn't like, and you'd better duck. If Lasorda thought you were important, he had all day for you. If not, don't let the door hit you on the way out. This trait hardly made Lasorda unique among major league managers; he just carried it to extremes. Some called him moody. Others were harsher: They called him phony.

One oft-told story goes back to the day longtime Dodger owner Walter O'Malley died. Lasorda sat in his office with the cameras rolling and talked about how much he'd loved O'Malley. He cried, the tears rolling down his cheeks. He called O'Malley the greatest man he'd ever known and talked about his joining the Great Dodger in the Sky. Then, as soon as he'd finished, he looked up, spotted one of the clubhouse kids, and yelled, "Hey, where's that fuckin' linguini I told you to get me?"

In a profession where using the word "fuck" at least a hundred times a day is generally considered part of the job description, Lasorda might be the most profane man of all. His temper is explosive, and when he gets mad he stays mad. He can carry a grudge with the best of them.

Consider the case of David Raymond, who, for the last fifteen years, has been the Phillie Phanatic. If there is one thing everyone in baseball agrees on it is the Phanatic. No mascot is funnier, better prepared, or more fun to watch. For years, Raymond and Lasorda were friends, especially after Raymond went to Japan with a Lasorda-managed All-Star team one winter.

Three years ago, Raymond pulled his four-wheel bike in front of the Dodger dugout one evening carrying a doll dressed in a Dodger uniform. This was one of his favorite routines. To the tune of "Beat It," Raymond proceeded to pummel the Dodger doll. About midway through the routine, Raymond became aware of someone in the dugout screaming profanities at him. He glanced up just in time to see Lasorda, face contorted, charging at him.

"At first I thought he was just getting in on the act," Raymond said. "I like it when guys on the other team come out and give me a hard time. But Tommy was crazed. He started pounding on me, screaming, 'You stop that, you motherfucker!' Even then, I thought he must be joking, but then he tried to twist my head off. I said, 'Hey, Tommy, enough!' But he kept doing it until finally a couple of his guys pulled him off. That's when I realized he was serious. He was still red and screaming when they dragged him away."

After the game, Raymond went looking for Lasorda to try to clear up the misunderstanding. "I wanted to explain to him that it was all in fun," he said. "I didn't even get the chance. He started screaming at me to get the fuck out of his office and that if I ever came back he'd kill me, and on and on. I just said the hell with him and left."

Now, whenever the Dodgers come to town, Raymond gets a can of Ultra Slim-Fast, which Lasorda endorses, and crushes it underneath the Phanatic's foot in front of the Dodger dugout. The players, he says, love it. "Tommy just curses me out some more," he adds. "That's fine."

Lasorda needs attention the way most people need air. He craves company so much that, at the World Series, he will sit in his hotel lobby and talk to anyone and everyone who comes by. Peter Schmuck, now of the Baltimore *Sun,* but then the Dodger beat writer for the *Orange County Register,* remembers bumping into Lasorda in the team hotel at two-thirty one morning in Pittsburgh.

"Walk with me, Pete," Lasorda said.

"I was exhausted," Schmuck said. "But I was a twenty-six-year-old beat reporter and Tommy Lasorda wanted my company. So, I went.''

The two men walked from bar to bar, restaurant to restaurant. Anyplace that was open, Lasorda went in. "If they didn't recognize him, he would walk up and introduce himself," Schmuck said. "Everyplace we went, he was the center of attention within a few minutes. It wasn't like an ego trip or anything the way most of us think of those things. He just *needed* to be the center of attention.

"A lot of people don't like him because they think he's a phony. I can see that. But I don't think it's that simple. Tommy just can't help himself. It's not malicious with him. It's just the way he is.''

A large portion of Lasorda's preseason crankiness was being attributed to his battles with Claire and his contract situation. There was something to that. But it wasn't that simple. Tommy Lasorda was a wounded man. Eight months earlier, his only son, Tommy Lasorda, Jr., had died. The California death certificate listed pneumonia as the official cause of death but went on to say the pneumonia was brought on by the human immunodeficiency virus—in other words, AIDS.

Lasorda refused to acknowledge the truth about his son's death. When Tommy Junior first became ill during the winter of 1991, Lasorda actually told several reporters that his son had cancer. When Tommy Junior died, the Dodger manager pleaded with the local media not to report that he had died from complications caused by AIDS. The *Los Angeles Times* decided to go along with that request—on the grounds that Tommy Junior was not a public figure—and the rest of the mainstream media followed suit.

That decision sent shock waves through the gay community in Los Angeles. In an era in which obituaries routinely mentioned that people had died due to AIDS-related complications, the manager of the Dodgers was being allowed to act as if his son had died of pneumonia because he didn't want to deal with his sexuality.

During spring training, Lasorda was interviewed by Peter Richmond of *Gentleman's Quarterly* for a piece that would appear in the fall of '92. Richmond asked Lasorda how he felt about Tommy Junior being gay. "My son *wasn't* gay!" Lasorda roared. But if he refused to accept his son's sexuality, Lasorda never refused to accept his son. Tommy Junior frequently visited him at the ballpark. He was well liked by the players, who all assumed that their manager's son was gay, based on what they'd heard, who he hung out with, and his appearance: If you just glanced at Tommy Lasorda, Jr., you were very likely to mistake him for a woman.

Yet, except for one brief period, there was never any estrangement between the effeminate son and the macho father. No one ever doubted how devastated Lasorda was by his death. Players, coaches,

and reporters learned to make a lot of noise, before walking into
Lasorda's office after Tommy Junior's death; otherwise there was a
good chance you would catch Lasorda crying.

That the hurt was still there in 1992 was apparent. What happened on one steamy night in Atlanta says a lot about how Lasorda
felt. The Dodgers were in the middle of a June road trip that would turn
into a Bataan death march, burying them in last place for the duration
of the season. At one point during the series in Atlanta, Lasorda had
become so frustrated he had tried walking back to the hotel after a
game rather than riding the team bus.

On *this* particular night, Orel Hershiser's two sons, Quinton and
Jordan, were in the clubhouse waiting for their dad to finish talking to
the press after a 2–0 loss. Quinton is seven, Jordan almost four.

As they stood waiting, Lasorda stalked out of his office, a fierce
look on his face. Earlier in the day he'd put his team through a ninety-
minute workout in searing heat, a response to a horrendous three-
game series in Cincinnati. His mood was as sour as could be. But
when Lasorda saw the two boys, his face went soft.

"Hey, Quint, Jordan, c'mere," he said, hugging them both. "You
guys want something to eat?" He began pulling food off the table in
the middle of the room and feeding it to the boys. "What else you
want? You want something to drink?" The boys kept nodding and
Lasorda kept feeding, oblivious to anything else going on in the room.
As they ate, he watched for a couple of minutes, then pulled them into
another hug, kissing them both intensely.

"I love you guys, you know that?" he said. "I really love both of
you."

There were no TV cameras around, no national columnists. As far
as Lasorda knew, no one was watching him. For one moment at least,
Tommy Lasorda was completely and totally real: a broken-hearted
father reaching out to two little boys for love.

VOICES

The afternoon of March 6 was no different from most spring days on the west coast of Florida. It was sunny and breezy, a little cool in the early morning, but warm and comfortable by the time the Chicago White Sox and Detroit Tigers began preparing for their exhibition game.

Rick Rizzs and Bob Rathbun didn't notice the weather. As they drove from Lakeland to Sarasota, they didn't take note of the sights and sounds. They had scouted the trip a day earlier to make certain they wouldn't get lost en route to the ballpark. In their briefcases they had packed just about every fact and figure they could find on the two teams.

"You want to know how many times Charlie Hough threw over to first base last year?" Rizzs asked. "Three hundred and thirteen. Not that we've overresearched this game or anything."

Rathbun and Rizzs pulled into the parking lot at Ed Smith Stadium at a little after ten in the morning.

"This is a first in the history of baseball," Rathbun said. "For the very first time the seventh game of the World Series will be played on March sixth."

To Rizzs and Rathbun this was the World Series. The pinnacle. With all the ensuing pressure. Camera crews trailed them everywhere. Reporters chased them, wanting to know how they felt. They were about to do something each had fantasized about doing for years. And they were about to do something each had dreaded for months.

Both had dreamed that this day would come: a day when they were the voices of a major league baseball team. But both knew from the minute they were hired that they would be doing something no one in their right mind would want to do: They would be replacing the legendary Ernie Harwell, longtime Voice of the Detroit Tigers.

"Not replacing," Rizzs said firmly. "Following."

•

Only in baseball do broadcasters become part of the family.

It is not by coincidence that most of the great names in sports broadcasting have been associated with baseball: Red Barber, Mel Allen, Jack Brickhouse, Curt Gowdy, Vin Scully, Harry Caray, and Ernie Harwell—to name a few. Other sports have their legends—Cawood Ledford in college basketball, Marv Albert in pro basketball, Marty Glickman in pro football—but baseball, more than any other game, lends itself to the pace of radio. Only rarely do people sit around and *listen* to football or basketball; they *watch*. Baseball, where so much of the romance comes from the imagination, is the sport to listen to. Corny or not, baseball does become a companion. The season is long, there always seems to be some meaning to any particular game—even if a team is hopelessly out of a pennant race, there is always the chance to find out how the young players look when they come up from the minors in September.

Almost every city has a Voice; some have two. And more often than not, once someone has settled in somewhere, he isn't likely to leave. Vin Scully has done the Dodgers for forty-three years. Jack Buck has been with the Cardinals for thirty-nine. Bob Murphy has done the Mets for thirty-one. Rich Ashburn has worked for the Phillies for thirty. His partners, Harry Kalas, Andy Musser, and Chris Wheeler, have been with him for twenty-one, seventeen, and sixteen years.

The list goes on and on. Managers and players come and go but the Voice stays. And he—or in cases like the Phillies, they—becomes the team's identity.

Nowhere was this more true than in Detroit. In 1991, Ernie Harwell, at seventy-three, completed his thirty-second year with the Tigers. Paul Carey, his sidekick, had been with him for nineteen years. But before that season had started, Harwell and Carey had been called in by management and told that they would not be back in 1992.

And an entire city went into shock.

Almost all of the controversy centered on Harwell. He was, after all, the symbol. To this day, there are at least ten different versions of what led to his dismissal. Different sources blame different people. The bottom line to the fans was a simple one: Ernie Harwell had been dumped. It didn't matter if it was the doing of team president Bo Schembechler (since dumped himself); of WJR, the team's flagship station; or of George Bush (who no doubt would have blamed Congress).

Throughout 1991 there were tributes to Harwell both at home and on the road. There were ceremonies and gifts and hundreds of thousands of kind words. One moment stands out in Harwell's memory.

"It was during my last home game," he said, sitting in a hotel room one morning, the familiar southern lilt in his voice. "I always did the first three innings of a game, Paul did the middle three, and then I came back for the last three.

"We got to the top of the seventh, I came back into the booth, and, just as Paul was turning the mike back over to me, all of a sudden, everyone in the crowd stood up, turned toward the booth, and started to clap. It was completely spontaneous. Most of them knew that I was taking the mike for the last time in Tiger Stadium and so they just turned around, I guess, to say thank you and good-bye. I really had a hard time keeping my composure right there."

Composure is a Harwell trait. He started in the business as a newspaper man, working for *The Sporting News*, while he was still in high school, as their correspondent on the old Atlanta Crackers. The Crackers were his heroes as kids. "One of the great days in my life was finding out that one of the Crackers had moved into a house on our block," he said. "To me, being around the Crackers was the ultimate."

Harwell broadcast the Crackers on radio after he got out of the marines and then was *traded* by the Crackers to the Brooklyn Dodgers for a player, catcher Cliff Dapper, in 1948. It had never happened before; it has never happened since that an announcer was traded for a player. Harwell learned under Red Barber, moved on to the Giants, the Orioles, and, in 1960, the Tigers.

"I didn't mind being a number-two guy, especially under someone like Red," Harwell said. "But the chance to be number one was irresistible."

He stayed number one until October 6, 1991, when he broadcast the last game played at Memorial Stadium in Baltimore, an 8–1 Detroit victory. Ironically, Harwell had also broadcast the first major league game played there, in 1954, when he made his debut with the new Baltimore franchise.

During the '91 season, Harwell approached several number-two broadcasters in other cities and urged them to apply for his job. Rick Rizzs was in his ninth year as the number-two man in Seattle. He had grown up outside of Chicago and had known by the time he was fifteen that he wanted to be a broadcaster. He even wrote a letter to Jack Brickhouse telling him so. When Brickhouse wrote back to him, Rizzs followed up with another letter asking if he could come to the station and meet him. "One of the great thrills of my life then and now," Rizzs said. "I've stayed in touch with him ever since then."

He was flattered when Harwell turned to him behind the batting cage one night and said, "Rick, why don't you apply for the job?"

Rizzs loved the idea, but felt uncomfortable, since everyone in baseball knew Harwell was being pushed out of the booth. "Don't give it a second thought," Harwell said, reading his mind. "It isn't my job anymore. Someone has to do it."

And so Rizzs applied for the job.

Bob Rathbun didn't want Harwell's job. He wanted Paul Carey's. Baseball broadcasting is very structured. There is no doubt in any booth who the number-one man is. Rizzs, with eight years in the minor leagues and nine as a number-two in the majors, was a logical choice to make the move to the number-one slot. Rathbun was looking to break into a major league booth as second in command.

He had grown up in Salisbury, North Carolina, and, like Rizzs, knew at a very young age that he wanted to be a broadcaster. There wasn't any Jack Brickhouse in Salisbury, but there was a man named John Bolcer, the Voice of Salisbury, on WSTP radio. When Rathbun was twelve, his parents took him to the station one Sunday to meet Bolcer and, from that day forward, Rathbun spent his Sundays there.

The sports director was a twenty-five-year-old hotshot named Marty Brennaman. Rathbun became Brennaman's stats man on games at Catawba College and during American Legion games that summer. As a reward for all his hard work, Brennaman let Rathbun call the seventh inning of a game one night.

"The team we were covering, Rowan City, wasn't very good," Rathbun said. "In fact, they hadn't hit a single home run all season. Marty introduces me, hands me the mike, and up comes the first baseman, Joey Brown. He steps in, takes a pitch, and then hits the next pitch over the right-field scoreboard! Marty was livid. He kept saying, 'I can't believe I waited all summer to call a home run and when they finally hit one I've given the mike to a twelve-year-old punk!' "

Brennaman did survive the trauma, moving seven years later to Cincinnati, where he has now been the Reds' Voice for nineteen years. Rathbun went on to Catawba College, became a college basketball play-by-play man, and did the broadcasts of the Mets' top farm club, the Tidewater Tides. But a major league job was elusive. Five times he finished second in the auditions for number-two jobs, including twice

in New York. He did get some major league work as the backup
play-by-play man for Oriole cablecasts but by the fall of '91, Rathbun
was thirty-seven (a year younger than Rizzs) and wondering when his
chance would come.

And then it came.

The press conference announcing their hiring was chaotic, as
might be expected. They had been briefed on how to handle the
questions, so nothing caught them off guard until one TV type asked
them if they thought they were being brought in as sacrificial lambs.

"What kind of a question was that?" Rizzs said months later.
"We've got three-year contracts and I think it's fair to say the Tigers
want and expect us to do a good job. Otherwise, why would we be
here?"

Rizzs and Rathbun couldn't wait for the games to start. Both
assumed that once they did, the attention would begin to die down.
When they arrived in Lakeland, they were encouraged by the number
of fans who stopped them at workouts and said things like "We loved
Ernie, but we wish you boys all the best."

"That's all we ask," Rathbun said. "Rick isn't going to be Ernie
and I'm not going to be Paul. We *can't* be them. We just want to be
ourselves. The sooner the games start and we get the first reviews
behind us, the easier things will be."

That was why March 6—the first spring-training game—was so
important. They both knew there'd be one more media blitz for their
regular-season debut in Tiger Stadium on April 6, but at least the
beginning of the season meant that the end of the questions was in
sight.

As one o'clock approached, the two men finished their pregame
work on the field, accepted good-luck wishes from a number of people,
and headed for the booth. They had done all the interviews and intended to lock themselves in so they could focus on the broadcast.
Public relations director Greg Shea had warned them that one last TV
crew had asked to come into the booth briefly to shoot them at the
microphones just before they went on the air.

Their stomachs were churning as they walked the steps to the
booth. They settled in, spread their notes around, and began to prepare. The clock ticked down. One minute to air. A knock on the door.
The TV crew Shea had told them about. An engineer opened the door.

But it wasn't the TV crew. It was Dick Vitale, the nonstop-talking
ESPN basketball announcer, who lived in Sarasota. "Hey, guys, you
ready to go? Ready to do it?!" Vitale shouted. "This is a big one, baby!
Everyone's listening to you guys!"

Rizzs and Rathbun looked at Vitale as if he had just landed from
Mars. Neither said a word. They turned back to their work. Vitale got

the message. He looked around for a moment, saw the engineer counting down, and left. At 1:05 P.M. they were on the air.

"Good afternoon from Ed Smith Stadium in Sarasota," Rizzs said.
"I'm Rick Rizzs along with Bob Rathbun, welcoming you to another
season of Detroit Tiger baseball."

Rizzs paused. "Folks, I'm sitting in the chair of a Hall of Famer,
Ernie Harwell, and Bob is sitting in the chair occupied for nineteen
years by Paul Carey. Gentlemen, I hope you're both listening and we
both hope we can continue in the great tradition of Tiger broadcasters
such as the two of you."

Rizzs had written his little speech weeks ago. It was out, and now
it was time to talk baseball. He was relieved. So was Rathbun. The
worst was over.

Or so they thought.

7

SENIOR AND JUNIOR

As spring training wound down, different stories made headlines in both Arizona and Florida. In addition to the rape/masturbation saga of the Mets, Jean Yawkey, the owner of the Red Sox, died on February 26, leaving the financial future of the team in flux; Bo Jackson retired—sort of; Rob Dibble, the Reds' talented but often overwrought reliever, had shoulder troubles that landed him on the disabled list; Rickey Henderson whined about not making enough money—which hardly constituted a news story; and the owners continued to waffle about the proposed sale of the Seattle Mariners to a group of Japanese investors. The big trades, Smiley and Sheffield, created a stir. And a big nontrade, Barry Bonds to the Braves for David Justice, had all of Florida talking for several days.

"How come I pick up the *Pittsburgh* papers and I don't see any screaming headlines about this so-called trade?" Braves president Stan Kasten asked *Atlanta Journal-Constitution* beat writer I. J. Rosenberg one day.

"Because Pittsburgh isn't completely baseball nuts like Atlanta is," Rosenberg replied. "Why don't you just enjoy it—and while you're at it, make the damn trade."

Kasten rolled his eyes as if to say, "If we could have made the damn trade, don't you think we would have?"

Meanwhile, tucked away from all the noise and mayhem, the team with no home quietly prepared for the season. For thirty-two years, the Baltimore Orioles had trained at Miami Stadium, smack in the middle of downtown Miami. As the neighborhood worsened, the team began looking for an alternative place to train. Negotiations broke down in several places and by 1991, the team was, for all intents and purposes, without a headquarters.

To compensate, the Orioles began 1992 with *three* headquarters. During the pre-exhibition phase of the spring, they worked out at Twin Lakes Park in Sarasota, once the home of the Kansas City Royals Baseball Academy, the then-futuristic concept that folded after producing several major leaguers, including the brilliant Royals second baseman Frank White.

Twin Lakes was perfectly adequate for workouts but had no place to play games. That meant, after unpacking on February 19, the Orioles had to repack on March 5 and move thirty-five miles up the road to St. Petersburg. There, they worked out at the old Huggins-Stengel complex that had once been the Mets' home base, and played their games at Al Lang Stadium, sharing it, as the Mets once had, with the St. Louis Cardinals.

In the midst of all this, the Orioles were preparing for a move up north too: they were going across town, leaving Memorial Stadium for the new downtown park at Camden Yards. The new ballpark was scheduled to open with an exhibition game on April 3; the gala season opener was to follow on April 6.

In short, everywhere you looked, there was chaos.

Except in the corner of the clubhouse where Cal Ripken, Jr., dressed. Ripken is not a believer in chaos on any level. He was coming off a monster season in which he'd hit .323 and won his second MVP Award. This was all in spite of playing on a team that had been awful from day one, finishing the season with a 67-95 record.

To everyone in the Baltimore organization, he was never "Cal," only "Junior," just as his father, the third-base coach, was always "Senior." Junior was entering the final year of a contract that paid him a relatively paltry $2.1 million a year. During the winter, his agent, Ron Shapiro, and Orioles president Larry Lucchino had begun the mating dance that would ultimately decide Ripken's future. Almost no one believed he would leave Baltimore or that the Orioles would let him leave. The estimates on what Ripken would be paid ranged from as low as $5 million a year to as high as $8 million.

In other words, Ripken only had to wonder, as former Oakland pitcher Mike Norris had once put it, walking into an arbitration hearing, whether he was going to be "rich or richer."

Money really wasn't Ripken's concern, though. After all, if he ended up at the *low* end of the projected scale, he was going to have enough to buy several countries. As with most players, baseball had never been about money for Ripken. Most of the time, baseball had been about his father.

Cal Ripken, Sr., looks as if he has just stepped out of a casting call for the grizzled old coach in any baseball movie ever made. His skin is tanned and wrinkled from years in the sun and he looks a good deal older than fifty-six. Stories about his toughness and stubbornness are legendary.

Once, the Ripkens' garden was being destroyed by a gopher, who showed up every night and burrowed away until daylight. The only way to catch the gopher was to wait up all night for it. Senior did, shotgun in hand, and blew the little critter away when it made the mistake of showing up once too often. On another memorable occasion, Senior got a serious cut while plowing snow out of the front yard. But he wouldn't go to the hospital until he'd finished the damn plowing. He tied a bandanna around his forehead to stem the flow of blood, finished the job, and *then* went to have the gash attended to.

Senior signed with the Orioles in 1957 as a catcher, and played six years in the minor leagues, finishing with a career batting average of .253. In 1961 he became a player-manager at Class-D Leesburg, Florida, and spent the next fourteen seasons managing different teams in the Baltimore system.

Junior has an older sister and two younger brothers. When he was very young, he had only a vague idea that his father was associated with the local baseball team in places like Elmira, Rochester, Dallas–Fort Worth, and Asheville.

"At first it was kind of fun," he said, sipping a cup of coffee on a cool Florida morning. "It made you feel special. But after a while, I came to resent it because it was taking my father away from me. By the time I was playing Little League, it seemed like my dad was never around. My mom was the one who came to all my games because Dad was always on the road. That feeling of being left alone is something I think about a lot in terms of my own children."

The way the Ripken story is told, Junior learned baseball by hanging out at clinics with Senior and around the ball clubs he was managing. But, according to the son, it wasn't the game that drew him to the ballpark, it was the father.

"My brother Fred [a year younger] was always very mechanical. That's where he and Dad connected. They would work on things around the house together. I had baseball. I can remember my father coming into my room very early in the morning and saying, 'You want to go to the park with me for the clinic?' Well, the answer was no. I actually thought the clinics were kind of boring.

"But the time in the car going to the park and then coming back was my only chance to be alone with him and really talk to him. I went to the clinics for the twenty minutes in the car with my dad. That was all I really cared about. I just picked up the baseball because I was sitting there with nothing else to do but listen."

Whether by osmosis or otherwise, Junior learned to play. And how to ask questions. By the time he was twelve, his father was managing in Double-A. Every day, Junior would test the players, asking them questions about how to do something on the baseball field. He would take their answers back to his father. If his father said a player's answers were right, Junior went back for more. If he said they were wrong, that player was scratched from the list for not taking the youngster's questions seriously.

"The year in Asheville was the first time I thought in terms of being a baseball player," Junior said. "Of course to me, Double-A was the ultimate because the players made enough money that they didn't have to work in the winter. To me, that was unbelievable. Dad had always worked two jobs in the winter, usually driving a beer truck or working in a drugstore. These guys didn't have to work. I thought that was the best thing I'd ever heard."

Senior scouted in 1975, then joined Earl Weaver's staff in Baltimore in '76. Settled in at last, Junior blossomed as a player. He shot up to six feet four and suddenly, as a high school senior, was a prospect. Scouts showed up to watch him pitch and play shortstop; he wondered if the Orioles might draft him.

When they did, in the second round, "everyone said it was just because of Dad. In the minor leagues, my first year, I really struggled. So I heard the same stuff again. It was only after I hit .300 the next year in A-ball that people started to quiet down."

Junior inherited every bit of Senior's competitiveness, plus an analytical side that he can't quite explain (or analyze). The product that is Cal Ripken, Jr., today—role model and milk drinker—is quite different from the Cal Ripken, Jr., of a few years ago.

"You wouldn't believe I was the same person," he said, laughing. "I was the worst winner *ever*—and a worse loser than that. I had to win at *everything*, all the time. My mom would invent games to entertain us and I had to win them all. When we went bowling, if we lost, I would blame it on everyone else and they'd all get mad at me. Mom would say, 'Cal, the point of the game is to have fun,' and I would say, 'It is not, the point is to *win!*'

"When I played canasta with my grandmother I used to hide cards and cheat. I *had* to win, no matter how I did it. To this day, when we play cards on a plane, my brother [Orioles second baseman Billy Ripken] will sometimes look at me as if he thinks I'm cheating. I have to tell him I don't do that anymore."

Hearing the barbs about his father made Junior that much more driven to prove himself in the minor leagues. He was constantly screaming at umpires, throwing bats, smashing helmets. "You see, to me it wasn't just an out, it was someone else holding me back. I had to prove myself, had to become my own person. If someone missed a call or something, they were preventing me from doing that. *Nothing* was going to get in my way."

Nothing did. He reached the major leagues in three years, making his debut August 10, 1981, two weeks before his twenty-first birthday. "Even then, I still had a lot of anger in me, I still had to prove myself, still wanted to throw things. But I watched Eddie Murray and Ken Singleton, the way they would handle a strikeout. Almost always, they would just walk back to the dugout without saying a word. I wondered if I could do that.

"One night I struck out in the first inning and kind of lost it. I don't know how I didn't get ejected. I was angry about it the whole game. That night on the news, I saw myself on the highlights and I thought, 'This is *awful*.' I knew I couldn't continue that way—I had to work at keeping things more in control. I think that's where the whole image thing started with me, seeing myself that night."

The Streak thing started during that first half-season in the big leagues, too. This was the year, 1981, when the player strike split the season in two. When Junior was called up after the strike, the Orioles were trying to win the second-half pennant. Weaver played him sparingly—twenty-three games, thirty-nine at-bats. More often than not, he was a late-inning replacement. Sitting on the bench, he was miserable.

"Oh God did I hate it," he said. "I couldn't stand having to just sit there and chew sunflower seeds and watch. I remember making a promise to myself that once I got in there, I wasn't coming out. When the streak began [on May 30, 1982], before it became The Streak, there'd be days when I might be a little banged up or sore or tired or even hurting. But every time I thought of coming out I would think back to how much I hated sitting and just push myself to keep playing."

The Streak has now taken on a life of its own. By the end of 1992, Junior had played in 1,735 straight games, the last 1,708 of them at shortstop. If he stays healthy, he will break Lou Gehrig's record of 2,130 straight games in June 1995. Even in the spring of 1992, more than three years away from the record, Ripken was keenly aware of the attention he was going to receive as he drew closer to Gehrig.

And he was aware of the controversy. "That's one reason why last season meant so much to me," he said. "I know people were starting to say that The Streak was hurting me, that I was playing tired, because my numbers had dropped off. I never believed that. I had some mechanical problems I had to fix and I'd lost confidence. Sometimes, when you get into a slump you overanalyze it and start to think you're never going to get another hit. I know I did that at times."

There are few people in the world more analytical than Junior. If someone says "Hello" to him one morning, then "How are you" the next, he will wonder why the greeting changed. He constantly examines people, especially successful people. During spring training, he was reading *The Man to See,* the biography of Edward Bennett Williams, the onetime Orioles owner who died in 1988. It brought back memories for him.

"I always remember EBW coming into the clubhouse once or twice a year and giving us his speech on contest living. I used to watch him when he gave us that speech, trying to picture what he was like in the courtroom. I noticed that he liked to catch someone's eye, then fix on him. He would just keep staring right at the guy until he would make him look away. I always thought that was part of the contest he was talking about—make the other guy look away.

"One year, when he came in to give the speech I decided if he looked at me, I wasn't going to look away no matter what. Sure enough, he fixes on me. So I just stared right at him. Stared and stared. He kept staring right back. I have absolutely no idea what he was saying because it took all my powers of concentration to keep staring at him. He never stopped and neither did I. Finally, when the speech was over, he just walked over, shook hands with me, and left. Never said a word. But I felt good about it. It might have been the hardest thing I've ever done."

That stubbornness is a huge part of Ripken's personality. It's part of what defines him as a player and as a person. Never would those characteristics play a larger role in his life than in 1992. As spring training ended, Ripken was busy analyzing—and wondering—exactly why the Orioles hadn't signed him yet. Were they hoping he would have a mediocre year and drive his price down? Was there a chance they didn't want him back? Or was he just worrying too much about being rich or richer?

None of it seemed to matter much as spring training ended. The Orioles looked like a much better team than they'd been the disastrous year before. The young pitchers, Mike Mussina and Ben McDonald, were healthy; Rick Sutcliffe, the thirty-six-year-old ex-Cub, was throwing well and had added stability to the young staff. Back home, the new ballpark was already receiving rave reviews.

And then, just before camp broke, the Orioles decided to release Dwight Evans. At thirty-nine, ex–Red Sox legend Evans was near the end, though most people thought he'd last one more year as a fourth outfielder and DH. But manager Johnny Oates was concerned about a spot player who had days when he was just too sore to play. After lengthy meetings and considerable soul searching, a decision was made.

Oates said later that it was "one of the toughest things I've ever had to do as a manager. Dwight Evans was never anything but a class act."

The release of Evans shook Ripken. He was the other wise old head in the clubhouse, someone he could relate to. Brother Billy was there, but he was still a younger brother. Glenn Davis and Storm Davis, who did everything together, were veterans, but Ripken wasn't close to either of them. Evans's disappearance created a void for Ripken. He wondered if the always-money-conscious Orioles had decided that $900,000 was too much to pay for an extra player when they were going to need somewhere in the neighborhood of $30 million to pay their shortstop. *If* they were going to pay their shortstop.

Ripken understood that players coming and going was part of baseball. He had seen it happen his entire life. Still, he wondered . . . and wondered . . .

PART II

PLAYING FOR REAL

BEGINNINGS

As the teams worked their way north, stopping in various places for final exhibition games, the expected pecking order was not all that different from what it had been at the end of 1991.

Almost everyone expected the Toronto Blue Jays to repeat in the American League East. The team had added Jack Morris and Dave Winfield to an already strong group. Third baseman Kelly Gruber made the comment that if the Jays stayed healthy, they would win the division by fifteen games. No one thought him crazy.

"We're all playing for second place," Tigers manager Sparky Anderson said. "When I look over there and try to figure out why they've got so much more talent than we do, it don't take me long to get an answer: about twenty million dollars."

The consensus pick to give Toronto a race: Boston, which had tied the Tigers for second in '91. Dark horses? Maybe the Tigers, if Sparky could work his magic again. The Orioles and Milwaukee Brewers would be better if their young pitchers stayed healthy, but they wouldn't be in the race.

In the American League West, the race was considered a toss-up between the White Sox and Twins. Chicago had entered spring training the favorite but the loss of Bo Jackson, Carlton Fisk's continuing foot problems, and Minnesota's pickup of John Smiley had changed that. The Rangers were the dark horse if their pitching held up. Their hitting was as good as anyone's. The Athletics? Too old. And too fragmented—they had fourteen potential free agents.

The National League West was pegged as a two-team race. The Cincinnati Reds had probably improved themselves more than anyone in baseball, picking up two quality starting pitchers, Tim Belcher and Greg Swindell, and Bip Roberts, who brought great speed and versatility. They also had a big-time Rookie of the Year candidate in Reggie Sanders. The Braves had the game's best starting pitching and the hunger that came from winding up the last season ninety feet shy of winning the World Series. The Dodgers were possible contenders if Darryl Strawberry and Eric Davis had huge years. The Astros were a lock for last.

The mystery race was in the National League East. Was *anyone* good enough to win? The Pirates had lost Bobby Bonilla and Smiley. The Cardinals still looked a year away. The Cubs, Phillies, and Expos all had obvious holes. The pick then was the Mets, even after all their spring-training troubles. Gooden's elbow was coming along. That meant a rotation that included Gooden, Cone, Saberhagen, and Sid Fernandez, all of them potential Cy Young Award winners.

"The spring's behind us," Jeff Torborg said on Opening Day at Shea Stadium. "We expect to have a lot of fun this season."

•

In no city was Opening Day greeted with more enthusiasm than Baltimore. The project that had become "Oriole Park at Camden Yards" (by the end of April almost everyone had dropped the "Oriole Park" portion of the name and simply called the place "Camden Yards") had been a controversial one.

If you cut through all the political mumbo-jumbo and hype, what had happened was simple: Edward Bennett Williams, then the team's owner, had blackmailed the State of Maryland into building him a new ballpark. How had he managed this? By threatening to take the team elsewhere.

Williams's cause was aided considerably by the memory of Colts owner Robert Irsay moving his football team out of Baltimore in 1984—literally sneaking them out in the middle of the night—and resettling them in Indianapolis. Baseball's transfer rules made that particular scenario impossible, but Maryland and Baltimore officials couldn't afford to call Williams's bluff and chance losing their baseball team, too. Thus was the Camden Yards project born and financed—even though Memorial Stadium, with some nips and tucks, could have remained a serviceable ballpark for many years.

But Williams wanted lucrative luxury boxes—and plenty of them—and to get them he needed a new ballpark. As was almost always the case throughout his life, what Williams wanted, he got. In this instance, however, he didn't live to see what he had wrought.

If he had, he would have been proud. Camden Yards was *not* the Sistine Chapel, as some people claimed during those first euphoric days. It wasn't even the Eiffel Tower or the cathedral at Chartres. It was, however, the best ballpark anyone had built in more than thirty years. What made Camden Yards particularly significant was what it *wasn't:* It wasn't a multipurpose stadium with artificial turf that was closed in all the way around to assure maximum seating capacity. It wasn't a suburban colossus, situated in the middle of nowhere. It wasn't a dome and it wasn't built from the same round cookie cutter that had produced the stadiums in Atlanta, Pittsburgh, Cincinnati, Philadelphia, and St. Louis.

It *was* a ballpark, a part of the city's downtown. The famed Bromo-Seltzer clock tower, the one real signature in the Baltimore skyline, hung over the left-field fence. The grass was green and real. The B&O Warehouse looming in the right-field backdrop gave the place a unique character and look, as did the old-time advertising on the scoreboard and in right field.

There *were* flaws. The Holiday Inn that was part of the backdrop was an eyesore, as was the silly HIT IT HERE sign posted on the outfield fence by Maryland Lottery officials. A number of the seats in left field faced center field instead of home plate, and parking—as at Memorial Stadium—was no picnic.

But on a scale of 1 to 10, Camden Yards was at least a 9.8. The clubhouses were huge, most of the facilities excellent. The players had two early complaints: The infield was the slowest in baseball and the showerheads were inadequate. The water pressure was so high that players were getting bruised.

Naturally, the first person to figure out a solution to that problem was analytical Cal Ripken, Jr., who brought his own shower head to the ballpark. Though he'd come up with the answer, he wasn't capable of putting the shower head on—so Senior did it for him. The next problem came when the other players realized what Junior had done.

They immediately lined up to use the new shower head. When Junior stepped into the shower on the first night after the installation, he found Rick Sutcliffe luxuriating under it.

"Hey, Sut, *I* brought that thing in," Junior announced.

"Squatter's rights," Sutcliffe answered.

Junior looked over at the six-foot-seven-inch, 240-pound Sutcliffe, analyzed the situation—and decided to let him finish his shower.

"If that's the worst problem we have with the place, I think we'll be okay," manager Johnny Oates said. "Unless Junior decides to fight Sut for the shower head."

At forty-five, Oates was another ex-catcher turned manager. He was a onetime first-round draft choice of the Orioles who had spent eleven years in the big leagues, mostly thanks to his smarts and toughness. He'd never had more than 322 at-bats in any one season (averaging closer to 150 per year), but he'd always been a winner, playing on four division titlists in three different cities (Philadelphia, Los Angeles, and New York). By 1981, his arm had so little left in it that Yankee coach Birdie Tebbetts spent spring training teaching him how to throw the ball to second base on a hop.

Because he was the only healthy catcher on the roster, he began that season as New York's starter. When the other catchers got healthy, however, Oates was released. "I'll never forget Gene Michael [then the Yankee's manager] coming over to me in the clubhouse and saying, 'Johnny, you got a minute?' " Oates says. "I told him, 'Gene, I don't want to talk to you today.' I knew what it was about. But when I came out of Gene's office, [Yankee vice president] Bill Bergesch was standing there. He said the team wanted to offer me a minor league coaching job. I was fired and hired within five minutes."

Oates had known during his last several years as a player that he wanted to stay on in baseball. "I can remember the exact moment when I first thought about it. It was during the pennant race in 1978. I was sitting on the bench—as usual—and Tommy [Lasorda] made some kind of move. I turned to [coach] Monty Basgall and I asked, 'Why's he doing that?' And Monty looked at me and said, 'That's why you'll manage someday.' "

When Oates was released by the Dodgers in March 1980, he went to his old friend Basgall and said, "Monty, am I done?" Basgall looked at him and said, "Johnny, you're done."

"Of course, as soon as he said that I was convinced he was wrong and set out to prove it. I called every major league club until finally the Yankees gave me a shot. I lasted more than a year with them. Of course, Monty was right. I *was* done."

Oates's sense of humor is so dry that people often miss it. Although he likes to portray himself as an unsophisticated hick from the little mountain town of Sylva, North Carolina, he has as sharp a mind as anyone in the game.

"He's got the look," Sparky Anderson said one night, sitting in the visiting dugout at Camden Yards. "Don't ask me what it is, but I know it because I seen it before. LaRussa has it. Leyland has it. This kid has it, too."

Anderson was LaRussa's role model and LaRussa was Oates's role model. The O's manager studied LaRussa the way an archeologist studies hieroglyphics. Ten years after he'd run his first team in Nashville, managing had become Oates's passion. But it hadn't always been that way. In fact, for two years, Oates was convinced he was in the wrong job.

"I just couldn't deal with cutting people or sending them out," he says. "I remember my first spring training with Nashville. We'd all sit down at night and make decisions on which players were going to move up, which would move down, which would be released. Each manager was responsible for telling his own guys what was happening.

"Every morning, all the minor league managers would stand outside the complex while the players were coming in from the parking lot. You'd have to call the guys over to tell them what was going on before they went inside. When a player heard his name called, he *knew* what was going to happen next. I had guys come over to me with tears in their eyes.

"What you were doing right at that moment, in many cases, was saying to a guy, 'Your dream, the thing you've worked for all your life, is over.' At the Double-A level, a lot of times you were dealing with guys who'd been in the game for four or five years. If you sent them back to A-ball or released them at that stage, the message that they were done with baseball was pretty clear.

"In a way, you were doing them a favor, because it was probably time for them to get on with their lives. But every time I had to cut someone I always hoped he would be as stubborn as I was and call every team before he gave up. You should never give up on your dream just because someone else tells you to.

"I got to the point where I couldn't sleep at night. I had nightmares about it. I kept thinking, 'This is my first year—it'll be better next year.'

"The next year, I was at Columbus and it hadn't gotten any better. A few weeks into the season we had a numbers problem—several young pitchers who'd started the season with the Yankees had been sent back to us. We had to send Tim Burke [who later became an All-Star in Montreal] back to Double-A, even though he deserved to be in Triple-A.

"This time I not only couldn't sleep, I couldn't eat. I had no appetite and no energy. I seriously thought about quitting. The word got back to New York and Clyde King came down to talk to me. We sat behind the dugout one afternoon for two hours and he told me all the right things and I felt better. Much better. Then he left and an hour later I was miserable. But I felt I owed it to the Yankees to finish the season. If I didn't feel better about managing by then, I would ask for a coaching job in New York."

Oates did that but was told that no decisions on coaches were going to be made until Billy Martin's status as manager was determined. In those days, that was like waiting for Godot. So when Jim Frey called Oates and offered him a coaching job with the Cubs, he jumped at it.

Coaching was perfect for Oates. He got to be around the game, he got to teach and see players get better, and he didn't have to cut anybody. But after four years, Don Zimmer became the manager and decided to bring in his own staff.

Oates had worked during the offseasons as a salesman for Ha-Lo Advertising Specialties. On the day the Cubs told him he wouldn't be back, his boss offered him a full-time job, for very good money, with Ha-Lo. It was tempting. His wife and three children all liked living in Chicago. Maybe, he thought, the time had come to give up the dream.

Then came a phone call from Doug Melvin, the Orioles' farm director. The club needed a manager at Rochester. Oates was torn. After four years as a coach, he thought he might be ready to deal with making cuts when he had to. He liked the Baltimore organization and Rochester was one step from the majors. But his kids were all in school, and moving would be tough on them. As often happens when baseball men are confused, it was Oates's wife who convinced him that getting out would be a big mistake.

"She just sat me down and said, 'This is what you do. You love it and you're good at it and if you walk away now, you'll regret it. Don't worry about moving. We'll deal with it.' "

Oates accepted the job, did well, and was promoted to Frank Robinson's major league staff in 1989. That was where he was on May 23, 1991, when the Orioles asked him to replace Robinson as manager. But Oates wasn't sure he could do that.

It was Robinson who convinced him that taking the job was the right thing to do. "Frank called me and said, 'It's not my job anymore. Someone's going to do it and I would just as soon it be you.' "

In 1975, the Cleveland Indians had made Robinson baseball's first black manager. As a Hall of Fame player, he was known as tough and gruff, sometimes mean. But he is also bright and sensitive, someone who understands the mores of the game as well as anyone. In 1977, when the Indians made him the first black manager to be fired, it was Jeff Torborg, one of his coaches, who was offered his job. Torborg didn't accept. He thought taking it would be disloyal to Robinson.

"Phil Seghi was the general manager," Torborg recalls. "My father had died the previous winter and when I said no, Phil said to me, 'Jeff, I think your father would want you to do this.' And I said to him,

'Not over the body of the man who gave me my first shot at coaching he wouldn't.' I was really hot. It pissed me off that he invoked my father's name in that situation.

"So, I said, 'No, I won't do it.' Then Frank came and found me."

Robinson said almost the exact same thing to Torborg that he would say to Oates fourteen years later. Torborg took the job. So did Oates. The Orioles then lost their next four games and Oates dropped sixteen pounds. Things got better after that, but not much. The final record was 67-95. "The last two months of the season felt like they took twenty years," Oates said. "The offseason felt like it lasted about ten minutes. There's just so much to do."

Like a lot of young managers, Oates found that time management was the toughest thing for him to handle. The demands of managing at the major league level are like nothing else in baseball. Every single day—from March until October—there must be time made for the media before *and* after the game. Every local TV station wants an exclusive standup. The coaches need time and, of course, so do the players. Then the front office must be dealt with, especially if players are being moved.

Oates wrestled with the problem. He tried coming to the park earlier and earlier. He made lists each morning and checked things off as the day went along. He was getting his job done as a manager, but, as the 1992 season got under way, he was convinced he wasn't getting the job done as a husband and father.

Early in May, Glenn Davis gave Oates a book called *The Man in the Mirror*. Like Oates, Davis is a born-again Christian and he thought the book, filled with Christian themes, might help Oates deal with some of his dilemmas. He was right. One line stood out for the manager.

"It said, 'Figure out who would cry most at your funeral,' " Oates said. "Those are the people who should be number one on your list of priorities. So I sat down and thought about it and realized my priorities were exactly the opposite of what they should be. That had to change, period."

While he was changing his personal priorities, Oates was also changing his baseball team. The Orioles had been awful in 1991 because their pitching had completely fallen apart. From 1966 to 1983 no team in baseball produced more good young pitchers than the Orioles. Those pitchers were the touchstone for a team that won seven division titles, six pennants, and three World Series. But the pitching and the once-proud farm system had broken down and, as 1992 began, the Orioles had not won ninety games since 1983. They had been over .500 only once in six years. Their ERA in 1991 had been 4.59—the starters giving up more than five runs per game.

One of Oates's first moves at the end of the '91 season was to promote Dick Bosman, the Rochester pitching coach, to Baltimore. A former major leaguer who had once led the American League in ERA, Bosman was so competitive that he had to force himself not to talk to his pitchers after a bad game. "When they make dumb mistakes, it drives me crazy," he said. "If they get beat, they get beat—I can handle that. But if they do something stupid, I have to get the hell out of the clubhouse before I say something I'll regret. By the next day, I'm cool enough that I can talk to them about it without biting their head off."

The Orioles felt they had two potential stars in Ben McDonald and Mike Mussina. Both were very young, though. McDonald, the number-one pick in the country in 1989 when he came out of Louisiana State, was twenty-four and had fought arm problems throughout '91. Mussina was a year younger. He had come out of Stanford in 1990 and, like McDonald, been a first-round draft pick. Talented as he was, he'd been in the big leagues for less than half a season.

Oates felt strongly that he needed a veteran pitcher, one who came with a real portfolio and could anchor the staff, give the young pitchers someone they could look to as an example. The year before, Jack Morris had done it for the Twins staff, leading them to a championship. This year, Kirk McCaskill, the talented but oft-injured California Angel, was available and interested. Rick Sutcliffe, who had missed most of the last two seasons with shoulder problems, was also available—but not particularly interested.

It was Sutcliffe whom Oates wanted. The two men had become friends when Sutcliffe was the ace of the Cubs staff and Oates a coach there. Although a number of other clubs had shown more interest in Sutcliffe, Oates convinced him to fly into Baltimore just before the Christmas holidays to meet with general manager Roland Hemond and see the new ballpark.

Oates had convinced Hemond that Sutcliffe was the man they needed. McCaskill was scheduled to fly into Baltimore the next day, so Oates planned to pitch Sutcliffe hard. He wanted a firm commitment from him. He arranged to have the tarpaulin taken off the infield at Camden Yards so Sutcliffe could stand on the mound and imagine what it would be like to pitch in the new park. He and Hemond showed Sutcliffe the seats where the kids from the Sutcliffe Foundation (Sutcliffe buys fifty season tickets each year for underprivileged kids) would sit. And Oates told Sutcliffe—repeatedly—that in spite of the Orioles' horrendous record, they weren't that far from being a contender. Maybe just a Rick Sutcliffe away.

"It was Johnny who convinced me," Sutcliffe acknowledged later. "He believed in me, in spite of the arm problems I'd had, and he was asking me to believe in him. I did."

Sutcliffe had not planned to make any decisions that day. But after seeing the park and talking to the Baltimore brass, he made up his mind. Before the day was over, he'd come to terms with the O's, actually signing the contract on a beverage cooler in a hallway. Hemond had to race back to his office to call McCaskill and tell him not to get on a plane the next day.

Even with Sutcliffe in camp, the Orioles were still full of pitching questions. Sutcliffe was old (thirty-six in June) and had experienced arm problems; McDonald was young but had also had arm trouble. In fact, he'd spent most of the fall learning to shoot a gun left-handed because his right shoulder was so sore by the end of the season that he couldn't hunt right-handed. Mussina was healthy, intense, and very, very green. Bob Milacki and José Mesa had flashed potential at times but both had spent time in the minors in '91. It was a staff that had potential both for success and for disaster.

That delicate balance made Sutcliffe's 2–0 shutout of the Indians on Opening Day significant for reasons that went well beyond the gala occasion. The veteran had set a tone for the others. McDonald also pitched a shutout that first week, and although the Orioles went 1-4 on their initial road trip to Toronto and Boston, the pitching was solid. Unlike '91, where the team all too often had been out of games in the third inning, the starters were carrying them deep into games with a chance to win.

That pleased Oates. If the starting pitching held up and the shower heads got fixed it was possible that Sparky Anderson's prediction—that everyone but the Blue Jays was playing for second—might be, if not inaccurate, at least premature.

•

Nothing seemed premature in the early going when it came to the Tigers. Bob Rathbun and Rick Rizzs had hoped that the team would get off to a fast start, especially with six straight home games the first week, and take the media focus off the radio booth and put it on the field.

It didn't quite work out that way. The Blue Jays came to Tiger Stadium for three games—and swept. Okay, not a good start but at least it was Toronto. The Yankees, picked by many people for last, came next. *They* swept. The Tigers' record at the end of one week: 0-6.

"I'm just glad I've been doin' this twenty-three years," Sparky said. " 'Cause if this was my first year, I'd probably be out of my mind by now."

Ironically, as his team did its first-week pratfall, Anderson *was* counseling a first-year manager going through a similar start. Bill Plummer had been Johnny Bench's backup catcher during Anderson's years as manager of the Cincinnati Reds. Now he was a rookie manager in Seattle, the one team in baseball that conceivably had worse pitching than the Tigers. When the Mariners started 0-4, Anderson called Plummer.

There was no answer. When the tape machine beeped, Anderson said, "Plum, I know you're there. Pick up the damn phone."

Plummer followed orders. "Whatever you do, don't change your plan," Anderson instructed. "If you do, then you aren't being yourself, you're being somebody else. That won't work."

"I remember my first year in Cincinnati," Anderson said later, recounting his talk with Plummer. "I was so cocky I told my coaches we'd win the damn thing by ten. They thought I was crazy. We won by fourteen. I thought I knew more about the game than anyone who ever lived. I didn't think we could lose and the club picked up on that."

Anderson laughed and took a deep puff on his pipe. "I wish I *didn't* know what I know now, about how many things can happen during a year. But that's the fun of it, when you're so damn nervous you can't hold your coffee and you're scared to death. When I get out, that's what I'll miss, that feeling. It makes you feel alive."

There has never been any doubt about the life that George Anderson brings to the ballpark every day. He is the Casey Stengel of his generation, able to sit for hours and tell stories, fracturing the language as it's rarely been mangled before. He is fifty-eight but looks older. When he started managing in 1970, he was thirty-six—with the same white hair; it was his trademark then as it is now—and he looked *much* older.

But dig just a little beyond the twinkling eyes and the funny stories and you will find a manic competitor, someone who never misses anything and never, *ever* forgets.

"I'm gonna tell you why John Oates is good," Sparky said on a cold, rainy April morning in Baltimore. "Last night, he had my ass beat [8–0] and he gets a man on first in the eighth inning. I put my first baseman behind the guy. He can steal second base easy. But he doesn't. See, that's smart. Because if he does steal that base, I'm gonna remember and I'm gonna find a way to kick his ass someday. Baseball's like that. Everything comes around. John Oates knows that."

Above his desk in his Tiger Stadium office, Anderson has a sign that says, EACH 24 HOURS THE WORLD TURNS OVER ON SOMEONE WHO IS SITTING ON TOP OF IT.

Anderson is living proof of those words. He was a journeyman big leaguer who had 104 major league hits—"and thirty-four RBI," he points out quickly—during his playing career. He won a National League pennant his first season out as a manager. During his first seven years in Cincinnati he won five division titles, four pennants, and back-to-back World Series titles in 1975 and 1976. His reward for that extraordinary performance? At the end of the 1978 season, the Reds fired him. Anderson went home to California and figured, at forty-three, he could live without baseball for a while.

"I woulda been in shock but the phone never stopped ringing for three days," he said. "I was amazed all the people who called. Really made me feel great."

One of the calls was from a Los Angeles TV station. They wanted him to do live pregame reports from the ballpark before Dodger and Angel home games. Anderson liked that idea. He would drive to the game, do his report, watch the first six innings from the press box, and listen to the rest of the game on the radio driving home. He was content. Occasionally general managers would call him, ostensibly to ask his opinion on someone but also to find out if he had any interest in managing again. "I always told 'em no," he said. "Because that was how I felt."

He felt that way until the night of May 28, 1979—he picks the date out of the air as if it is hanging there—when he found himself sitting alone in the press box watching the Dodgers play the Cardinals. "All of a sudden it hit me that baseball was going on down there and I wasn't part of it in any way, shape, or form. The game was going merrily along without me. Of course, the game goes along without everyone. It went along without Babe Ruth and Joe DiMaggio so it sure as hell was gonna go along without George Anderson. But it was like one of those revelations. I went home that night and said to my wife, 'Hon, it's time.' "

Over the next few weeks, Anderson let it be known that he *might* be ready to come back to the game—for the right deal. Two weeks after Anderson's revelation, Jim Campbell, the Tigers' general manager, called. Was Sparky interested in managing the club?

"Jim," Anderson said. "You don't want me. My terms are too tough."

"What are they?"

"Five years—guaranteed."

"Fine. When can you start?"

Anderson was brought up short. He wanted back in but not so quickly. "Tell you what, Jim. If you still want me when the season's over, I'll take the club next spring. But I can't do it right now."

Campbell wasn't buying. "Sparky, I can't look Les Moss in the eye for the rest of the season if I know I want you to manage the club. It has to be now."

Anderson wrestled with the idea for a few more days, then finally decided—he was back in. Five years later, the young team he had taken over in '79 matured. Kirk Gibson, Alan Trammell, and Lou Whitaker were stars, Darrell Evans provided stability, Jack Morris was the best starting pitcher in the American League, and Willie Hernández was so dominant as a relief pitcher that he won both the Cy Young Award and the MVP. The Tigers went wire to wire, going 35-5 in their first 40 games, and won 104 games in the regular season. They swept the Kansas City Royals in the play-offs and easily beat the San Diego Padres in a five-game World Series. Anderson became the first manager in history to win World Series titles in both leagues.

And then he almost quit managing.

"It was the worst year of my entire life," he said softly. "Early in the season, my daddy died. Doesn't matter how old you are, you lose a parent, it does things to you. I didn't understand it then, but after he died I became a maniac. I was obsessed with winning that year and becoming the first manager to win it all in both leagues. I lived in fear of blowing it. I was awful to be around. I didn't sleep. I couldn't get it out of my mind.

"Of course I figured out later that I was facing mortality. But that was the way I dealt with it then. When we finally won it, I was exhausted and miserable. I told my wife I was quitting, that I had to get out. She said, 'Give it thirty days. If you still feel the same way, I won't argue with you.' Two weeks went by and I had some time to rest and think and figure out what had been going on. One night we were standing in the kitchen and I looked at her and said, 'You know, you were right. I'm not going to make that call.' "

The Tigers made it back to the play-offs in 1987, catching the Blue Jays during the last week of the season. Anderson still says that was his greatest thrill as a manager, "because that club had no right, no way of winning." It did, though, only to lose to Minnesota in the play-offs. Since then, the Tigers hadn't been close to postseason play. They had become an old team, losing 103 games in 1989, a season that aged Anderson considerably. But the acquisition of Cecil Fielder in 1990 helped the team climb back to respectability and, in 1991, Detroit stayed in the pennant race until the final two weeks, ultimately finishing seven games behind the Blue Jays.

"We did better than I thought we would," Anderson admitted. "I thought we were a fifth-place club when the season started. But, let's face it, the only reason we were anywhere close to Toronto was because they *let* us stay close. There's no comparison between our club and theirs."

Sometimes Sparky will poor-mouth his team to get it going. But early in 1992, it was apparent that that was not the case. The Tigers had lots of power, led by Fielder. Trammell and Whitaker were still around but aging and, in Trammell's case, often hobbling. There was only one solid starting pitcher—Bill Gullickson.

Like Fielder, Gullickson had spent a year in Japan before returning to find success in the major leagues. Gullickson was a remarkable
story, a diabetic who had cowritten a book on the disease while in
Japan. "Over there, they treat kids with it like they're lepers," he said.
"The point of the book was to make people understand you can still
function quite well, even as an athlete, if you have diabetes."

Gullickson had won twenty games in '91, but his high ERA (over
four runs a game) made people question his ability to come close to
that total again. No one questioned Fielder, though. He had hit ninety-
five home runs and won back-to-back RBI titles in the two seasons
since his return from the Land of the Rising Sun. Fielder was six feet
three and weighed at least 240 pounds. He had been more of a football
player than a baseball player in high school but had decided to concentrate on baseball after a recruiting visit to Arizona State.

"I took one look at the size of the offensive linemen and said, 'No
thanks, I'd like to get to twenty-one in one piece. When I got drafted
for baseball [by the Royals] I figured, Why not give it a shot? My mother
wasn't very happy about me not going to school. I told her, 'Look, if
this goes wrong, you can tell me I told you so and I'll go back to
school.' "

Fielder was traded from Kansas City to Toronto after one year in
the system—a shock—and made it to the major leagues in 1985 as a
part-time player. In 1987, he platooned with Fred McGriff and hit
fourteen home runs. McGriff hit twenty and the Blue Jays decided he
had to play full-time the next year. George Bell was the DH. That didn't
leave a lot of at-bats for Fielder, who asked the Blue Jays to try to move
him at the end of the season. The Jays did—to Japan.

"Gord Ash [Toronto's assistant general manager] called me and
said the team had a deal that would make them money and make me
money," Fielder says. "I wasn't so sure I liked the idea. Then he told
me I'd be paid one million dollars plus expenses in Japan. I was making
a hundred and twenty thousand at the time. I said to Gord, 'When does
the plane leave?' "

Fielder wasn't overwhelmingly happy in Japan, but he played
well, hitting thirty-eight home runs. Those numbers were enough to
entice the Tigers, who signed him for 1990 with the idea that he was
capable of hitting twenty or twenty-five home runs. He hit fifty-one.
The next year he hit forty-four.

Those ninety-five homers made him a very rich man. In 1992, he
earned $4.7 million—and free agency was still two years away. But
Fielder, like Anderson, was troubled by what he saw when the Tigers
took the field. Their pitching, beyond Gullickson, was horrendous.
During a four-game weekend series in Baltimore, they allowed twenty-
eight runs—including twelve in the finale on Monday after three

straight third-inning home runs off Ben McDonald (by Trammell, Fielder, and Mickey Tettleton) had put the Tigers ahead 4–0.

Anderson called a team meeting after Sunday's 3–2 loss to remind the players that it was much too early in the season to panic, that they had to fight their way through their current frustrations. But the frustration was overpowering, etched on everyone's face.

When someone noted that they had played pretty well in the game, Anderson shrugged and said, "You *gotta* play good once in a while."

The final score on Monday was 12–4. The Orioles were 7-5 and beginning to feel as if they had a pretty good team. The Tigers were 3-11.

"I heard the word *salvage* in here tonight and we've only played fourteen games," Alan Trammell marveled, sounding confused and amazed all at once. "I know we'll score runs, but how soon? It's ugly right now. If we give in to the way we feel, it could be a terrible, terrible season.

"How many games out are we? Eight?" He shook his head. "Seems like Opening Day was about two months ago, not two weeks ago."

Down the hall, the Orioles were as giddy as the Tigers were perturbed. "Twelve games doesn't prove a thing," Oates said. He paused and smiled. "But it can provide some clues."

Of that there was no doubt—in both clubhouses.

9

THE TRIBE

I n most baseball cities, Opening Day has a magical quality to it. For weeks, fans have watched from afar as their teams prepared for the start of the season. They have read all the words of optimism about the veterans and devoured all the statistics of the new players, who are going to make such a huge difference during the coming season. Anticipation builds through March.

Opening Day is almost always a sellout, even in cities where the April weather can be raw and ugly. Opening Day is, after all, a big party, a chance to see your team when it is still fresh, still hopeful, and still convinced that *this* will be the year.

And, the joke goes in Cleveland, it is also a chance to see your team before it is mathematically eliminated from the pennant race.

Bob DiBiaso winces when he hears that joke—and all the *other* Tribe jokes that come with the territory when you work for the Cleveland Indians. DiBiaso is vice president/public relations for the Indians, a job that is, by definition, difficult. He is thirty-seven, a native of Cleveland who has spent most of his adult life working for the ballclub. Since he was born in 1955, DiBiaso missed being alive for the last Cleveland pennant in 1954.

"I do have memories from the womb," he said, sitting in the dugout on Opening Day. "But, the truth is, I am part of the generation that has never seen an August that mattered."

The Chicago Cubs haven't won a National League pennant since 1945. But the Cubs *have* contended—winning two National League East titles and coming reasonably close a couple of other times. The Indians haven't finished within ten games—ten games!—of first place since 1962. Since division play began in 1969, their highest finish has been fourth. During that time, they have won more than 81 games exactly once—in 1986 when they were 84-78—and that brief moment of glory was quickly followed by a 61-101 debacle the next season.

The negative numbers appear to stretch on forever. The last time the team drew more than two million fans was 1949. In 1991, attendance barely passed one million. In mid-September, the Indians and Red Sox played a makeup game. The team announced that anyone who wanted to see the game could show up, pay five dollars, and sit anywhere they wanted to in the stadium. A total of 1,695 accepted the offer. At one point during that game, a beer man in right field called out "Beer here!" and a fan sitting behind the third-base dugout yelled, "I'll take one."

As a huge Opening Day crowd made its way into dreary Cleveland Stadium for the '92 opener, there was both hope and concern. The concern centered on 1991, a 57-105 disaster that had ended with the team trading off many of its best-known players for younger (read: *cheaper*) players. If those players were not ready for the major leagues, the Tribe could disappear off the map before April was even over.

No one was more aware of that than Mike Hargrove. The previous July, with the team in complete disarray, Hargrove had replaced John McNamara as manager. Cleveland was 25-52 when Hargrove took over. That meant the 32-53 record he produced was a noticeable improvement. However, that was a long way from good—or even *pretty* good—and Hargrove began 1992 with a one-year contract. In other words, if the ship sank, he was going to need a very seaworthy life vest.

"I don't have a problem with that," he said, studying a lineup card in his small office several hours before the opener. "I would hope that we're going to be better than last year. If we're not, I'm not sure I'll make it through the year anyway. We have some talent here. Not as much as we'd like to have, but still there are some good players."

Hargrove had been a pretty good player himself. He had grown up in the tiny town of Perryton, Texas, where it was so hot in the spring and summer that his high school didn't even have a baseball team. He had gone to college on a basketball scholarship and ended up playing football, basketball, and baseball. The summer after his junior year, he played summer league baseball and was spotted by several major league scouts who told him he should drop football and focus on baseball in his senior year. A scout from the Cubs went a step further, offering him an $8,500 contract.

"But it was all in incentives," Hargrove said. "He wouldn't even guarantee five hundred dollars of the money. I decided to turn it down." A year later, in 1972, the Texas Rangers drafted Hargrove on the twenty-fifth round and offered him $2,000—guaranteed—to sign. "I was so excited I forgot to ask for incentive money," he said. "The way I figure it, I'm still sixty-five hundred dollars behind in this game."

Since most incentives are keyed to making the major leagues, Hargrove would have collected that money quickly. After struggling so much his first season in the minors that he seriously thought about going home to find a teaching job, Hargrove took off, hitting .351. A year later, he was in Texas, where he batted an extremely impressive .323 as a rookie. He ended up playing twelve years in the majors, retiring just before the start of the 1986 season with a career .292 batting average.

Of course, that isn't what most people think of when they think of Hargrove. "The human rain delay," he said, shaking his head. "I was a pretty good hitter in my time, but that's what people remember."

It was former Cleveland announcer Joe Tait who put the nickname on Hargrove when he was playing for the Indians. While he was still in the minor leagues, Hargrove had hurt his thumb—"I got jammed four straight times one night," he said. "I doubled every time, but my thumb hurt like hell afterward"—and had invented a special bandage to protect himself while hitting.

Each time he stepped in, he had to carefully wrap the bandage. Shortly after that, Hargrove popped up—off a pitcher he thought he should have hit—because he was distracted by his own flapping shirt-tail. "I just decided after that happened that I wasn't stepping in until I was completely ready." Hence his routine: wrap the thumb, check the shirttail, check the bat, dig in. Time after time. The human rain delay.

Most people call Hargrove "Grover." He is forty-two, with a face and body rounded somewhat over the years by too many meals in baseball clubhouses. He might not be in baseball today if the Texas bank he worked for—in the offseasons near the end of his career—hadn't failed.

"I wanted to be prepared for the end of my career," he said. "That's why I took the bank job. But towards the end, I started to think managing might be worth a shot. The day I stopped playing [in the spring of '86 with Oakland] was about as bad a day as I can ever remember. I thought I was prepared, but I wasn't. It's devastating.

You go from being a big-league ballplayer to nothing. There's nothing that can prepare you for that.''

That is one thing Hargrove tries to tell his players. Although they are making breathtaking money, the day they can no longer play *will* come—and it will be tough to take. Every ballplayer lives with the knowledge that his career is a fragile and finite thing.

Hargrove was offered a job managing in the Cleveland farm system and jumped at it. He moved up the ladder until he was named to McNamara's staff in 1990. That wasn't a bad year in Cleveland— seventy-seven victories—but from the very start the following year, everything went as wrong as it could go.

"I looked around and wondered if Mac was going to get through the year," Hargrove said. "I had all sorts of mixed emotions. I wanted to see things get better, but I think I knew deep down they probably weren't going to. I knew if they made a change, I might have a shot—but I also worried we might *all* get fired.''

On the night of July 5, after yet another loss, general manager John Hart asked Hargrove if he would come to team president Hank Peters's office the next morning at ten-thirty. Hargrove knew immediately what it was about. "I was either going to be hired or fired," he said. "I didn't know which one. I got home and told Sharon that Peters and Hart wanted to see me in the morning. She looked at me and said, 'But you'll miss Andy's Little League game.'

"For some reason, that really pissed me off. Twenty-two years we've been married [they first met in seventh grade] and she didn't get it. I just walked into the living room and sat down. Fifteen minutes later she ran in and said, 'I just figured out what you were trying to tell me. What do you think is going to happen?'

"I tried going to sleep at about eleven-thirty but by four-thirty I gave up. I went downstairs and took an hour run. Then I came back and sat in the kitchen drinking coffee until it was time to go.'

Fortunately for Hargrove, he wasn't so caffeine-jagged that he couldn't understand Peters when the team president asked him if he would take McNamara's spot. "I hesitated only because of the way I felt about Mac," he said. "He had been very good to me. But I was also dying for the chance. It was very bittersweet.''

It was made less bitter by McNamara. After his meeting with Peters and Hart, Hargrove walked downstairs to his new office. Sitting on the desk was a note:

"Mike—Good Luck. If there is anything I can do to help, don't hesitate to call. I will always remember your loyalty and your help . . . Mac.''

The note, framed, hangs in the wall in Hargrove's office. Right next to it is a picture of a cowboy. Underneath the cowboy is the following: ''There were a hell of a lot of things they didn't tell me when I signed on with this outfit.''

In truth, Hargrove didn't need to be told much. Anyone who manages the Indians knows *exactly* what he is getting into.

•

Opening Day in Cleveland was as dreary as the old ballpark itself. Built sixty years ago, Cleveland Stadium was called ''the most spectacular stadium in the country'' when it opened. Now, it is a white (actually gray) elephant that has all the problems of an old ballpark—obstructed seats, tiny, dirty bathrooms, outdated facilities for the players—without any of the charm. Fenway Park and Wrigley Field make you nostalgic for the old days. Cleveland Stadium makes you long for 1994, when the new downtown ballpark is supposed to open.

''There's probably not a franchise in baseball that needs a new park as much as we do,'' DiBiaso said. ''Even when we put a decent crowd in here, say twenty thousand, the place looks empty because there are seventy thousand seats.''

More than sixty-five thousand of those seats were filled for the Saturday home opener (the Indians had not opened on a Saturday since 1985). The lights were on when the game began and things quickly turned comical for the Tribe. Just as Dennis Cook prepared to deliver the first pitch of the season, a stripper named Lulu Devine popped out of the first-base box seats and raced to the mound. Ms. Devine gave Cook a juicy enough kiss to leave him looking nonplussed as the security guards took her away. Their decision to escort her out through the Boston dugout caused a mad scramble as Red Sox players raced from their seats for a better view.

Cook took a deep breath and threw strike one. A huge cheer erupted from the faithful. He took another breath, threw again, and Wade Boggs crushed a double into the gap. Two batters later he scored. The Red Sox led 1–0. Could Ms. Devine be persuaded to do an encore?

By the third inning it was 5–0. Cook was as far gone as Lulu and many fans had already started to entertain themselves by making paper airplanes and tossing them onto the field. It was cold and raw— and there were still eighty more home games after this one.

Then, suddenly, the Tribe came alive. Kenny Lofton, the rookie center fielder, singled home Mark Lewis, the rookie shortstop. Glenallen Hill, the twenty-seven-year-old leftfielder, doubled Lofton home. Mark Whiten, the other young outfielder acquired with Hill in the trade that had sent Tom Candiotti to Toronto, now drove in a run. Then, in the seventh, Carlos Baerga, the talented twenty-three-year-old second baseman, started a rally with a bunt single and the Indians scored twice more. It was 5–5. The paper airplane parade stopped. The young players had shown them something.

The Indians' bullpen had shut the Red Sox down since the third and it continued to do so. But the Boston pitchers kept pitching out of jams. The Indians got the winning run to second in the tenth, the thirteenth, *and* the fourteenth. Darkness began to fall. Boggs stepped on a stray balloon bobbing past his post at third base and everybody booed. Some left, many stayed. The temperature dropped into the forties.

Dinnertime came and went. In the fifteenth, the Indians got the winning run to third with two out, but Lofton popped up a drag bunt attempt. "Nothing wrong with the play," Hargrove said later. "If the ball hits the ground, the game is over."

Back in Boston, where he had been left to prepare for Monday's home opener, Roger Clemens went out for a run. He returned in the bottom of the seventeenth to find that manager Butch Hobson had Mike Gardiner, who was scheduled to start one of the games of the Sunday doubleheader, pitching for the Red Sox. Clemens found an American League directory and dialed the clubhouse in Cleveland. The clubhouse man switched him to the dugout.

"Butch, do you want me to fly out there and pitch the second game tomorrow?" Clemens asked.

Hobson thought about it for about five seconds. "Absolutely," he said. Clemens hung up and immediately booked a flight to Cleveland.

Gardiner struck out Whiten and catcher Sandy Alomar on called strikes. Whiten argued at length. Hargrove joined him. Plate umpire Dale Scott, who had been on his feet for more than six hours and had seen twenty-five batters strike out, looked at them wearily and said, "Fellas, it's been a strike for eighteen fucking innings and it's *still* a strike." Later, Scott would smile and say, "I hope I don't have to say *that* again any time soon."

The Indians left the bases loaded in the eighteenth. Finally, in the nineteenth, Tim Naehring, a late-inning substitute at shortstop, hit a two-run home run, his first since 1990, and the Red Sox won 7–5. It had taken six-and-a-half hours for the Tribe to lose its home opener.

"Can't do anything but hope they play as hard every day," Hargrove said afterward, sipping a beer. "The effort was there all day. They battled back. All we can do is try to come back tomorrow." He smiled. "Kind of tough to play eighteen the day after you play nineteen."

Especially, someone noted, when you have to face Clemens instead of Gardiner.

"Clemens?" Hargrove said. "What about Clemens?"

The story about Clemens's call to the clubhouse was repeated to him. "You sure?" Hargrove asked. He leaned back in his chair and smiled wanly. "You play nineteen innings and the reward is Clemens. Isn't baseball a great game?"

•

One of the first arrivals at the ballpark the next morning was Sandy Alomar. On most days, even when it means leaving the house by 8 A.M., Alomar is in the clubhouse at least four hours before game time.

He is twenty-five and, on a team filled with young players, he is the veteran, a two-time All-Star, and one of the few Indians who is not a question mark. He is a given.

As good a catcher as he is, Alomar will be the first to tell you that he isn't even close to being the best baseball player his family has produced. "Robby is the star," he said softly. "Always was. When he was eight he was taking ground balls from big leaguers. He took his bat everywhere he went."

Roberto Alomar, twenty months younger than Sandy, is now the All-Star second baseman for the Toronto Blue Jays. When he first came up with the San Diego Padres, Robby Alomar was considered one of the best young players in the game. Now, he is simply thought of as one of the best players—period.

The Alomars' father, Sandy Senior, played in the major leagues for fifteen years. Robby is the heir apparent; like his father he is an in-fielder. Strangely, Sandy always wanted to be a catcher.

"I liked the equipment," he said. "When I first saw it, when I was seven, I asked my father for it as a Christmas present. After that, I was always a catcher. I never got to hit very much, though. Since I was the only one with catching equipment, I always had to catch for both sides."

By the time he was thirteen, Sandy was bored with baseball and quit. While Robby played every day, he worked at a gas station. Three years later, he was working one afternoon when a local coach pulled in and asked him if he wanted to play in a tournament that weekend. His catcher was hurt and he remembered Sandy's strong arm.

"I figured, 'Why not?' I hadn't played, but I could still throw. Someone from an American Legion team saw me and asked if I wanted to play for them that summer. Again, I just figured, 'Why not?' By now, I had grown a lot and I hit with a lot more power, so it was more fun."

A little more than a year later, the San Diego Padres offered him a contract. Alomar wasn't sure. His boyhood friend from Salinas, Puerto Rico, Benito Santiago, was with them and Santiago was far more advanced as a catcher than he was. Sandy Alomar, Sr., stepped into the picture. "He told me not to worry about Benito," Alomar said. "He said there were twenty-six teams in baseball and I only had to be good enough to catch for one of them."

Catching was never a problem for Alomar. Hitting, during his early years in the minors, was. Between Santiago and his hitting woes, by the end of 1989 he was beginning to wonder if his father's advice had been so wise. Finally, the Padres traded him, along with Carlos Baerga, to the Indians for Joe Carter. Most players moan when they're traded to Cleveland. Alomar was thrilled.

"All I wanted was to play," he said. "The first year was great because we were getting better. I like it in Cleveland, I even bought a house here. Then last year was rough. I was hurt, the team was bad. All I did when I was on the disabled list was sit around and eat popcorn. Drove me crazy."

The Indians were convinced that Alomar was the heart of their team. That concept was important when they came up with a plan during the winter of 1992 to give the franchise some stability. The idea focused on the notion that a team in a small market cannot afford the $40 million annual payrolls that now abound in larger markets. A team in Cleveland has to find a way to keep young stars around long enough to build a contender. The centerpieces of the plan were Alomar and Baerga.

"We wanted to find a way to make our young players happy but also not put ourselves in the position of losing them after a few years," general manager John Hart said. "So, we decided to offer them multiyear contracts *before* they were eligible for arbitration."

Most baseball players become eligible for arbitration at the end of their third year in the majors. At that point, the balance of power between player and club shifts. During his first three years, a player has no choice but to accept whatever management offers him—unless he wants to sit out. After the third year, if a player doesn't like what he is being offered, he can do something about it. The player submits a figure to an arbitrator and the team submits one. The arbitrator picks one or the other; there is nothing in between. The system makes it impossible for teams to lowball players. If they do, the arbitrator will simply choose the player's figure.

The Indians decided to give a number of their key young players leverage prematurely, offering them multiyear contracts for more money than prearbitration players normally make. The gamble, from the players' point of view, was at the back end of the deals. If a player like Alomar or Baerga had a superb third year, he would probably be able to make more money—by going through the arbitration process— than the Indians were now offering. The difference was that the Indians were guaranteeing the money *now,* regardless of performance.

"We all talked about it a lot," Alomar said. "We understand what the club is trying to do. They're making a commitment to us and asking for a commitment back. Baseball isn't like that these days. That's why the idea is so different."

Hart and team president Rick Bay spent most of February and the first ten days in March working on the deals. They focused first on Alomar and Baerga because they felt the others would be more open to the concept if the two stars were on board.

"We knew it would be a topic of discussion in the clubhouse," Bay said. "Young as they are, those two guys are the team leaders. There were a lot of long days involved in getting this done, especially when we got to spring training. But we thought it was important."

On March 10, the Indians made their dramatic announcement: Alomar, Baerga, Mark Whiten, and the team's top pitcher, Charles Nagy, had agreed to three-year deals with an option for a fourth year. Four more pitchers—relief closer Steve Olin, Dave Otto, Dennis Cook, and Scott Scudder—along with Glenallen Hill, had signed two-year contracts with a third-year option. And pitcher Rod Nichols had signed for one year with an optional second year. The only player the Indians wanted who chose *not* to sign was Albert Belle, the moody power hitter.

Belle was one of those players whose career could go either way. He would not turn twenty-six until August but had already proven himself a man with huge power (twenty-eight home runs and ninety-five RBIs in just 461 at-bats in 1991), a huge ego, and a penchant for getting into trouble.

He had gone through alcohol rehab two years earlier and had been suspended in '91 after throwing a ball at—and hitting—a fan who had been ragging him in the outfield about it. He was often guilty of not running balls out or not chasing balls in the outfield and battled often with Hargrove—or almost any authority figure who tried to discipline him.

Belle had so much self-confidence that he turned down the Indians' offer of guaranteed money to wait for arbitration—even though he was still two years away from it. "Albert honestly believes he's better than he is," Hargrove said later in the season. "He is very good and can be better. But almost no one on the planet is as good as Albert thinks he is. That's part of the reason why he's successful. Almost nothing can hurt his self-confidence."

With the exception of Cook, who was twenty-nine, the newly signed players all ranged in age from twenty-three to twenty-seven. Suddenly, the Indians had a base from which to work. Cleveland fans, who had been subjected to years of propaganda about rebuilding plans, now had two pieces of concrete evidence that the future might be brighter—the contracts and the foundation being laid for the new ballpark.

Maybe that was why 20,480 of them showed up for the doubleheader the day after the nineteen-inning marathon—even though the temperature when the first game began was 41 degrees. Normally, the second-day crowd in Cleveland is closer to 5,000. It was McDonald's Day at the ballpark and Ronald McDonald threw out the first pitch. More than a few people couldn't help but note that Ronald wasn't the first clown the Indians had sent to the mound in recent years.

The team's game-one starter in no way resembled any sort of circus performer. At twenty-four, Charles Nagy was starting to come into his own as a major league pitcher. He had pitched better than his 10-15 record in 1991 indicated and was growing in confidence each time he pitched. He had excellent control and an assortment of breaking pitches. Matt Young, who had become a favorite target of the Fenway Park boo-birds during his two years with the Red Sox, was his opponent.

The Indians scored in the first when Lofton walked, stole second and third, then scored on an error.

That was a typical Lofton run. A superb athlete, Lofton had played basketball at Arizona when the Wildcats had one of the top teams in the country. He played on Arizona's 1988 Final Four team and was noted for his quickness and great hands on defense. But he was too small to make it as an NBA guard and had opted instead for baseball.

In 1991 he had hit .308 at Tucson before being called up to the Astros in September. The Indians had gotten him in a trade for catcher Ed Taubensee during the winter. That swap would prove to be one of John Hart's best moves. In return for a catcher he had picked up off the waiver wire, Hart got a twenty-five-year-old center fielder who would finish second in the Rookie of the Year balloting, proving to be a superb outfielder and the catalyst for the Cleveland offense.

The Tribe scored again in the third when Mark Lewis walked, moved to second on a walk to Lofton, took third on a Hill grounder, and scored on a Baerga fielder's choice. That was enough for Nagy, who pitched superbly, holding the Sox to one run. But while Nagy was doing that, Young was steadily retiring the Indians. In the seventh inning, first baseman Mo Vaughn turned to Young on the bench and said, "Man, they don't have any *hits.*"

They didn't—and they never got any. Young pitched a no-hitter and *lost,* 2–1. The Indians, who had gotten twenty hits the day before in a loss, got no hits in a win. Technically, Young's effort was not recorded as a no-hitter. A rule—an idiotic rule—passed the previous winter stated that a pitcher could not be credited with a no-hitter if his team lost the game. So, Young pitched the first non-no-hitter in history.

"It's a little bit like being in purgatory. I really don't know how to feel," a stunned Young said. "On the one hand, guys were congratulating me. On the other hand, we lost the game. To me, a no-hitter is supposed to end when you strike someone out and the catcher runs out and jumps into your arms. This wasn't quite like that. It was kind of anticlimactic."

Surreal is what it was. Between games, the media went down to the Red Sox clubhouse to talk to Young. They were kept waiting on the public concourse while Boston officials tried to decide whether Young would be made available immediately to help the Boston writers deal with their first-edition deadlines or be held back until game two was over.

Ten minutes passed. Finally, the clubhouse door swung open. A guard came out and held out his hand to indicate that no one was to move. Then, Ronald McDonald and the Hamburgler were escorted out. Michael Gee of the *Boston Herald* watched them leave and said, "Does anyone here besides me think we're in a Fellini movie?"

At least there was one thing that could still be relied on: Clemens dominating the Indians. He was 15-2 lifetime against them and had little trouble making it 16-2 with a brisk two-hit, 3–0 shutout that quickly got everyone out of the cold.

The two hits were the lowest total *ever* for one team in a doubleheader. Even so, the Tribe had split. When it was all over, all Hargrove, no fan of Fellini, could think to say was "Like I was saying yesterday, baseball's a great game."

Even after thirty-seven innings played in thirty hours in Cleveland.

10

THE ATLANTA
FOUR

On a rainy afternoon in late February, Richard Griffin, the public relations director of the Montreal Expos, stood in the third-base dugout at Municipal Stadium in West Palm Beach and waved an arm toward the first-base dugout.

"All you ever hear over there is 'worst to first, worst to first,' " he said. "What is the big deal about going from worst to first? All you have to do is walk from here to there. Boom! You've gone from worst to first."

Griffin's Expos, who used the third-base side of the ballpark as their spring-training headquarters, had been the worst in the National League East in 1991. The Atlanta Braves, who used the first-base side, had been the champions of the National League. Of course, as everyone who had ever heard of the sport of baseball knew by now, the Braves had gone from worst in 1990 to first in 1991—in the standings, not just using the Griffin method of walking from one dugout to the other.

The Minnesota Twins had achieved the same feat in the American League and had become the world champions. But their climb was not as dramatic as that of the Braves. The Twins had been world champions only five years earlier, in 1987, and had won ninety-one games in 1988. Their last-place finish in 1990 was an aberration.

The Braves were a completely different story. After winning the National League West in 1982, they had gone steadily downhill. They won eighty-eight games the next year and finished three games behind the division-winning Dodgers. In 1984, the record was 80-82. Then came the collapse. During the next six seasons, the Braves' *best* record was 72-89 (1986).

In 1988 they were an embarrassing 54-106. That year was the first of three straight in which the team failed to draw a million people at home. The Braves' attendance for those three years *combined* was a little more than 2.8 million—less than the Dodgers, Blue Jays, and Mets were drawing in *single* seasons during that period.

Most nights, Atlanta–Fulton County Stadium looked like a ghost town. The WTBS Braves commercials, which shouted, "Watch America's Team in action!" sounded like parodies.

"Some nights it hurt to watch," said Stan Kasten. "No, make that a *lot* of nights."

Kasten had become team president at the end of 1986. Bobby Cox had just completed his first year as general manager and the two men sat down to talk about Cox's plan to rebuild. "It was all pitching," Kasten remembered. "Everything centered on getting young arms and developing them. The hardest thing to do during the next four years was grit your teeth and stick to the plan. But we did it."

A perfect example of how the Cox plan was executed took place during the first winter that he and Kasten worked together. The team had to decide whether to re-sign Doyle Alexander, a thirty-five-year-old pitcher who probably had a couple of decent years left but certainly wasn't going to be around when the Braves became contenders again. What's more, Alexander was a headache, one of the few players who negotiated his own contract, a tough guy to deal with and not terribly popular in the clubhouse.

Cox re-signed him, for one reason: He believed that when August rolled around, the team would be able to trade Alexander to a contender for a young pitcher, maybe two. Sure enough, come August the Tigers needed a pitcher for the stretch run. To get Doyle Alexander, they were willing to part with a twenty-year-old pitcher who was considered a bright prospect, but was still a long way from being ready for the major leagues.

The prospect was broken-hearted when he heard about the trade. He had grown up in Lansing and had spent his boyhood going to Tiger games. "I couldn't believe they traded me," he said. "Then Doyle went nine-and-oh and won the pennant for them. I remember saying to myself, 'Someday, this will be a good trade for the Braves. Some-day.' "

The prospect was John Smoltz. The day came.

By 1989, the young pitchers were starting to show potential. Tommy Glavine was winning 14 games for a bad team at the age of twenty-three. Smoltz won 12 with an ERA of 2.94. A teenager named Steve Avery was 12-7 with an ERA around two pitching in Durham and Greenville. Pete Smith, twenty-six days older than Glavine, was also in the majors, although he was struggling. Still, there was hope.

Kasten wondered if he had the right manager in place. Russ Nixon had taken over from Chuck Tanner early in the disastrous 1988 season and the team had played better for him. But every time Kasten looked at Cox he saw a man whose reputation as a manager in Toronto had been exemplary.

Tony LaRussa has a word he uses to describe the best managers: "deep." Not as in deep thinkers but as in thinking beyond the surface of one inning or one game or even one week. To LaRussa, the best managers "go deep" when they make out a lineup. They think about how a start for an outfielder on Wednesday might affect the lineup for Sunday. Or they'll stick with a pitcher for an extra batter because something in the way he pitched to the previous guy tells them that he'll get the next batter out—even if logic says he shouldn't.

Cox, according to LaRussa, is deep. Kasten knew that a lot of baseball people felt that way, and he had a sense that Cox missed the dugout. Occasionally, he would ask Cox if he was interested in manag-ing again. Every time the answer was the same: "I'll do whatever you and Ted [Turner] want me to do."

"I probably asked him the question seven hundred times," said Kasten, who is also the president of Turner's basketball team, the Atlanta Hawks. "I've always believed that basketball coaches and baseball managers are the same in one sense: No matter how many times they say they want to get out and do something else, they aren't telling the truth. Deep down, they *never* want to do anything else."

Sixty-five games into the 1990 season, Kasten decided that he and Ted wanted Cox to manage again. Nixon's frustrations were making the clubhouse a very tense place; Kasten didn't think it was the right atmosphere for a young, developing team. So, with the Braves 25-40, he asked Cox to go back to the dugout.

"I was nervous about the move," Kasten said. "I was concerned that it might be too soon. Any manager, no matter how good, only has so much credibility in terms of wins and losses. If Bobby went back there too soon, I might be setting him up for a fall. But I thought it was time. And I was almost certain he was the right manager, especially since he had put most of the players into place as the general man-ager."

Now Kasten had to find a general manager. He began calling around and doing some research. He still hadn't gotten very far when he went to New York in August for a Player Personnel Development Committee meeting at the commissioner's office. The Royals were playing the Yankees that afternoon and John Schuerholz, the Royals general manager, had ordered a car to take him to Yankee Stadium as soon as the meeting was over. He asked Kasten if he wanted to come along.

"I figured, why not?" Kasten said. "I hadn't been to Yankee Stadium for years."

Kasten and Schuerholz spent the afternoon talking about general manager candidates for Atlanta. By the end of the day, Schuerholz had made it clear to Kasten that there was one candidate he hadn't thought of: Schuerholz.

The thought of leaving Kansas City was traumatic for Schuerholz. He had been one of the architects of the Royals, joining the club in 1968 prior to the expansion draft that stocked the team. He'd started his baseball career in Baltimore (where he grew up) as an assistant farm director with the Orioles. To get into baseball, he left his $6,800-a-year job as a junior high school teacher and took a $2,100-a-year pay cut.

Two years later, when Lou Gorman left the Orioles to become the farm director with the expansion Royals, he took Schuerholz with him. Schuerholz stayed twenty-two years, rising to the general manager's job in 1981. Two years after that, the Royals went through a drug scandal that landed four players in jail. They recovered from that nadir to win the World Series in 1985. Five years later, the team was struggling again and Schuerholz was feeling some heat.

"Maybe I was just paranoid but I felt there wasn't the kind of unification of support for my decisions that there had been in the past," Schuerholz said. "Or maybe I was just a little bit stale after twenty-two years with the same organization. Our expectations had become very high—which is what you want—but there were times I just didn't feel comfortable. It was nothing blatant. It wasn't as if Herk Robinson [Schuerholz's assistant] was running around trying to get my job. It was more of a subliminal thing. In any event, it was bothering me. I was bringing it home with me.

"When Stan started talking about what he was looking for, I began thinking, 'This is the move for me.' I remembered a talk I once had with [then Royals president] Joe Burke in which we were talking about the franchises that should work but don't. The two we came up with were Atlanta and Texas."

When Schuerholz expressed interest to Kasten, he was surprised and intrigued. He knew things had gone off the track a little in Kansas City but he also knew that Schuerholz was a driven, intense workaholic—characteristics he could relate to. He also thought Schuerholz might be a perfect fit with the more laid-back Cox. Several weeks after their day in New York, Kasten offered Schuerholz the job.

Schuerholz had already talked about the move with his wife. She was all for it. The Royals had made it clear they would not stand in his way. Still, Schuerholz wasn't sure. He loved Kansas City and he hated the idea that people might think he was fleeing a sinking ship.

Five days after the season ended, Kasten got a call from Schuerholz: He had decided to stay in Kansas City. Kasten was somewhat surprised, somewhat disappointed, but prepared. He had a backup name in mind—and he probably would have given the backup name to Ted Turner that day if not for the fact that he had to go to Deion Sanders's house for a contract negotiation. He spent the afternoon preparing for Neon Deion and decided to wait until Monday to recommend a general manager.

On Sunday afternoon, Kasten came back from a workout to find that Schuerholz had called. "My wife took the call and John said to her, 'Has he hired someone else yet?' " Helen Kasten said she didn't think he had. "Well then," Schuerholz said, "ask him to call me if he's still speaking to me."

Kasten called. After turning Kasten down, Schuerholz had met with the Royals and with his family again. Both factions had told him he'd made a mistake. Kasten hired Schuerholz the next day and took him straight to Cox, who was in the hospital after knee surgery.

"Bobby had both his legs up in the air in stirrups," Schuerholz remembered. "He wasn't very comfortable, but he had a lot of ideas. We went over the entire club that day."

Schuerholz left the hospital filled with ideas. The Cox plan had produced one of the game's bright young pitching staffs. But there was more to do. Cox, an old third baseman, thought the team needed a third baseman who could catch the ball. So did Schuerholz. The same was true at first base.

Before the year was over, Schuerholz had signed two free agents he hoped would give the team some defensive stability. Both were thirty and both were considered risks; they'd each had injury problems in the past. But both could sure catch the ball. Young pitchers need to feel that the people behind them can make plays. Sid Bream could make plays at first base: Schuerholz gave him a three-year contract. Terry Pendleton had lost his third-base job in St. Louis, but he was a two-time Gold Glove winner. He signed for four years.

Pendleton's career batting average was .259. If he stayed healthy, hit that much, and played third the way he was capable, the Braves would be thrilled. Kasten, Schuerholz, and Cox felt, as they approached spring training in 1991, that the Braves were ready to take a big step forward. They had won sixty-five games in 1990. They would have to win sixteen more games in 1991 to finish at .500. That was the unstated goal going into training camp—eighty-one wins.

•

The Braves didn't win eighty-one games that year. They won ninety-four and the National League West title. Then they won four more in the National League Championship Series against the Pirates and three more against the Twins in the World Series before coming up one run short in Game Seven.

Pendleton didn't hit anywhere close to .259—he hit .319, won the MVP Award, and became the unquestioned leader of the young team. David Justice and Ron Gant emerged as stars and Greg Olson became one of the National League's better catchers.

Schuerholz made two more crucial trades. On April 1, he picked up Otis Nixon, a thirty-two-year-old journeyman outfielder from the Toronto Blue Jays, in a deal that most expected to be little noted nor long remembered. Nixon could steal bases and could be a late-inning defensive replacement. That was why Schuerholz picked him up.

No one dreamed he would end up becoming the catalyst for the entire offense, hitting .297 and stealing seventy-two bases before his season was shut down on September 16 when a drug test came back positive. His loss seemed critical at the time, but the Braves were deep enough and confident enough by then that they were able to hold off the Dodgers down the stretch.

They might not have done so had Schuerholz not swung another seemingly innocuous deal on August 29, picking up another journeyman, thirty-two-year-old relief pitcher Alejandro Peña, from the Mets. Schuerholz and Cox felt they needed *someone* in the bullpen after Juan Berenguer went on the disabled list and, just as Jeff Reardon would be the best man available a year later, Peña was the guy in '91. Peña was almost perfect, winning two games and saving eleven in the crucible of the pennant race.

But none of those performances would have meant anything if not for the Atlanta starting pitching. If Pendleton was the heart and soul of the club, the starting pitchers were the foundation. Everything began with them. Great things had been expected—eventually—from Tommy Glavine, Steve Avery, and John Smoltz. Little had been expected from Charlie Leibrandt.

The four of them were, in a word, magnificent. None of them missed a start. Combined, they started 141 of the Braves' 162 games, making the lack of a consistent fifth starter almost irrelevant. They were 67-45, an impressive number under any circumstances but even more remarkable in light of the fact that Smoltz was 2-11 at the All-Star break. Every night, the Braves took the field almost certain that their starter was going to keep them in the game and give them a chance to win. All four were fast workers, which made it that much more fun to play behind them.

It was also fun to watch *them* play once they left the field. They were the Atlanta Four, each very different but united by two things: their common cause on the field and the desire to beat the hell out of one another at anything—and everything—off the field.

If you walked into the Atlanta clubhouse at any given hour, the odds were decent that you would find two, three, or four of the starters fighting over a card game. Or arguing over that day's round of golf. Or involved in a putting contest from one corner of the room to another. Or arguing about their hitting. Or making a friendly wager on a college basketball game.

It never stopped. "They just *find* things to compete at," said Olson, their catcher. "I get exhausted sometimes just watching them. If you ever wonder why they pitch the way they do, just play golf with them sometime. Or do *anything* with them."

Each of the Four had a clear role. Glavine was the leader, the Cy Young winner. He was not as loud as Smoltz or as experienced as Leibrandt, but there was never any doubting his competitiveness. "Payback is a bitch with Tommy Glavine," pitching coach Leo Mazzone said one night. "Just look into his eyes sometime."

Smoltz was the target, always bragging, always telling the others how much better he was than they were. This was due, in part, to the psychologist he had worked with in 1991 after his 2-11 start. No matter what, he constantly told Smoltz, always believe you are the best.

Smoltz did just that. At the beginning of the season, the four starters each put up $100 for the pitchers' hitting pool. When Glavine built a big lead by midseason, Smoltz pressed him, adding $100 to the bet. When Glavine pulled even farther ahead, Smoltz pressed again for *another* $100. Only the end of the season prevented him from going for his wallet one more time.

When Smoltz came up with two hits *and* stole a base in the play-offs, Glavine didn't want to hear about it. "I kicked his ass all season," he said with a grin. "Now, I'm going to hear about one game forever."

If it was Glavine's job to keep Smoltz under control with his bat, it was Leibrandt's job to do it with golf clubs. Both were excellent players, good enough to break 80 on almost any golf course (and there weren't many golf courses that they missed). Midway through the season, Smoltz got into the habit of playing on the day before he pitched. Technically, this was a violation of team rules. But Smoltz was pitching so well that he was afraid to stop. If Cox or Mazzone knew what was going on, they didn't let on. No doubt they were just as superstitious as the pitcher.

Smoltz was frustrated, though, because Leibrandt continued to lead him in their battle to be club champion. Leibrandt was the old man of the group, the wily veteran, who might not have as much talent as the others—with a baseball *or* a golf club—but usually figured out how to get things done. Everyone on the team knew how hard Leibrandt worked at his craft; he was as respected for his ability to win with less talent as the others were respected for their talent alone.

Avery was the kid, the wide-eyed youngster who had turned twenty-two just after the season started and didn't even look that old. The odd friendship that developed between Avery and Deion Sanders was as much the result of Avery being awed by Sanders's flash and glitz as anything else. Avery was the quietest of the group, shy, always polite, but very much a man on the mound and when things went wrong. One thing about all four, they never hid from adversity. If they pitched well, they were there to talk about it. If they pitched poorly, they were also there to talk about that.

They were like four brawling brothers: Leibrandt was the oldest and steadiest, Glavine was the star, Smoltz was the brilliant troublemaker, and Avery was the prodigious baby, the one who starts speaking in sentences at fifteen months.

"The competition works for us," Glavine said. "Every time one of them goes out to pitch, I'm rooting for them to pitch a shutout. But you can be certain if they do, when I get the ball, I'm going to want to pitch better than the last guy did. If I don't, I know I'll hear about it. That keeps you going."

Although Smoltz and Avery probably had more pure "stuff" than Glavine, he had always been the most precocious of the group, arriving in the majors when he was twenty-one and being thrown right into the rotation of what was then a bad team. Avery was actually younger than Glavine when he reached the majors, but by then he had several good pitchers around him for emotional protection.

Glavine had none of that. In 1989, when the Braves only won sixty-three games, he was 14-8. He was, in many ways, a typical young lefty, sometimes brilliant, sometimes awful. But he fit none of the other lefty stereotypes. He didn't throw that hard, he wasn't wild, and he didn't do weird things off the field. He was quiet and thoughtful and analytical, a superb athlete who had been drafted in both baseball and hockey after graduating from high school in Billerica, Massachusetts.

Glavine liked hockey. He had started playing it when he was four and, as in baseball, had become a star as much through smarts as natural ability. He understood the game, knew how to be in the right place at the right time, and knew how to make other players better. The Los Angeles Kings chose him on the fourth round.

The Braves took him on the second round. At the same time, the University of Lowell offered him a full scholarship to play hockey. Fred and Mildred Glavine left the final choice up to their son and, as always, he examined the question from all sides before making a decision.

"I liked the idea of going to college where I could have played both sports," he said. "If the Braves had not offered good money, that's probably what I would have done. I didn't make my decision based strictly on money, though. Sure, I knew that baseball players made more than hockey players, but I wasn't thinking, 'Well, in baseball I might make three million dollars a year someday.' It was more the idea that there's more longevity in baseball. I guess, in a sense, that has to do with money but I didn't look at it that way."

There are occasions when Glavine has hockey pangs. Every once in a while he will recognize on TV someone he once played against now playing in the NHL; every now and then he will catch himself fantasizing about what it would have been like to play on a line with Wayne Gretzky. But there is no second-guessing his decision to play baseball.

Stardom has meant adjustments for Glavine. When he started to make a lot of money, he wanted to take care of his parents. Fred Glavine worked in construction, eventually starting his own small company. He always kept his four kids fed and happy, but obviously never made the kind of money his third child is making now. When Tom started to give his parents things, they balked.

"In a way it was difficult for them," he said. "I know how hard and how long my dad worked to get where he did. Now, I come in at twenty-five and I'm making more money than he ever dreamed of making. I honestly believe my parents would miss a payment on something before they would ever come to me for money. It took me a while to convince them that they should let me do things for them. Role reversal can be tough for both sides. Now, I think they're a little more comfortable with it."

Glavine is more comfortable with being a public figure, too. The Braves' dramatic turnaround made everyone on the team into a celebrity in 1991, but none more than Glavine. Rich, single (then), good-looking, and a star, Glavine found that going out in public could be a chore.

"My first few years in the majors, I might get stopped for an autograph away from the park a couple times a week," he said. "But in 'ninety-one, when we started winning, it got to be where going to the market to buy milk became a half-hour process. I stopped going out at night because it was too much of a hassle for me and for my girlfriend [who became his wife last November 7]. We'd walk into a place and people would literally start shoving her out of the way to get an autograph.

"I mean, in a way, it's a nice problem to have, especially after all those years of playing in front of seven thousand people every night. But sometimes it gets to be too much."

Glavine vividly remembers the night he knew that his days of being able to go out for a quiet dinner were over. "It was the night we clinched in 'ninety-one," he said. "A bunch of us wanted to go out and celebrate what we'd done. We figured wherever we went some people would recognize us and we'd sign some autographs and then have dinner. Wrong. We walked into a place, tried to sit down, and the next thing we knew, we were in the middle of a card show. It's been kind of like that ever since."

When Glavine won the Cy Young Award after going 20-11, there were some in the media who commented that Glavine might have been the first pitcher in history to win the Cy Young who was the third-best pitcher on his own staff. The comments irked Glavine. He doesn't question the talent that Avery and Smoltz have, but he has figured out that there is more to pitching than how hard you throw the ball. When he is on, Glavine is a joy to watch; he mixes his pitches up so well and seems able to make the baseball go to any spot he wants it to. His change-up is as good as there is in the game and makes his fastball and curve much tougher to hit. He hides the ball from the hitter until the last possible second and is rarely outsmarted on the mound in any confrontation.

What's more, he's always learning. Early in '91, after pitching well in his first outing and not so well in his second, Glavine was frustrated; he seemed unable to pitch consistently start after start. Informally, he began interviewing hitters on the Braves whom he respected—Pendleton, Bream, Lonnie Smith—asking them what made a pitcher tough on them.

Their answers varied. Different pitchers beat you with different things. On the night of April 20, sitting on the bench between Bream and Smith, Glavine watched the Reds' Tom Browning mow the Braves down with ease. Browning didn't throw the ball hard, none of his pitches looked unhittable. "And yet, he'd go out there, give up six or seven hits and, after two hours he'd have a complete-game victory," Glavine says. "At least that's the way it seemed against us."

On this particular night, Browning shut the Braves out 3–0. As the game wore on, Glavine turned to Bream and Smith and asked, "What's he *do* out there?"

Glavine doesn't remember who said what exactly, but he does remember the words: "Comes right after you. Pitches fast. Makes you hit his pitch. Sets up every batter. Always has an idea about what his next pitch will be. Stays ahead in the count. Hits spots all the time.''

All basics. Glavine listened. And watched—closely. And decided that if Tom Browning could pitch that way, *he* could pitch that way. From that moment on, Glavine was a different pitcher. Three days later, he shut the Dodgers out 4–0. In his next start, he lost to the Astros 2–0, despite pitching a complete game. And then he won six straight starts with an ERA of 1.76.

Glavine is occasionally accused of being too serious. He radiates intensity on the mound. As Mazzone says, check out the eyes. ''People always say to me, 'Why don't you smile more, have fun out there?' I *have* fun—when I'm getting guys out.''

In the clubhouse, Glavine is right in the middle of the give-and-take among the Four and enjoys getting on Smoltz as much as anyone. But, perhaps because of his New England upbringing, or perhaps because it's just his nature, Glavine simply cannot take anything for granted.

''I remember when I was a kid I was always pretty good at both baseball and hockey and in the back of my mind I knew I wanted to take a shot at playing one or the other professionally,'' he says. ''But whenever we had to write papers or give reports on what we wanted to be when we grew up, I never said an athlete. I always said policeman or fireman or whatever. I just figured the chances of making it were, being realistic, pretty remote.

''Once I got to high school, there were scouts at all my games and I figured that I was going to at least get a shot to prove myself. But I always thought there must be a hundred guys out there who are as good as I am who I'm just not seeing, being from a small town in Massachusetts. I guess that's always been my approach. Every level in the minors, I wondered if I was going to be good enough. For a long while I wondered if I would make it in the majors.''

Now he has made it. *More* than made it. *Now* does he take it for granted? ''Not for one second,'' he said. ''For one thing, pitching is such an unnatural act, your career can be over in a second. We all know that.''

He smiles. ''And I know one more thing. If I let down for one second, those other three guys will be all over me. I can assure you, *that* is the last thing in the world I want to deal with.''

And that may be why the Braves fully expected to win again in 1992. They were talented, experienced, and, still flushed with the memories of 1991, cocky almost to a fault. Most important, almost every night, they sent one of the Four to the mound, each one knowing that as he pitched the other three were watching . . . and waiting.

11

LEYLAND AND
LARUSSA

On the afternoon of April 24, Tony LaRussa sat in the middle of the visiting clubhouse in the Minneapolis Metrodome, staring at the television set propped on a shelf a few feet away from him. Outside, the weather was cold and raw. Inside, it was toasty, warm and comfortable.

LaRussa has the kind of piercing eyes that quickly give away his emotions. If the eyes are windows to the soul, LaRussa's is a soul that smolders. Within the Oakland Athletics organization he is known as "the Load," because everything that happens every day is so damn important.

Now, the Load was focused clearly on a game taking place two hundred miles away in Chicago, where the Pittsburgh Pirates and Chicago Cubs were locked in a 2–2 tie. Both managers had been LaRussa coaches: Jim Lefebvre of the Cubs remains a friend; Jim Leyland of the Pirates is LaRussa's soul mate. They talk constantly—about the game, their teams, their families. They talk about situations they have faced and decisions they have to make.

"A lot of nights I walk out of the ballpark knowing I fucked up and maybe no one else knows it,'' Leyland says. ''I call Tony, tell him what happened, and he gets it right away. He knows how I think, I know how he thinks. That comes from spending so much time talking all these years.''

The two men had talked the previous night. LaRussa's A's, picked to finish in the middle of the pack by most people in preseason, were 11-5 and two games ahead of the second-place Chicago White Sox. Leyland's Pirates, after a tumultuous spring training, had roared out of the gate, going 12-3. They had a three-and-a-half-game lead over the favored New York Mets. Did that mean the two friends were happy?

LaRussa shook his head at the question, keeping one eye on the television as he talked. ''In this game, you don't stay happy, you stay concerned. It's just too long a season to ever get happy about things. You feel good about your team if it has the right feel to it. Like this team right now, I just feel like we're breathing, we're alive. These guys come to play. That doesn't mean we're going to win, it means they're doing everything they can to get the job done.''

Note the use of the word *they.* LaRussa is almost hyper about making sure credit for his team's success is given to the players. Part of this is philosophical. He and Leyland are both great believers in the notion that a manager is far more capable of screwing up a good team than rescuing a bad team.

Leyland is quick to note that his first Pittsburgh team lost 98 games in 1986. ''Did I manage bad that year?'' he asks rhetorically. ''I don't think so. You don't have good players because you managed good. The reason you manage good is because you have good players.''

LaRussa points to 1991, a year in which his team was 84-78 and finished fourth after winning three straight American League pennants. ''Remember that José [Canseco] hit forty-four dingers and Eck [Dennis Eckersley] saved forty-three,'' he said. ''Those are great years. We still finished fourth. It takes a lot of elements to win.''

At first blush, both managers sound disingenuous. After all, it's part of the job description for any coach or manager to publicly insist that the players deserve all the credit—just before they wink at their pals in the media and explain how they succeeded even though the other guy had so much more talent.

But LaRussa and Leyland not only believe what they say, they know it's crucial that their players understand how they feel. ''You watch a guy who starts taking too many bows, regardless of the sport,'' LaRussa said. ''Sooner or later it will catch up with him. Especially in this sport. The minute you think you have this game licked it will come back and humble you. Guaranteed.''

The last part of that statement is almost a mantra for LaRussa. He chafes at his image as some kind of baseball Renaissance man. ''All that stuff about being a lawyer is bullshit," he says, his "Load" voice firmly in place. "I'm a baseball guy every day. I think it, eat it, sleep it. Maybe during the offseason I do some other things—a little—but that has more to do with my wife and family than anything else. To imply that I'm somehow different from the other guys in my profession is just wrong."

Not entirely. Anthony LaRussa, Jr., grew up in Tampa, a baseball hotbed. His father was a ballplayer, a good catcher in his day, and Tony was playing with friends and cousins by the time he was six. He benefited from the excellent coaching of a man named Andrew Espolita, a Nicaraguan, who taught the kids fundamentals. "I always looked like a ballplayer because I had been taught right from the beginning," he said. "And I played. During the summer, you could play on four or five different teams a day if you wanted to. That's what I did."

He played against another highly regarded prospect named Lou Piniella in high school, and with Piniella in summer league. Like Piniella, he grew up bilingual. His mother spoke only Spanish so LaRussa learned that first, then learned English in school. His parents never pushed him to play ball but they encouraged it. Tony LaRussa, Sr., was up at two-thirty every morning to drive a wholesale milk truck. Whenever he could, he got home in time to watch his son play in the afternoons. When he wasn't around, Oliva LaRussa would play catch with her son in the alley behind their house.

By the time he was a high school senior, LaRussa was being watched by almost every team in the big leagues. He was a smooth-fielding shortstop who could hit. This was in 1962, three years before the draft, so he had his choice of teams. Cleveland, Pittsburgh, and the Kansas City Athletics showed the most interest. Charles O. Finley, the team owner, came down to meet LaRussa and his family and that was enough to convince them to sign with his team. On the night he graduated from high school, LaRussa signed with the A's for a package worth about $90,000, huge money in those days.

It wasn't quite that simple, though. His mother wanted him to go to college. She not only insisted that money be put aside for his education, she elicited a promise from her son that he would use the money during the offseason to go to school. For seven straight winters, LaRussa attended Florida State to keep his promise.

There is a clue there to the LaRussa character. He was not, by any means, the first or the last son to promise his mother to go back to school on the day he signed a professional sports contract. But, unlike most athletes, he not only went to school, he graduated. LaRussa does not believe in doing part of a job. If, as he claims, he is not exceptionally bright, he is, without question, exceptionally dogged.

"You have to understand one thing about Tony when you watch

him manage a game," says Wally Haas, the president of the A's. "It's almost impossible to catch him unprepared, no matter how the game goes. He's already gone through just about every situation in his head the night before or that day. When a game starts, he's already managed it—one hundred times."

LaRussa never became the star the A's had envisioned when they signed him. He hurt a shoulder playing in a pickup league during his first winter home and didn't get it treated properly. The shoulder never healed and LaRussa had to move from shortstop to second base because he couldn't make the longer throw.

Most of his sixteen years as a player were spent in Triple-A, although he spent parts of five seasons with the A's in both Kansas City and Oakland. He also had brief stints with the Cubs and Braves. He only came to bat 176 times in the big leagues and got 35 hits—a batting average of .199. Always a good Triple-A player, he was an MVP three different times.

Dave Duncan, LaRussa's longtime pitching coach, and Rene Lachemann, his third-base coach until the expansion Florida Marlins hired him as their first manager, both joined the A's organization shortly after LaRussa. Both like to point out that one of the scouts who signed LaRussa, Charlie Gassaway, was fired shortly thereafter. "They always say it was because he recommended me," LaRussa says, a smile flickering briefly across his face.

By 1972, LaRussa knew it was time to look for a real job. He was making decent money in Triple-A but that wasn't going to last forever. He liked reading and he liked trying to figure out problems. He also liked the idea of being a litigator because that was another form of competing. So he applied to law school and was accepted at both Florida State and Miami. He opted for Florida State. This time, it took him five offseasons to get the degree.

While he was in law school, LaRussa continued bouncing around Triple-A ball. In 1975 he played in Iowa, on a White Sox Triple-A team for a man named Loren Babe. He was thirty that season and Babe made him a player-coach. "Right there was where the managing thing started for me," LaRussa said. "Loren was a fabulous teacher. He would sit next to me on the bench every game and explain what was going on, no matter what the situation."

It was under Babe that LaRussa first learned the concept of "going deep." "Loren taught me that every decision you make as a manager is a matter of levels."

Some of those levels are fairly basic. For example: "If a pitcher isn't going well in the first, you can't just bang him [take him out] because that will affect your entire staff not only that day but for *several* days. Almost every decision you make as a manager, there can be two, three, four, or five levels involved. Sometimes it's the fifth level where you make the decision. The best guys are the ones that go the deepest. Loren was deep. Sparky [Anderson] is deep. Bobby Cox is deep. Leyland is deep.''

And, by watching, observing, and assimilating, LaRussa became deep. Other managers will tell you that LaRussa's greatest strength is the way he handles his pitchers and uses his bullpen.

''It don't take no genius to run Eckersley out there,'' Anderson says. ''But it takes great feel to know exactly when to get a starter, when to ride with him, who to bring in and how long to leave him in there. That's where Tony's great.''

Johnny Oates, an ardent LaRussa disciple, is more direct: ''He almost never lets you face a pitcher who shouldn't be out there. He's got an absolute feel for when to make a change.''

LaRussa says it isn't that simple, that the way he handles pitchers is, like so much of what he does, something he learned by watching someone else. ''When I was still playing, Vern Rapp was managing in Indianapolis. He always had a fresh pitcher on the mound. It wasn't like there was a hard and fast rule that a guy came out after five or six innings, it was more the idea that you didn't leave a guy out there till he was gasping. Soon as he looked a little bit tired, you thought about getting him.''

After fourteen years of managing in the big leagues, LaRussa's approach isn't nearly that simple. He will watch for other clues: Is a pitcher working more slowly than normal? Is he still going after hitters? Is he throwing a first-pitch ball to every batter? But the concept— using the entire bullpen—began to germinate twenty years ago, with Vern Rapp in Indianapolis.

LaRussa's playing career ended in 1978, just as he was finishing law school. Because he had to wait six months to take the bar exam and because he had become interested in continuing in baseball as a manager, he wrote to most of the major league teams looking for work. Some might say his approach was a bit arrogant: He wanted to manage, but only at the Double-A level or higher.

''The reasonable thing for someone who had never managed was to start in rookie ball or A-ball,'' he said. ''But I had the law degree as a backup, so I figured I could afford to shoot a little higher.''

He figured right. Roland Hemond, then the White Sox general manager, was fascinated by the notion of a ballplayer who had finished law school during the offseason. He had also known LaRussa as a player in the Chicago system. He offered LaRussa the job in Knox-ville—Double A. The team had won fifty games the previous year. In 1978, it won forty-nine—during the first half. ''Would have been fifty,'' LaRussa said, ''except Chris Bando hit a homer off us in the last game [most minor leagues are divided into seventy-game half-seasons], so we won forty-nine. We had a lot of talent on that team, guys who made the majors."

LaRussa was promoted to Triple-A Iowa the next year. In August, Don Kessinger resigned as manager of the White Sox and Hemond asked LaRussa to take the team. "It was too soon, I wasn't ready," he said. "I had managed just a little more than a year in the minors. But I remembered picking up a *Reader's Digest* a few years earlier and reading a story in there about a guy, a writer, who had been offered an assignment totally out of his area of expertise. He turned it down, because he didn't think he could handle it. He never got another chance. The point of the story was that you had to take your shot, no matter what, because you might never get another one. And the more you're exposed to pressure, the better you deal with it. I still have the story someplace."

Clearly, he also still has it in his mind. Throughout the season, LaRussa will challenge his players to deal with pressure. Often, before the rubber game of a three-game series, he will tell them to treat the game as if it is the seventh game of the World Series, a game they absolutely must win. "If you don't win two out of three enough times, when you get to September you're going to be out of the race," he said. "If you do, and you take that approach, when you get to September where every game does matter, you've already dealt with pressure so it isn't anything new." *Expose yourself to pressure.*

LaRussa handled the pressure of managing in the majors. The White Sox were 27-27 during the final third of 1979; that was good enough to convince Hemond to bring LaRussa back. Slowly—70-90 the first year—but steadily, the White Sox improved. By the third year they were 87-75. The next year, after a sluggish start, they ran away with the American League West, going 99-63 to win the division by 20 games.

It was in 1982 that LaRussa hired Leyland as his third-base coach. Leyland had managed in the minor leagues for eleven years and, at thirty-seven, was beginning to wonder if he would ever get a shot at the majors. He *really* began to wonder when the first three games of his major league coaching career were rained out. "He was convinced he was some kind of jinx or something," LaRussa said. "I've never seen a guy more nervous about a baseball game than Jim when we finally got to play."

LaRussa and Leyland quickly discovered that there was a lot of common ground between them. They were almost exactly the same age, LaRussa having been born ten weeks earlier in 1944 than Leyland. Although LaRussa had been a better player than Leyland, neither had known a lot of success. Both had explosive tempers: It took less to send

Leyland off but he was less likely to hold a grudge afterward. Each had been divorced and was remarried. And, perhaps most important, each had an almost insatiable desire to learn.

"We were always looking for guys to listen to, guys who had something to say, as opposed to guys who thought they knew it all," LaRussa said. "We would sit up for hours talking about what we had done but also what we had seen other people do."

They were a strange-looking couple: LaRussa, tall and dark with the law school background; Leyland, shorter, his hair gone gray, with a tendency to fracture the language. Clearly, though, they spoke the same dialect when the topic was baseball. In a sport where machismo is considered at least as important as hitting a curveball, they weren't afraid to say they loved one another.

"If I have one memory in this game that will never leave me, it's the moment right after we clinched in 1983 when Tony hugged me," Leyland says. "The damn thing meant so much to both of us and to be able to share it that way . . ."

"There's a picture somewhere, I've seen it, but I can't find anyone who has it, of that hug," LaRussa says. "I've been trying to track it down because it means so much to both of us. I can talk about Jim Leyland for hours, but there's only one thing that really matters: He's the best there is. Absolutely, the best. He's a perfect manager and a better guy. Now, if someone wants to make fun of that, let 'em."

Leyland left the White Sox after the 1985 season to take on the job of resurrecting the Pirates. LaRussa was gone soon after that, fired 64 games into the '86 season when the White Sox struggled to a 26-38 start. He wasn't home for long. Almost as soon as he became available, A's general manager Sandy Alderson was on the phone. The A's wanted him to take over—immediately.

LaRussa wasn't ready. "I was carrying some baggage," he said. "I understood what the White Sox did. Heck, there had been a couple other times where there had been pressure on them to bang me and their response was to extend me. But even so, when you put your heart and soul into something and one day someone says to you that isn't good enough, it hurts. That organization was like a family to me. I believed in it and in the people in it. To be told one morning you're out of the family, that hurts."

One of the first callers was Sparky Anderson. "You'll be hired again in five minutes," Anderson said. LaRussa believed him, "because I always believe Sparky." Now, Alderson was proving Anderson right. Only LaRussa wasn't sure. He asked Anderson if he could wait until the next spring. Just as Jim Campbell had done with Anderson in 1979, Alderson said no, it had to be now. So, LaRussa jumped back in. *Take the chance when it's there because it may not come again.*

The A's were an evolving team. José Canseco was a rookie when LaRussa took over. Mark McGwire would arrive the following season. Dave Stewart had been signed to a Triple-A contract five weeks before LaRussa was hired, having been released by the Philadelphia Phillies. One of LaRussa's first moves was to put him into the starting rotation. Dennis Eckersley came from the Cubs the next spring. LaRussa convinced him to give closing a shot.

The A's were a game out of first place on September 1 in '87 before fading to third. The next year there was no fade. They won 104 games and swept the play-offs from Boston. But they were stunned in the World Series by the Los Angeles Dodgers when Kirk Gibson hit his famous ninth-inning pinch home run to beat Eckersley in Game One. In 1989, battling injuries most of the season, they won again. This time the World Series was marred by the San Francisco earthquake, but nothing could stop the A's from sweeping the Giants in four games.

It was the following season, while the A's were en route to their third straight pennant, that George Will's book *Men at Work* came out. LaRussa was one of four men Will used as centerpieces. The others were Cal Ripken, Jr., Tony Gwynn, and Orel Hershiser. Will's point was to write about someone who was outstanding at one aspect of the game: Ripken was the fielder, Gwynn the hitter, Hershiser the pitcher.

And LaRussa was the manager. He was also the cover boy when *Sports Illustrated* excerpted the book that spring. The cover line said simply: "The Mastermind."

When Will called to tell him what was on the cover, LaRussa was furious. "If you're in baseball for a long time, it's kind of a dream to be on the cover of *Sports Illustrated* or *The Sporting News*," he said. "Now, here's my one shot at *Sports Illustrated* and I'm pissed off about it.

"The point of what he [Will] wrote was not that I did things that no one else did or that my way was the best way or the only way. It's pretty obvious that isn't true. The point was, here's a guy who has had some success and this is what he does. Period. End of story. I guarantee you if you sat down with Sparky or Leyland or Cox or Tom Kelly or any decent manager you would find out that we all work hard, try like hell to prepare and, most of the time, have a pretty good idea what we're doing.

"Do I think I do a good job—yes. But the game belongs to the *players*. It absolutely does. Jim Leyland is a great manager every year of his life, but he isn't going to win every year because some years his players won't be good enough. So here I am on the cover of *Sports Illustrated* and it says, 'The Mastermind.' Was I embarrassed? No. I was *very* embarrassed.

"If you want to talk about guys who are masterminds or geniuses or whatever you want to call it, you've got to look at guys who have done it again and again for years and years. Pat Riley's won four times in the NBA. Bill Walsh won three Super Bowls. Bob Knight has won the Final Four three times. Sparky's won three times with two different clubs. I am *not* a goddamn genius. I think I'm good because I work very hard. I did well in law school because I worked hard, not because I was smarter than anyone else. That's the way I've always been. But I've won one World Series. Count 'em up—one.''

LaRussa doesn't even like to joke about the mastermind tag. Late in the season, after a key victory, a reporter walked into LaRussa's office and made the mistake of opening the conversation by saying, "Tony, when people call you a genius . . .''

"I ask 'em what goddamn place did we finish last year?'' LaRussa answered. "You got anything else?''

•

The Cubs and Pirates were now in the bottom of the ninth. The Pirates, after leaving runners in scoring position in both the sixth and seventh, had finally pushed a run across in the eighth to lead 3–2. LaRussa watched the TV intently. "Jim won't sleep if they don't win this one,'' he said. "So many chances. I know he's got a lot invested in this game. Look at him.''

The camera had panned to a shot of Leyland, who, as usual, looked pale and exhausted. Jerome Walton, the Cubs center fielder, was on first base with two out. Ryne Sandberg, the $7-million second baseman, was at the plate. Stan Belinda checked Walton and threw to the plate. Walton took off. But Leyland had called a pitchout. Catcher Don Slaught stepped outside, grabbed the pitch, and whipped it to second baseman José Lind who tagged Walton to end the game.

"Look at that!'' LaRussa screamed. "He guessed right! Can you believe the guy! Unbelievable!''

If LaRussa had made the same call himself to end a game he could not have been more animated. Calming down, he pointed at the television set. "Now *there*,'' he said, "is an example of a manager helping his team win. The players won the game, but the manager helped.''

LaRussa tried to do the same thing that night. He watched his team build a 5–0 lead on the Minnesota Twins but, as if to prove his thesis valid, his players couldn't hold on. After Canseco struck out with Rickey Henderson on third base in the ninth, the Twins won it 6–5 in the tenth. Goose Gossege walked the leadoff hitter and he scored.

Basics of the game: Get the run home from third with less than two out; never walk the leadoff batter, especially in a tie game. LaRussa had managed on every pitch but his players, on this night, weren't good enough. Of course he didn't see it quite that way. He felt he hadn't handled Ron Darling, his starting pitcher, correctly.

Darling had taken a 5–2 lead into the fifth inning but he couldn't hold it. A double by Pedro Muñoz and a two-run triple by Scott Leius tied the game before LaRussa went to get Darling. Most of the Oakland writers figured that LaRussa had wanted Darling to get through the fifth inning so he could get credit for a win (he'd left his two previous games with leads only to watch the bullpen blow the saves).

After a loss, especially a tough one, LaRussa will usually shower before meeting with the press. It gives him a few extra minutes to calm down—but it rarely works. Every time someone asks a question, the muscles on his neck bulge with tension.

"Tony, were you trying to get Ronnie a win . . ."

"I was trying to get a win—period." The answer was snapped off, the tone—to be polite—brusque.

The next morning, sitting in the clubhouse at nine o'clock eating a bowl of fruit, LaRussa was calmer. "I *did* mess up with Darling last night," he said. "But it wasn't in the fifth. It was earlier. I could see in the third, even the second, that he wasn't himself. He was working slowly. He didn't want to throw strike one. That's where I blew it. I should have gone out there and talked to him, at least once, maybe twice, just to tell him to work faster and throw strike one.

"You lose sleep after a game like that. I sat up and watched Cincinnati–San Diego [a sixteen-inning game that ended at almost 3 A.M.], then I sat up and read for a while. I don't do that all the time but sometimes, especially when I know I've got an afternoon game, I'll just stay up.

"That's what's tough about the job. You play a hundred and sixty-two and the odds are, all but about fifty of them are going to be like last night."

He smiled. "We made mistakes last night but I still like the approach. I liked the approach in spring training and I like it now." He paused and took a deep breath. "I just hope I still like it in August."

12

EARLY RETURNS

The team that the Athletics were facing during that final weekend in April hardly had the look one would expect from the defending world champions. The Minnesota Twins had staggered to a 6-9 start; already people were wondering if the five players who had not returned from 1991 were being missed.

Most notable among the missing were two of the World Series heroes: Jack Morris, who had pitched so brilliantly in the seventh game, and Dan Gladden, the left fielder who had scored the winning run in the tenth inning that night.

On paper, both had been replaced. John Smiley had come from Pittsburgh in the stunning March 17 trade that had so shocked the Pirates. Gladden had been allowed to leave via free agency (to the Tigers) because the team felt that Pedro Muñoz was ready to step into his spot.

Muñoz justified the team's faith in the early going, hitting .308. Shane Mack, supposedly ready for stardom, was also doing his part, hitting .368. But Smiley, unhappy in his new surroundings, had been bombed in his first three starts. More important, Kent Hrbek hadn't played in a single game. He'd injured a shoulder while foolishly trying to stretch a double into a triple during a spring exhibition game in St. Petersburg.

Hrbek and Kirby Puckett were the Twins' main men, their leaders, the players manager Tom Kelly expected to pick the team up when it was down. Hrbek's injury was as much an emotional setback as a physical one. It provided a perfect example of how delicate the balance can be on a team, even a very good one.

Good teams don't panic in April, especially ones that have won two World Series in five years. Even so, there was a curious mixture—part leftover euphoria, lingering from 1991, and part tension, building slowly as the '92 team struggled—that was easy to feel when one stepped inside the Metrodome.

There may be no building in baseball that has been derided more than the Metrodome. If the Seattle Mariners ever improve to the point where a key series is played in their Kingdome, that monstrosity would be recognized as the worst in baseball. For the moment, thanks to the scrutiny of having played host to twelve postseason games in five years, the Metrodome tops the list.

Opened in 1982 at a cost of $55 million, the place had been intended for football. Only twelve thousand seats were located between the baselines. The rightfield fence was a giant Baggie. Players often had difficulty with the lights. The ball often took weird bounces on the turf. All these things provided an atmosphere more conducive to an amusement park than a ballpark.

Still, the place did have character, unlike many of the domes and donut parks. The Baggie in right field *was* unique. And games there did have a little bit of the Fenway Park/Wrigley Field aura, if only because no lead was safe in the park that came to be known as the Homerdome.

Even at 6-9, the Twins were still a confident group.

"It helps knowing you've had success against someone," the Twins' Gene Larkin said before the second game of the series, referring to the fact that the A's had not won a season series in Minnesota since 1988. "We know the A's are good, we respect them, but we also know they have to respect us. We're still pretty damn solid."

Larkin was one example of why the Twins were solid. He was a player who improved a little bit each year, the first graduate of Columbia University to play in the majors since Lou Gehrig. That was no mean feat considering that he'd been a twentieth-round draft choice.

"Actually, I never thought of myself as any kind of pro prospect until I was a senior," he said in a voice still thick with his Long Island upbringing. "I was just an average hitter until I started switch-hitting in college. Even then, I figured they drafted me just to be a body around to work with the real prospects."

Larkin continued to improve as a left-handed hitter, to the point where he made it to the Twins in 1987 as a pinch-hitter and utility player. That was his role and he accepted it, although he was bitterly disappointed when a sore knee kept him from starting Game Five of the '91 World Series.

He was still on the bench as Game Seven unfolded. By the eighth inning, he sensed that he might play a role in the final outcome. "It seemed as if no one was ever going to score," he said. "It was easily the longest, toughest game I've ever had to sit through. In the eighth, Jarvis Brown ran for Chili [Davis] and I thought to myself that if his turn came around with anybody on, Tom would probably send me up to hit."

Larkin's instincts were right. Dan Gladden led off the tenth inning with a bloop double and Chuck Knoblauch bunted him to third. Not surprisingly, the Braves walked Puckett intentionally. Larkin fully expected Bobby Cox to bring in a left-hander to pitch to Hrbek and try to induce a double play. "Herbie was struggling with lefties," he said. "But they decided to walk him, too. As he tossed his bat away, he just looked at me and said, 'End this shit, will you?' "

Larkin had to wait for the chance. Catcher Greg Olson went out to the mound to talk to pitcher Alejandro Peña. Again, Larkin figured a pitching change was coming. "I thought they'd want to make me hit righty," he said. "But they stuck with Peña."

As Olson walked back to the plate, he looked at Larkin. The two men are friends from Olson's days in the Twins organization. In fact, Olson taught Larkin how to hunt. Now, though, when Olson looked at Larkin, all he saw was a blank stare. "It was as if he didn't recognize me," Olson said. "He was in a trance or something."

Trance or no trance, Larkin had to wait still longer while Terry Pendleton raced around, setting the defense in both the infield and outfield. Finally, Peña was ready. "All I did was look fastball," Larkin said. "He'd been throwing it past us all Series."

He didn't get one past Larkin, though. He hit Peña's first fastball deep enough to right center field that none of the Braves even chased it. "Normally a routine fly," he said. "But not this time."

This time it made the Twins world champions, it made Larkin a hero in his adopted home state, and it left the team and the city convinced it could happen again in 1992.

Saturday's game was on CBS, a chance for the network brass to get a second look at its new broadcast team of Sean McDonough and Tim McCarver. McDonough had replaced Jack Buck, the longtime St. Louis Cardinals voice, after Buck, whose style was more suited to radio, had spent two fairly uncomfortable years working with McCarver. At thirty, McDonough was something of a wunderkind, much like Bob Costas with NBC a decade earlier.

There are some baseball people who do not like McCarver. They think he talks too much, analyzes too often, critiques too strongly. The simple fact is that McCarver is the best analyst in the history of the sport. He understands the game as well as anyone and his ability to communicate that understanding is unique.

He is articulate and funny. Yes, he may reach too far for the puns he loves so much. And baseball people grumble that McCarver sometimes states the obvious. But sometimes the obvious needs stating. At least as often, he disturbs those same baseball people with his opinions, which are often pointed and tough.

McCarver is not a second-guesser, he is a *first*-guesser. He will raise questions about strategy before the play unfolds: Why is the outfield so deep? Why is the third baseman guarding the line when a single can hurt as much as a double? Why is the first baseman holding a runner who wouldn't steal second on a bet? He will question trades before they have been proven right or wrong. In baseball, this is breaking the code: Ex-players are supposed to be supportive of both current players and management.

Criticism from the media is different; players don't like it, but they expect it because reporters don't know any better, they aren't part of the club. Ex-players who become announcers are, generally speaking, *not* considered part of the media. The rules that apply to the media in the clubhouse do not apply to them. Routinely, they will walk into the training room or the players' lounge, areas that are strictly off-limits to the regular media.

Most ex-players turned broadcasters don't *want* to be cast with the media; to them, that would be a decided step down. McCarver, who played twenty-one years in the majors, has never shied away from his role as a reporter, not during his ten years doing New York Mets games or his eight years working for the networks, first at ABC, now at CBS.

Not surprisingly, it didn't take him long to upset someone during the Saturday telecast. Just as they'd done on Friday, the A's jumped to a quick lead, scoring six runs in the first three innings to lead 6–0. The Twins came back with two in the fifth and another in the seventh, but the A's held on this time to win 8–3.

In the bottom of the fifth, Twins general manager Andy MacPhail stalked out of his box in search of a cup of coffee. "Jesus, you should hear McCarver," he said angrily, pouring the coffee as if he wished the cup were McCarver's head. "Listening to him is like being in purgatory. He keeps saying, 'I just don't know if the Twins can replace Gladden's fire.' Forget the numbers, right? Forget that he was the least productive leadoff hitter in the league last year. Was he with us in 1990 when we finished last? Where was the fire then?"

If MacPhail could have taken *his* fire onto the field, maybe the Twins wouldn't even have noticed Gladden's absence. The mini-outburst was instructive because MacPhail is not a man given to revealing his emotions. At thirty-eight, he wears the label of boy-genius general manager, having taken over the team in 1987 at age thirty-three.

MacPhail is third-generation baseball royalty. He is the grandson of Larry MacPhail, the man who brought night baseball to the game, and the son of former Baltimore Orioles and New York Yankees general manager Lee MacPhail, who later was also president of the American League. MacPhail has been around baseball and baseball players since he was a toddler. He is rightfully proud of what he and the Twins have accomplished in a relatively small market. But he clearly doesn't appreciate first-guessing very much.

Actually, MacPhail had a right to be a little edgy. He was trying desperately to wind up negotiations that would ensure Kirby Puckett's presence in Minnesota until the end of his career. With the possible exception of Cal Ripken, no player in baseball is more a part of his city's fabric than Kirby Puckett. He is not only the team's best player, he is its most approachable, a roly-poly five-foot-eight-inch, 215-pound kid whose joy at doing what he does is still evident.

On the morning of the finale of the Oakland series, Puckett was the first player in the Minnesota clubhouse. His mission was a tough one—clean out his locker, which overflowed with shoes, shirts, pants, and socks he didn't need. He called over two of the clubhouse kids and began doling out equipment as if he was dealing cards from a deck.

"Got to give myself some breathing space," he said, smiling.

Only rarely does Puckett *not* smile. There is irony in the fact that he and Ripken are so connected in the public's mind because it is unlikely to find two people more different. They do have the same agent, Ron Shapiro. They both have two-year-old daughters whom they hate leaving. They both have many children named after them in the cities where they play. The similarities end there.

Where Ripken is serious and analytical, Puckett is deliriously happy to be who he is and where he is at all times. His attitude about his contract was simple: If the Twins came up with the money, he would be thrilled to sign and spend the rest of his life right where he was. If they didn't come up with the dough, someone else would. It might even be the Cubs or White Sox.

"Remember, I grew up nine blocks from Comiskey Park," he said. "We never walked to the ballpark, we *ran*. Baseball was always my first love. I was never big enough to really play the other sports, so I played baseball all day long. If I hadn't, I'd probably be dead, coming from where I do. It was baseball or a gang; I chose baseball."

Puckett was the ninth of nine children, six years younger than his closest brother. "I was an accident," he says, laughing. He grew up in the Robert Taylor Homes of south Chicago, an area once described by a policeman who worked the neighborhood as "the place where hope comes to die." Puckett never felt that, though. He remembers playing baseball until dark every night. "When my mother wanted me to come home she would walk outside the house and yell, *'Kirby!'* Wherever I was, someone would tell me she was calling for me and I would run home."

His father, William Jack Puckett, had been a left-handed pitcher before becoming a postman. He made sure his youngest always got the glove he needed or the bicycle he wanted. The pro scouts and the college recruiters never came to Calumet High School looking for baseball players—"they would risk coming into the neighborhood for basketball, but not for baseball," Puckett says—so Kirby went to work at a Ford plant when he graduated from high school. He made $540 a week until he was laid off—the day before he would have been eligible to join the union.

Just for fun, he went to a tryout camp in Kansas City that summer. There, Dewey Kalmer, the baseball coach at Bradley University, liked the quick bat he saw and offered Puckett a scholarship. Peoria was close enough to Chicago to suit his parents, so off he went to college. Three weeks later his mother called: One year after retiring, his father had died of a heart attack. Kirby dropped out of school to go home and take care of his mother. He wanted to go back to work but his mother said no. "You have a chance to play baseball," she said. "We spent too much money on bats, gloves, and balls for you to stop now."

He enrolled for the spring semester at nearby Triton Junior College, a baseball hotbed. In the meantime, the Twins, having seen him play summer league ball, drafted him number one in January 1982.

"They offered me four thousand dollars to sign," Puckett said. "I told them I made more than that working at Ford. They came back with six thousand dollars. I told them I could make more on the street."

Instead of signing, he went to Triton for the spring semester and hit .472. This time the Twins' offer was $20,000. "Now we were talking real money," he said. "I knew Calvin Griffith liked to move players through the minors quickly, so I figured I'd have a chance."

Puckett arrived in Minneapolis in 1984, six weeks before Griffith sold the team to Carl Pohlad, and in what seemed like a matter of hours became the team's mainstay in center field. He hit .296 that first year but didn't hit a single home run in 557 at-bats. Two years later, he hit thirty-one home runs, and has averaged ninety-five RBIs per season dating back to '86.

If there was any doubt about Puckett being an official state treasure, it ended on the night of October 26, 1991, when his eleventh-inning home run off Charlie Leibrandt won the sixth game of the World Series. Now, everyone wanted to get Puckett signed, including Puckett and Shapiro.

"In some ways, this would be easier if Kirby wasn't the person he is and if his agent wasn't as reasonable as he is," MacPhail said. "If they were in here asking for ludicrous money, we could just say, 'No, we can't afford that.' But they aren't likely to do that. They're going to want a lot because Kirby deserves a lot. The question is, can we pay it? I hope so."

Kirby fever would grow in the Twin Cities as the negotiations dragged on. They nearly ended in May when Puckett accepted $27.5 million for five years—but then continued when Pohlad withdrew the offer. That decision infuriated the fans and frustrated almost everyone connected with the team. "When I think that he may not be back," MacPhail said, "I feel very sad."

The only one who seemed unbothered was Puckett. He continued to put up hitting numbers that made the dollar numbers climb higher. "If I test the waters, I test the waters," he said. "Either way, I'm going to have fun."

In that sense, Kirby Puckett is the rarest of the rare: Somehow, in going from projects kid to millionaire ballplayer, he has never quite forgotten how to have fun.

•

The Twins came from behind again in the final game of the series with the A's, winning 8–4 on Sunday afternoon. Most disturbing for LaRussa and the A's was the fact that it was Dave Stewart who could not hold the early 2–0 lead. LaRussa was convinced that his team could not win without an effective Stewart.

That had certainly been the case a year earlier when Stewart's string of four straight twenty-victory seasons had come to a crashing halt. He had gone 11-11 with a 5.18 ERA. Now, at thirty-five, on the last year of his contract, he was off to a 1-2 start and his ERA was hovering around 4.00.

"Stew needs to smell twenty in August to be at his best in September," LaRussa said. "He wasn't that bad today [four of the runs had been unearned], but he knows and I know he can be a lot better. Still, it's early."

The last three words—"Still, it's early"—are as much a part of baseball's vocabulary as runs, hits, and errors. In *August* you'll hear players and managers say, "Still, it's early." Almost everyone in baseball swears that they pay no attention to the scoreboard until September. Almost everyone in baseball lies.

Everyone knows where everyone else is from Opening Day on. When the Toronto Blue Jays open the season 9-1, the rest of the American League East notices. When the Kansas City Royals start 1-16, they are crossed off everyone's mental checklist of contenders. When the Atlanta Braves are 6-10, or a few weeks later, 20-27, people wonder what the hell is going on.

Of course, it *is* still early. A quick start ensures nothing. The New York Yankees were 5-0 after one week but no one was making plans to be at Yankee Stadium in October. The Houston Astros played their first fifteen games at home because of the August odyssey that had been created for them by the Republican National Convention, and were 9-6. That put them in first place. Anyone betting on the Astros to win the National League West?

April and May are the table-setters for the season. They're important because starts like Kansas City's can put a team in a hole so deep that the rest of the season becomes nothing more than a drive to pad statistics. They can also mean a lot to a team like the A's who are unsure of what to expect in a season. A fast start by the Orioles—especially with good pitching—can send a signal to the team that it is good enough to compete. The same is true of the Pirates, where a 12-3 record can remind the players that when Jim Leyland told them in March that they were good enough to win without Bobby Bonilla and John Smiley, he wasn't kidding.

Poor starts can also get managers fired. In 1991, six managers had been fired before the All-Star break, three during one seventy-two-hour period in May. In all, thirteen of the twenty-six teams started 1992 with different managers from '91.

The first manager to go in '92 was Tom Runnells, who had replaced Buck Rodgers as the manager in Montreal on June 3, 1991. Twelve days short of a year later, Runnells was gone. The Expos weren't playing horribly—they were 17-20—but Dan Duquette, the Expos boy–general manager (he turned thirty-four four days after firing Runnells), felt that the team wasn't playing to its potential. A move had to be made quickly before the season slipped away.

More often than not, managerial changes in midseason are meaningless. If the players aren't good enough, no one, not LaRussa, not Kelly, not Leyland, not Casey Stengel, can make them win. But the Expos' situation was a rare case; a change could make a difference because the change was so radical.

Runnells was a great believer in discipline. He thought a young team needed rules to follow, so he had dozens of them. He even had curfews on the road, curfews that were often enforced by bed checks. Runnells had tried to dispel the notion that he was an all-work-and-no-play guy on the first day of formal workouts in the spring when he had arrived in a military jeep wearing army fatigues. Everyone got a good laugh out of the joke—but once the season began, the Expos were an awfully tense group.

In baseball, tension rarely makes anyone play better. Mike Flanagan, the longtime sage of the Baltimore Orioles, points out that the hardest thing to do in baseball is to deal with a slump by *not* trying harder. "You have to try *easier*," he says. "Loosen your grip on the bat or the ball and relax. The other way never works."

Enter Felipe Alou. At fifty-seven, Alou had long ago given up hope of ever managing in the big leagues. The oldest of three brothers who had played in the majors, Alou had hit .286 during a lengthy, distinguished career and had retired with 2,101 hits. He had coached and managed in the Montreal organization for years and had been brought back to the majors by Runnells as his bench coach.

Duquette decided to give Alou a shot. On May 22 he made him the first Dominican manager in major league history. Alou promptly renounced all of Runnells's rules except one: players had to be on time. Even that rule was flexible—as long as the player in question proved himself ready to play once the game started.

The Expos didn't exactly turn into a juggernaut as soon as Alou took over; they lost five of their first eight games under him. Privately, he wondered if Duquette might make another switch at the All-Star break. But, slowly, things began to turn around. The tension in the clubhouse lightened. A fourth outfielder named Moises Alou was given a chance because of an injury to Ivan Calderon and he began to hit a little bit like his father—the manager—once had. The Expos began creeping up on the Pirates, the Mets, and the Cardinals.

At the same time, the Reds and the Padres began moving on the quick-starting-but-beginning-to-fade San Francisco Giants in the NL West and the Twins began to assert themselves in the AL West. The Blue Jays continued to lead in the AL East but the Orioles stayed right with them. The O's even slipped briefly into first place a couple of times before the Jays, like an annoyed older brother, shouldered past them.

On June 1, the standings were beginning to take shape: The Blue Jays led the Orioles by one in the East with the Yankees and Red Sox not far back and the Milwaukee Brewers hanging in at .500. In the West, the Twins were in a virtual tie with the A's and the Texas Rangers. The White Sox were two-and-a-half back.

In the National League, the surprise team was the St. Louis Cardinals, who had come back from a rash of early injuries to take a one-game lead over the Pirates. The Mets, seemingly recovered from their spring miseries, were only a half-game behind the Pirates. The Reds, Giants, and Padres were in a virtual tie for first in the West. The Braves continued to struggle at 24-27. Even so, they were only four games from first place.

Late in his team's disastrous 1-8 West Coast trip, Pittsburgh manager Jim Leyland called a rare team meeting. "I prefer to talk to guys one-on-one," he said. "That way, you know you've got the attention of the guy you're trying to get a message to. When you talk to all twenty-five of them, you don't know who's listening and who isn't."

Leyland *will* call his team together when he feels he has something he has to say to all of them. This time his message was clear and simple: "I'm not panicking and I don't expect any of you to, either," he said. "We were a good ball club the first few weeks of the season and we're still a good ball club. Just keep working and we'll be fine. There's a long way to go before anything is decided for us this season."

No doubt. It was, after all, still early.

13

THE CRASH
OF '92

O n the night of May 20, the California Angels suffered what
cliché-mongers call a "heartbreaking loss." They blew a late
3–2 lead to the New York Yankees, eventually losing the game 4–3 in
thirteen innings.

It was a bitter defeat for a struggling team. Six games into a
nine-game East Coast swing, the Angels dropped to 1-5 on the trip,
including three straight losses to the Yankees. Their record for the
season was now 19-20.

"We were a pretty discouraged group coming out of there," relief
pitcher Bryan Harvey said. "I think we were all kind of thinking, 'When
are we going to catch a break?' "

Not soon. Shortly after midnight, the Angels boarded two char-
tered buses that would take them to Baltimore. Bus trips between
cities are rare in baseball these days; most teams fly by charter, meaning they can come and go as they please and not have to worry about
airline schedules. But there are some trips that are too short to bother
to bus to the airport, unload, reload onto the plane, unload again, then
get on another bus to the hotel or ballpark. In the National League,

teams usually bus between Los Angeles and San Diego and between New York and Philadelphia. In the American League there are three bus routes: Milwaukee–Chicago, Cleveland–Detroit, and New York–Baltimore.

Late at night, the trip from Yankee Stadium to the Angels' hotel across from Camden Yards shouldn't take much more than three hours. There were thirty-seven members in the two-bus traveling party; they divided themselves up more on choice of movie than anything else. The first bus would show a tape of *Delta Force II,* a Chuck Norris kick-'em-up flick; the second would show *Dances with Wolves.* Some in the group didn't care which movie was on. All they wanted to do was sleep.

Eighteen men got on the first bus, the rest onto the second. Two players, Hubie Brooks and Luis Polonia, had been given permission to stay behind and spend the team's off day in New York. Manager Buck Rodgers and his coaches rode bus number one. The manager always rides in the first seat on the first bus. Tradition.

They were rumbling down the New Jersey Turnpike at 1:50 A.M. when a number of players on the first bus felt what they thought was a skid. The skid became a long slide. Suddenly there were crashing sounds as the bus slammed through a guardrail and then, frighteningly, flipped over on its side.

"It felt like we were in a washing machine," shortstop Gary Disarcina said the next day. "We were all being tossed around like a bunch of dolls. It was terrifying."

The bus driver, Carl Venetz, would tell police that he had swerved to avoid something in the road. The way the accident occurred, it was also possible that he had fallen asleep at the wheel. For obvious reasons, both Venetz and the bus company vehemently denied that suggestion.

It was after crashing through the guardrail that the Angels, a team beset by horrible luck and tragedy throughout their thirty-two-year existence, finally got lucky. When the bus flipped, it came to rest in a small grove of trees. If the trees hadn't been there, the bus would have dropped all the way down to a creek a hundred feet below.

The driver of the second bus immediately pulled over to the shoulder of the highway. Players who were awake roused those who were sleeping; everyone raced in the direction of the first bus. All the team's pitchers—they do stick together—were on the second bus. Chuck Finley, Jim Abbott, Mark Langston, Bert Blyleven, and Harvey led the way.

What they saw stunned them. The door of the bus had collapsed completely. Windows were broken. "I thought for sure we were going to have some dead boys in there," Harvey said. "If we had stood there and thought about what was going on, we probably would have just started to cry. But there was no time for that.''

The baseball-team-turned-rescue-squad worked quickly. Some teammates were pulled from the bus uninjured. Others were clearly hurt. Trainer Ned Bergert, cut and bleeding himself, began working on those who were most seriously injured. Within a few minutes, almost everyone had been pulled free.

Except the manager. Sitting in that front-row seat, Rodgers had been pinned against the windshield. It took several players to pull him out. ''He looked awful,'' catcher Ron Tingley said later. ''He had blood all over his face and his leg and arm looked like they had been crushed. Seeing him like that shook us all up.''

Tim Mead, the team's vice-president of public relations, rode in the ambulance with Rodgers to the hospital. Rodgers, although clearly in a tremendous amount of pain, was able to speak lucidly about what had happened. By the time the team reassembled at the hospital, it was apparent how lucky they had been. Rodgers would need surgery on his leg and his elbow; infielder Bobby Rose had suffered a serious ankle sprain. First baseman Alvin Davis bruised a kidney, as did Bergert. A number of other players needed stitches. Everyone was shaken. But it could have been much worse.

''We went back to the site to get our luggage,'' coach John Wathan said later. ''And when you looked at the way the bus was resting on those trees, it gave you the shudders. It was amazing that we didn't crash all the way through.''

It is more amazing, perhaps, that with all the travel that goes on in professional sports, accidents like this—and worse—do not happen more often. In a strange twist of irony, the subject of travel and accidents had come up on the NBC comedy series *Seinfeld*—on the night of the Angels' trip. Keith Hernandez, the ex–New York Met, had made a cameo appearance. Seinfeld's sidekick, George, muttered to Hernandez that he often wondered how it was that with twenty-six teams playing 162 games a year in baseball, no one ever got into an accident.

Tim Mead's wife told him about that line when he called home early Thursday morning. ''It made me cringe,'' Mead said.

The overall feeling of the Angels when they finally reached Baltimore on Thursday morning was relief. Given the team's history, they were entitled. Four times in the past, active players had been killed in automobile wrecks. Another, star outfielder Lyman Bostock, had been shot to death in Gary, Indiana, in 1978. And, in 1989, Donnie Moore, their onetime relief ace, committed suicide. Moore had given up the 1986 play-off home run to Dave Henderson that denied the Angels their first American League pennant. Many people believed that his suicide was due, at least in part, to his being unable to deal with that failure. The last trauma had occurred during spring training: hitting coach Deron Johnson, after a long bout with cancer, had died at the age of fifty-three.

This time, at least, no one died.

•

Hubie Brooks was asleep at his mother-in-law's house the next morning when a friend called, wanting to know what he had heard about the bus crash. Brooks had heard nothing. He called the hotel in Baltimore but couldn't reach anyone. Finally, he turned on CNN. After waiting a few anxious moments, he heard that all of his teammates were alive. A shot of the bus lying in the woods flashed on the screen. Brooks felt sick to his stomach. Everyone in baseball woke up that morning to the news, the shots of the bus, and the same sick feeling that Brooks had. Baseball players travel in the lap of luxury everywhere they go, and even though baseball, like all professional sports leagues, has an emergency plan to deal with a disaster, no one ever gives much thought to it.

"You do start to think you're invulnerable to it all," said Ron Tingley, the backup catcher. "There's a sense, because you're on charter airplanes and in first class and traveling in luxury, that nothing can happen. Then, in a matter of seconds, you find out just how vulnerable we all are."

The crash was not Tingley's first. Twelve years earlier, when he had been playing in Reno, a car had crashed into the team bus, sending it spinning off the road. That had not been as serious, but the bus crash brought back memories for Tingley, who had probably spent more time riding buses in his career than anyone on the team.

Tingley, who turned thirty-three a week after the crash, was in his sixteenth season in professional baseball. He is, in some ways, a real-life Crash Davis, except that, unlike the character in *Bull Durham*, Tingley did indeed make it to the Show. But it wasn't easy.

On more than one occasion, he thought he was finished. In 1984, two days after his wedding, he slid into second base in Salt Lake City, felt his leg get stuck under the bag, and emerged with torn knee ligaments. He missed almost the entire season. In 1986, the Atlanta Braves released him. He was twenty-seven and had been in the major leagues for eight games, going 2-for-20 during a brief stint in San Diego in 1982.

But Tingley still believed he was good enough to play in the big leagues. He signed a minor-league contract with the Indians and in 1988 thought he had the team made out of spring training. Then, a week before the season started, the team traded Mel Hall to the Yankees for Joel Skinner, a backup catcher. As soon as Tingley heard about the trade, he knew he was in trouble.

"I went in to [manager] Doc Edwards and I said, 'What gives?' "
Tingley said with a wry smile. "He told me that they really thought
that Skinner was good enough to push Andy Allanson into being a
great catcher. I just laughed at him and walked out thinking, 'If you're
going to lie to me, at least come up with a better lie than *that.*' Andy
Allanson was never going to be a great catcher and Joel Skinner
wasn't going to push him into anything. They just didn't have faith in
me. It was that simple."

Tingley thought about quitting then, but decided to hang on a
little bit longer. The Indians recalled him on July 30; four days later
they gave him a start. In his first at-bat, Tingley hit a two-run homer—
just like in the movies. But—back in real life—a month later he was
traded to the Angels. He began both 1990 and 1991 in the minors but
was called up both years. Finally, in 1992, after sixteen tries, he made
a team out of spring training. Seven weeks later came the crash.

The Angels' clubhouse in Baltimore was a quiet place on Friday.
Players talked among themselves, subdued, or to reporters. Strangely,
this was one of the rare situations in which the media were not viewed
as vultures. The Angels *wanted* to talk about what had happened. It
seemed to be cathartic.

When Hubie Brooks walked into the clubhouse and saw his teammates, many of them with cut-marks on their faces, he started to cry.
"It just hit me," he said. "We all talk about keeping baseball in perspective. Most of us don't. This was like a slap in the face. It made you
realize that any game could be your last one. When I walked in, I just
wanted to hug every guy and say, 'Thank God you're all here.' "

John Wathan, who had been named acting manager in Rodgers's
absence, refused to use the manager's office. Shortly after the team
bus arrived from the hotel, someone flipped on the television set. A
M*A*S*H rerun flickered onto the screen. No one even cracked a
smile.

"The tough thing is we can't sit around and feel sorry for ourselves," Wathan said. "We have to try and go out and play tonight as
if nothing happened. Of course, that's impossible. But I would think,
in a way, playing would be therapeutic for us right now. One thing we
can't expect and don't want is sympathy. The Orioles would be crazy
not to come out here and try to kick our butts."

The Orioles did just that, winning 5–1. The Angels did manage to
bounce back and win the following evening but they lost the finale
before flying home, hoping to put the horror of the crash behind them.
It wasn't to be. They dropped seven of nine on the homestand and
never really recovered.

Though the Angels stopped winning, to label them losers would
be unfair. Aside from the crash, this was a team full of men who had
dealt with adversity and refused to be set back by it.

Tingley was but one example. Bert Blyleven, who had come back from rotator-cuff surgery at the age of forty-one, was another. Rene Gonzales, released by Toronto and thought finished at the age of thirty, had signed a minor-league contract with the team and had become the starting second baseman.

On most teams, Bryan Harvey's story would have been the most remarkable of all. Harvey had grown up in North Carolina and, after graduating from high school, had gone to the University of North Carolina–Charlotte on a baseball scholarship. After one year, he dropped out. His record as a freshman was 3-11 and he was convinced he was going nowhere. He went to work in a tire-retreading factory, got married, and moved into a trailer park.

Almost two years went by and Harvey's only connection to baseball was playing slow-pitch softball for the same team his father had played on for many years. Then a friend came by one day and asked him if he would be interested in pitching in a semipro game that Sunday. His team had lost a pitcher and his friend remembered that Brian had once thrown a baseball pretty hard. "I just figured, 'Why not?' " Harvey said with a shrug.

A bird-dog scout for the Angels happened to be at the game that Sunday and when he saw how hard Harvey threw he asked him if he would be interested in attending a tryout camp. Harvey's reaction was the same: Why not? He was impressive enough at the camp that the Angels offered him a contract—for $2,500.

"I figured it was worth it for the trip to spring training," he said. "I didn't figure on making the team, but I thought it might be a nice way to get away in the winter."

It almost turned out exactly that way. Harvey hurt his arm early in spring training and the Angels were about to release him. But Joe Coleman, who was then the minor-league pitching coach for the Angels, saw something in Harvey and convinced the team to hold on to him.

"I thought if I could teach him to throw a forkball we might have something," Coleman said. "As it turned out, he was a great learner."

Harvey went to Quad City once he was healthy and began working on the new pitch. Three years later he was in California, and three years after that, in 1991, he saved forty-six games and was the top closer in the American League.

Of course life is never that simple or perfect, especially for a California Angel. Harvey and his wife, Lisa, have two children. Their son, Christopher, is eight. Their five-year-old daughter, Whitney, is the victim of an extremely rare disease, known in a strange twist as "Angel's syndrome." Very little is known about the disease, which is caused by a deletion of chromosome number fifteen. "It's so small you can barely see it with the human eye under a microscope," Harvey said.

There are less than five hundred known cases of the disease in the United States, although researchers now think there may be quite a few undiagnosed cases (the disease has symptoms similar to those of cerebral palsy). Children with Angel's syndrome are unable to speak; they also have serious learning disabilities. "At least we know what we're dealing with," Harvey said. "It's slow and tough, but she's making progress."

Since Whitney was diagnosed at age three, Harvey not only has worked to try to help her, he has become a national spokesman for the disease. He works tirelessly to raise money to find a cure as well as to make more people aware of Angel's syndrome. Shortly after a story on Whitney appeared in the *Los Angeles Times,* and solely because the story ran, an eleven-year-old was properly diagnosed. Her parents and doctors had wondered for *years* why she couldn't talk.

Harvey's soft drawl becomes almost a whisper when he talks about his daughter. "She's really something," he said. "I can come home after I lose a game or pitch poorly, so angry I can't even see. She'll come running into my arms and that's it, nothing else in the world matters. How can it? She's helped me grow up a lot, shown me how good I have it. A lot of guys in this game spend a lot of time feeling sorry for themselves, thinking that getting beat or striking out or giving up a home run is tough. They don't have any idea what tough is. I know I didn't."

•

The reason Harvey's story is only the *second* most remarkable on the Angels is Jim Abbott. But Jim Abbott doesn't see it quite that way.

When he was twenty-one, they wanted to make Abbott's life story into a movie. His response? "That's ridiculous." Every year since then, someone has approached him about doing a book. "I would like to think that twenty-four is a little bit young to write my life story." He smiles. "It's especially silly since the odds are that I'll feel differently today about something than I felt about it last Saturday. How in the world can I be qualified to write a book?"

With that attitude, Abbott is probably far more qualified to write a book than most people—especially athletes, who crank out autobiographies the way General Motors used to crank out cars. At least GM tests their cars. Most athletes don't even read their own autobiographies.

Abbott *is* special. A young pitcher with outstanding talent and extraordinary maturity, he has an almost limitless future. He was also born without a right hand. That's why all the movie and book people keep bugging him.

"The way they all want to tell the story is that I overcame all these obstacles and people telling me that I couldn't reach my goals or do the things I wanted to do," he said. "But that isn't the way it was. The fact is I was surrounded by people—my family, my friends, my coaches—who always encouraged me. I had some ability and I had a lot of help. That's all there is to it."

Perhaps not quite all. It is encouraging, as Abbott points out, that the time has come when a physical handicap is not automatically thought debilitating. But watching Abbott pitch, holding his glove at the end of his right arm, throwing the ball home, switching the glove onto his left hand—so he can field—so quickly that it's impossible to see if you aren't looking right at him, it is very apparent that he is someone who has worked very long and very hard to get where he is.

Abbott doesn't like to promote himself but he does try to respond to the mail he gets from handicapped children and their families. "If my story helps kids understand that they can do anything they want to, then that's great, I *love* that part of it," he said. "But the hero stuff I can live without. I've never thought of myself that way and I've never wanted to be treated that way."

What Abbott is treated like now is one of the best young pitchers in baseball. When he graduated from high school, he was drafted on the thirty-sixth round by the Blue Jays. The only reason he was taken so late was because he had made it very clear that he planned to go to college. Even so, Jays general manager Pat Gillick coaxed him up to Toronto to try to convince him to sign. And Gillick almost pulled it off.

"The Jays really were great," Abbott said. "But, growing up in Flint, I had two dreams. One was to go to Michigan, the other was to pitch in Tiger Stadium. I wasn't ready to give up on Michigan at that stage."

He spent three years at Michigan. Pitching for the school team, he was 48-19 by the end of his junior year, when the Angels drafted him on the first round. He spent that summer with the U.S. Olympic team, winning the gold medal game in Seoul. "The feeling after the last pitch, everyone piling on top of me, is like nothing else I can remember in my life," he said. "I'd like to have that feeling again on this level."

Abbott got to this level—the majors—without even stopping for a cup of coffee in the minors. He made the Angels out of spring training in 1989 and each year he has steadily improved. In 1991, he was 18-11 with a 2.89 ERA. He was even better in 1992, but that wasn't reflected in his record—7-15—because the Angels didn't score any runs for him.

"If you're going to be a top pitcher, you have to go to the next level," he said quietly. "That means winning games one–nothing if you have to. Pitchers who complain about lack of run support usually aren't very good pitchers."

Abbott is a very good pitcher. During the summer, even when he spent time on the disabled list, several teams called about acquiring him. He was easily the most marketable member of the team. The Blue Jays wanted him—again. So did the Yankees. The Angels held out, hoping to sign him to a long-term contract or get a package of players they could build around in return for giving up their star pitcher. Finally, in December, they got their package: three top Yankee prospects for Abbott.

Like everyone else on the Angels, Abbott was shaken by the crash. Not surprisingly, when he, Finley, and Lee Stevens were mentioned as the most heroic members of the rescue squad, he laughed. "None of us even thought about what was going on," he said. "There were guys who needed help. Our teammates. We didn't do anything different than anyone else would have done."

Perhaps. But athletes face situations every day in which they must react without stopping to think of the consequences. They have little understanding of physical fear. Many people, faced with what those on the second bus saw, would have frozen or run to get help. The Angels did neither. They just did what they had to in order to get their teammates free.

The morning after the crash, Tim Mead called Gene and Jackie Autry, the team's owners, to fill them in on what had happened and how everyone was doing. At the end of the conversation, Mead added an editorial comment to his news report. "I just want you to know something about your team," he told the Autrys. "I don't know what place we'll end up in this year, but this is one group you should be very proud of."

When Mead hung up, he wondered for an instant if he had sounded corny. "Then I thought back to what I had seen at the crash site," he said. "I remembered my very first thought: that I was going to have to announce the names of the dead players to the press. And then I knew I hadn't been too corny."

A bunch of millionaire ballplayers went crashing through windows to rescue their friends, not knowing whether or not the bus was going to topple through the trees. Certainly the response of the Angels doesn't quite fit the image of the modern ballplayer. Were the Angels heroes?

"No," said Jim Abbott.

"Absolutely not," said Chuck Finley.

"Of course not," said Bryan Harvey.

Without question, say the facts. If that's corny, so be it.

14

HAVING THE
NECESSITIES

It is known now simply as "Campanis": a historical reference not much different—at least in the world of baseball—from Vietnam or Watergate. When the topic of minority hiring in the game comes up, someone inevitably begins a sentence by saying, "Since Campanis . . ."

The man for whom this watershed moment is named is seventy-two now, a frail figure who still shows up at almost every Los Angeles Dodgers or California Angels home game. He still calls the Dodgers "we" in conversation and will occasionally mention that a couple of clubs have talked to him about coming back. Half Italian, half Greek, he still answers to "Chief," the nickname players hung on him because he had the complexion of an Indian.

"If they're looking for someone who can teach the game and will work hard, I'm the right guy," Al Campanis says, his eyes bright with hope. "You know, I've always thought that time is a great healer."

In all likelihood, there won't be enough time for Campanis to heal the wounds he opened up. On the night of April 12, 1987, he was the Dodgers' general manager. He had been with the team for more than forty years, and was one of Jackie Robinson's first friends when Branch Rickey decided it was time to bring a man of color to the major leagues.

"Spring of 1946, Branch Rickey called and asked why I wasn't in camp," Campanis says, sipping a cup of decaf. "I told him there was no point, I couldn't beat out Pee Wee Reese, that I was going to stay home in New York and teach. I had taught at City College before going into the service and enjoyed it. Mr. Rickey said to me, 'Al, I want you down here. Baseball is your destiny. I have plans for you.' "

Those plans included Robinson, whom Campanis worked with, first at Montreal in 1946, then the next year when he was brought up to Brooklyn. Campanis speaks proudly of his friendship with Robinson, reminding people often that when his son graduated from elementary school, Jackie Robinson was the speaker.

April of 1987 marked the fortieth anniversary of Robinson's arrival in the major leagues, and ABC's *Nightline* decided that was a good reason to put together a show examining where blacks were in baseball. At the time, there had been three black managers in the game's history. None of them—Frank Robinson, Maury Wills, and Larry Doby—was then still managing. There were no black general managers, either.

Al Campanis was asked to appear on the program. When the question arose about the lack of black managers, Al Campanis uttered the four words that made him into a historical benchmark: "They lack the necessities."

He says now and has said often that he meant to say, "They lack the necessary experience," but being nervous on live national television, it came out wrong. That may be true. But when he went on to talk about blacks being poor swimmers because they lack the necessary buoyancy as another example of what he was talking about, his career in baseball was over.

The Dodgers fired him in the midst of a storm of controversy set off by his comments. Suddenly, America woke up one morning and wondered, perhaps for the first time, Why in the world *aren't* there any black managers? In the blink of an eye, minority hiring became an issue in the commissioner's office. Newspapers and magazines assigned major stories on how all of this could have—or couldn't have—happened.

Whether he misspoke because of nerves or made a foolish, thoughtless comment, Campanis will never escape "Campanis." He insists that he doesn't want to. "If what happened made people more aware of minority hiring, I'm glad it happened," he says, trying to sound convincing. "Things *have* gotten better in baseball since then."

He pauses and looks around the room. "If Jackie had been alive when it happened, he would have set people straight," he says. "I don't think he would have been very happy with what happened to me."

•

There is a lot in baseball that Jackie Robinson would be unhappy with today. As the 1992 season began, five years after "Campanis," there were two minority managers in the major leagues—Hal McRae in Kansas City and Cito Gaston in Toronto.

Both had grown up in the South—Gaston in Texas, McRae in Florida—and both had seen more than their share of racism. Neither complained much about it, though. "You never thought about segregation as a problem," McRae said. "That's just the way things were. You didn't really give it much thought. You just dealt with it."

Gaston is forty-eight, a year older than McRae, a shy, softspoken man who rarely betrays much emotion. There is little doubt, though, that he is sensitive to criticism, stung when he reads or hears that he is not a good manager.

"I stopped reading the papers in Toronto," he said one June morning. "I realized after a while that if I read something that pissed me off and then the guy who wrote it came into my office that night, I was probably going to get into it with him. I would rather not know and just deal with everyone the same. I didn't get into baseball to sit around all day and argue with people."

Like most people, he got into baseball simply because he liked to play and was good at it. He was the third of six children (the only boy) and first remembers thinking he wanted to be a big leaguer when he was nine years old. As early as eighth grade, it occurred to him he might really have a chance.

"I was always a real big kid and I pitched," he said. "In seventh grade, I pitched two or three no-hitters. The next year the parents in the league got up a petition to keep me from pitching. So, that year I was a catcher."

He graduated from high school in 1962, three years before there was a major-league draft, and signed with the Milwaukee Braves, who weren't quite sure whether he was a pitcher or an outfielder. They bounced him back and forth for a couple of years before sending him to Batavia in the New York–Penn League in 1966 as a full-time outfielder.

There, Gaston blossomed. He hit .330 with 28 home runs and 104 RBIs. Even so, his memories of that summer are darkened by what happened on the last day of the season.

"I had a chance to win the Triple Crown for the league," he said. "The last couple of weeks I began to notice guys I was fighting for the

RBI lead getting some questionable ones. You know: A ground ball that should be fielded goes through someone's legs and they call it a hit and a guy on second scores. That sort of thing.

"I didn't worry about it much but then the last weekend of the season, the batting title came down to me and a kid from the Dodger organization. I can't remember his name now. We went into the second-to-last game tied. I got four hits. He got three and reached on an error on a ground ball our third baseman just kicked. They gave him a hit. So, we were still tied. The next day I was one-for-four. He came up for his last at-bat needing a hit to beat me. He popped up. Somehow, our guy dropped the ball. A clear error. They gave him a hit and I lost by a couple hundredths of a point. That was the first time I saw blatant racism in baseball."

Eleven years later, on the major-league level, Hal McRae would have a similar experience when a Twins outfielder named Steve Braun allowed a ball to drop in front of him on the final day of the season, giving McRae's teammate George Brett the batting title by one point. Like Gaston, McRae shrugs now when the subject comes up.

"For two days, I was upset, disappointed," he said. "But I got over it. It never caused any trouble between George and me because George had nothing to do with it. The guy just let the ball drop. Some people said that was a bad reflection on baseball. I don't think so. I think it was just a reflection of the fact that baseball is part of society and society is like that sometimes."

Gaston was able to use his season at Batavia as a springboard to the big leagues—at least briefly. He made it to Atlanta in 1967 before being sent back to the minors the following year. Then, during the winter of 1969, he was selected by the San Diego Padres in the expansion draft—their final pick—and finally made it to the majors to stay. He spent six years with the Padres before being traded back to the Braves. He played there for a little more than three years before finishing his career in the Mexican League in 1980.

When he returned to the Braves, his roommate was Hank Aaron. The two men became friends. "He had always been my hero," Gaston said. "To be his roommate, to this day that awes me. He was a huge influence on me in more ways than I can count."

He was also the reason Gaston stayed in baseball. Even though he had played in the majors for more than nine years, Gaston left the game with a bad taste in his mouth. He had been strictly a pinch-hitter in his final years in Atlanta and had felt capable of more. Many players feel this way to some extent when they retire: "If I'd just been given more of a chance . . ." But Gaston felt it more than most.

He planned to leave baseball behind, but prior to the 1981 season he got a call from Aaron, who had become the Braves' farm director.

"He wanted me to come to work for him as a hitting instructor," Gaston said. "I told him no thanks." Aaron persisted. He called again; Gaston refused again. Finally, on the third try, Gaston decided to give it a shot. He was a roving instructor for the Braves in 1981 and found he enjoyed the work. When Bobby Cox was fired by the Braves at the end of the season and hired to manage the Blue Jays, he asked Gaston to go along with him as the team's major league instructor.

Gaston held that job until May of 1989, staying on under Jimy Williams after Cox left Toronto in 1985 to return to Atlanta as general manager. Then, on May 15 of the 1989 season, his life changed dramatically.

The Blue Jays were struggling. They had just returned home after losing a three-game series in Minnesota. That dropped their record to 12-24. Rumors about Williams's status had been flying, but Gaston hadn't paid very much attention; rumors about Williams had been popping up periodically ever since the Blue Jays had dropped their last seven games of 1987 to lose the division title to Detroit.

Gaston was up making coffee at nine o'clock that morning when Jays assistant general manager Gord Ash called to say that GM Pat Gillick was on his way over. Gaston didn't think much of it; Gillick lived right down the street from him and could be coming by for any number of reasons.

When Gillick got out of the car, however, Gaston knew this was not a social call. Ash had neglected to mention that Gillick was bringing team president Paul Beeston with him.

"When I saw Paul get out of the car, I knew something was up," Gaston said. "Of course, for a split second I thought maybe I was going to be blamed for what was going on and they were going to fire me as hitting instructor. But then I thought, no, not likely. I just waited to see what would happen next."

He didn't have to wait long. Beeston is a direct man. He and Gillick sat down across from Gaston, and Beeston began the conversation by saying, "Cito, we just fired Jimy."

More coffee, Paul?

"Even with our record, I was surprised," Gaston said. "I don't think I said anything because the next thing Paul said was 'We want you to be interim manager.'

"I told them thanks, but no thanks. We had several coaches with plenty of experience and there was no reason one of them couldn't do it. But as I was going down names, Paul kept shaking his head."

Beeston finally looked at Gaston and said, "Cito, you're it."

"For how long?" Gaston asked.

"No more than two weeks. Maybe less."

"The sooner the better."

Sooner still hasn't arrived. The Blue Jays quickly turned around under Gaston and sixteen days after he took over, the "interim" was removed from his title. The team went 77-49 the rest of the way and won the division. Even after losing to the Oakland Athletics in the play-offs, Gaston was hailed for his calm handling of a tough situation. His laid-back, hands-off style was just what the Blue Jays needed, said the experts.

A year later, the team was 86-76 and lost the division title to the Boston Red Sox. Now, the same experts said that Gaston wasn't aggressive enough, didn't use enough players. When the team won the division again in 1991 only to lose the play-offs to the Minnesota Twins, it was because Gaston didn't get his players emotionally up for big games. They needed someone more intense to get them through postseason.

For a long time, Gaston laughed at the second-guessers, accepted them as part of the job. But by '91, the tension was beginning to show. He had serious lower back problems that were so painful he had to miss thirty-three games. After the season, surgery relieved a lot of the pain. Sparky Anderson, for one, told Gaston his back pains were more emotional than physical.

"You can see it in his face," Anderson said. "The guy keeps it all bottled up. He can't win no matter what he does. He goes one-sixty-one-and-one they'll want to know how the hell he lost the one game. I told him to relax. But I don't think he can do it."

Managing a team that will be judged a failure unless it wins the World Series—especially when you're in the last year of your contract—is not likely to relax anyone. And yet, when Joe Carter and Pat Tabler came to Gaston in spring training and said they wanted to have T-shirts made up that said "Three for Three," Gaston told them to go ahead.

"Three for Three" was symbolic of the three steps the Blue Jays wanted to take—division title, American League pennant, World Series. A lot of managers would have shied away from making public that kind of goal. Gaston thought it was a good idea.

"As long as they don't start thinking that the first step is a lock," he said. "I think you should set high goals and walk away at the end of the season knowing you did everything possible to reach them. If you don't get there, but you gave it all you had, there's no reason to feel bad. This is an experienced team. The players know what they're doing."

That basic philosophy—that the players knew what they were doing—would continue to get Gaston second-guessed throughout the season. It bothered him. By the time the pennant race began to heat up he had gotten into the habit of retreating to his office after games and shutting the door, sometimes after talking briefly with the media, other times not talking to them at all.

Even in postseason, after victories, when managers traditionally sit around for long periods rehashing the game, Gaston would make his appearance in the interview room—as he was required to do—and then shut his office door. One night when a reporter knocked on that door, he found Gaston and coach Gene Tenace talking quietly, each man sipping a beer.

"None of you will ever know how much fun I'm having right now," Gaston said. "I love what I'm doing and there's nothing anyone can do to change that."

His voice was, as always, quiet, but there was anger in it. Tenace stood up. "None of you understand Cito," he said. "He does more to keep us loose than anyone. Tonight, [pitching coach] Galen Cisco wanted to check to see if we had the right guys up in the bullpen. He turned to the TV [in the dugout] and someone had turned it off. It was Cito. He was just messing with us to keep us from getting too tense."

Turning off a TV may not qualify as high humor, but in the middle of a World Series game, it's unusual. Certainly it's different from the image people have of Gaston. "Image is something *you* guys make up," he said. "It has nothing to do with who I am or what I am."

What he has become is a very good major-league manager, one who is judged only by wins and losses. Five years after Campanis, that is no small feat.

•

Whenever the Blue Jays win a game, Dusty Baker smiles. That isn't surprising since Baker and Cito Gaston were teammates at Austin in 1967 and again in Atlanta in 1975. But Baker also takes pleasure whenever the Kansas City Royals or the Montreal Expos win.

"Every win is a small step towards busting the stereotypes," he said, sitting in the San Francisco Giants dugout on a frigid (what else?) evening in Candlestick Park. "You have to understand one thing about blacks in baseball. We *do* try to look after each other. Always have. When I was playing, when we went into a town, we usually got together with the black guys on the other team. It wasn't any big thing. But we did have shared experiences."

Experiences that white players, or for that matter, today's black players, can't begin to imagine. Being turned away in southern restaurants and hotels, having to stay in the colored sections of town in places like Greenwood, South Carolina; Shreveport, Louisiana; and Richmond, Virginia.

"I remember the day before the draft, praying that I would be chosen by anyone but Atlanta," Baker said. "I knew Atlanta meant the

South and this was 1967. I dealt with it, though. It helped me become a man."

Almost every baseball player of Baker's generation can tell stories about being forced to stay in seedy hotels, especially in the South, because even in the '60s and into the '70s there were still hotels that were either "whites only" or made it so clear that they didn't want blacks staying there that blacks chose to stay elsewhere.

"In every city there were restaurants we would go to on the black side of town," Baker said. "You almost never ate with your white teammates. I can still remember a place called the Soul Shack in Shreveport. It was a dump, but the food was unbelievable. It was easier back then not to make trouble, not to fight it even if you knew it was wrong. Even in the majors, most guys were more comfortable going into places where blacks hung out. That's just the way it was."

It is different now. No hotel or restaurant would dare refuse someone on the basis of race, and blacks, Hispanics, and whites mingle fairly comfortably in baseball's clubhouses. But, as Marge Schott would prove with chilling insensitivity during the winter of '92–'93, racism is still a pervasive part of baseball—and society.

"One thing you have to remember is that baseball is part of society," McRae said. "You aren't going to change society overnight, or, for that matter, baseball. I know there are always going to be people who judge me as a *black* manager rather than as a manager, and there are going to be people who want me to fail just because I'm black. Does that upset me? Sometimes. But you can't let it. If you do, you're giving them what they want."

Eddie Murray, the Mets first baseman who will be in the Hall of Fame someday, doesn't like talking to the media. He doesn't think reporters understand baseball or baseball players and especially not black baseball players. Most baseball beat writers are white males.

"*You* can't understand what I feel," he said one morning, sitting in front of his Shea Stadium locker. "You think that racism died in the sixties when the laws were changed. Of course it didn't. If I go into a hotel in the South *today*, I still face resentment. We all do. And with athletes, successful athletes, it's especially true because people resent our success."

Deion Sanders is a perfect example of what Murray is talking about. He is prejudged by many because he is black and wears a lot of gold and oozes cockiness. During spring training, Sanders had gone on a fishing trip with relief pitcher Kent Mercker. Sanders was following Mercker in a black Jaguar when he was pulled over by a cop. Neither man had been speeding. But the cop, seeing a black man in an expensive car, stopped Sanders.

"In a way, it was good that that happened," Sanders said later in the season. "Sometimes you can tell white folks about what it's like to be black, but they can't really understand it. Kent *saw* it that day. The guy stopped me for one reason and one reason only: I was black. And if Kent hadn't seen what happened and come back to help, I probably would have ended up in jail—for nothing."

In 1992, the Boston Red Sox began the season with exactly three black players on their roster. During parts of 1990, the only active black players on the Mets roster were Darryl Strawberry and Dwight Gooden. That has changed somewhat since then: The Mets started 1992 with seven black players on their roster.

Yes, there has been progress. But in some places, it is still slow, grudging progress. Life wasn't easy for a black man when Dusty Baker was drafted by the Braves. It may not be as difficult in 1992, but it *still* isn't easy.

Baker played in the major leagues for sixteen years and, although he had some bad times, he emerged as a man respected by those he played with and against. When he retired after the 1986 season, much like Gaston, he thought he had been around baseball long enough. So, he went to work as an investment broker.

And then "Campanis" happened.

"Every club was looking for blacks to hire," Baker said. "I really wasn't that interested. I was thinking of buying a farm and going off and disappearing. I had separated from my wife and thought I wanted to go someplace and just start over.

"But when the Giants came after me, I thought it was at least worth thinking about. I called my father and asked him what he thought. He said to me, 'Son, you have too much knowledge of this game and too much to offer to just go off and disappear. God wouldn't have given you all this knowledge if he wanted you to disappear.' "

Johnnie B. Baker, Sr., had always been an important influence on his son (Dusty is a nickname put on him by his mother because he was always rolling in the dust as a kid), dating back to the days when Dusty was cut from his Little League team three straight years because he had a bad attitude. The coach of the team was Johnnie B. Baker, Sr. So when his father told him to take the job, Dusty took the job.

Four years later, Baker was one of the most respected hitting coaches in the game. Kevin Mitchell, now with the Cincinnati Reds, credits Baker with turning him into one of the best power hitters in the game. Most of the current Giants swear by him. Corey Snyder, given up on by three different teams, came back to have a solid year in 1992 and credits Baker with giving him his confidence back.

"I care about these guys and I think they understand that," Baker said. "I know what it's like to play on teams where the coaches don't really want to do anything but collect a check. That's not why I'm in the game. I think the players know that about me and they respect me for it."

Baker doesn't stop caring about a player when he leaves the Giants. As Mitchell struggled during the first half of '92 after being traded to Seattle, Baker watched him on television. When he spotted what he thought was the problem, he immediately dug into his tape library. He pieced together some tapes of Mitchell at his best and sent them to him with a note telling him to compare these to what he was doing now.

"He wasn't rocking his foot," Baker said. "He needs to do that to sit back enough to see the pitch. I could have told him that on the phone, but I figured he would be better off seeing it for himself. That's why we use tape, so they can *see* what they're doing wrong."

Mitchell was touched when he received the tapes and, shortly after viewing them, began to find the range. "You work with a guy for four years, you don't just tune him out of your life if he gets traded," Baker said, smiling. "Of course, if he was in our league, I might have had to wait until after the season."

Anyone who has worked with Baker will tell you he is ready to be a major-league manager. Baker thinks he is ready too, but knows it isn't as easy as all that. "When I was a kid my mother always told me I had to be twice as good as the white kids because I was black," he said. "I think there's still something to that. We're making progress. Felipe Alou getting hired and doing so well certainly helps all of us. But look how long it took for him to get a chance. There's still a long, long way to go. The fact that people only became aware of what was going on—or wasn't going on—because of something negative [Campanis] tells you that the problem is pretty serious."

It is probably not coincidence that two of the minority managers in the game work in the sport's two Canadian cities. It is also probably not a coincidence that the Blue Jays and Expos have more Hispanics and blacks than most of their American counterparts.

"I think people in Canada are less race-conscious than people in the states are," Blue Jays general manager Pat Gillick says. "I think people in Canada are less judgmental. It's a more comfortable environment for a minority player and, obviously, for a minority manager. I think the good news for us is that when people criticize Cito, whether I agree with them or not, it's strictly on the basis of baseball and nothing else. I'm not sure that would always be the case in an American city."

Fay Vincent, the now-deposed commissioner, also thought the problem *very* serious. He pressured major league owners to hire more minorities at all levels of the game.

"Right now we have two minority managers," he said during

spring training. "Let's say by next season we have five. People will say, 'Wow, what great progress.' But in fact, all it will really be is a Band-Aid." Going into 1993 the number was six: Baker was hired to manage the Giants. Don Baylor got the expansion job in Colorado, and Tony Perez was hired in Cincinnati. Still, Vincent knew there was a long way to go.

"If you look at business in this country there are almost no minority CEOs," he said. "The reason? There are almost no minority executive vice-presidents. We have to get teams to hire more minorities to manage in the minor leagues, to coach at all levels, to be in the front office at every level. We not only don't have a single black general manager in the game, we only have *one* black assistant general manager. Five years after Campanis that's an appalling number.

"People tend to hire people they are most familiar with. That's human nature. White general managers tend to know more people in the game who are white, so they hire white managers. Most of the white managers know more whites too, so they hire white coaches. It's only in the last few years that we've started to see a few black third-base coaches. That's how tough it's been to get the thing turned around. It will happen. It *must* happen. But it isn't easy."

Technically, Dusty Baker doesn't have, as Campanis meant to say, the necessary experience, since he has not managed in the minor leagues. But neither had Phil Garner when he was hired in Milwaukee before the 1992 season, and, for that matter, neither had Cito Gaston.

Preparation to manage in the major leagues can take many forms. Jim Leyland managed in the minor leagues for eleven years; Tony LaRussa for barely more than a year. Joe Torre was a great player; Jim Lefebvre a good one; Sparky Anderson barely made it to the majors. Felipe Alou and Hal McRae both had more than two thousand major-league hits; LaRussa had thirty-five, Leyland zero.

They all have one thing in common, though, something that is apparent very quickly in conversation: Each of them, without any question, has the necessities.

Whatever they may be.

PART III

SUMMER IN THE CITIES

15

RACES

Baseball players like to say that there is no such thing as a key series or a pennant race until after the All-Star break. There is truth in that. To be a serious contender, a team must prove itself capable of dealing with hot weather and injuries, with the building pressures of August and, finally, the crucible of September. But by June there is, at least, a sense of slowly mounting tension. Everyone has played everyone else. Early-season experiments have either panned out or been discarded. April euphoria has faded. And when the contenders do meet, there *is* a heightened sense of drama. These games will not decide the pennant, but they may set the stage for what is to come later. They may be a chance for a veteran team to reassert itself or for a young team to announce that it has arrived. They may also turn out to be nothing more than enjoyable teases, games that appear important at that moment but, as the races unfold, prove to be insignificant.

The point is, no one knows.

"For us to say that we aren't aware of the Reds would be silly," Tommy Glavine said before an Atlanta-Cincinnati series in June. "By now, it's pretty apparent that we're good and they're good. Does that mean we count out the other teams? No. It *does* mean that we assume that when September rolls around, we're going to be there. And the odds are decent that they'll be there too.''

In Baltimore, the arrival of the Toronto Blue Jays for a June weekend series was a major event. In Toronto, the same three games might be regarded with a raised eyebrow or two—''Oh, are the Orioles in town? They're playing rather well, aren't they?'' At Camden Yards, the presence of the haughty Blue Jays was seen as nothing less than the beginning of a summer-long war.

The Blue Jays and Orioles had played Alphonse-Gaston since the middle of April, trading first place back and forth. To the Orioles, contenders only once in the previous six years, this was joyride stuff. They were giddy and confident and their manager Johnny Oates kept telling them that was exactly the way they should feel. ''No one expects us to win,'' he kept saying. ''We can't lose anything. All we can do is win something no one is picking us to win.''

Privately, Oates believed that although the Blue Jays were more talented than his team, they were vulnerable. He looked at the Toronto pitching staff and saw an impressive list of names. But he also saw Jack Morris, Jimmy Key, Dave Stieb, and Tom Henke starting to show some age. He saw a team that felt the pressure of ''Three for Three'' every day.

''I really believe we can hang with them,'' he said. ''And if we're still there in September, who knows what will happen?''

The Blue Jays' clubhouse was, in many ways, a prickly place. Any suggestion that this was a key series was met with a sarcastic laugh or a dirty look. Mention past failures and the answer was always the same: That has nothing to do with *this* team. That was, of course, entirely untrue, since *this* team was going to have to hear those questions until *those* past failures were exorcised.

Dave Stieb, the club's all-time leader in wins with 173, was coming off back surgery and was fast approaching thirty-five. He had not pitched well all season and there were whispers he might be dropped from the rotation. Kelly Gruber, the third baseman who had driven in 118 runs in 1990, was barely hitting .200. Todd Stottlemyre, a fifteen-game winner in 1991, was struggling.

Even so, the Jays were 33-20 and had a one-game lead on the Orioles. They *were* in first place—but they were *not* living up to Gruber's prediction that they would have the race put away by Labor Day.

The opening game of the series had a September atmosphere—whether the Blue Jays liked it or not. By now, Camden Yards had become *the* place to go in the Baltimore-Washington area. Every game was a sellout, a phenomenon that would continue for the rest of the season. On a warm, muggy night, 45,803 fans showed up to see if the Orioles really could play with the Blue Jays.

They could. The game was a superb pitchers' duel between Jimmy Key and Rick Sutcliffe, who had become the backbone of the Baltimore staff. For seven innings they both threw zeros, although Sutcliffe needed some extraordinary help to match Key. In the fifth inning, right fielder David Segui went back to the fence, leaped, and barely pulled Candy Maldonado's drive back into the ballpark.

In the sixth, Mike Devereaux made a catch that defied belief. It came after Roberto Alomar had walked with one out. Joe Carter came up and absolutely crushed Sutcliffe's first pitch on a line toward the left-center-field bleachers. None of the walls at Camden Yards is very high, partly because low outfield walls make for better spectating out there, but also because low walls give outfielders the chance to make spectacular catches.

In Devereaux and Brady Anderson, the Orioles have two outfielders who take great pleasure in running into walls or jumping over them. In fact, Anderson loves nothing more than running *up* the wall. Sometimes he does it on balls hit way over his head just for the hell of it.

Now, Devereaux took off in pursuit of Carter's ball, running full-bore straight at the wall. For a split second, it looked like a futile effort; the ball looked as if it were going several rows deep into the bleachers. It might very well have done so, if not for Devereaux. Just as the ball was about to clear the fence, he launched himself into a full-length dive, his body parallel to the ground.

The ball was not dropping at that stage. It still had plenty of steam on it. But as it disappeared into the crowd, Devereaux went with it, clearing the fence with his leap, his arm and glove stretching several rows into the seats. For a moment, no one knew what had happened. And then there was Devereaux, coming back to earth, waving the ball.

"I saw the replay and I still don't know how he did it," Carter said. "Amazing catch."

The Blue Jays were stunned. It was almost as if the Orioles were saying, "Take your best shot, we've got an answer." Sutcliffe retired the next seven batters he faced before an Alomar single leading off the ninth caused Oates to bring in his closer, Greg Olson.

By then, the Orioles had managed to piece together the one run they needed off Key on three straight eighth-inning singles by Anderson, Devereaux, and Junior. Olson, who usually liked to make things suspenseful, induced the still shell-shocked Carter to ground into a double play. After pitching carefully to Dave Winfield and walking him, he got Gruber to pop to left for the last out.

As soon as the ball settled into Anderson's glove, Camden Yards exploded. The Orioles were in first place by percentage points. More important, they had played the kind of baseball that brought back memories of the dominant '66 to '83 Baltimore teams. Olson, usually a stoic, shot a fist into the air as his teammates came out to celebrate.

It was one baseball game—one *June* baseball game—but it was a special night. It reminded everyone in the ballpark how good baseball can be.

The Blue Jays won the second game 4–3, getting all four runs early, then not having a base-runner for the last 6 2/3 innings. That was barely enough for Morris, who overpowered no one, but hung in for six innings before turning the game over to the bullpen of Duane Ward and Tom Henke. Cal Ripken, Sr., made the highlight films in the ninth inning, racing onto the field after second-base umpire Chuck Meriwether called out Mark McLemore, the potential tying run, trying to steal second.

Replays were too close to call but there was little doubt that Ripken's explosion was fueled by the fact that Billy Ripken, the team's best bunter, had popped up a bunt seconds before, forcing McLemore to try to steal the base. The ejection that followed was the thirtieth of Ripken's career and a continuation of his long-simmering feud with American League umpires.

Sunday's explosion came from Dave Stieb. Pitching in a 1–1 game in the bottom of the fifth, Stieb gave up a leadoff single to catcher Chris Hoiles. Then Billy Ripken made up for his gaffe the previous evening with a perfect sacrifice. Anderson walked, but Stieb got Devereaux to fly to center for the second out. Up came Cal Ripken, who already had two hits for the day.

Stieb worked Junior to 1-2, pitching him away. Then he came inside with a gorgeous curveball. Ripken, fooled completely, never moved. Stieb saw strike three and took a step toward the dugout. Umpire Ted Hendry saw ball two and never moved. Maybe the pitch fooled him too.

When Hendry called the pitch a ball, Stieb lost it. Always high-strung, even at his best, Stieb not only wanted that strike, he *needed* it to escape the inning. He began screaming at Hendry. Gaston came out to calm Stieb down and ended up shouting at Hendry himself.

Ripken waited, knowing that Stieb was out of sorts. He now had to be patient and wait for the pitcher to make the kind of angry mistake that had been a trademark his entire career. Stieb threw ball three, still clearly upset. The next pitch was away, which was where Ripken had guessed Stieb would go. He punched the ball to right to drive in Hoiles. The Orioles led 2–1. Stieb was now berserk. He grooved a fastball to Glenn Davis, who drove in another run with a double into the corner, then he gave up a two-run single to Randy Milligan. It was 5–1. The final would be 7–1 as Mike Mussina, getting better every time out, cruised to his seventh win of the season.

Stieb was in street clothes by the time the game ended but he was still seething. Someone asked him if he had lost control. Eyes steely, Stieb shook his head.

"No matter what it looks like I'm always under control," he said. "I don't have to bend over and take that bullshit, though. I was throwing him [Ripken] shit low and outside and I had him diving over the plate. [Catcher Greg] Myers called a curve and I said I'm going to throw it inside and that's exactly what I did. I threw it exactly where I wanted and locked him right up. Everybody in the fucking ballpark saw it except for one motherfucker who didn't call it. It was pathetic."

Stieb tossed an empty beer can into his locker. He was completely under control. As long as Ted Hendry didn't appear in front of him any time soon.

"I thought it was a fun series," Gaston said. "Until that pitch."

The Orioles thought the whole thing was a gas. They were back in first place and on Friday night they had gone over the million mark in attendance. Only one other major-league team was over a million in attendance—Toronto, which had gotten there three days earlier.

Everywhere the Blue Jays turned, there were the Orioles, nipping at their heels.

Of course this was just June. Early June at that.

•

The toughest race to get a handle on was, without question, the National League East. It seemed as if this were the division that no one wanted to win.

The Pirates, after their quick start, had spiraled downward through most of May and had finished the month out of first place, the first time since the end of the 1989 season that they had ended a month anywhere but atop the division.

The team that had overtaken them was the St. Louis Cardinals, something of a surprise since the Cardinals had been fighting injuries from the very first week of the season when they lost four key players in four days, including their two second basemen, José Oquendo and Rex Hudler. They had also played most of the first month without their best power hitter, Felix José, and were getting very little production out of the aging Pedro Guerrero.

Guerrero's one notable moment had come after a loss to the Cubs, when he'd invited one of the Chicago players, Sammy Sosa, into the Cards' clubhouse. Todd Worrell, who had pitched that day, didn't think Guerrero should be whooping it up with a member of the opposition after a tough loss—and said so. Guerrero didn't think it was any of Worrell's business—and he said so. A moment later the two team-mates were wrestling one another to the floor while everyone else tried to pull them apart.

Joe Torre, the manager, called them both in to straighten things out. By the time the meeting was over, Worrell and Guerrero had hugged and made up and Torre had new rules about outsiders in the clubhouse.

"It actually worked out well because it gave me a reason to shut things down," Torre said. "I've always thought the clubhouse should be kind of a sanctuary, not overrun with people hanging around. So, I sat down with the team and we decided no one from another team is allowed in and no ex-players can come in, except ex-Cardinals who don't work for another team. I put that in because I'm not going to be the guy who tells Stan Musial he can't come in the clubhouse. Family can come in to look around, but not linger, and they have to be out by the time the bus arrives on the road or when BP [batting practice] starts at home."

The Cardinals were the third team Torre had managed. He had played for eighteen years in the majors with three teams—the Braves, the Cardinals, and the Mets. He had now managed in the majors for eleven years with the same three teams. At fifty-two, he still sounded like the kid who had grown up in Brooklyn hating the Dodgers and loving the Giants. He was sharp-witted and funny, a good storyteller with a self-deprecating sense of humor.

"If you really want to find out the truth about me, you should talk to my ex-wives," he said one day. "They can probably tell you a lot more than I can."

His first marriage—to a *Playboy* bunny—lasted two years and produced a son. His second marriage produced a daughter. His third marriage came after much thought and five years of living together. It has produced happiness.

Torre's parents were divorced when he was thirteen. His father was a cop who retired from the force and convinced the Milwaukee Braves to hire him as a scout—at the same time they were signing Torre's older brother Frank. Joe, the youngest of five children, was almost nine years younger than Frank, the second youngest. When his parents split, Frank became older brother/father/mentor. To this day, his opinion means more to Torre than anyone else's.

"If every newspaper in the country writes that I'm doing a good job, it doesn't mean as much as Frank saying so," Torre said. "I always wanted to impress him. The year I won the MVP [1971] he was on me all the time about things I could do better. Then I would hear from other people what he said to them, which was quite different."

Torre was a big, powerful kid who could always hit and liked to catch. At sixteen, he had a forty-inch waist. "My mother said I was big," he said. "Everyone else said I was fat."

In 1959, the Giants, who were in San Francisco by then, offered him $10,000 to sign. Torre would have done it if they'd thrown in a car. They didn't. He figured he would go to St. John's. Then the Braves, urged on by his father, offered him $22,500 to sign. He took the money, paid off his mother's mortgage, and *bought* a car. "Didn't have a nickel left," he said. "Over and out."

Two years later he was in Milwaukee as the starting catcher. His most vivid memory of that season is from spring training. "I wasn't a Yankee fan growing up, but the Yankees *were* the Yankees," he said. "We're playing them, I'm catching, and here comes Mickey Mantle up to hit. *Mickey Mantle!* I thought I was going to pass out or something. Later in the game, I come up and Whitey Ford is pitching and I hit a home run.

"God, I can still see it in my mind's eye, because as the ball goes over the fence, who's standing there watching it? Mickey Mantle. I'm twenty years old and this is happening. It was incredible."

Torre stayed with the Braves until 1969, when a vicious contract dispute with Paul Richards got him traded to the Cardinals. Bing Devine, the St. Louis GM who made the trade, told him later that, as he sometimes did before making a deal, he had asked Bob Gibson, the Cardinals' Hall of Fame pitcher, what he thought about the idea of trading for Torre.

"Gibby told him, 'Yeah, that's a good idea, trade for Torre if you can,' " Torre said, smiling at the memory. "A week later Bing gets me—for Orlando Cepeda. And Gibby goes up to him and says, 'I told you to trade for Torre, but I *didn't* tell you to trade *Cepeda* for him!' "

Torre made Devine look good by making a smooth transition to first base and driving in more than 100 runs each of his first three seasons in St. Louis—including 137 in 1971. He was traded to the Mets in 1975 when the Cardinals thought Keith Hernandez was ready to take over at first. He played in New York until the middle of 1977, when he became the manager in the midst of a huge shakeup, The biggest change was that Tom Seaver was traded two weeks after Torre took over the team.

"The only thing good about it is that I can say I'm the only manager Seaver ever went undefeated for," Torre said. "He was three-and-oh for me."

No one else came close to that during the next five years. Working with a nearly bare cupboard, Torre tried to keep the Mets afloat. When the team was sold and Frank Cashen became general manager, Torre knew he would bring in his own man—which he did after the '81 season. Torre landed in Atlanta and promptly won the division title the next year. The Braves just missed winning the pennant again in 1983, then struggled to an 80-82 record in 1984. Ted Turner, never known for his patience, fired Torre.

"I figured the phone would ring any minute," he said. "I thought I would have another job in no time."

He did—as a broadcaster for the California Angels. It was five years before the phone call Torre had been expecting finally came. By then, he wasn't sure if he wanted to manage again.

"We liked California," he said. "There was definitely something to be said for going home every night without being all that concerned about who won or lost. I worked hard at the job and I think I got better at it. When Dal [Maxvill] first called after Whitey [Herzog] quit, I told him I would talk to him but I really wasn't sure if I wanted the job. Ballplayers today are different. They can be tough to deal with. I wasn't certain I wanted to get back into it and put up with the headaches. My wife wasn't too excited about it either. Then, she ended up talking me into it."

Alice Torre saw a look in her husband's eyes that told her he had to take the job. So Torre became the Cardinals' manager in August of 1990. In 1991, he took them to a surprising 84-78 second-place finish. The surprise was that they improved so fast with so many young players.

In 1992, they started the season with a spate of injuries. But they'd gotten José back in May and their pitching had been superb. On May 24, they had gone into first place by winning for the fourteenth time in twenty-one games. The next day—Memorial Day—before a packed house in Busch Stadium, they blew a 4–2 lead to the Dodgers, fell behind 5–4, then won the game 6–5 in the ninth. They were 26-18 and rolling.

Or so it seemed. But the Dodgers came back to win the next two games of the series and the Cardinals hit the skids. They lost twelve of their next fifteen and Torre began shuffling the lineup to keep them afloat. The young pitchers who had looked so good in May—Donovan Osborne, Mark Clark, Rheal Cormier—suddenly looked like young pitchers. The bullpen—particularly setup man Worrell, back after two years of shoulder miseries, and thirty-five-year-old Lee Smith, perhaps the greatest closer of all time—went from untouchable to very touchable. José cooled off and Guerrero never got hot. Todd Zeile, the young third baseman who was supposed to be approaching hitting stardom, couldn't hit his weight.

The only Cardinal who seemed unaffected by the losing skein was Bob Tewksbury. Nothing, it seemed, could bother Tewksbury, who at thirty-one was living proof that throwing hard was not a prerequisite for success as a pitcher.

The Yankees had given up on him because he couldn't throw hard enough. The Cubs had given up on him because he couldn't throw hard enough. The Cardinals had signed him to a minor league contract, figuring he threw just hard enough to be useful in middle relief. His career record entering 1992 was 22-25, but in 1991 he had shown signs of becoming a very good pitcher. He finished the season at only 11-12 but his ERA was an impressive 3.25.

"Everything Bob does is simple," said pitching coach Joe Coleman. "There's no mystery. He almost always throws strike one. His control is unbelievable. Not only is he not going to give up walks, he's going to throw the ball exactly where he wants it almost all the time."

Tewksbury remembers having good control even as a Little Leaguer. "The funny thing is, back then, I pitched slower than most kids because I was always concentrating so hard on throwing the ball exactly where I wanted it to go," he said. "Now, I pitch faster than most guys because I throw strikes and I have confidence that I can throw the ball to a spot."

When Tewksbury is on, throwing one of his nine-inning, ninety-pitch complete games, he is an artist on the mound. Which is appropriate, since he is also an artist *off* the mound. His father, an auto mechanic, enjoyed sketching and, although he was talked out of pursuing art as a career, always liked to sketch cars. His oldest son inherited the talent and took art courses in high school and college.

Now, Tewksbury enjoys drawing and cartooning and says that his drawing helps his pitching. "To draw something, you have to see it in your mind before you draw it," he said. "When I go out to pitch, I try to see what I'm throwing before I throw it. If I can visualize it, I can usually throw it. Usually, I can tell very quickly in a game if I've got it. Actually, to be accurate, I can tell if I haven't got it because the vision just isn't there."

Most of the time, Tewksbury does have it. But it hasn't always been that way. Although he was a hard thrower in high school, no one drafted him and he went to college, first to Rutgers, then to St. Leo's in Florida. In 1981, the Yankees drafted him on the nineteenth round and he signed, wanting to find out if he was good enough to pitch professionally.

Injuries slowed him down. He hurt an elbow in 1982 that cost him some velocity and he was on and off the disabled list for each of the next three years. But in 1986, he made the team out of spring training, thanks to an 0.93 ERA. He was in the rotation when the season started but it soon became apparent to Tewksbury that manager Lou Piniella didn't think he threw hard enough to be an effective big league pitcher. He started eight times, went to the bullpen, then went back to Triple-A. He came back and finished the season 9-5 but didn't feel the Yankees really wanted him to be in their rotation.

He got one start at the beginning of 1987, then was back in the bullpen. Then he was back in the minors and, in August, he was in Chicago with the Cubs. He spent almost all of 1988 in Triple-A before signing a minor league free-agent contract with the Cardinals in '89. He spent that year at Louisville, where he was 13-5 with a 2.43 ERA.

"That was the year I got my confidence back," he said. "All the bouncing around with the Yankees and the Cubs, wondering if I threw hard enough to make it in the majors, affected me. I lost confidence in my fastball, which is always going to be my best pitch if I throw it where I want to. But I kept hearing that you couldn't get by throwing eighty-three or eighty-four in the majors and I began to believe it."

Tewksbury made the team in '90 but was sent back to Louisville after being used a couple of times in relief. That was when he thought about quitting. "I was twenty-nine and I was tired of Triple-A," he said. "I had already proven I could pitch there. I wanted a chance to prove I could pitch in the majors because I was convinced I could do it. I decided to give it a month. Then, I was either going to go home or look at going to Japan."

Tewksbury was in Louisville for three weeks. He pitched forty innings and walked *three* hitters. The Cardinals brought him back and put him in the rotation. He beat the Expos in his first start and in August went 4-1 with a 1.60 ERA. He was in the majors to stay. When Torre joined the team, he brought Coleman with him and Tewksbury found someone he could talk to for hours about pitching. By 1991 he was keeping a chart of every pitch he threw to every batter. "I actually started doing it in Triple-A because I was bored," he said. "Now, I really use it."

There was no better example of a Tewksbury game than his victory over the Mets in New York on June 20. He threw ninety-two pitches. With games averaging close to three hours, this one lasted 2:22. Tewksbury made one mistake: a hanging slider that Eddie Murray hit over the center-field fence in the fourth. The Mets got five hits. Tewksbury struck out four, didn't walk anyone, and threw a strike on the first pitch to twenty-two of the thirty-one hitters he faced. That was the stat that most impressed Coleman: "They know he's going to throw strike one and they still can't do anything about it."

In 1991, according to his charts, Tewksbury had thrown his fastball 46 percent of the time. His goal at the start of '92 was to throw it 55 percent. At the conclusion of this game, he had thrown it 66 percent of the time. "I throw it about eighty-five [miles per hour]," he said. "That's not that hard. But I throw it right where I want to. If I do that, I'm going to get outs."

Tewksbury was now 7-2 and on his way to making the All-Star team. The victory put the Cardinals back at .500—33-33. It dropped the Mets, who had held a players-only clubhouse meeting *and* a Jeff Torborg–called clubhouse meeting earlier that week, to 31-36. Things were getting ugly at Shea. Howard Johnson was booed after misjudging two fly balls on the night of Tewksbury's masterpiece, and even Torborg had to admit he didn't blame the fans for being frustrated. "Why shouldn't they boo?" he said. "We've been awful."

Things would get worse for the Mets. As for the Cardinals, they were hoping to get going again soon. Torre sensed the division was there to be won. The Pirates led by five but only because no one else was playing over .500. "Any one of the six is good enough to win," Torre said. "I know that's a cliché, but in this division it's true. I just don't see anyone dominating. There's no Atlanta or Cincinnati in this group."

•

Atlanta and Cincinnati *were* in the National League West. And, as the weather began to turn hot, so, it seemed, did their race for the division title.

The first two months of the season provided some false hope for the other teams—especially the Giants. They had been the team that had gotten the fast start and they had remained in first place until early June, when an injury to Billy Swift, who had gone 6-0 after being acquired in the Kevin Mitchell trade, began to slow them.

There was also the not-so-little matter of where they would play. On June 2, voters in San Jose rejected a bond issue to build a new ballpark there for the Giants. Owner Bob Lurie, having been rejected four times by Bay Area voters, said he would look for a buyer for the team—from anywhere. Any city, any state. It may have just been coincidence but the Giants went 7-20 in the four weeks following the vote and Lurie's announcement.

The Astros, the youngest team in the division, had also started well but were quickly fading to their appointed spot near the bottom— and they still had the twenty-six-game road trip in August to look forward to. The surprises were the Dodgers and Padres. The Dodgers had been 23-23 on June 2, then, beset by injuries, proceeded to lose 17 of their next 24 and dropped into last place. The Padres, with Gary Sheffield bolstering the lineup in the number-three spot, were hanging on the fringes of the race, still only five games back as June came to a close.

That was all well and good but there was little doubt in anyone's mind that this was destined to be a two-team race. The Braves had worried a few people by starting 20-27. The main problem was the bullpen. Alejandro Peña, their savior the previous September, was either hurt or couldn't get anyone out. Mark Wohlers, the closer-in-training, still needed more training. Everyone else was struggling. On May 10, the bullpen blew an 11–2 lead in St. Louis and lost 12–11. The next day the lead was 5–1 and the final was 6–5—Cardinals.

That dropped the record to 15-17. Terry Pendleton called a team meeting the next day to remind everyone not to take winning for granted. Everyone listened and nodded but it was another three weeks before they really began to turn things around.

"The team really wasn't playing that badly," said Kent Mercker, one of the beleaguered relievers. "We were scoring runs, the starters were pitching okay, we just weren't closing the games out. None of us were getting it done. We all sort of knew it was just a matter of time until we broke out. It was frustrating, though."

The Braves finally broke out the final weekend in May when they went into New York and swept the Mets. That started a skein in which they were almost unbeatable. They reeled off twenty-one victories in twenty-four games, including three of four against the Reds when they came into Atlanta for a weekend series. Each of those games was close and tense and had the same kind of feeling the Toronto-Baltimore series had had two weeks earlier.

Lou Piniella was impressed by what he saw that weekend, but not overwhelmed. "They're very good and they're playing great baseball right now," he said. "But they've gone twenty-one-and-three and they still haven't quite caught us. We're still in first place."

And now the Braves were coming to Cincinnati for three games. The Reds had swept three from them the first time they had come to Riverfront Stadium but that had been the second week of the season. It was so early it almost didn't count. Now, smarting from the previous weekend in Atlanta, the Reds would find out something about themselves.

Piniella is not a man who demands a lot from life. A beer, a cigarette, a place to play golf, and an occasional trip to the track will usually keep him pretty happy. Throw in a healthy baseball team and, most days, he will be positively delirious.

In 1990, as a rookie National League manager, Piniella had led the Reds to the World Series title. A year later, with several key players hurt, they collapsed in the second half of the season and finished an embarrassing 74-88.

During the winter, Piniella and general manager Bob Quinn had made major changes. Gone were Eric Davis, the oft-injured superstar; Randy Myers, the left-handed closer in a bullpen that had too many closers; Jack Armstrong, an All-Star in 1990, a bust since then; and Scott Scudder, like Armstrong a young pitcher with potential that had never quite been realized.

In their places were Bip Roberts, a versatile leadoff hitter who

could play just about any position on the field; Tim Belcher, a solid
veteran starter; Greg Swindell, who had pitched well for miserable
teams in Cleveland, and Dave Martinez, a reliable fourth outfielder
with speed and moxie. Throw in Reggie Sanders, who many people
thought might be the most talented rookie in the league, and the Reds
looked as if they had reloaded quickly.

"I like the look of this team," Piniella said, sitting in his office a
few hours before the first game of the series with the Braves. "Since
we've gotten healthy, we've played well. Hell, we played well last
weekend in Atlanta. They just played a little better."

The Reds had spent most of April putting people on the disabled
list—seven players in all, including Barry Larkin, their All-Star shortstop; José Rijo, their number-one starter; starting infielders Hal Morris
and Chris Sabo; and Rob Dibble, their right-handed closer/angry
young man. By the end of May, they were all healthy and the team was
in first place. With the Braves in town, things were starting to get
serious—at least a *little* serious.

"This is fun," Piniella said. "This is what you get into managing
for. You want to start to feel the race a little about now, really get into
it by the end of July, and then spend the last two months feeling
nervous. That's what it's all about—the chase."

Piniella has always enjoyed the thrill of the chase. His other passion is the stock market. He often spends his mornings on the phone
making deals and has often thought about trying to buy a seat on the
New York Stock Exchange.

"It's just another way of competing," he said. "I like challenging
myself. I liked to play the game because hitting is such a challenge.
Everyone knows that's what I loved doing when I played. I got into
managing because that was a challenge too. The stock market is the
same kind of thing."

In one sense, Piniella has had it very easy as a manager. After
playing in the majors for almost eighteen years, he never had to go
back to the minor leagues as a manager or coach. He became the
Yankees' hitting instructor after retiring and was told by Billy Martin,
then the manager, that George Steinbrenner had told him to groom
Piniella as his replacement.

In 1986, Piniella did replace Martin—who, of course, in turn replaced him two years later—and won 179 games in two years. He
didn't win the division either year but the Yankees were in the chase
both times. At the end of 1987, Steinbrenner made Piniella the general
manager. That lasted a half season. Piniella went back to the dugout
for another half season, then spent 1989 as a broadcaster/roving instructor. Pat Gillick wanted him to replace Jimy Williams as manager
in Toronto that year, but Steinbrenner wouldn't let him go. At the end

of the season, when Quinn, another of Steinbrenner's ex–general managers, was hired in Cincinnati, he asked Piniella to be his manager.

They were an odd couple. Quinn, a recovering alcoholic, was quiet and studious; Piniella, loud, boisterous, and temperamental. But they put their mark on the National League quickly, running away with the division title, then upsetting the Pirates and A's to win the world championship.

Having worked for Steinbrenner, Quinn and Piniella were probably better equipped to deal with the wishes and whimsy of Reds owner Marge Schott than most people. For all of his bluster and paranoia, Steinbrenner did have his defenders in baseball. He was considered loyal—by some—and smart by others. Schott, on the other hand, was respected by almost no one.

Part of this was, no doubt, sexist. Baseball is an old-boys' club, especially in the ownership ranks. If a woman does own a club, she is expected to behave the way Joan Payson did when she owned the Mets: Be sweet and kind to all and let men like M. Donald Grant run the club—even if the club gets run into the ground.

Schott was not sweet or kind and she was as hands-on as any owner in the game. She wasn't Steinbrenner—she didn't call meetings after every game to discuss what was wrong with the ballclub—but she was extraordinarily cheap, often checking phone records herself to see if anyone made personal calls at the expense of the team. In 1992, she had even taken Quinn's box away from him—and he was the general manager!—forcing him to sit in the press dining room during games.

Schott battled constantly with the media. If she didn't like what a member of the local press wrote, she would ban that person from the ballpark's media dining room. No fewer than seven local reporters met this fate in 1991. Naturally, T-shirts to commemorate the occasion were made for the banned seven.

Before Game One of the 1990 World Series, Schott took the PA microphone to assure the crowd that everyone was thinking and worrying about "our boys in the Far East." She was referring to the troops stationed in the *Middle* East, following Saddam Hussein's occupation of Kuwait. As she babbled on, then-commissioner Fay Vincent sent one of his aides to tell Schott that it might not be a bad idea for her to give up the microphone.

"Tell the commissioner," Schott told the aide, "to mind his own goddamn business."

And then, of course, there were the dogs. The joke in Cincinnati, ever since Schott had owned the team, was that the Reds were the one ball club in the world where you wanted to be treated like a dog. Schottzie was Marge's best friend, her pride and joy, and nothing was too good for the dog. When Schottzie died at the age of eight, she was replaced by Schottzie 02.

The players really didn't mind Schottzie. She was a calm, docile dog who was content to sit in the owner's box and mind her own business. The new dog was a lot friskier and Marge insisted she be allowed to romp on the field before games. Often she left quite a mess for the ground crew to deal with. The players didn't have anything against the dog, but she was a pain in the butt.

When Tim Belcher commented to Jerry Crasnick of the *Cincinnati Post* that the dog sometimes made it difficult for players to get their pregame work done, Crasnick wrote it. He promptly joined the banned-from-the-dining-room crowd. Belcher, as other players had done in the past, responded by having food sent to Crasnick in the press box.

For Belcher, being in Cincinnati after four years in Los Angeles was an adjustment. "The ironic thing is I grew up a couple of hours from here," he said, sipping coffee in the dugout one morning. "And there's no doubt this is a better club than the Dodgers. But when the trade happened, it was real tough for a while."

Part of it was timing. On the day before Thanksgiving, Belcher had taken his wife, Teresa, who had just miscarried six weeks into her pregnancy, to Columbus for a D&C. On the quiet drive home from the hospital, the Belchers heard a report on the radio that the Reds were about to announce a major trade and that rumor had it Eric Davis was going to the Dodgers for Tim Belcher.

"If it's true," Teresa Belcher said, "just take me out and shoot me like a horse."

"You have to understand, we were very happy in L.A.," Belcher said. "The Dodgers are a great organization to play for and they're great to the wives. They treat them like gold. They're always welcome on the charters, everything is done first-class.

"I told her not to overreact to what we had heard on the radio, but in my mind, I was thinking that this made sense. When I'd first heard some rumors that they might trade me, I really didn't think they were true. Mike Morgan had left for the Cubs, Orel [Hershiser] was still kind of a question mark, and Ramon [Martinez] had been kind of iffy at the end of the season.

"But when I heard the report on the radio I thought it was probably true. Eddie Murray had signed with the Mets that day and they had already lost Morgan. I know that [Dodger GM] Fred Claire is very PR-conscious. Bringing Darryl [Strawberry] and Eric [Davis] back together would wipe out any negative publicity from losing Murray and Morgan.

"I walked into the house and the message light was on. Now, I was certain. I put Teresa to bed, went down to the basement, and checked the message. Sure enough, it was from Fred Claire. I called him back and he said, 'Tim, we've made a trade.' I hung up, poured myself a shot of Crown Royal, and went upstairs to tell Teresa. I put a big smile on my face and said, 'Guess what, dear, my lifelong dream of pitching for the Reds has come true.' She didn't buy it.''

What made it tougher on the Belchers was seeing all their relatives the next day and realizing how excited they all were about the trade. They would now be able to see every home game Tim pitched.

"We kind of liked spending six months a year away from home," Belcher said. "It's like Teresa said to me, 'For six months a year, I had you to myself. Now, I'll spend *twelve* months a year being Tim Belcher's wife.' That's a tough thing for wives, the idea that they lose their identity because they're married to a celebrity. Where we lived in Los Angeles, she had her own group of friends who really didn't care that much that I pitched for the Dodgers.

"Teresa understands the ups and downs of this life better than anyone. We grew up three miles from one another and first knew each other as toddlers. She went through the minor leagues with me so she's seen it all. Being with the Dodgers was pretty close to perfect for both of us. That's why the trade, even though I knew it was a good thing in a baseball sense, was a shock for us.''

Belcher had recovered from a slow start and was pitching well. He had adjusted to the fact that life with the Reds was different from life with the Dodgers. The Reds were one of the few teams in baseball that still flew on commercial flights sometimes. Wives were *not* welcome on the road. Dogs perhaps, but not wives.

•

The Braves did go on charters wherever they went, but they might not have needed the plane that brought them to Cincinnati. The team was hot, cocky, and convinced they were on a roll that wasn't about to end on a steamy summer weekend in Cincinnati.

Deion Sanders, hitting an astounding .346 for the season, showed up in the clubhouse before the opener wearing not one but two earrings.

"What the hell is that supposed to mean?" John Smoltz asked when he saw the new attire.

"It means, I am too cool for words," Sanders answered.

The way he was playing, no one was likely to argue. The Braves were cool, too, but it was the Reds who came out hot against Steve Avery. In the first inning, they got three straight infield singles, one by Reggie Sanders, one by Bip Roberts, and one on a bunt by Barry Larkin. Avery managed to strike out Chris Sabo but then Glenn

Braggs, after hitting a ball just foul deep into the seats, hit a ball very fair and very far for a grand slam.

Braggs had come into the game hitting .220. But against Avery he was Mickey Mantle: now 11-for-23 for his career, with three home runs. The Reds cruised from there to a 6–3 victory. The next afternoon was more of the same. Charlie Leibrandt was gone in less than two innings and the Reds led 7–1 after two. This time the final was 10–3. The one-game lead was now three.

"Why are people getting so excited?" Barry Larkin said afterward. "Don't they know this is June?"

His manager wasn't getting overly excited but he *was* having fun. "You know, when they started their twenty-one-and-three run, they were four-and-a-half games behind us," he said. "If we win tomorrow, they'll be four games back." He smiled and lit a cigarette. "No big deal. But it's something for them to think about."

The Braves were no doubt thinking a lot of things the next afternoon when Glavine, their ace, was touched for three first-inning runs. That meant the Reds had outscored the Braves 10–0 in the three first innings during the series. Glavine did settle down after that and the Braves finally made one of the games competitive. They pulled even at 4–4 in the eighth when Norm Charlton walked Damon Berryhill with the bases loaded.

But the Reds came back with two runs in the bottom of the inning. The second run was the result of a controversial play at third: Sabo was called safe trying to steal the base when it appeared Greg Olson's throw beat him by several feet. Both Terry Pendleton and Bobby Cox argued at length with umpire Jeff Kellogg, Pendleton clutching the ball in his glove the entire time as if to prove he had made the play. The call and Sabo's run proved crucial when Olson homered in the ninth. The final score: 6–5.

"He tagged the dirt, not the man," Kellogg said afterward.

"I tagged him from the tips of his fingers right up to his head," Pendleton said. "I've looked at the replay seven thousand times and he was out every time. I've never had an umpire tell me that I tagged the dirt in my entire life. The play wasn't even close. The ball was there, I made the tag, that was it. Sabo just stood there and didn't say anything. He knew he was out."

Sabo ducked the question when it was raised. "I had my head down, sliding," he said. "I really don't know what happened."

What galled the Braves—in addition to being swept—was that Kellogg was working the game because crew chief Terry Tata had been called away for the day. Tata had been scheduled to work third base.

"Where the fuck was Tata?" Bobby Cox asked. "Look, it was a

horseshit call, he blew it, but the umpire didn't beat us. We gave up two-out hits the whole weekend. That was the story, not the umpire. The Reds just beat us.''

The Braves were too experienced to lose their cool over one call, one game, or even one three-game sweep. ''We made a point last week and they came back and made a point right back this week,'' Glavine said. ''That's baseball. We knew coming in here they were good. We still know it going out.''

Cox can never sit down after a game. He's too wound up. He paced up and down in his office, sipping a beer. ''We were horseshit for three days,'' he said. ''It's three games we'd like to have, but still, just three games.

''Hell, we're four out. I'll take four out at the break.'' He paused, then turned for the door. ''But I'd rather be four ahead.''

16

THE COMMISH

While the pennant races were beginning to take form in June, so was the confrontation that likely will define baseball in the 1990s. On June 7, the commissioner of baseball was asked to voluntarily remove himself from any potential negotiations with baseball's labor union, negotiations that might or might not take place in 1993.

In no uncertain terms, the commissioner declined.

Thus, the battle that would ultimately lead to his resignation three months later was publicly joined. Baseball's owners needed a fall guy and Fay Vincent was anointed to play the role.

If you listened to his enemies, most of whom chose to hide behind anonymous quotes as the summer wore on, Fay Vincent was power-hungry, paranoid, a bully, overzealous, a manipulator of the media, and not to be trusted. Most of the ills of baseball—and mankind—had been caused by Vincent. If only Bart Giamatti had lived, they moaned, he would have understood our problems and none of this would have happened.

"Bart, now there was a guy who really loved the game," Milwaukee Brewers owner Bud Selig said one summer day. "We used to have long talks about the future of the game. He just *cared* so much about the game. Not the business of the game, the *game*."

Selig was one of the leaders of the Dump Fay Movement, along with Jerry Reinsdorf of the Chicago White Sox and Richard Ravitch, the head of the Player Relations Committee, which was the owners' negotiating arm. It was Ravitch's hiring which first tipped Vincent off that he and the owners who employed him might be coming to a parting of the ways. The fact that the owners decided to pay Ravitch a salary of $750,000—$100,000 more than they were paying Vincent— was a fairly obvious clue.

Vincent, having been CEO of both Columbia Pictures and Coca-Cola, didn't care what the owners paid him; he didn't need the money. But the salary was a warning sign, a signal that the new man was seen as some kind of savior.

"A lot of these guys think they're smarter than everybody else," Vincent would say later. "They always think they're going to outsmart people—the union, the networks, the public, anyone you can think of. And each and every time they think that, they find out that they're wrong; usually the hard way."

The owners had tried to break the union before. They had locked the players out in 1990 and had gotten nowhere. For that, they blamed Vincent, who had interceded to end the lockout before the regular season began. During the mid-1980s, they had colluded against the game's free agents and ended up paying fines totaling $280 million after an arbitrator found them guilty of collusion. For that, they blamed then-commissioner Peter Ueberroth.

Now, with television revenues about to take a precipitous drop, with clubs overpaying mediocre players on a regular basis, and with other sports challenging baseball's supremacy as the national pastime, the owners were panicking. Someone had to take the blame and it wasn't going to be any of them. Vincent was elected. Or, as things turned out, unelected.

•

Baseball was always a part of life for Francis Thomas Vincent, Jr. His father had been captain of the baseball team at Yale and, in fact, spent the afternoon on which his son was born playing in a semipro baseball game.

"I don't think my mother ever quite forgave him," Vincent said with a smile. "My father knew she was due and took a chance. It was an issue for quite a while."

Vincent was never a great athlete, but it was sports that allowed him to bond with his father. He can still remember weekend trips from their Connecticut home to Yankee Stadium, the feeling of awe he felt walking into the huge ballpark and how much he enjoyed holiday doubleheaders. In 1992, there wasn't a single doubleheader scheduled on a holiday. Some teams didn't even *play* on Memorial Day.

"The game misses traditions like that," Vincent said. "I understand the business aspect of it, not wanting to give up a home date, but sometimes in this game we don't look past the numbers often enough."

When Vincent's father's playing days were over, he umpired baseball games and refereed football games. Watching his father umpire, Vincent gained an appreciation for the craft, an appreciation that carried over to his days as commissioner. He played both football and baseball in high school, pitching and playing first base, but his playing days were ended when, in college, he fell off a two-story building ledge in the midst of a fraternity prank and broke his back, an injury that has made walking very difficult and painful for him throughout his adult life.

He became very successful and very rich and eventually became friends with A. Bartlett Giamatti, the president of Yale. Vincent still enjoys recounting the now oft-told stories about how he and Giamatti would go out to dinner together and talk about working with one another someday. When Giamatti moved into baseball, first as president of the National League, then as commissioner, he brought Vincent in as his number-two man.

"The lure of baseball was Bart, not the job itself," Vincent said. "I had been a CEO, so being the number-two man was new for me. But I was happy and prepared to do it because it meant working with my best friend."

Giamatti and Vincent were not really prepared for the baseball world they found. When they had talked about their new jobs, they thought they were going to have fun, work hard for a few years, have the best seats in the house, and then move on, probably to write. It was almost a way to ease into early retirement.

"We had no long-term strategy," Vincent said. "We weren't sure how long we were going to stay. We were both reasonably free and it seemed like an interesting thing to do for a while. We had no major plans and no foresight. We really didn't know much when we took over. Neither one of us ever dreamed it would be as intense as it was. We expected this to be *less* intense than our previous jobs. It wasn't. The [Pete] Rose thing happened right away and it's never really calmed down since then."

The Pete Rose gambling scandal was dumped in the laps of Giamatti and Vincent on April 2, 1989, the day Giamatti took office. Vincent was Giamatti's point man on the investigation and, later, on the difficult negotiations that led to Rose's banishment from baseball.

Throwing baseball's all-time hit leader out of the game wasn't easy. Both Giamatti and Vincent were exhausted at the press conference announcing Rose's banishment. A few days later, though, with Labor Day weekend coming up, Vincent and Giamatti, along with Vincent's sister and Giamatti's son, flew to Cape Cod on a private plane.

This had become a weekend routine with Vincent and Giamatti. Vincent would charter a plane, drop Giamatti off at his home on Martha's Vineyard, then go on to his house on Cape Cod. On Monday morning, the plane would pick Vincent up, stop for Giamatti, then deliver them both back to New York. "It was a way for us to get some time away on the weekends," Vincent said. "If we had driven, with summer traffic and all, it would have been too exhausting."

Vincent can still remember the flight up that Friday. Giamatti's mood was as good as it had been for months. "We were high," he said. "We finally had the Rose thing behind us. The pennant races were beginning to shape up and we were thinking that we could really enjoy the postseason now that this was over."

Vincent dropped Giamatti off around lunchtime, went on to the Cape, and did an early-afternoon interview there with a local reporter. At approximately three o'clock, the phone rang. It was Bobby Brown, the president of the American League.

"They had just gotten a report that Bart had had a heart attack and that it was very serious," Vincent said. "I honestly can't remember exactly what he said to me, but something in his voice told me that Bart had died. Bobby's a cardiologist, so he knew what the doctors were dealing with. I don't know if it was terminology or his tone, but I know that when I hung up the phone, something in my gut told me Bart was gone. Bobby said he was going to call the hospital and try to talk to the doctor.

"I turned the radio on to WFAN [the all-sports station in New York]. A few minutes later, before Bobby could call me back, they announced that Bart had died."

The rest of that weekend is something of a blur for Vincent. He can remember television crews showing up on his front lawn, as if by magic, within minutes of the announcement that Giamatti was dead. Vincent only had one phone line in his house and it wouldn't stop ringing. He was trying to find out where Giamatti's wife and family were but the phone kept ringing. State troopers finally showed up to take control of things outside. Fred Wilpon, the Mets' co-owner, flew up in his private plane to pick up Vincent and then stopped to get Giamatti's wife.

Vincent was in shock. One minute he had been celebrating the end of an ordeal with his friend and now he was facing a much bigger

ordeal without him. "During those early days the one emotion I remember is missing Bart," he said. "We had gotten into this thing to
be together. Now, I was there without him. The only thing that really
saved me was that there was so much to do that my mind was occupied."

Vincent was quickly elected as Giamatti's successor and distinguished himself during the San Francisco earthquake that turned the
World Series he and Giamatti had so been looking forward to into yet
another nightmare. The crises kept coming: the lockout of 1990; the
dwindling TV ratings, which made it apparent to just about everyone
but the owners that baseball was going to take a huge hit when the
network contracts ran out in 1993; spiraling salaries; the George
Steinbrenner/Howie Spira fiasco of 1991 and its never-ending aftermath; and then, as 1992 began, the specter of another lockout that
could endanger the 1993 season. That cloud hung heavily over Vincent
even as he made his annual tour of spring training.

Sitting poolside on the morning of March 6, Vincent smoked a
cigar while he read a newspaper story quoting Don Fehr, the executive
director of the player's union, as saying that both baseball and the
networks were crying wolf when they claimed that the networks were
taking huge losses on the game. "It's a normal thing to claim losses as
a bargaining position," Fehr was quoted as saying.

Vincent put the story down and shook his head. "We can't turn
this into a morality play again," he said. "If we have another problem,
and I suspect we will, it is going to be bad for both sides. The public
will see this as a battle between a bunch of cheap billionaires taking
on a group of whiny millionaires. That is not going to be very attractive
or very good for a game that already has serious image problems.

"I like Don Fehr and I think he's a bright guy. But he has to come
into this negotiation, whenever it takes place, not just thinking like a
union leader. He has to think like a businessman and as a statesman.
Baseball has to change, one way or the other. It can change civilly or
it can change by force after a prolonged confrontation. The worst way
is confrontation.

"The best thing for everyone involved is to look up and say,
'That's an iceberg and we are the *Titanic*. If we hit it, some of us will
live and some of us won't, so let's do something before we hit it.' "

Why, Vincent was asked, should Fehr and his union believe that
the owners, having lied in the past about their financial problems,
aren't lying again?

Vincent smiled. "Because this time," he said, "they aren't lying.
Look at what's happening this spring. The marketplace is already
starting to correct itself. Look at all the players in camps on minor
league contracts. The rich are still getting very rich, but the middle

class is being wiped out. Owners just aren't going to pay .260 hitters two million or three million dollars a year anymore. If Don is working for *everyone* in his union, then he realizes changes have to be made."

Vincent struggled slowly to his feet. "Come on, Don Fehr!" he shouted, looking up at the sky and waving the newspaper clipping over his head. "You're better than this, Don. Get serious! Get real! You know what the dollar figures are! Don't be stupid! To say this is a bargaining position is ludicrous and you know it!"

He looked around, embarrassed for a moment, wondering if anyone had noticed him. No one had. He smiled. "Now comes the part of the job I like," he said.

It was time to go to a game.

•

Watching Fay Vincent at a baseball game, it was quickly apparent that when he said, "My joy is the games," he was not kidding.

Everywhere he went, the home team provided him with a golf cart to take him onto the field. In itself, this was a departure. No commissioner in history had ever been as accessible to players, managers, coaches, umpires, and the media as Vincent. He would sit in the golf cart behind the batting cage and chat with anyone and everyone. He liked baseball players and he liked the media. But he also thought part of his job was being available to them.

"I have always believed that a commissioner should be the commissioner of everyone in the game, not just the owners," he said. "I know I'm elected by the owners and it is almost inevitable in this job that you are going to piss some of them off. I think baseball recognizes that fact: You need three fourths of the owners' votes to be elected, but only a majority to be reelected.

"If you are trying to run a business, you have to have a relationship with everyone in that business, not just the board of directors. If I didn't enjoy talking to players and the media, I would do it anyway. As it is, I do enjoy it."

That he enjoyed being visible and talking to people other than owners would become an issue with his detractors later in the season. They would whisper that Vincent spent too much time softening up players and the media and not enough time making *them* happy. It was a charge he would not deny.

Once seated in the stands, Vincent was besieged by autograph seekers. He signed gladly—between innings. "I once asked Bart if he ever signed an autograph while he was president of Yale," he said, as he signed a baseball. "I wish more of this job was just sitting and watching games."

He pointed toward the field, where Lou Whitaker, the Tigers' second baseman, had just kicked a ground ball. "What's nice about baseball is that it acknowledges human frailty. Errors are part of the game. We allow for errors."

The White Sox used women from a restaurant called Hooters as hostesses and ball girls. Clearly, it was not politically correct to have women in halter tops and shorts running around the field.

"I guess that's true," Vincent said, smiling in the direction of his wife, who was a few seats down from him. "But let's be honest—it's tough to be against Hooters girls."

Vincent always stayed for the entire game. When this one, in Sarasota, was over, the umpires made a point of stopping to say hello to him. Several reporters returned while a number of fans lingered for autographs.

"The closer you get to baseball, the better off you are," Vincent said as he was driven away from the ballpark. "Your feeling about the game has to change when you're commissioner. When you're at the ballpark you look around and see things that need to be done better and you worry about them. As a fan, obviously, you don't do that. The thing about being commissioner is, you should enjoy the game. I know there have been commissioners who really didn't like baseball that much. If nothing else, I do love the game."

But his relationship with the men who owned the game was changing—and eroding. By mid-May, Vincent's frustrations were beginning to become more apparent to his friends and to those around him.

"The problem with the owners," he said one afternoon, sitting on another golf cart in another ballpark, "is that they can't make up their minds what they want. One day they want one thing, the next day they want another. They don't really care about each other, they only care about themselves. That isn't a good way to do business."

He paused and was quiet for a moment. "There are good guys in this business," he said finally. "And there are bad guys, too."

Two weeks later, some of those guys asked Vincent to remove himself from future contract negotiations. Vincent sensed that Ravitch and Reinsdorf were planning an all-out war with the union and felt they needed to get him out of the way to wage that war. He was so discouraged by the approach of the PRC that he was ready to quit right then and there.

But several owners, including Fred Wilpon of the Mets, Haywood Sullivan of the Red Sox, Claude Brochu of the Expos, and Walter Haas of the Athletics, talked him out of it.

For the very reasons that the PRC wanted him out, they argued, he needed to stay. But things got worse as the summer proceeded. Vincent had, against the wishes of some of the owners, ordered the

National League to align its teams into geographically sensible divisions. But a court ruling wiped out his order and that was a big blow. The controversy over his handling of the Steve Howe case also hurt.

Vincent had suspended Howe, the Yankees' talented but perennially troubled left-handed reliever, after Howe had pleaded guilty to drug possession during an offseason incident in Montana. Since the suspension was the pitcher's seventh, and since Vincent had a letter from Howe, written in 1989, asking for one *last* chance, he banned him for life.

Although Howe had pledged in his letter to Vincent that he would walk away from the sport voluntarily if he ever used drugs again, he appealed the ban. When several Yankee officials, including general manager Gene Michael and manager Buck Showalter, testified at the hearing *against* baseball's drug policy, Vincent was furious.

"I have no problem with them testifying for Steve Howe," he said. "I *do* have a problem with them testifying against a drug policy that is part of the Basic Agreement. Mark Connor [the Yankee pitching coach] testified, too, but all he said was that Steve Howe was a good guy. Period. He had no problems with me. But when the others criticized something that is written into their contracts, in my view, they resigned from the game.

"It's like a cop deciding that the Fourth Amendment is a pain in the ass, that he shouldn't have to get a warrant, that if he knows someone is guilty he can just go and knock their door down and start beating heads in. He may have the right to disagree with the Fourth Amendment, but if he acts on it that way, then he has to be prepared to be fired."

Vincent was so upset with Michael, Showalter, and Yankee vice-president Jack Lawn (a former Drug Enforcement Agency official) that he summoned the three of them to his office on the morning of August 6, even though the Yankees were playing at one o'clock that afternoon. The incident caused a huge brouhaha, especially when Showalter didn't get to the ballpark until the bottom of the first inning.

Here, Vincent had made a mistake. If he had waited until the next day, when the Yankees were playing at night, he could have had the meeting with far less fireworks. The fact that he insisted on holding the meeting right away made it look as if he was throwing a temper tantrum. He *was* angry—and perhaps was entitled to be angry—but he had overreacted.

"I don't think I did overreact," he insisted. "I called George [Steinbrenner] on the phone to tell him I was calling these people in and he said, 'If I had been running the club when they testified, I would have fired them.' So, in a way they were very lucky that all that happened to them was getting called in here by me."

But no matter what the owners said publicly, none of those incidents had anything to do with the revolution against Vincent that reached fruition on September 3. On that date, in Chicago, the owners voted 18–9 (with Marge Schott abstaining) to ask for Vincent's resignation. Vincent had written the owners on August 20 to say that he would not resign and, under the major league agreement, could not be fired or removed from office until his contract was up in April of 1994. He knew that Ravitch and Reinsdorf, having failed to convince him to voluntarily remove himself from future negotiations, were now trying to get him out of the way for good.

"They've inflamed a lot of the other owners by convincing them that I would order the camps opened if there was a lockout," Vincent said, eating a tuna sandwich at his desk three days before the vote. "That's not true. There is no point to ordering the camps opened because there would still be no contract. I've told them that. No commissioner in his right mind would do that.

"But they *like* the issue more than they like the solution. It's like being soft on communism. It's easy and it's no-lose from their point of view. They're accusing me of being soft on labor."

That was the real issue when the owners met at their special session in a Chicago hotel. Vincent had committed the greatest crime of all: He had not been their toady. So they voted him out. For four days he held his ground, but after a weekend on Cape Cod, he concluded that it was silly to try to run the game when it was clear the owners were not really going to let him run it. He could have continued to sit in his office in Manhattan and hold the title but if he couldn't affect policy, there was no point. Even so, it was an extremely difficult decision.

"For a long time I felt like resigning was taking the easy way out," he said afterward. "I felt that if I quit and ran off to Europe and sat by a fire and smoked cigars, I wouldn't feel very good about what I had done, that I had let people down. I felt resigning would change the commissioner's office forever, that his right to 'act in the best interests of the game' was vital to the game itself. But then I realized that even if I somehow did hang on until my term was up, there was nothing to prevent the owners from restructuring the office before they hired the next commissioner anyway."

So on September 7—Labor Day—Vincent addressed a letter to the American and National League owners. It was three pages long and quite direct.

"I strongly believe a commissioner should serve a full term as contemplated by the major league agreement," he wrote. "Only then can difficult decisions be made impartially and without fear of political repercussions. Unfortunately . . . some want the commissioner to represent only owners, and to do their bidding in all matters. I haven't done that, and I could not do so, because I accepted the position believing the commissioner has a higher duty and that sometimes decisions have to be made that are not in the interest of some owners.''

There was more: ''Simply put, I've concluded that resignation—not litigation—should be my final act as commissioner, 'in the best interests' of baseball. . . .

''I bear no personal ill will towards any of the owners and I wish them well. At the same time, I remind all that ownership of a baseball team is more than ownership of an ordinary business. Owners have a duty to take into consideration that they own a part of America's national pastime—in trust. This trust sometimes requires putting self-interest second.''

Vincent's resignation was both dignified and eloquent. The owners who had pushed for his removal were absolutely giddy over their triumph. They elected Milwaukee Brewers owner Bud Selig as their figurehead interim leader the following week and Selig talked about what great feeling everyone now had for one another. The wicked witch was dead. The owners were almost certain, it seemed, to reopen their contract with the union on or before the December 11 deadline. Reopening would quite possibly lead to a 1993 lockout and the war that Reinsdorf and Ravitch appeared to covet.

The next six weeks would surprise and disturb the victorious owners. Everywhere they went, it seemed, they were asked by friends, business acquaintances, and strangers, ''Why did you fire Fay Vincent?'' They were almost universally ripped by the media. Perhaps they should have listened to one employee of major league baseball, someone who has been around for several years but never worked closely with Vincent:

''I never knew the man well,'' he said. ''But I do know this: I never saw him treat anyone who worked in the office with anything but complete respect. He was a rich man who never acted as if being rich made him privileged or gave him the right to treat people poorly. I think some of the owners who fired him might have learned some things from watching him in action. I think it was a sad day for baseball when he walked out of here. I hope someday the owners understand that.''

Someday, they might. But don't count on it.

17

BUDDY AND
THE BREWERS

Very few players cared much about Fay Vincent's ongoing conflicts with the owners. They were vaguely aware of the possibility of a lockout in 1993 and they knew the owners were complaining about losing money. But, with the exception of each team's player representative and a few others, no one was overly concerned with baseball's finances. In the clubhouses, where only a few players made as little as $109,000 (the major league minimum) and the average salary was slightly more than $1 million, the game's finances looked fine.

That was not the view from the office of Allan H. "Bud" Selig. If there was one man in baseball who seemed to know everything about every issue, it was Bud Selig. If there was a committee or a study group, Selig was on it. Stacked up behind his desk were reports and folders; stacked behind them were *more* reports and more folders. "Can't really discuss these things," he told visitors. "It's all very ongoing."

Ongoing and onboring. Selig had owned the Milwaukee Brewers for their entire twenty-three-year existence and was baseball's committee-aholic. Need someone to run the PRC? Bud would do it. Need an owner to cochair the owner/player economic study group whose report was months late and seemed like it might never quite get done? Appoint Bud. The executive council? Bud. Ownership committee? Bud. Need someone to be on the board of the Green Bay Packers? What the heck, Bud would do that too. If the owners had a party committee, there's no doubt who would be in charge of ordering the balloons.

"Just can't say no," he said, walking around the desk in his tiny, cluttered office. It was a Thursday morning and the Brewers were playing at one-thirty. Selig stood on a footstool so he could get his chin above the high windowsill and check the walk-up crowd at the box office. It was a bright, cool June afternoon.

"Looks pretty good," he said, swiveling his head to survey the area. "We should get close to twenty-five thousand." The actual crowd that day was 24,774. Selig has an almost uncanny knack for guessing attendance figures. He makes regular forays into the press box during games—something almost no other owner in the game would think of doing—and usually engages the local media in an informal guess-the-attendance contest. Selig is very good. Of course, he has the advantage of knowing how many tickets were bought in advance.

He got his nickname at birth, when his mother, Marie Selig, told his brother Jerry, who was four at the time, "Now you'll have a buddy." He was Buddy then, Bud now. His father, Benjamin Selig, made a lot of money selling cars. He talked his son out of teaching and into joining him in business after Bud had graduated from Wisconsin and been in the service.

But it was Marie Selig who introduced little Buddy to baseball. A Russian immigrant, she was a baseball fanatic who started taking her younger son to watch the Milwaukee Brewers of the American Association play at Old Orchard Field when he was three. Once he was old enough, he started riding the bus there by himself on days when his mother couldn't go. He dreamed of playing baseball until he was fifteen. "Someone hit me in the head with a curveball and that was it for me," he said. "Of course a lot of people claim that has a lot to do with me being the way I am today."

Today, he is the owner of a small-market franchise at a time when the small markets are struggling to survive. "I often kid some of my colleagues who own teams in big markets that just for a thrill they should spend one year running the Milwaukee Brewers," he said, laughing. "They would be shocked. This is a different world." He waved his hand around the office. "I mean, look at these offices."

There is nothing pretentious about the Brewers' offices. Selig's office is considerably smaller than that of many public relations directors in bigger cities. Milwaukee–County Stadium itself is outmoded, much like the ballpark in Cleveland. Selig is trying to put together the funding to build a new park, though he knows it won't be easy. But then, nothing with the Brewers ever has been.

Selig and his backers bought the team on March 31, 1970—six days before the season began. The team that had gone to training camp as the Seattle Pilots came north as the Milwaukee Brewers, the stitching on their caps literally torn off to replace the "S" with an "M." The purchase of the team ended a five-year-long attempt by Selig and the city, an attempt begun when the Braves decided to flee to Atlanta. Selig, who had just turned thirty, became the leader of the movement to bring another team to Milwaukee. In 1969, they thought they had the White Sox, but the deal fell through. Over the five-year period, exhibition games and several White Sox regular season games drew well, but the group was running out of steam.

"The Pilots were our last gasp," Selig said. "I had said we wanted baseball back in Milwaukee in the worst possible way and that's how we got it—in the worst possible way."

The Brewers have been a solid franchise during most of their existence. They won a mini-division pennant during the 1981 strike year and won the American League pennant the following year, before losing the World Series in seven games to the Cardinals. They have had great players: Hank Aaron finished his career here, as did Sal Bando, now the general manager. Rollie Fingers won a Cy Young Award and went on to the Hall of Fame, and Pete Vuckovich won a Cy Young Award before arm problems cut his career short.

Robin Yount, a certain Hall of Famer, has been with the team since 1974, Jim Gantner since 1976, and Paul Molitor, who may yet get to the Hall of Fame, since 1978. Those three have been the backbone of the franchise. The Brewers drew just under 2.4 million people in 1983, the year after their pennant.

That is the only time the team has drawn more than two million people. In some ways, the Brewers are almost like a mom-and-pop grocery store; people can walk into the team's offices and put in a request to have their names mentioned on a radio broadcast. In the Brewers' case it is actually a pop-and-daughter store: Selig has anointed his thirty-two-year-old daughter Wendy as his successor.

"We really are a family operation," he said. "We just can't create the revenues they can in New York, Chicago, or Los Angeles. We have no cable TV and believe me we've tried everything to get it. Our broadcast revenues are a fraction of what the big markets have. There is just no way for teams in markets like ours to compete financially with the teams in the big markets. What everyone has to realize is that the institution is only as strong as its weakest franchise. There are more have-nots than haves right now. We've got a lot of difficult times ahead of us."

The current season had not been easy by any means. On Opening Day, a couple was run down in the parking lot by a departing school bus. The man had been killed; the woman crippled. Then, on June 3, a two-year-old boy named Michael Harrison was run down and killed by an usher in a golf cart outside the ballpark before an afternoon game with the Tigers. Both deaths shook Selig and the franchise, especially that of Michael Harrison.

"It was a beautiful Wednesday afternoon," Selig said. "Here comes this young father, bringing his son to his first baseball game ever. The Brewers and the Tigers, an afternoon at the ballpark. Everything we want the game to be. And then this little boy dies. God it was awful."

Two days after the accident, Selig got a phone call from Christ Harrison, the boy's father. The Brewers had announced that there would be a moment of silence in Michael Harrison's honor that night. Christ Harrison wanted to know if he could throw out the first ball in his son's memory.

"I thought it was a strange request," Selig conceded. "But who was I to sit in judgment of this man at this moment? You know what, though? It really was a wonderful thing. We introduced him and he walked out there and all of a sudden the whole crowd was on its feet. I had so many emotions that night. I mean, this sort of thing just shouldn't ever happen but the emotion we all felt . . ."

The two eerie accidents overshadowed the fact that the Brewers were playing better baseball than most had expected them to. Picked to finish in the middle of the pack in the Eastern Division, they began the season full of question marks. Selig had overhauled his management team the previous year, firing longtime general manager Harry Dalton and replacing him with Bando. In turn, Bando had fired Tom Trebelhorn, the popular young manager of the team, and replaced him with Phil Garner, a onetime teammate in Oakland.

"I can't give you a reason why I fired Treb," Bando said. "To some extent, I did worry that some of the players were taking advantage of his goodness. But, really, to be honest I made the change for the sake of change.

"Knowing I was doing it for that reason made it very tough to do. I didn't sleep the night before I told Treb. When I told him, he asked me why and I couldn't give him a reason. Plus, I knew if I did, he'd have an answer because he's so bright."

The Garner hiring had drawn criticism. Garner had played for sixteen years and been a coach in Houston for three. But he had never managed. Many people thought that Don Baylor, who'd been Trebelhorn's batting instructor, should get the job. At a time when major league owners were citing lack of experience as one of the reasons there were so few minority managers, Bando had hired an old friend with no experience.

"We were never really that close," Bando said somewhat defensively. "I called Phil because he was someone I had played with and someone I knew. That's true. I hired Phil because of the way he handled the interview and because I had a gut feeling he was the right person, not because we had played together."

Garner took over a team considered too old—Yount, Molitor, Gantner—*and* too young to compete for a division title. Bill Spiers, his projected shortstop, went down before the season started and Garner had to put Pat Listach, ticketed for Triple-A, in his spot. Teddy Higuera, the onetime staff ace, continued to have shoulder problems and wouldn't throw a pitch all season. Gary Sheffield was traded ten days before the opener.

And yet, Garner was convinced his team could compete. He was determined to play "National League" baseball—run, run, and run—and he made it apparent to the players very quickly that 1) he had a plan, and 2) that plan would be followed. Anyone who didn't believe in the plan could play someplace else. The Brewers started slowly but as they got accustomed to one another and their new style of play, they began to pick up. By the end of June they were a solid third behind the Blue Jays and Orioles. If they could stay there the rest of the season everyone in Milwaukee would be quite happy.

•

"That's a bunch of crap," Phil Garner said, pulling an unlit cigar out of his mouth. "They may be playing better than we are right now, or at least getting better results, but don't try to tell me they're a better team than we are. Don't tell me *anyone* is better than we are."

The Brewers had just dropped a second straight game to the Orioles and one of the local writers had wondered if perhaps these two games had brought Garner's team back to earth a little bit after a hot streak. Garner wasn't buying it. "They're good," he said. "They play well, catch the ball, pitch well. But so are we."

Tom Haudricourt, the beat writer for the *Milwaukee Journal,* had called the Brewers "The not-ready-for-prime-time players" that day. Garner gets along well with the media and probably has a better understanding of its role than most baseball people. But he wasn't about to let that one ride.

"Not-ready-for-prime-time players, my ass," Garner grumbled.

"It wasn't a sloppy loss?" Haudricourt shot back. "You guys couldn't hit José Mesa, for crying out loud."

"Hey, I'll tell you what," Garner said. "You put a major league uniform on someone, there's going to come a night when he'll get your ass out.''

''Bad baseball,'' Haudricourt said.

Garner grinned. ''Okay, fine. But when we kick their ass tomorrow, you better be right back on the goddamn bandwagon.''

Garner is forty-three, but looks younger, even behind the mustache he grew years ago to make himself look older. He is a Baptist minister's son, very much the product of a small-town puritan upbringing in the Smoky Mountains of Tennessee. He is an avid reader who loves a good argument, whether the subject is baseball, the weather, business, or politics.

''I'm used to people telling me what I can't do,'' he said. ''The only reason I got a college scholarship [to Tennessee] is because my high school coach went down to Knoxville and told them they were crazy if they didn't give me a chance.

''When the Expos drafted me in 1970 they kept telling me I wasn't any good. The scout was Red Murff. Same guy who signed Nolan Ryan for the Mets. He came down to see me and I told my dad I was going to sign for whatever he offered me. So, he tells me I can't play but here's a bus ticket to spring training. I said, 'What else?' He said, 'That's it.' I said, 'I'm not signing for any less than thirty thousand dollars.' I didn't want thirty thousand dollars, I hadn't even thought about how much I wanted. But he pissed me off and I was cocky so I demanded thirty thousand. That ended the negotiations.''

Garner spent that summer in Liberal, Kansas, playing summer league ball. The Expos sent another scout, Red Patterson, to talk to him. The first night Patterson was in Liberal, Garner hit a three-run home run in the eighth inning to win a ball game. Patterson took him out to eat afterward and asked him how much he wanted.

''I said thirty thousand,'' Garner said, waving his cigar. ''He looked at me and said, 'Now, son, one home run doesn't make you a great player.' By now I was *really* cocky so I just looked at him and said, 'Come on back tomorrow, I'll hit another home run.' You know, like Babe Ruth.''

Patterson came back the next night and Garner hit another three-run homer. ''As I was rounding third base I looked up in the stands and saw him get up and leave,'' Garner said. ''That was the last I ever heard from the Expos.''

The Oakland A's drafted him the following January and he signed—in about two minutes—for $15,000. Three years later, he was the starting second baseman on a team that had just won three straight world championships. Bando remembers one thing about him: ''He wasn't the least bit intimidated by anything. He thought he was as good as we were.''

Garner doesn't deny it. "I'd been called up in September the year before," he said. "I'm out there with Reggie [Jackson], Sal, [Bert] Campaneris, [Joe] Rudi, that whole crew. After three days I came home and told my wife I was good enough to play with these guys."

He played with them for two full years, then went to Pittsburgh for five. There, he played in the 1979 World Series and went 12-for-24 as the Pirates beat the Orioles in seven games. When his career ended in 1988, Garner was offered a job coaching in Houston. He stayed three years until Bando called.

"I was shocked when he called," he said. "I never thought he'd consider me. And, to tell you the truth, with two of my kids in high school I wasn't all that thrilled about moving my family. But opportunity doesn't always knock twice."

Garner did not expect Listach to play as well as he'd played, but he *had* told his team all season that it was good enough to compete with anyone. And with each passing day, the Brewers seemed to believe in themselves just a little bit more.

They had won three out of four from Cleveland to push their record to 36-30 when the Orioles came to town and promptly beat them twice. That made the finale extremely important; the Brewers were leaving that night to begin a thirteen-game road trip. Many thought that would go a long way toward deciding whether they could stay within shouting distance of the leaders.

Ricky Bones was the Milwaukee pitcher, the same Ricky Bones who had been the key to the Sheffield trade. He had not pitched well thus far. He had a 3-3 record and an ERA of close to five runs a game. But, with Selig pacing up and down in the back of the press box almost the entire game, Bones shut the Orioles out for eight innings. Doug Henry came in with two men on in the ninth to get the last three outs and preserve a 1–0 victory. The Brewers' only run came on a sacrifice fly in the seventh inning by—who else?—Robin Yount.

Yount was three months shy of thirty-seven and closing in on three thousand hits. He didn't really want to discuss either topic, or much of anything else, for that matter. As taciturn as he appeared to be in public, there was little doubting his importance to the Brewers, even if he was nowhere close to being the player he'd been in his MVP years (1982 and 1989). He was still the leader and the role model, even if Molitor had succeeded him as the best player.

"Boy, that was a big one," Selig said after Henry had gotten the last out. He had spent almost the entire game trying to crack jokes to keep loose, for the most part failing. "I'm fifty-seven years old and I still have trouble sleeping at night after losses," he said. "It's kind of silly for me to deny that I live and die at the games because all you have to do is look at me for five minutes and it's pretty apparent."

Garner's approach was more relaxed—except when Haudricourt ventured into his sight line.

"Hey, asshole!" he yelled.

Grinning, Haudricourt walked into the office. "Not ready for prime time?" Garner asked.

"Afternoon game," Haudricourt responded.

Garner had to give Haudricourt points for being quick. He put his stocking feet on his desk and smiled. "We'll win a few at night before it's over," he said.

"I'll check with you in September," Haudricourt answered.

Garner leaned across the desk and pointed the cigar at Haudricourt. "You do that," he said. "You just be sure and do that."

VIEW FROM
THE BASEMENT

B y the time the All-Star break approaches, the pecking order for a baseball season has been pretty well established. Only rarely do teams that have foundered in the first half find a miraculous elixir and race to a pennant in the second half.

It does happen. The 1991 Braves limped off to the break nine-and-a-half games out of first and ended up winning the division. But they only had two teams ahead of them and both, the Dodgers and Reds, started the second half horrendously, practically begging the Braves to get back into the race.

Generally speaking, any team that is not in the first division on the Fourth of July—or among the top four in the seven-team American League divisions—isn't going to contend. Teams below .500 tend to stay that way. That would certainly be the case in 1992. Fifteen teams were at or below .500 on July 4. The one team at .500—the Yankees— would finish the season ten games under. One other, the Astros, would finish exactly at .500. Only one of the fifteen—the Cardinals, who were 38-40—would finish above .500. They would end up 82-80.

On the other side of the ledger, only one of the eleven teams above

.500 on that date—the Texas Rangers—would finish with a losing record.

Order had been established. The contenders and pretenders had assumed their roles. Three of the four teams that would finish last were last. The exception to this was the Boston Red Sox, a team many had thought in preseason to be the only club with a chance to challenge the Blue Jays for the division title.

The Red Sox lurked around the .500 mark for most of the first half of the season. On May 1, they were 9-9. On June 1, 24-21. By July 1 they had slipped to 35-38. Every time the team appeared ready to really hit a slide, Roger Clemens would pitch brilliantly and things would brighten in Boston. Then would come a string of 2–1 losses and everything would go dark again.

What was strange about this Boston team was that unlike in past years, it could pitch but it couldn't hit. Wade Boggs, who entered the season with a career batting average of .345, was struggling to stay over .250. Jack Clark, the prototype right-handed power hitter whose game was made for Fenway Park, looked helpless at the plate. Tom Brunansky was not the power hitter he had once been. Tony Peña was still an excellent catcher, but not nearly the hitter he'd been in the National League. Mike Greenwell and Ellis Burks were hurt (and not terribly productive *before* they were hurt). The younger players looked overmatched most of the time.

The batting order had gotten old in what seemed like the blink of an eye. Boggs was thirty-four, Clark thirty-six, Peña thirty-five, and Brunansky almost thirty-two. Greenwell and Burks were only twenty-nine and twenty-seven but their banged-up bodies felt much older. The team batting average at the end of the Fourth of July weekend was .242. Collectively, the Red Sox had hit thirty-five home runs—only eight more than Oakland's Mark McGwire.

The reason the Red Sox weren't any worse than 36-40 on July 4 was their pitching. Clemens had been virtually unhittable until an injured foot slowed him late in June. Even so, his ERA was 2.11. Frank Viola, picked up as a free agent from the Mets, had pitched consistently, and Joe Hesketh had been surprising. Overall, the team led the league in ERA at 3.36. But there was no sense that this was a team that was going to turn around in the second half. The mood in the city bordered on surly. Butch Hobson had been the manager for less than half a year and was already getting booed.

If the boos bothered him, Hobson wasn't about to tell anyone. He did slip once when he admitted that he had warned his family about "hearing the wolves" when they came to watch the team play.

Hobson would turn forty-one in August. He had white hair, piercing blue eyes, and a handshake that could make your knees buckle. He had grown up in Alabama, worshiping Bear Bryant, and had played quarterback for him in college. In high school, he had played for his dad, who had also been an Alabama quarterback.

"I loved baseball and I was good at it," he said. "But in Alabama, when you get to high school, if you don't play football you're nothing. So I played football and fell in love with it. When I had a chance to go to Alabama, there just wasn't any doubt about doing it."

Although baseball became his vocation, Hobson's training, his background, and his approach was pure football. He almost never raises his voice in conversation and his accent still hints strongly of his upbringing. He talks constantly about execution and giving 110-percent effort and never lying down. His role models aren't Sparky Anderson or Tony LaRussa; they are Clell Hobson, Sr., and Paul William Bryant.

"I have a picture on my wall at home of Coach Bryant," he said after an intense hour of extra batting practice in midday heat. "It was taken my freshman year, 1969. Back then, freshmen weren't eligible to play, so we sat in the stands. A couple hours before every game the coaches and team would come out and walk around the stadium in street clothes. It was one of Coach Bryant's traditions.

"We were four-and-four at the time and when the team came out people started to boo. I realized after a few seconds that they were booing Coach Bryant. I couldn't believe it. After all the years and the national championships and all he meant to the state, they were booing him. Whenever things get tough for me, I look at that picture of him in the stadium that day and I realize if *he* could get booed, *anyone* can.

"I knew when I took the job it would happen, so when it does I don't let it bother me. Coach Bryant used to say the leader has to take the responsibility. I don't have a problem doing that."

The Red Sox had fired Joe Morgan and hired Hobson in his place the previous fall; they thought Hobson could bring toughness and discipline to the team. That had been his reputation during five years as a minor league manager. But appearances can be deceiving. If anything, Hobson wasn't tough enough. In spring training, he delayed roster cuts by forty-eight hours because he dreaded giving the bad news to players being sent out. During the first half of the season, as the older players continued to flounder, Hobson steadfastly insisted that they would come around. It was as if he thought if he said it enough times it would come true.

To be fair, Hobson was dealing from a weak hand. The team had given him little choice but to stand by the fading players. On July 7, Michael Gee, in a back-page column in the *Boston Herald,* put his finger squarely on the dilemma: If general manager Lou Gorman had not pushed the panic button and fired Morgan at the end of the '91 season, he could have brought Hobson in after the slow start in '92 and moved the old players out along with Morgan. That would have left Hobson with a clean slate and a mandate to play the youngsters.

But it hadn't happened that way and now Hobson was tied to the failings of the current team. Boston is not a patient town when it comes to the Red Sox. Since the miracle pennant of 1967, the team has been a contender most years. Only twice in twenty-five years had the Red Sox finished below .500—in 1983 and 1987, each year going 78-84. They had won three division titles in the past six years, advancing in 1986 to the World Series that still haunts all of New England.

In short, the people of Boston had, for the most part, seen a lot of good baseball over the years. They had *not* seen a World Series champion and they had read over and over and *over* again—since the Red Sox and their failures are a favorite of the overwrought literati—about the disappointments of fall that led to bleak New England winters. The works of Shakespeare have probably not been as analyzed as often as the Curse of the Bambino and Billy Buckner's Boot.

Boston hadn't won a world title since that noncursed 1918 season, but the Red Sox were hardly the Indians, Cubs, or White Sox. Perhaps that was the problem: Being close so many times without getting the final victory had left many people a little angry, even bitter.

The Red Sox were 37-41 when the Kansas City Royals came into Fenway Park immediately after the July 4th weekend, a mediocre record but certainly not hopeless. Still, there was a definite pall over the ballpark. It was as if the fans, having watched this team in action for half a season, knew that things were only going to get worse.

The attendance for the opening game of the series—28,495—was an indicator of the town's malaise. Traditionally, the Red Sox *never* draw under 30,000 for a game between Memorial Day and Labor Day; most nights they play before full houses of just under 35,000. The attitude of the fans seemed to be: Show us improvement before we begin to believe in you again.

Booing had become part of the routine. Boggs kicked a ground ball in the second and got booed. When the error led to an unearned Kansas City run, the boos grew louder. Jody Reed missed a sign in the third, leaving Tony Peña a dead duck at second. Boos. Jack Clark grounded into a double play in the fourth. Loud boos. Hobson went to get starting pitcher John Dopson in the seventh. Loud, lusty boos.

The only real cheer of the night came on a Mo Vaughn home run in the seventh that closed the Kansas City lead to 6–3. The crowd was so into the game at that point that it decided to do the wave. One could almost hear Ted Williams looking up from his fishing somewhere to say: "What the hell is that?!" (The best line ever delivered by a baseball player on the wave came from Graig Nettles, the ex-Yankee third baseman who said, "The wave is the worst thing to hit baseball since Bowie Kuhn.")

The wave was nowhere in sight by the ninth. There were some final boos for the road when Phil Plantier struck out looking, but by then most of the crowd was on the way home. It was a beautiful summer night, the Prudential and John Hancock buildings highlighting the skyline of downtown Boston beyond the right-field fence, the Citgo sign lighting up over and over again behind the Green Monster. Postcard stuff.

On Butch Hobson's office wall hung a schedule for his old team, the Pawtucket Red Sox. If Hobson had been sending a postcard that night it might very well have read: "Wish I were there."

•

On the morning after that loss dropped the Red Sox to 37-42, there was little talk in Boston about the continuing futility of the ballclub. All eyes and thoughts were focused instead on someone who had never left the clubhouse the previous night: Roger Clemens.

It has been said in Boston that if Roger Clemens has a headache, everyone in town takes two aspirin. There is a good reason for this: Clemens is the best pitcher in baseball. In 1991 he won his third Cy Young Award, and during the first two months of 1992 appeared well on his way to a fourth.

Then came the toe injury. In June, Clemens started to feel pain when he landed on his left foot. He continued to pitch but became less and less effective. When the White Sox reached him for five runs in less than four innings on July 2, it was time to step back and decide what to do next.

When the team returned from Chicago, Clemens asked team doctor Arthur Pappas to come to Fenway to take a look at the foot. At the same time he called the people at Reebok; he asked them to see if there was some way to add some protective padding to the shoes they made for him.

Two representatives from Reebok arrived in the Boston clubhouse at four o'clock in the afternoon. Their conversation with Clemens lasted for twenty minutes. While they talked in front of his locker, the media hovered, watching, waiting, wondering.

Pappas arrived as the Reebok people were leaving. As he and Clemens headed for the training room, reporters trailed the Reebok reps into the hallway. "No comment," they kept repeating. "Talk to Roger."

It had not been a great week for the shoe manufacturers. The previous week, their overhyped "Dan and Dave" Olympic decathlon campaign had blown up in smoke when Dan O'Brien failed to make the Olympic team. Now, Roger Clemens's foot hurt—and all of Boston was ready to blame the shoes.

"The shoes aren't the problem," one of the Reebok men insisted after the Boston reporters had left. He turned to his partner. "Maybe we should have said something."

While they were debating what to do next, Clemens returned to his locker. Through the years there has been considerable tension between Clemens and the Boston media. As the focal point of a baseball team that is the focal point of sports life in New England, Clemens performed in a spotlight that often got white hot. It was tough to take for a country boy from Texas who simply wanted to get the baseball and go throw it.

For a long time, Clemens would only talk to the media after he pitched. Now, after nine years, he has become far more accommodating. He understood that his foot pain had left a couple of million people limping. So, when he finished with Pappas, he sat in front of his locker and patiently explained the problem—and, he hoped, the solutions.

He would throw on the sideline Tuesday in a specially padded shoe Reebok was going to make for him. If all went well, he would pitch again Friday. Resting for the last few days had already helped. Clemens answered every question. He was patient, friendly, even funny. He understood it was part of the deal.

"I can usually handle pain pretty well," he said. "But this has gotten to the point where I'm just not getting the job done."

That's what sets Clemens apart from other pitchers with great stuff—his obsession with getting the job done. He is almost never satisfied, has never taken his success for granted, and is always looking for an extra edge to stay ahead of everyone else.

"I probably get that from my mom," he said, sitting on a staircase outside the Red Sox clubhouse one night to avoid the media horde. "My father died when I was nine and she worked two or three jobs so that my younger sister and I were taken care of. I can remember every year around Christmas, she would go out and get work at night to make sure that we had everything we wanted at Christmas. She always used to tell us, 'Whatever you do in life, try to be the best at it. Always try to get better, every day.' "

Clemens was the fifth of Bess and Woody Clemens's children. His brothers were grown up by the time their father died, but they found time to get Roger involved in sports, putting him into a nine-year-old baseball league when he was seven. "I was always a big kid," he said. "Right from the start, I liked competing with older kids."

He played all sports until his senior year of high school when he had to give up basketball; the football coaches had made him bulk up to 245 to play defensive end and he needed the time in the winter to get back down to his pitching weight of 205. Several major league teams showed interest in him but Clemens decided to stay home for a year and attend junior college. Then he went to the University of Texas; it was only 150 miles from home and he wasn't ready to go any farther away than that.

"One scout came to our house and gave my mother this big speech about how if I didn't sign right away, I'd never get another chance because major league teams wouldn't be interested in me after college," he said. "My mom said, 'There's no need for him to be riding buses all over Appalachia when he's eighteen. Don't let the door hit you on the way out.' "

In his sophomore year in college, Clemens grew from six feet two to six feet four, got on a weight program, and saw his fastball go from eighty-four miles per hour to ninety-one. He pitched the clinching game of the College World Series in 1983 and, later that month, signed with the Red Sox, who had made him their number-one draft pick.

Eleven months after that, he was in the major leagues. He was 9-4 that year but was on the disabled list twice in 1985 before finally giving in to shoulder surgery at the end of August. The pain and the surgery scared the hell out of him.

"I kept thinking the pain would go away, that I could just pitch through it," he said. "But it wouldn't quit. I went out to pitch one night in Anaheim and I just couldn't beat it. I got into the runway and just tore my uniform off, I was so frustrated. I can remember sitting outside the locker room that night with [former Red Sox pitcher] Al Nipper and crying. I was devastated and I was scared. I was a power pitcher and I couldn't throw with any power. What was I going to do, become a breaking ball pitcher at twenty-three?"

The surgery corrected things and Clemens has worked hard at arm and shoulder exercises since then. But the memory of the pain and frustration is still vivid. "Right now, the way we're playing is tough to take," he said. "I hate it. I go into the training room and ride the bicycle for an hour most nights before I go home because if I don't exhaust myself completely I won't sleep. But I know things can be worse than they are because I still remember 'eighty-five."

It was in 1986 that Clemens became a superstar, going 24-4, striking out twenty Seattle Mariners one night, winning his first Cy Young Award, and leading the Red Sox to within one strike of winning the World Series. A blister forced him to leave Game Six in the seventh inning with a 3–2 lead. He had to sit and watch as the extraordinary events of that evening, culminating with Buckner's infamous error, unfolded.

"I still have people send me computer printouts on what the odds were of us getting to two strikes with two outs three times and not getting the third strike," he said, forcing a smile. "It still hurts some. Maybe next time, we can just freeze the frame and figure out how to get it right. I'd like to know what it feels like to get that last out."

Since that 1986 season, Clemens has had to deal with the fishbowl life of a superstar athlete. At times, it has not been a comfortable existence. He made headlines when he and his brother were arrested in a Houston bar in 1989; memories of his 1988 play-off confrontation with umpire Terry Cooney still linger (Clemens was ejected—to the nation's shock—after vehemently arguing Cooney's ball and strike calls). He has had his share of blowups with reporters and the *Boston Herald* even started a feature called "The World According to Roger," quotes taken from his postgame comments that, printed verbatim, make Clemens sound like a modern-day Yogi Berra. (Example: "My intensity was really intense tonight.")

Clemens *is* always intense. He talks the way he pitches: fast and hard, the words tumbling out so quickly that sometimes he might repeat himself or speak an imperfect sentence or two. Most of us do that all the time but no one is taking notes or creating a World According To in our honor. He wants to do everything well. In 1986, he took up golf as a way to escape the pressures of the game during the season. Six years later, he is a seven handicap. That means he's talented, but it also means he's worked maniacally at the game.

"The great thing about golf is that I can really get away from things for a few hours," he said. "I used to do that by running through the streets but people actually figured out my running pattern and would wait for me to get autographs or try to talk to me. On the golf course, I can usually hit it far enough into the woods to get some time to myself. 'Course when I do that, I get pissed because I don't like to lose."

That is apparent every time he pitches. When he's healthy, he almost never has a truly bad outing. If he's on, forget it—pack the bats up and try again tomorrow. If he's not on, you still have a long night on your hands; Clemens will battle on every pitch.

"The games that give me the most satisfaction are the ones where I don't have my good fastball or my control isn't quite there and I still find a way to win the game," he said. "You're more likely to see me smiling, walking off the mound, after I give up nine hits and win 4–3 than after a shutout. I think what makes you a great pitcher is finding a way to win on the nights when it isn't easy. There's nothing to it when you have God-given talent and it's all there that night.

"I know I have a certain amount of talent but what I'm proud of is how hard I've worked to develop it. I do little things in my garage that I haven't even told my teammates about because I want every edge there is. I've always taken the approach that there's plenty of time to party in the offseason. During the season, you get the ball maybe thirty-six times and you should make the most of it every single time out. I've become a tedious person, pitching, preparing, pitching, preparing.''

"The way I look at it, what if I go out one day and feel lethargic? There are days when that happens to all of us. But what if there's a guy who's driven a hundred miles to the game with his family and this is the one game they'll see all year and I go out and just pitch lousy and I'm blown away in the third inning? Is that fair to that guy and his family? I don't think it is. I know that sounds corny, but I really feel that way. *That's* what I owe the public, not all the stuff out of uniform, but everything I have when I'm *in* uniform. If baseball was just collecting the check for me, it would have been time to get out long ago.

"When I think of my baseball career, I think of what my mother said to me about being the best at whatever I became. Well, to me, there's one step left and that's the Hall of Fame.

"You pitch in high school, you want to go to college; in college you want to be a pro; you get to the minors, you want to get to the majors. You get up here and you're around for a while, there's one thing left to do. Sometimes, when we're in a crowd and people are pushing and shoving, I look at my little boys [now six and four] and I wonder what they must think of all this. Well, one way to explain it all to them years from now would be to take them to the Hall of Fame. That would mean a lot to me. The game goes on without you, but it's nice to feel like you've left a mark.''

With 152 wins at the age of thirty there's little doubt that Clemens is leaving a mark. Even in a year when things turned completely sour in the Back Bay, Clemens was still worth buying a ticket to see. Even if his team wasn't.

19

UMPS

Baseball's All-Star break lasts three days. It is viewed by most teams and players as some sort of oasis halfway through a long trip in the desert. By mid-June, managers will begin to say things like, "If we can just get to the break at .500." Or, "As long as we're within five at the break, we'll be okay."

For the game's best players, the break is not a break. They must fly from wherever they play on Sunday to the site of the All-Star Game, go through a day of workouts and press conferences and official events on Monday, play the game on Tuesday, and then figure out the best way to rejoin their team in time to play on Thursday.

The 1992 game was further complicated by George Bush's decision to show up. With fifty thousand people descending on a stadium where a president is going to be appearing, the Secret Service, paranoid on its best days, becomes totally crazed.

In this case, they created one of the great gridlocks of modern times: Long before Bush's arrival, they shut off all access roads around the ballpark, making it nearly impossible for people to get into the parking lots. They even went so far as to issue *instructions* to the media on how they were to behave if they happened to come within one thousand miles of the president. Everywhere in the ballpark were areas that were off-limits. The players were given notices by the leagues on how to act when the president came into the clubhouses.

The saddest part of the whole situation was the insistence on the part of Bush's people that he be introduced with Ted Williams.

The entire All-Star festival had been a Williams love-in. San Diego was where the Red Sox great had grown up and now he was coming home a hero to throw out the first ball—except that Bush's people managed to throw cold water on what should have been the warmest moment of all. Because their man was doing horrendously in the polls (he was even behind in nearby arch-conservative Orange County that week), the Bush spin-doctors didn't want him booed lustily in front of a national television audience. So they went to Major League Baseball and insisted that Bush and Williams be introduced *together*. Most of baseball's staff people were horrified: The highlight of the pregame ceremonies was to have been the introduction of Williams.

But Fay Vincent, an old friend and supporter of Bush's, agreed to the plan. So, as the fans were rising to greet Williams at the end of a flowery introduction chronicling his extraordinary career, they were stopped short when the public address announcer said, "And joining Ted Williams is the President of the United States . . ."

The boos thundered down from the stands. Even Williams couldn't rescue Bush. The magic of the moment was lost as Bush, a stunned grin frozen on his face, walked out with Williams.

Oh yes, the American League won for the sixth year in a row, 13–6. The only person who had a worse night than Bush was Tommy Glavine, the National League starter, who gave up seven straight hits in the first inning.

"I should have stayed home," he joked later.

He wasn't the only one.

For everyone else in the sport, there is a respite, but it is brief. It is more the concept of starting over that is important than the actual rest itself. The players, who have seen each other virtually every day since February, actually get a break from the daily routine of the clubhouse or the road. They get to eat dinner with their families and they don't have to check the standings. Everything stands still, if only for a little while.

Even the umpires—except for the six selected for the All-Star Game—get to go home for a few days. No one needs the rest more.

"Things have gotten a lot better for umpires the last few years," said Bruce Froemming, who has been in the National League for twenty-three years. "But most people still don't understand how difficult the job can get, especially the travel. The players are almost always on charters. Their bags are taken care of. So are their hotels. We do everything ourselves. Is that awful? No. It just isn't that easy."

As is the case in most sports, umpires are a fraternity. They know what their brethren are up to and they network constantly. When Cal Ripken, Sr., an umpiring nemesis, was knocked down by a baseball (that the Indians were throwing around the infield following an out) as he charged onto the field to argue a call during a mid-June game in Cleveland, every American League umpire had heard the story within twenty-four hours.

Umpires are more accessible to the media than officials in any sport. If there is a controversy in a game that a reporter wants to ask about, all he has to do is knock on the door of the umpires' room and ask what happened. Most umpires are as accessible before games as the players. They usually ask for privacy only thirty minutes prior to game time—much like the players.

That does not mean they are deep in contemplation of the upcoming contest. How a crew approaches a game usually depends on the crew chief. Froemming is a big believer in never discussing problems at the ballpark. If someone in his crew has made a mistake he will wait until the next day to discuss it with him. When Froemming's in charge, the omnipresent pregame card game may be dealt until seconds before the national anthem.

Other crew chiefs will let whoever is working the plate that night decide on the pregame atmosphere. Rich Garcia, who has been in the American League for eighteen years, is a believer in letting the "plate man" decide what he wants. "That's the guy who's going to have all the pressure," Garcia said. "If he wants the TV on, blaring, he gets it. If he wants it quiet, he gets it."

Garcia is fifty, an ex-marine who grew up in Key West, Florida. He is fourth-generation Cuban and spoke both Spanish and English growing up. Baseball was always his passion, and when he got out of the marines, he got into coaching. At the same time, to pick up some extra money, he began umpiring and refereeing in the Key West area. He did all sports at all levels. In 1970, working a junior college baseball game, he ejected a man named Bill Cates, a local coaching legend. After the game, the coach of the opposing team walked up to Garcia and said, "Anyone with the guts to eject Bill Cates in Key West ought to be a professional umpire."

Garcia was flattered. "You really think so?" he asked.

The coach shook his head. "Well, maybe not," he said. "How tall are you?"

"Five-eight," Garcia answered.

"Too bad," the coach said. "You have to be five-ten to get into umpire's school."

In those days you had to be at least five-ten, a high school graduate, and not wear glasses to get into the umpires' development school. Garcia lied on his application, put lifts in his shoes, and stood up as straight as possible every time a supervisor looked in his direction. He graduated five weeks later and was assigned to the Florida State League. When he went into the league office to sign his contract, George McDonald, Sr., the umpiring supervisor, asked him how tall he was.

"Well, you have to be five-ten," Garcia answered.

"I didn't ask you how tall you *had* to be," McDonald said. "I asked how tall you *are*."

Garcia set his jaw. "My application says I'm five-ten."

McDonald smiled. "Well, I know you aren't five-ten, so I'm putting down that you're five-nine." To this day, Garcia is listed as five feet nine.

Umpires have been closely scrutinized and oft-criticized in recent years. Many people think they have become too aggressive, particularly in not walking away from on-field arguments. In some cases, the scrutinizers believe the umps have *prolonged* the arguments, even when a player or manager has walked away. Some players and managers think that baseball officials have become so cowed by the umpires' union and its very effective leader, Richie Phillips, that they're afraid to discipline umpires who make mistakes. The last three commissioners—Peter Ueberroth, Bart Giamatti, and Fay Vincent—have all been viewed as pro-umpire. The umpires agree with that—and think it's been a long time coming.

"For years, we were treated very poorly," Froemming said. "I think the 1979 strike, when they brought in scabs to work in our place and things were so bad that the players were begging for a resolution, helped our standing. But I also think the last three commissioners, especially Fay Vincent, have really tried hard to make things better for us."

Things *are* better for the umps. These days, a full-time umpire in his first year in the major leagues will make approximately $70,000. The highest-paid crew chiefs make about $150,000. That doesn't begin to compare to what the players make, but it's a long way from what umpires' salaries were in the not-so-distant past.

Froemming, who became a professional umpire at the age of eighteen, made it to the National League in 1971. During his last year in Triple-A, he made $3,200. When he jumped to the majors the next year, he made $10,000. When Garcia reached the majors in 1975, rookie umpires were up to $14,500.

"Things didn't begin to change until the strike," Froemming said. "Before the strike, the highest-paid umpire in baseball was Augie

Donatelli and he made $38,500. It took a lot of ugliness to turn that around. But it was necessary.''

Umpires are far more outspoken than officials in other sports. When Bobby Bonilla was ejected from a June game in Atlanta for arguing with Harry Wendelstedt on a called third strike, Wendelstedt commented after the game that he thought Bonilla wanted to be ejected. When everyone in baseball acted as if the Houston Astros' twenty-six-game road trip was the twentieth-century version of the *Odyssey,* the umpires snickered openly. ''They ought to try eighty-one straight days and see how *that* feels,'' Joe West commented.

Arguments tend to get more personal in baseball, especially after an umpire has ejected someone. At that point, the ejected player or manager has little to lose—so he is likely to really let loose.

Garcia, who was, by his own admission, a little hot-tempered when he first got to the big leagues, remembers ejecting Dick Williams during his second major league game behind the plate. Garcia was working in a crew that included Armando Rodriguez, the first Latin umpire to work in the majors. Williams and Rodriguez had never gotten along. As Williams turned to leave he said to Garcia, ''I'm sick and tired of you fucking Latin umpires!''

''I'm more American than you are!'' Garcia yelled back.

''Like hell you are!'' Williams screamed. ''You never served this country!''

''I sure as hell did!''

''Oh yeah, well I was a marine!''

''So was I!''

Fifteen years later, Garcia ran into Williams at a party. ''He introduced me to his wife and said, 'Rich was in the marines, you know.' He had a big grin on his face. All the arguments he was in, I couldn't believe he still remembered that one.''

Garcia was in his share of arguments during his early years as an umpire. In fact, he ejected *seven* people during his first two plate jobs. He was a very aggressive umpire, perhaps too aggressive. ''Part of it was some of the managers you worked with back then,'' he said. ''You had guys like Earl Weaver, Billy Martin, Dick Williams, Sparky [Anderson] when he was younger, who would try to intimidate you. If you didn't let 'em know that you weren't gonna back down from them, you were in trouble.''

Weaver, the longtime Baltimore manager, was one of the great umpire-baiters of all time. Garcia remembers throwing him out of a game in Oakland one time only to have Jim Marshall, the A's manager, come out and tell him that Weaver was still in the dugout.

''I went over looking for him and he wasn't there,'' he said. ''Suddenly I noticed Frank Robinson and Lee May standing in front of the bathroom door, arms folded, trying to look casual. I went over there and pushed the door open. No Earl. Then I saw some smoke. He was tucked in under the sink smoking a cigarette. I had to go in there and pull him out.''

Garcia says he has learned from his mistakes over the years, and that managers don't try to intimidate the way they used to. He has also learned to deal with situations more calmly. He was quite proud of the fact that he didn't have a single ejection in 1991. As a crew chief, he now finds himself in the role of peacemaker and big brother. Early in the 1992 season, Tim Welke, one of his crew members, got into a shouting match with Cleveland manager Mike Hargrove. Angry at some bench jockeying, Welke took off his mask and screamed at Hargrove about what a lousy team he had. Hargrove charged out of the dugout and was met by Garcia.

"That's wrong, he can't say that,'' Hargrove said.

"I know,'' Garcia said. "You're right. I'll take care of it.''

Hargrove left without further incident. That night at dinner, Welke looked at Garcia and said, "I screwed up today, didn't I?''

"Yeah, you did,'' Garcia answered. "You never pick on the guy who's down in this business. These guys are working their ass off just like we are and they're frustrated. You know how tough things are in this town.''

Welke nodded. "You're right. I'll apologize to Mike tomorrow.''

Garcia was pleased with that response. "You should never apologize unless you really feel it in your gut,'' he says. "Doing it because you think it will quiet a guy down is wrong. Doing it because you aren't sure is wrong. But if your gut tells you it's the right thing to do, then you should do it. The reason Tim Welke is a hell of an umpire is because he had the right gut feeling without me saying a word.''

Umpires are taught to react not only to what they see and hear but to what they feel in their gut. That's why ejections sometimes happen so quickly: An umpire feels he must do something to get the game—or a team—under control. They also happen quickly when a player or manager drops the now-famous magic word—motherfucker.

"A guy curses me, he's gone, simple as that,'' Froemming says. "I don't see any need to take that kind of abuse. Someone has a problem with a call and they want to discuss it, that's okay, but a guy curses me, that's it.''

Froemming is one of the most popular umpires—and people—in the game. He is short and chunky and outgoing. As with most people who are good at what they do, there is no doubt that he loves his work.

"The travel beats you down,'' he said one night in Philadelphia. "Thank God they let us fly first-class now and we get a three-week vacation during the season. When I was younger, before any of that, you'd get to September you were so tired you could barely stand up. And that meant you weren't doing your best work on the games that mattered the most.

"Even now, you get wiped out at times. The games are longer now and sometimes if you try to sneak home on an offday, you're even more tired when you get back because you've added another day of flying. But the games make it worthwhile. We all love baseball and to be a part of it is a great thing."

Froemming got a rest he hadn't counted on or wanted during the 1992 season. In early June, he took a stress test as part of his annual physical and was shocked when the doctor told him there was a 98-percent blockage in the main artery leading to his heart. He recommended an angioplasty to open up the blockage. On June 15, Froemming checked into Lenox Hill Hospital in New York and had the procedure done. He was surprised—and touched—by the reaction of the baseball world.

"It was amazing," he said. "People came by, called, sent flowers, the whole works. Partners [Froemming refers to other umpires as his partners] called from all over the country. It was the kind of thing that made you feel good."

On the day after the procedure, Froemming received flowers from Mets co-owner Nelson Doubleday. The card said: "Checked upstairs and you don't have any reservations, so everything must be all right." The next day, a second bouquet arrived from Doubleday. This time the note said: "Checked downstairs and, while they're quite familiar with you, there are still no reservations in your name."

Froemming was in the hospital for a week and back at work in seventeen days, relieved and happy to be back with his partners doing what he loves to do.

Do umpires hold grudges?

"No, absolutely not," Froemming said. "You can't afford to. You wouldn't survive."

That may be true, but umpires are human—and they have memories. Proof of that can be found in an incident involving Cal Ripken, Jr., and umpire Drew Coble. During a game in Toronto in August, Coble and Junior—who had had run-ins before—argued over a called third strike. On the television replay, which Coble didn't have the benefit of seeing, the pitch looked to be at Ripken's ankles.

Ripken, in the middle of one of the worst slumps of his career, stood and stared at Coble for a moment. "You can't possibly believe you got that one right," he said.

"Yes I do," Coble answered. "It was a good pitch."

Ripken continued to argue briefly before walking slowly to the dugout. Once in the dugout, Ripken put his bat down and turned back to Coble. "One of us has to be wrong, Drew," he said. "I guess it must be me."

Was there some sarcasm in Ripken's voice? Probably. The smart thing for Coble to do would have been to point to Jack Morris and tell him to throw the next pitch. Instead, Coble took off his mask and charged back toward the dugout, screaming at Ripken. At that stage, manager Johnny Oates, not wanting his shortstop ejected, intervened. He leaped out of the dugout to meet Coble before the ump and his shortstop could exchange any more words.

What Coble said next could be seen clearly by anyone watching television who had even a cursory ability to read lips. "You tell that motherfucker to shut up . . ."

Oates, a devout man who almost never uses profanity, couldn't allow Coble's comment to pass. He screamed back at Coble and got himself ejected. He was still upset after the game, as was Ripken. "I went out there because I didn't want Junior ejected," Oates explained. "What he [Coble] said was unacceptable."

The next afternoon, seeking solitude, Ripken spent some time underneath the stands in an area where players can hit a ball off a tee into a batting cage. He was swinging left-handed, hoping that by reminding himself how hard it was to swing lefty, he would convince himself that by comparison, swinging righty was easy.

As Ripken swung at ball after ball, Coble and his crew arrived at their dressing room a few feet away. Hearing footsteps, Ripken turned just as Coble reached the door of the umpires' dressing room. He looked right at Coble for a moment. Coble froze and looked right back. No words were exchanged, just hard "I'm not backing down from you" looks. Finally, Coble followed the other umpires inside.

"What bothered me about the whole thing was that he wouldn't even concede that he might have missed the pitch," Ripken said later in the season. "Umpires miss pitches just like I miss pitches that I should hit. So if a guy says to me, 'I called it too quick,' or 'Maybe I missed it,' what can I say back to him? But he was so insistent that it wasn't even *possible* he was wrong. I don't like to argue with an umpire unless I'm one hundred thousand percent sure I'm right. Because if I argue and then go back and find out later I was wrong, I feel terrible."

Did Ripken worry that Coble held a grudge? "It's the kind of thing you can't afford to worry about. If I start thinking that *any* umpire is holding a grudge against me, it'll affect me."

In other words, Ripken is too smart to say that an umpire can hold a grudge. But they do. They do not—as José Canseco claimed during the '92 season—call one another and say, "Get that guy," but they do talk to each other about those athletes who are "problems." Umpires don't like players who show them up—Rickey Henderson is one who does it often—and they don't like bench jockeys who don't know when to quit.

More often than not, though, umpires are hardworking men who love what they do and want to do the job well. They respect the players and ask for the same respect in return. Another Coble incident is an example of how the game works when things are done correctly. .

During a game in Anaheim in July, Jack Morris gave up five runs in the bottom of the fifth inning, turning a 3–0 lead into a 5–3 deficit. He finally appeared to be out of the inning when Junior Felix hit a routine ground ball to second base. Seeing the ground ball, Morris began jogging to the dugout with his head down. As he did, he accidentally bumped Felix, who was running the ground ball out, and threw him off stride for a split second.

Felix was out by a step at first base but Coble, the home plate umpire, followed the play down the line and saw Morris obstruct Felix. He correctly awarded him first base. Morris was already in the dugout and didn't even see Coble make the call. When Coble went over to tell him that he had to come back to the mound, Morris went crazy.

"He started screaming at me that it was a horseshit call to make," Coble said after the game. "I told him, no, he was the one who was in a horseshit position. He kept screaming at me that I was horseshit and I got mad at him and said, 'Look, I'm working my ass off for you behind the plate so don't give me any more shit.' "

By then, manager Cito Gaston had arrived in the role of peace-maker, telling his pitcher to get back on the mound and pitch and trying to calm Coble down too. Morris finally got the third out and the Blue Jays—as they often did for him throughout the season—rallied and won the game, 9–5. After it was over, Gaston went looking for Coble.

"I told him I was sorry about what had happened," he said. "Jack was wrong and he was right. Jack made a mistake. And I also told him that I thought he really did do a good job behind the plate and didn't let the incident affect him. I meant it, too."

Coble was appreciative. "We do try to work hard for the players," he said. "Jack was frustrated and he made a mistake. I had to make the call. For Cito to come over and say what he did was a classy thing to do. All we ask of the players is that they be fair with us because we're trying to be fair with them."

Most of the time, umpires *are* fair. And an amazingly high percentage of the time they are right—as instant reply has proven. But sometimes they are too sensitive and some—not all—have trouble admitting mistakes. That was apparent during the World Series when both Jim Joyce and Bob Davidson made glaring errors.

Davidson made a call that cost the Blue Jays the first World Series triple play in seventy-two years—and he willingly admitted the next day that he'd missed the call. Joyce, on the other hand, called Roberto Alomar out on a play at the plate when he was clearly safe—and continued to insist that Alomar had been out.

More often than not, umpires get along with players and managers. In 1992, when American League ump John Hirschbeck was faced with huge medical bills after his two young sons were stricken with a rare and debilitating genetic disease, a group of managers put together an offseason auction to raise money for the family. Many players agreed to fly into Chicago for the day while other players and managers from both leagues volunteered their help.

One of the managers involved in organizing the day was Tony LaRussa, who has had as many battles with the umpires as anyone. "Let's face it," LaRussa said. "Everyone in baseball has two things in common: We love the game and, if we're lucky enough to have them, we love our kids. Those things go beyond whether a pitch is a ball or a strike."

20

MASCOTS

I t has been a long drought in Philadelphia. Since the Phillies won their last pennant in 1983, the club has finished over .500 just once—in 1986—and most of those years it has been out of the pennant race long before the All-Star break. In fact, in that one winning season, when the Phils were 86-75, they were out of the pennant race just as early as in other years because the Mets ran away from the division before July was over and ended up winning 108 games.

The 1992 season was more of the same. Injuries devastated the pitching staff very early. Starter José DeJesus went out for the entire season while fellow starter Tommy Greene was out *almost* the entire season. Even though Terry Mulholland and Curt Schilling pitched well through most of the summer, they weren't nearly enough. Closer Mitch Williams, coming off a superb 1991, was inconsistent throughout '92. During one amazing stretch, he threw 282 pitches in thirteen innings, meaning he went to 3-2 on just about every batter he faced. Center fielder Lenny Dykstra broke a wrist on Opening Day and didn't really start to hit until midseason.

"I spent all winter trying to quit smoking," said manager Jim Fregosi, in the raspy voice of a man who has been a chain-smoker his entire adult life. "I didn't touch a cigarette for months. Then on Opening Day, Dykstra breaks his wrist and I had to put Williams in the game to pitch." He held up a cigarette. "I started again that day."

The Phillies were not without stars. Darren Daulton ended up leading the league in RBIs and John Kruk led the league in hitting for more than half the season. Dykstra, when healthy, was one of the game's best leadoff hitters and Mulholland, Schilling, and a third young starter, Ben Rivera, certainly gave the team hope for the future.

But for the fifteenth straight season, there was little doubt about who turned in the best performance night in and night out in Veterans Stadium: David Raymond. Well, actually it wasn't David Raymond, it was his alter ego, a giant green bird described in the Phillie media guide as "6 feet, 300 pounds, mostly fat."

David Raymond is the Phillie Phanatic. Or the Phanatic is Raymond. Sometimes it's difficult to tell which came first. Raymond himself gets confused at times. Several years ago, while making an appearance at a shopping mall, the Phanatic accidentally broke a plate glass window in the front of one of the stores. The police came and filled out a report. The Phanatic signed it, finished his act, and went in the back of one of the stores to change back to Raymond. When he came outside, the cop who had taken the report was waiting for him.

"Hey buddy, you signed this report 'Phillie Phanatic,' " he told Raymond. "We need your real name."

"But officer, I didn't break the window," Raymond protested. "The Phanatic did."

The Phanatic is, without question, baseball's best and funniest mascot—and is also one of the reasons the Phillies have continued to draw close to two million fans a year even with such mediocre teams. When you go to a game at Veterans Stadium, the Phanatic makes you laugh. He'll do it by coming out with a Deion Sanders doll and beating it up while the PA plays "Too Legit to Quit," the signature song of Sanders's buddy Hammer. He'll do it by sticking his stomach out at opposing players who won't play catch with him. Or he'll do it just by getting on the motorcycle the Phanatic rides around the ballpark.

The Phanatic is never boring. One of his biggest fans is Fregosi, an ex-ballplayer turned manager who would unhesitatingly describe himself as a baseball purist and traditionalist. Mascots are supposed to offend the senses of baseball purists and traditionalists.

"The guy is a hell of an athlete," Fregosi said. "He works at what he does, he's in great shape, and he's funny. He's good for the game."

He *is* a good athlete. Raymond, blond and as slender as the Phanatic is portly, still looks like he could punt for the University of Delaware, which he did—for a thirty-eight-yard-per-kick average—while playing there from 1975 to 1978.

The Phanatic was born in 1978 when the Phillies marketing department, encouraged by the success of Ted Giannoulis as the San Diego Chicken, decided to come up with a mascot. Raymond, who was finishing his junior year at the University of Delaware, had worked as an intern in marketing the previous summer. He was hoping to work for the Phillies again when promotions director Frank Sullivan called him.

"Actually, Chris Legault [Sullivan's assistant] called me first and said, 'Frank wants to talk to you about something and I want you to promise me you'll say no.' I had no idea what she was talking about but she kept saying, 'Just promise me you'll say no.' I said, 'Fine, I'll say no.'

"She said, 'You promise?' And I said, 'Yes, I promise.'

"So she put me through to Frank and he said, 'David, we've decided to have a mascot this year and we want you to do it.' And I said, 'Fine, great, I'd love to.' "

Raymond still kids Legault about what he would have missed if he'd kept his promise. "She was concerned that it was going to be something silly and I'd end up getting hurt by having people make fun of me," he says.

Of course it *was* something silly and people *do* make fun of him. But the Phanatic has been a star from the day he made his debut on April 25, 1978. He was named after the Phillies' marketing slogan for that season: "Become a Phillies Phanatic." Initially the plan was to give the Phanatic a name, but it was scrapped when the character became so popular so quickly.

The costume was designed by Bonnie Erickson, who had done many of the Muppet designs for Jim Henson. In many ways the Phanatic, with his huge nose, purple eyelashes, and bulging stomach, resembles a Muppet. There is no question that the costume is part of the reason the Phanatic works: Look at the costume and you laugh.

It was the costume that caused Raymond's father, Tubby, the longtime Delaware football coach, to make his now-famous comment about how the Phanatic changed his life. "Once, I was Tubby Raymond, football coach, University of Delaware," he said. "Now I'm the father of a giant green transvestite."

But the Phanatic, Raymond quickly points out, has a girlfriend.

"From the first day, the thing just took off," he said. "I mean it was as if the Phanatic was a rock star. That initial reaction, I think, was the costume. Then, after a while, he began to develop a personality."

He also learned to stay out of the upper deck. Since the Phanatic is supposed to be some kind of bird, customers in the upper deck sometimes wonder if the Phanatic can fly. "And, after four or five beers, there are always going to be some people who want to throw the Phanatic out of the upper deck to find out," Raymond said.

The Phanatic's personality—feisty, curious, occasionally arrogant—is Raymond's creation. He started out making twenty-five dollars a game and five dollars an hour for outside appearances. To a college senior that seemed like huge money. Now, at thirty-six, Raymond makes $150,000 a year plus another $10,000 to $15,000 annually for appearances (he sends a backup to do appearances on game days). He is absolutely worth every penny. And, like most athletes, he must deal with the fact that the end is in sight for him.

"Oh yeah, I'm very aware of that," he said one night, relaxing in his tiny dressing room, the Phanatic's head looming over the couch he was stretched out on as if listening to the conversation. "Each winter, it's a little bit harder to do all the work I have to do to stay in shape. I do all this jumping off of things and falling down and running around. It beats you up. I hope I'm not one of those guys they have to tear the uniform off. I don't want them wheeling me out one day or something like that. I hope I can do it a couple more years because I still love it. I mean, why grow up if you don't have to? But I don't want to stay too long."

The Phanatic has had his share of controversial moments. When Lonnie Smith was with the Phillies, Raymond developed a routine in which he would fall down and get up, fall down and get up. It was based largely on the trouble Smith often had staying on his feet in the outfield, trouble that earned him the nickname "Skates."

No one laughed harder at the routine than Lonnie Smith. But in 1983, when Smith was with the Cardinals, Raymond did the routine one night and looked up to find Smith charging at him, screaming hysterically. "He crashed into me full-bore, hurt my knee and my ankle," Raymond said. "It was the worst I've been injured since I started doing this. [He has missed seven games in fifteen years.] I couldn't figure out what had gotten into him. After the game, he came to see me and said he was really sorry, he didn't know what had happened, that he had just snapped. I looked into his eyes and thought, 'This guy's on something.' Two weeks later, he checked into rehab."

Raymond also had trouble with umpire Bob Engel. From the beginning, Raymond has been careful about making fun of the umpires. He does follow them around when they come onto the field; he will often clown with them between innings and he will make fun of those who are overweight. But he never incites the crowd or makes fun of a bad call. He doesn't use the old Chicken-eye chart (to check the ump's vision) or offer anyone glasses. Sometimes, he'll even hold his hands up to try and stop booing.

"My first year Doug Harvey sat me down and explained to me what I could and couldn't do with the umpires," he said. "He understood that I wanted them in the routine and I think most of them understand that when they clown around with me it makes them more human to the fans too. So, I'm always careful. But one night I was carrying water to the umpires between innings and I tripped [on purpose] and spilled water on Bob Engel's shoes. He went crazy. He called me in after the game and called me every name in the book and told me never was I to include him or anyone in his crew in my act again. So, I didn't."

Several years after the incident, Engel was caught shoplifting and lost his job.

There was also the aforementioned run-in with Tommy Lasorda—when Lasorda went berserk over the Phanatic's manhandling of the sacred Dodger doll—which still baffles Raymond; he had thought he and Lasorda were friends. "I tried to make it up to him even though he cursed me out again *after* the game," he said. "The next time they were in, I found out what his favorite restaurant in town was and I got them to deliver dinner to him before the game. I never heard from him. Finally, on the field, I asked him if he got the dinner I had sent him. He said, 'Yeah, I did. It was cold.' After that I just figured the hell with him."

And then, in 1992, there was Bruce Froemming. Of all the umpires, Raymond says he enjoys working with Froemming the most; it's obvious that Froemming has a sense of humor and enjoys the routines. Early in August, Froemming's crew came to town for a series against the Expos.

The first game was routine, the Expos winning easily. Late in the game, as he often does, the Phanatic climbed on top of the Philadelphia dugout and tried to throw hexes at the Montreal pitchers. They didn't work. The next night, Froemming arrived at the ballpark fuming.

"He went too far last night," he said to his partners. "That bullshit up on the dugout, getting on us like that. I don't like it and I'm going to tell him he better not do it again."

He turned to Kevin Steinhour, who runs the visitors' clubhouse and takes care of the umpires at Veterans Stadium. "Tell the Phanatic I want to see him."

A few minutes later the phone rang. "Bruce, it's David Raymond," said Jeff Kellogg, who was working on Froemming's crew that weekend.

"Who the hell is David Raymond?" Froemming demanded. Like a lot of people, Froemming has no idea who the Phanatic is when he isn't in costume. When he was told who Raymond was, Froemming stalked to the phone.

"Now listen up, David, I want to talk to you because we're friends," Froemming began. "See, I think you're going too far with this stuff on the dugout. I don't like you getting on us for balls and strikes and stuff. That's too far and you should know that.''

Raymond tried to explain he wasn't getting on the umpires, but on the opposing pitcher. Froemming broke in. ''Listen, David, I'm just telling you, don't mess with us. If you do, I'm gonna crush you like a fucking grape.''

He was angry now. Raymond was also angry—and confused. He hung up the phone and walked down the hall from his dressing room to the umpires' room. ''Bruce, I don't want to upset you, but I really think you misunderstood what I was doing,'' he said.

Froemming doesn't stay mad for long. This time, he listened to Raymond. They shook hands and Raymond was extra careful for the rest of the series about what he did with the umpires. ''Sometimes, you gotta remind guys not to go too far,'' Froemming said later. ''He's a good kid. He just needed a talking to.''

Raymond didn't see it quite that way. ''Sometimes, guys just don't have a sense of humor,'' he said. ''What's weird is, Bruce *does* have one. I'm not really sure what happened that night, but I think we're okay now.''

Raymond is very okay. The Phanatic has become the one thing the Phillies have going for them year in and year out. He has conducted the Philadelphia Pops and gotten his hair cut in a cameo appearance in the Broadway show *Shear Madness*. The Phanatic even has groupies. One groupie asked Raymond to autograph her breasts one night. He refused. ''Of course, the Phanatic probably would have done it,'' he conceded, laughing.

But Raymond has never gotten caught up in the fanaticism over the Phanatic. ''Every once in a while, maybe you start to think you're a star or someone important,'' he said. ''But there's always something that happens to bring you back to earth. A couple months ago I was asked to speak at my church. I thought that was very nice but I wondered exactly what I would say to all these people.

''Well, I brought the Phanatic's head with me to give people an idea of what the costume looked like and how I put it on and where I could see from [under the nose] and all that. I talked a little about my work and how much I liked working with kids and about my faith and what role it played in my life. All the usual stuff. Then I answered questions for a while.

''Everyone was very nice. But towards the end I noticed this older couple. They looked like they were arguing about something. Finally, the woman kind of pushed her husband aside and got up to ask a question. She said, 'Young man, you've been very nice and I'm sure you're a fine person but I have a question and I know quite a few of my friends are wondering about this, too.'

''And I said, 'Yes, ma'am, what is it?'

"And she said, 'Well, it's just that we have absolutely no idea who you are or what exactly it is that you do.'

"Before I could try to answer, her husband started screaming at her, 'Mildred, I already told you, he's the Phillies Phanatic out at the ballpark!'

"And she said, 'Dear, I already told *you*, I don't know anything about football.' And he screamed, '*Baseball, Mildred, I told you it was baseball!*' "

Does Raymond expect them to give him a day when he retires?

"Absolutely not," he said. "Because the Phanatic won't be retiring. It's just like baseball. Players leave and the game goes on. I'll leave and the Phanatic will go on."

Perhaps so. But in all likelihood, the Phanatic won't be quite the same without Raymond around. His uniform *will* be difficult to fill.

21

THE MEDIA

In the fourth game of the 1985 World Series, John Tudor pitched a four-hit shutout for the St. Louis Cardinals, giving his team a 3–1 lead over the Kansas City Royals.

As soon as the game was over, Tudor was ushered down a hallway into a curtained-off area underneath Busch Stadium; it had been designated as the interview room for the Series. For several minutes he answered the kinds of perfunctory questions that are endemic to such situations: What kind of stuff did you have? Were you surprised to pitch so well on three days' rest? Do you feel comfortable with a 3–1 lead? Will you be ready to pitch a seventh game if needed?

Tudor's answers were as perfunctory as the questions. The interview room serves two purposes at the World Series: It feeds a few quick, easy quotes to deadline-pressed writers who, because of the late-night starts, often stay in the press box and listen to the quotes as they are piped upstairs; and it gives TV and radio people immediate audio and video feeds for their stations.

Those who are looking for more go to the clubhouses. There, they talk to other players and wait for the stars of the game to return from the interview room so they can ask them more in-depth questions. When Tudor finished on this particular night, he walked back to the Cardinal clubhouse and found about fifteen writers standing by his locker waiting for him. John Tudor's story, his rise from journeyman left-hander with the Red Sox to twenty-one-game winner and postseason star with the Cardinals, was one many writers wanted to tell.

Tudor wanted no part of it. "What does it take to get a press pass around here, a driver's license?" he snarled when he saw what awaited him. "I already talked in the interview room."

Gordon Edes, then of the *Los Angeles Times,* stepped forward on behalf of his colleagues to try to explain to Tudor that this was the World Series and there were probably people out there in America who might want to know more about Tudor than what kind of curveball he thought he had that night.

Tudor glared at Edes for a moment, then turned to the other writers and said, "Do you guys really think I'm going to answer questions from a schmo like this?"

Before anyone could answer or step up to defend Edes—who is one of the best there is at what he does and a long way from being a schmo—a radio guy thrust a microphone at Tudor and asked some innocuous question about what a great bunch of guys the Cardinals were. Tudor smiled and happily answered the question. Then he went to take a shower. For those few writers who had time to wait that out, he did answer a few more questions. But almost everyone who tried to talk to Tudor walked out of the clubhouse that night empty-handed. Or, at least, empty-notebooked.

Tudor later apologized to Edes for the schmo crack. Three nights later, he did have to pitch a seventh game. He was shelled in the second inning and came into the dugout so upset that he smashed his hand against a small wall fan in the corner. When word filtered up to the press box explaining that Tudor had been hurt—and how his injury had occurred—Barry Bloom of the San Diego *Union/Tribune* shook his head and said, "Now the shit really *has* hit the fan."

That line has been repeated in baseball press boxes for seven years. It's a funny line—but it also goes a long way toward explaining the sometimes friendly, often uneasy, frequently adversarial relationship that exists between the baseball media and the people they cover.

"Baseball is the one sport left where the media has influence," says Peter Gammons, the ESPN commentator and *Boston Globe* columnist who, along with Murray Chass of *The New York Times,* probably knows more baseball people than anyone. "The reason we still have influence is that we have access. We can still find out what's really going on. A lot of the time, that's going to piss people off."

In professional football, coaches exert strict control over media access. Many locker rooms are closed on practice days or only opened

for brief periods of time. Practices are often closed or, if they *are* open
to local media, it is only after agreements are made that any new plays,
any fights or outbursts by coaches will not be written about.

Professional basketball is, generally speaking, more accessible
than football, but coaches will close practices, and with only twelve
players on a team, they can gag their players far more easily than a
baseball manager can. Occasionally a disgruntled player will speak up
in basketball, but not all that often.

Baseball is the one sport in which the media is in the clubhouse
every single day for long periods of time. Until recently, clubhouses
were closed to the media *only* during the forty-five minutes prior to a
game, during the game itself (except in spring training), and for a
ten-minute cooling-off period immediately after the game. Recently,
the rule has been changed. Now the media is kept out until three-and-
a-half hours before game time. This may sound minor, but often writers do their best work when they arrive five or six hours early and have
time to talk to early-arriving players.

Not all teams enforce the three-and-a-half-hour rule and even on
those that do, talking to most players is still fairly easy to do. But there
are tensions about media access. Many players deeply resent the
constant presence of reporters in the clubhouse.

"All they want to do is stand around and try and spy on you," says
the Mets' Eddie Murray, who will never be voted any Good Guy
awards by reporters.

Reporters *do* stand around baseball clubhouses. But it isn't for the
purpose of spying. Often players will take advantage of the many
off-limits areas: training rooms, player lounges, eating areas, weight
rooms—to avoid reporters.

If a reporter wants to talk to someone specific, he or she will often
find himself (or herself) doing nothing but standing around waiting for
the player to appear in an area where he can be approached. Most
reporters *hate* lingering in clubhouses—but they soon come to understand it is a big part of the job.

The best thing about covering baseball is its informality. More
often than not, a reporter can show up in a clubhouse and talk to
almost any player for a few minutes. If you need a longer interview, the
best approach is to see if the player has free time the next day or the
day after that.

It is here that the informality can become a problem. Sure, the
player will say, tomorrow would be fine. The reporter will ask for a
specific time. The player will give him one and then, almost without
fail, arrive forty-five minutes or an hour or—as once happened with
Kevin Mitchell—two-and-a-half hours after the appointed time. The
reporter has no choice but to be on time—and then wait.

What bothers baseball people the most about the media is that it is almost impossible to keep secrets from them. The season is so long and there are so many people in a clubhouse, nothing stays secret for long. If a player is feuding with another player or with the manager, it's going to come out. Someone is going to tell.

And it is going to make headlines. In baseball, where there are 162 regular season games, the stories *around* the games often become more interesting than the games themselves. If Carlton Fisk and Gene Lamont have a shouting match, it's going to make the papers. If Johnny Oates is upset because Glenn Davis has gone to a doctor other than the Orioles team doctor, it's going to make the papers. If the Blue Jays think that Kelly Gruber is dogging it, it will be in print.

As the season wears on, everyone gets tired. Baseball players see the beat writers who cover them close to two hundred days a year, starting in February and ending in October. It's only natural that there will be days when they don't want to answer questions. There are also days when the writers don't want to *ask* questions. But they have to: Someone back home wants answers.

"You learn after a while that most of the guys are good guys who are just trying to do a job," says Don Mattingly of the Yankees, whose relationship with the New York media has ebbed and flowed over the years. "Part of your job is to talk to them. But you also have to learn to say no to things because if you don't, you won't have time to get your work done. They have to understand when it's time to do your job. Most of the time, they do."

Cal Ripken's relationship with the Baltimore media has often been tenuous. During 1992, as he fought through his slump and the ongoing questions about his contract, Ripken began showing up in the clubhouse later and later for home games. The Orioles are due on the field to stretch before night games at five o'clock. By July, Ripken was showing up at 4:45 most days, giving him just enough time to get in uniform and onto the field.

Bobby Bonilla, who arrived in New York swearing that he would be accessible no matter what and wouldn't ever be bothered by anything people said or wrote about him, was one of the leaders of the Mets' media boycott—which took place before spring training was over. By July he was giving television interviews blaming the New York print media for his mediocre performance.

One player who has always seemed to understand the role of the media is David Cone, the ex-Met turned Blue Jay turned Royal. When Cone was subjected to one cruel joke after another in the aftermath of the lawsuit filed against him by the two groupies in March, he not only remained accessible to the media, he joked with them about his situation.

"I've always found that if you're honest with guys and don't take yourself too seriously, they'll treat you well," Cone says. "The guys I see have problems are the ones who try to throw bullshit at them or lie. They'll see through it most of the time and will resent you for it."

Things can get pretty tense over the course of a long season. The Mets' situation with the rape charges was the most obvious and difficult case in 1992, but there were others. Cito Gaston virtually cut himself off from most of the Toronto media during the second half of the season. Rickey Henderson announced on three separate occasions that he would not talk to the media anymore. He even drew "off-limits" lines around his locker.

Some teams have gone so far in recent years as to hire Andrea Kirby, a former TV reporter who is now a media consultant, to counsel their players on how to deal with reporters. Kirby's sessions—usually conducted during spring training—are, generally speaking, a more sophisticated version of Crash Davis's famous speech to Nuke La-Loosh in *Bull Durham* about how to deal with the media when he got to the Show: Always give credit to God and your teammates; never say anything bad about the opposition; look squarely into the camera and smile; and never say anything controversial.

Kirby sometimes uses real reporters to ask the questions during the mock interviews that are part of the sessions. She pays the reporters for taking part and also makes them sign affidavits promising never to repeat anything that they see or hear.

One person Kirby did have a positive effect on was Tom Kelly. The Twins' manager had little patience for silly questions and never hesitated to let the questioner know that. Questions can get particularly idiotic during postseason because a lot of writers who don't normally cover baseball do cover it then.

Kirby taught Kelly how to smile no matter how foolish the question, as well as how to give a pablum answer and move on without betraying his real thoughts. Now Kelly, one of the sharper, funnier people in the game, is also one of the more popular managers with the media.

Managers have to deal with the media more than anyone. Every day they are expected to sit down with their beat writers both before and after the game. Many new managers find this responsibility draining, especially on their time management. Most could spend four hours doing interviews every day if they chose to. None do because they can't afford to.

Generally, they set aside a time every day before batting practice. Tony LaRussa, whose team has as many reporters traveling with it as the New York teams do, will talk before BP begins; if there's anyone who has leftover questions he will talk to them while he hits fungoes.

Each manager has a different routine. Jeff Torborg did pregame and postgame radio shows in 1992. He was so roundly criticized for spending so much time on the radio that he canceled his pregame show for '93. His counterpart in New York, Buck Showalter, a Mississippi State graduate, read a school newsletter early in the season in which football coach Jackie Sherrill laid out his strategy for dealing with the media. One of Sherrill's recommendations was always to use the name of whomever you are talking to when answering a question because it would create a more friendly atmosphere. Showalter took that advice so seriously that he once called Yankee broadcaster Michael Kay "Mike" fourteen times during a five-minute pregame show.

Little things can easily become big during the course of a season. Early in 1992, Johnny Oates decided he wanted his team to have an extra five minutes of privacy before infield practice every night. So he decreed that the clubhouse would be cleared fifty minutes before each game, even though baseball's rules say forty-five. (Oates is not, by any means, the only manager to bend the media rules: The Tigers have signs posted that say their clubhouse is closed until three hours before game time and not open until fifteen minutes afterward; signs in both Comiskey Park clubhouses say the media must be out one hour before game time. These may sound like minor infringements but in an era when tracking down a player may take considerable time before a game, the extra five, ten, or thirty minutes can make a big difference.)

When Oates had signs posted saying that the clubhouse and dugout had to be cleared fifty minutes before game time, Peter Schmuck of the Baltimore *Sun,* the local chairman of the Baseball Writers' Association of America, pointed out the forty-five-minute rule to Oates. The two men, both mild-mannered and reasonable most of the time, ended up in a shouting match. *A shouting match over five minutes.* A compromise was finally reached: Oates would get his fifty minutes but, in return, those writers who did want to show up more than three-and-a-half hours prior to a game would have clubhouse access then.

That worked fine until later in the season when, with the Orioles in a pennant race, writers needed every minute they could find in the clubhouse. Jimmy Tyler, the Orioles' longtime clubhouse man, thought that 6:40 was the correct time to clear the writers out before a 7:30 game. But the official starting time for games in Baltimore is 7:35. When Tyler tried to kick Schmuck out of the clubhouse one night at 6:40 while Schmuck was in the middle of an interview, Schmuck pointed out that he had five minutes left.

It should be noted that most clubhouse men have little use for reporters. They see them as interlopers who make life difficult for the players they are paid to make life easy for. Reporters, on the other hand, view the clubhouse man as the second-to-last guy they want to have angry at them (the traveling secretary is last since he can make life on the road 1,000 percent easier for a reporter). Players are so dependent on the clubhouse man that if he's angry with a reporter, the players are likely to be angry with him too. In Atlanta, Bill Acree is the traveling secretary *and* the clubhouse man—which makes Governor Zell Miller the *second* most powerful man in Georgia.

When Schmuck told Tyler he had five more minutes, Tyler shook his head, pointed to his watch and said, "Six-forty, time to go."

"No Jim, we have until six-forty-five," Schmuck said. "The game is at seven-thirty-five. I've discussed this with Johnny."

"I don't care what Johnny says!" Tyler said, angry now because Schmuck was implying that someone had more authority than he did.

Schmuck could see he was going to lose the battle—and his interview—so he went and found Oates to try to win the war. Oates took Tyler aside and explained to him that 6:45 was, in fact, the deadline. Tyler was *not* happy. Neither was Schmuck. The players found the whole thing highly amusing.

Perhaps the whole confusing morass of baseball-media relationships was best summed up late in the season in Milwaukee. The Oakland Athletics were there, playing the Brewers, and scheduled a team dinner in a local restaurant. If the Minnesota Twins lost their game that night, the A's would clinch the Western Division title. If that happened, they all wanted to be together.

Traveling secretary Mickey Morabito gave the Bay Area writers the name of the restaurant and told them to show up near the end of the game if it looked like the Twins were going to lose.

"In other words, Mick," San Jose columnist Bud Geracie said, "you guys don't want us around until the last possible minute, right?"

Morabito grinned. "You know we love you guys," he said. "We just like to love you in small doses."

22

NEW KIDS
ON THE BLOCK

There was no doubt about who the two men in baseball most in need of a midseason break were: Dave Dombrowski and Bob Gebhard. They were the game's general-managers-in-waiting, two men who had franchises, staffs, offices, and ballparks, but no ballplayers.

"It's the strangest feeling to go to the ballpark day after day and not root for anybody," Gebhard said on a sunny afternoon at Wrigley Field. "You don't watch the scoreboard to see how other teams in your division are doing, you don't get that gut-wrenching feeling in your stomach when someone doesn't move a runner over. I've probably missed that more than anything."

Gebhard, the general manager of the Colorado Rockies, and Dombrowski, his counterpart with the Florida Marlins, were both in Chicago on an early August weekend; since both the Cubs and White Sox were at home they could see two games a day.

Gebhard and Dombrowski were in the process of doing what everyone who has ever followed baseball for more than fifteen minutes dreams of doing: putting together their very own teams from scratch.

Of course, there would be severe limitations on whom they could choose from and it had cost the men who'd hired them $95 million to get that opportunity, but it was still fantasy baseball come to life.

In hiring their general managers, the two expansion franchises had gone in very different directions. The Rockies hired Gebhard from the Minnesota Twins, where he'd been Andy MacPhail's top assistant for five years, a part of two World Series winners. Gebhard was forty-nine, an ex-pitcher who had spent a couple of years in the big leagues before becoming a pitching coach, a farm director, and then Mac-Phail's chief aide. Slightly overweight and a heavy smoker, Gebhard looks like he would be just as comfortable wearing a uniform and hitting pregame fungoes as wearing a suit. Maybe more comfortable.

By contrast, Dombrowski looks like he just stepped off a *GQ* cover shoot. He is an inveterate runner, still trim at thirty-six, tall and good-looking with dark hair and a cleft chin. Dombrowski was late for a ball game one afternoon in New York because it took forty-five minutes for a bellman to get all his clothes from his room to the curb. It is a fair bet that Gebhard never carries enough clothes on the road to need a bellman.

The oldest of three children, Dombrowski is still single (the only unmarried general manager in baseball), a fact that concerns his mother greatly. "And this hasn't exactly been a good year for starting a relationship," he said, laughing. "When I was young, my parents wanted me to marry someone who was Polish, Catholic, a straight-A student, and Miss America. Now I think just breathing would suffice. The standards have changed as I've gotten older."

Dombrowski never played baseball beyond the high school level. He was always driven—a straight-A honor society president growing up in the suburbs of Chicago's south side—and went to Cornell for a year before finances forced him to transfer to Western Michigan.

All through high school, when people asked him what he wanted to be when he grew up, Dombrowski answered, "A major league general manager." His honors thesis in college was titled "The Man in the Middle: The Role of the General Manager in Baseball." He started his quest for a general managership by looking for a job in baseball at the 1977 winter meetings in Hawaii, and was offered a position in the minor league scouting department by the Chicago White Sox. The pay was $7,000 a year.

Dombrowski, a White Sox fan as a kid, was thrilled. His mother was horrified. As an accounting major with an A average, Dombrowski could have walked into numerous jobs for three or four times as much money. His father was more sympathetic. "My dad worked for forty years in the parts department of a Chevrolet dealership and never enjoyed his work," Dombrowski said. "It was never more than a job, a way to make money. So, when I had a chance to do something I really wanted to do, he was on my side."

He and his father sat down and calculated what his expenses would be if he went to work for the White Sox. Paying relatively minimal rent by living at home, the total was $8,000. Dombrowski went back to Mike Veeck, the son of legendary owner Bill Veeck, and explained that while he was dying to take the job, he had to make $8,000 to break even.

"Mike leaned back in his chair and said, 'You know David, we don't usually start people at such high salaries, but for you, we'll make it eight thousand.' I was in heaven."

The next seven years were a joyride for Dombrowski, who became the organization's boy wonder. In less than two years, he was in charge of minor league scouting; by 1984 he was general manager Roland Hemond's right-hand man. But in the fall of 1985, Hemond was kicked upstairs by White Sox management, which had the brilliant notion that it could make Ken Harrelson into a general manager. Harrelson, the ex-player who was and is now again an announcer (and a huge homer) was gone within a year after a series of bizarre moves that damaged the organization, including the firing of Tony LaRussa.

Harrelson's promotion shocked Dombrowski. "Roland had been out of town. He called me and said he had to see me when he got back, that he needed to talk to me. I actually thought briefly that they were going to make him club president and give me the general manager's job. Of course that was probably pretty farfetched since I was only twenty-eight at the time."

Instead, Hemond had been shoved aside for Harrelson. Dombrowski's first instinct when Harrelson was hired was to quit. Hemond talked him out of it. "He told me, 'David, in baseball you never quit a job. If they fire you, that's different. Don't quit.' "

Dombrowski thought that over for a few days and decided to stay. But his instinct had been correct. Shortly after Harrelson took over, he decided to fire twenty-five people in the organization—and was going to do it via form letter.

"You can't do it that way," Dombrowski remembers arguing with Harrelson.

"Fine," Harrelson said. "If *you* want to call them, call them."

Dombrowski did. Things got no better after that. Dombrowski disagreed with almost everything Harrelson wanted to do. By the following June, the White Sox were in chaos. LaRussa was fired and, shortly after that, Harrelson fired Dombrowski too.

"It wasn't the wrong thing for him to do," Dombrowski acknowledged. "Our philosophies were totally different. He told me, one of us had to go and since he was the boss, I was the one going. I understood.

I was *crushed* but I understood. I went home and cried, then sat down to figure out what to do next.''

What he did next was relax. The White Sox were paying him for the rest of the season so he took advantage of the situation, learning Spanish and golf and doing some traveling. On July 27, his parents threw him a surprise thirtieth birthday party.

''Turning thirty didn't bother me at all,'' he said. ''In fact, having been thought of as 'the kid' all during my time in the game, I was sort of glad to have that number after my name. But I did start thinking about going back to work. Right or wrong, I'm one of those people whose identity is tied to his job. It started to bother me to have to say I wasn't working. Still, I didn't want to jump at the wrong thing.''

A number of teams contacted him but not with anything appealing. Finally, the week before Thanksgiving, Murray Cook, the Montreal Expos' general manager, called to see if Dombrowski would be interested in becoming the team's farm director. The reason for the opening: Bob Gebhard had left to join the Twins.

''My first thought was no, that being director of player development was a step back from assistant GM,'' Dombrowski said. ''But I liked Murray, I thought it was a good organization, and I thought it was time to get back to work. So I took it.''

Nine months later, Dombrowski thought he was in another Hemond-Harrelson dilemma. Cook left and was replaced by Bill Stoneman. Dombrowski had nothing against Stoneman, but he had signed on to work with Cook. He worried about being caught in a philosophy switch again. This time it was club president Claude Brochu who convinced him to stay. And this time, staying was the right decision. Less than a year later, Stoneman was replaced and Dombrowski, twenty-three days shy of thirty-two, was named as the Expos' general manager.

That officially made him baseball's boy wonder. Dombrowski traded for Mark Langston the following year to try to win a pennant but the Expos folded down the stretch. He personally liked living in Montreal, didn't mind the cold weather, but found that getting players to want to play there was difficult. Baseball players are not the most flexible of human beings and many are uncomfortable in a city that is largely French-speaking. ''It wasn't as if it made the job impossible,'' Dombrowski says. ''It just made it harder.''

His name was linked with the Miami job almost from the day the franchise was awarded. The late Carl Barger, who left Pittsburgh to become the team president, knew Dombrowski from having served on one of baseball's many committees with him. What's more, Barger leaned on Pirates manager Jim Leyland for advice and Leyland and

Dombrowski were old friends from their days with the White Sox. No one in baseball was shocked when Dombrowski got the job.

Once he was hired, he moved swiftly, hiring a number of his own front office people from Montreal to move with him. The Marlins' philosophy was to get rolling in a hurry. Before spring training had started in 1992, Dombrowski had twenty-five scouts in place and had set up an itinerary for himself that would include at least 150 games before the end of the season.

One thing he had not bargained for, as it turned out, was the perils of traveling in the real world. Having done 90 percent of his traveling with a baseball team, Dombrowski was used to charter flights, luggage being picked up at one door and dropped at the next, and never having to go through an airport the way most people do. Now, he was at the mercy of airline schedules and baggage handlers and air traffic control delays. It was a whole new world.

"Spoiled is what I was," he said one afternoon in New York. "The best thing about having a team next year will be going back to being that spoiled."

Dombrowski's worst trip came in June, when the expansion teams' two rookie league teams were making their debuts. He was in Toronto scouting the Blue Jays and Red Sox on a Sunday, drove three hours to Erie, Pennsylvania, on Monday to watch that team's opener—a fourteen-inning loss to, ironically, the Expos' rookie league team—then drove back to Toronto.

There, he got a call from the Player Relations Committee asking if he could come to New York on Thursday to testify in an arbitration case. He agreed, saw the last game of a Toronto-Detroit series on Wednesday, arrived in New York late that night, and was at the PRC at ten Thursday morning to testify. Things were backed up so it was three o'clock by the time he was called.

By the time Dombrowski escaped the PRC he had just enough time to get to the airport to catch the last flight of the night to Chicago. He arrived so close to departure time that he had to sign a form saying the airline wouldn't guarantee that his luggage would make the plane. (Gebhard would probably not have had *that* problem.) He raced to the gate and arrived huffing and puffing to learn the flight was delayed by bad weather. Three hours later, it took off.

Dombrowski finally got to Chicago at two-thirty in the morning. His luggage—naturally—wasn't there.

"You got there too late," the luggage inspector said, looking at his late luggage tag.

"Too late?" Dombrowski said. "The flight left more than three hours after I got to the airport!"

"Yeah, but you were late, sir, see what the tag says?"

Too tired to argue, Dombrowski got on the rent-a-car bus. When he got to the counter, there was one couple in front of him and, as you might expect at that hour, only one person working.

"The couple in front of me was German," Dombrowski says, able to laugh now at the memory. "They needed to have everything explained to them very slowly. To make a long story short, the thing I most remember is, after forty-five minutes, hearing the woman say, 'And what shades of gray did you say you had?' "

It was almost 4 A.M. when Dombrowski reached his hotel. He had no clothes but didn't care. All he wanted was a bed. "I went upstairs, put my key in the door, walked in and saw clothes lying on the floor. I thought, 'This is strange.' Then I took another step inside and I saw why the clothes were there: There was a couple sleeping in the bed!"

Before anyone woke up and the scene turned into a bad sitcom, Dombrowski fled. The embarrassed hotel people managed to come up with an empty room. The next morning his luggage arrived. Relieved, Dombrowski opened the suitcase—and found that all his clothes were wet. "I guess they had left the bag sitting on the tarmac during that whole delay in New York," he says. He finally found one wearable shirt, pulled out his hair dryer, and went into the bathroom. Thirty seconds later the hair dryer caught on fire—it was also wet.

"I wanted to sit down on my bed and cry," he says. "That day, for maybe the only time in my life, I wished I had never heard of baseball."

Gebhard has no horror story to match Dombrowski's. But he found the travel grind equally grueling as the season progressed. Yet he kept pushing himself not to cut any corners.

"There's always the temptation when a game is running long to duck out in the eighth inning and beat the traffic," he admits. "But suppose that's the night that a kid relief pitcher comes in who I should see and I miss him? Suppose the game runs long and someone who has just been called up gets in the game? I don't want to look back on this and say I didn't do everything possible to give us the best possible team. I've waited a long time for this."

Indeed he has. Gebhard grew up in a small town in Minnesota and won sixteen letters in four sports in high school before going to the University of Iowa on a baseball scholarship. He was drafted by the Twins in the very first amateur draft and made it to the majors with them in '71 and '72. The following year he was sent to the Expos and made it back to the majors briefly in 1974. A year later he retired and was offered a job as Montreal's minor league pitching coach.

"The funny thing is I had two education degrees but never once considered using them," Gebhard says. "I went straight from life as a pitcher to life as a pitching coach without ever looking back."

In 1982, when Montreal farm director Bing Devine suddenly re-signed, Gebhard was offered the job. That was where he was when the Twins offered him the chance to become MacPhail's assistant. Gebhard liked the idea of going back to Minnesota, especially since his family had lived there the entire time he was working in Montreal. "By then my kids were sixteen, twelve, and seven," he says. "I had really been on the road their whole lives. This was a chance to spend some time with them."

He was surprised when the call came from Denver asking if he was interested in interviewing for the general manager's job. "Actually, I had seen my name connected with the Miami job a couple times, but never Denver," he says. "I didn't even think I was in the mix."

Interestingly, no one who was interviewed for the Miami job was interviewed for the Denver job, and vice versa. Clearly, management had different ideas about what direction it wanted to go in. MacPhail gave the Rockies permission to talk to Gebhard after first receiving a written guarantee that if Gebhard was hired he would not be allowed to take anyone from the Minnesota organization with him for two years. Given Dombrowski's raids on the Expos, this was a smart, farsighted move.

Gebhard was interviewed by the Denver people on a Thursday in early September, asked in for a second interview three days later, and offered the job. He accepted the next day after team owner John Antonucci agreed to allow him to remain with the Twins until their season was over.

As it turned out, that wasn't until the seventh game of the World Series. "That was a tough time," Gebhard says. "I had a lot to do for the Twins, a lot of advance scouting, and I was very involved emotionally with what the team was doing. But there was also part of me that wanted to get going in Colorado because there was so much to be done."

The last night of the World Series was a particularly emotional one for Gebhard. For a while, it seemed the game might never end and he might never leave Minnesota. When the Twins finally won, he joined the clubhouse celebration, then took his son for a walk around the Metrodome, Gebhard's final stroll as a Twins employee. Leaving the ballpark, he broke down. At MacPhail's request, he rode in the victory parade the next day, then cleared out his desk and flew to Denver.

There was no time for nostalgia or looking back. Unlike the Marlins, who had a full staff in place before New Year's, the Rockies took a more methodical approach. "We hired people as we got to the point where we needed them," Gebhard says. "Different people have different ideas. Mine is that I would rather hire a guy I know I want than hire someone just to fill a position."

On the same night that the Marlins made their debut as a franchise in Erie, the Rockies played their rookie league opener in Bend, Oregon. As with the Marlins, all the team's brass, from Antonucci on down, was there. Down 4–1 in the eighth inning, Bend loaded the bases and catcher Will Scalzitti (who Gebhard says has a chance to someday be a major leaguer) hit a grand slam onto the roof of a grocery store behind the left-field fence.

"My God, you'd've thought we'd won the World Series the way we reacted," Gebhard said. "We were laughing and crying and hugging each other all night long. What a feeling."

Antonucci decided he had to have the home run ball as a memento. The young man who had climbed the roof to get the ball was tracked down. He was offered money for the ball. No, he wanted more. What? Four tickets to the Rockies' home opener *and* four airline tickets to get there. Antonucci wanted the ball a lot. He made the deal.

Both general managers spent most of the season focusing on players they thought might be available in the November 17 expansion draft. Each received the usual letters from people who insisted that, if they were just given a chance, they could make the major leagues. The Marlins held an open tryout camp in March at which several former professionals showed up, including onetime major leaguer Leon Durham. Afterward, they even signed a pitcher named Michael Anderson who had once been in the Mets organization. Unfortunately, the Cinderella story never went very far. Anderson, it turned out, was considerably older than he had claimed and didn't have nearly the experience he credited himself with on his résumé. He was a lot closer to being a wicked stepsister than Cinderella.

Predictably, both GMs were exhausted by the end of August from their nonstop travels. Dombrowski actually got a respite he hadn't planned on when he was stranded for two days at a friend's house in the aftermath of Hurricane Andrew, which swept through south Florida during the last week in August.

"We couldn't go out, we couldn't use the phones, the cables were down so we couldn't watch any television," he said. "The only thing to do, really, was sleep. I was amazed when I went back on the road how refreshed I felt. I hadn't realized just how exhausted I was until I got that chance to rest."

Overall, Gebhard seemed to be focused on putting a competitive team on the field quickly, while Dombrowski was looking further down the road.

That seemed to change on August 7, when San Francisco Giants owner Bob Lurie announced that he had sold his team to a group that would move the team to St. Petersburg. The Marlins were stunned. One of the cities they had beaten out in the expansion derby was St. Petersburg. Now they were being told that not only would St. Pete have a team but it would be an established one with names like Will Clark, Matt Williams, and Bill Swift in uniform.

The Marlins had not called themselves the *Florida* Marlins by accident. They were planning to market themselves throughout the entire state, not just in Miami. The Giants' move would be a huge setback. Publicly, owner H. Wayne Huizenga said he would vote in favor of the move. The public knew better, though. In the Tampa Bay area, Blockbuster Video stores (the source of Huizenga's millions) were boycotted and picketed. In the end, the Marlins were saved when the owners voted in November to force the Giants to stay in San Francisco.

That vote came a week before the draft and allowed the Marlins to go ahead with their original plan to draft—for the most part—young, talented prospects. Both teams chose more pitchers than position players in the seven-hour draft; before it was over, both general managers had also swung several trades. The only name player the Marlins drafted was Angels reliever Bryan Harvey. They went almost strictly for youth. The Rockies drafted more experienced players and, on paper, walking out of the Marriott Marquis hotel in New York on the night of the draft, they looked to be the stronger team for 1993. Time will tell which philosophy was the correct one.

Figuring out the best route to go in expansion is a total crapshoot. In 1961, the Los Angeles Angels won more games—70—than any first-year expansion team has ever won. The next year, led by such young stars as Bo Belinsky, Dean Chance, and Jim Fregosi, they won 86 games. Thirty-one years later, they have yet to play in the World Series. In 1962, the New York Mets were 40-120, easily the worst record in the history of baseball. And yet the Mets got to the World Series in their eighth season—faster than any other expansion team— and won it that same year, 1969.

The Mets have been in more World Series than any expansion team—three—and are the only one to have won twice. The Kansas City Royals reached the play-offs in their eighth year but didn't make the World Series until four years later—and they didn't *win* it until five years after that. The Toronto Blue Jays, generally considered the game's model franchise, made the playoffs in their ninth year but needed *seven* more years and three playoff failures before they made— and won—their first World Series.

In short, there is no answer that is right for everyone. Gebhard, the ex–major leaguer, hired Don Baylor, who played in the major leagues for nineteen years, as his manager. Dombrowski, the ex–intramural player at Western Michigan, hired Rene Lachemann, who had all of 281 major league at-bats, to manage his team.

They will both lose a lot of games in 1993. How quickly they improve will be the measure of both general managers. Both will no doubt enjoy having a team to root for again, even if a lot of the days and nights will be long ones.

And one thing is an absolute certainty: Dave Dombrowski will travel *with* his team every chance he gets.

PART IV

DOG DAYS

23

VIEW FROM THE
BASEMENT II

O n the night of July 16, the city of Seattle threw itself a party. It was certainly entitled. After more than a year of wondering whether major league baseball would flee for a second time, the fans knew that their team—the Mariners—was staying put. New ownership had been approved and all the talk of moving to Tampa had at last been silenced.

A cynic (realist?) might have made the point that losing the Mariners would not exactly be like losing a major league team. After all, during their first fifteen years of existence the oft-hapless M's had managed *one* winning season. That had come in 1991 when the club finished 83-79. Manager Jim Lefebvre, the man who had wrought this minor miracle, was rewarded with a request that he find employment elsewhere.

In his place, the Mariners hired third-base coach Bill Plummer, an ex-catcher whose main claim to fame in the big leagues had been playing the role of backup to Johnny Bench in Cincinnati. That meant Plummer got a little more work than the Maytag Repairman. The team hired Plummer because he was popular with the players, a change from the intense Lefebvre.

The now-happy Mariners were 10-11 in April. By the end of May they were 21-28 and a month later, 31-44. By the All-Star break the record was 36-53. Of course, the case could be made that the players had been distracted by all the controversy caused by the team's sale to Nintendo, the multibillion-dollar Japanese company, which had offered owner Jeff Smulyan $125 million to take the club off his hands.

Protectionists screamed long and loud about the evils of foreign ownership, even though most of the Nintendo people who would be running the team had lived in Seattle far longer than Smulyan, who, in fact, had first gotten interested in buying the team for the purpose of moving it to his hometown, Indianapolis. When baseball owners made it clear they wouldn't approve any such move, Smulyan bought the team anyway, watched it founder both on the field and financially, and came up with the notion of either moving it to Tampa or selling to a group down there. When the owners objected to that, Nintendo came up with the money to buy the team *and* keep it in Seattle.

When all the political posturing and pandering was finally over, the owners, pushed by Commissioner Fay Vincent to break with precedent and do the right thing, approved the Nintendo sale and the Mariners were locked into staying in Seattle.

That was the good news. It was also the bad news.

There may be no prettier city in the country than Seattle. Rumor has it that residents talk up the rain to discourage out-of-towners who see the place as Paradise Northwest. With Puget Sound on one side and snow-capped mountains on the other, with a relatively gentle (though allegedly wet) climate, Seattle has become such an attractive place to live that Californians have been migrating north in droves in recent years. This trend has so upset the natives and longtime residents that many of them will honk angrily whenever they see a car with a California license plate.

It is therefore a major dichotomy that in this beautiful city sits one of the ugliest places on the planet in which to play a baseball game. The Kingdome is poorly lit, the dirt-encrusted white tiles of the vaulted roof are singularly unattractive, and the dark red, blue, and orange seats just don't make it. Some people call it America's only overcast domed stadium. Others call it far worse things. If there has ever been a city with a crying need for a domed stadium with retractable roof, this is it. Going inside to watch baseball on a sunny day in Seattle is a crime against nature.

Of course, watching the Mariners can often be a crime against the senses. They joined the American League in 1977 (along with the Toronto Blue Jays) as part of baseball's payback to the city, which had seen the Seattle Pilots stolen away in 1970 after just one year. While the Blue Jays steadily built a solid franchise, the Mariners floundered.

Ownership changed hands, managers and general managers came and went, but the result was always the same. After drawing more than 1.3 million fans in their first season, the team drew less than a million for six of the next seven years—barely cracking the million mark in 1982 when they won more than seventy games (seventy-six) for the first time ever.

In 1991, the Mariners drew more than 2.1 million fans. Or at least sold that many tickets. With Smulyan threatening to move the team, local corporations bought blocks of tickets to swell the attendance. The no-show factor was actually fairly minimal since, for the first time, the product on the field was respectable.

That all came to a crashing halt at the start of 1992. The Mariners slipped quietly and steadily toward their accustomed spot in the basement of the American League West, even as the sale to Nintendo was being approved.

The pitching, which had been the franchise's hope for the future, was in tatters. Kevin Mitchell, whose acquisition had helped create the pitching chaos, showed up at training camp looking like a Thanksgiving Day Parade balloon and never came close to hitting the fifty home runs predicted for him in the cozy Kingdome. Mitchell's weight was listed in the Mariner media guide at 210. That *might* have been true if his arms, legs, and head had been cut off.

The star of the team was Ken Griffey, Jr., one of baseball's great talents, a twenty-two-year-old who did everything—except run out ground balls if he wasn't in the mood. The Mariners could hit but they couldn't pitch or field (except for Griffey and shortstop Omar Vizquel), and, most important, they didn't appear to really care very much about whether they hit, pitched, fielded, or won.

If they joked about Lefebvre behind his back and complained about how wound up he was, they also played hard for him. Plummer was everybody's pal, someone who wasn't taken very seriously. And yet, all of that was shoved to the background on that giddy first night back after the All-Star break. It was somehow appropriate that the Blue Jays, who had taken all the right turns while the Mariners were taking all the wrong ones, were the opponents on what was billed as "Opening Day II."

All over the Kingdome were signs that said "*Our* Mariners." The words were even painted on the on-deck circle. Bunting had been put out and a crowd of 52,212—about 37,000 above average—showed up. Naturally, the Mariners lost the game, 7–2. They did manage to win the next night but then lost the next two to drop to 37-56.

Plummer decided that to talk to the players about winning the West—they were now 20 games out of first—was going to be pretty futile, so he came up with a new goal for them: finishing at .500. That meant they needed 44 victories in their last 69 games, a rather large order for this group. Nonetheless, Plummer wrote the number 44 on the clubhouse blackboard, intending to change the number as it dwindled.

The Detroit Tigers came to town. After one night, the number was still 44. After two nights it was still 44. After three—44. It was beginning to look as if the Mariners might still be on 44 with 43 left to play.

"You can't keep saying, 'If this or if that,' " a disgusted Plummer said after the third loss to the Tigers, a 3–2 "if" job. "At some point, someone has to step up and make the big play, get the big hit, or throw the big pitch."

He slumped in his chair, reached under his desk for a beer, and shook his head. "God, this is frustrating," he said. "Every time I think we may get over the hump, we slip right back. We're beginning to run out of time here. We've got to get something going."

The Mariners' biggest problem was the players' *lack* of frustration. On the morning after the third loss to the Tigers—which made five in a row and six of seven since the high hopes of Opening Day II—the players arrived at the Kingdome early for a one o'clock game.

Randy Johnson, the six-foot-ten-inch left-hander, who in many ways was symbolic of the unfulfilled potential of the Mariners, had gone out and bought some firecrackers. He began the day by setting a bunch of them off behind second base, using a time delay mechanism so that he would not be standing on the spot when the explosions hit. Most of his teammates left the clubhouse to come out to the dugout and watch.

As smoke fumes billowed in every direction, they all sprinted for the clubhouse, laughing hysterically. A few minutes later, Johnson, aided by Kevin Mitchell, blew a hole in a fifty-gallon trash can that had been sitting in the runway area between the clubhouse and the dugout.

"We missed Fourth of July," Griffey said. "So I guess those guys wanted to make up for it."

The only person who didn't find Johnson and Mitchell's antics wildly funny was Henry Genzale, the clubhouse man. He stalked into Plummer's office, fuming. "Dammit Plumm, they did this last year and the fire marshal got all pissed off about it then."

"I know," Plummer said. "I'll talk to him."

He did, walking into the clubhouse just as the players, still giggling, were heading for the field. "Hey Randy," Plummer said.

"I didn't do it," Johnson said.

"I know," Plummer answered. "But don't do it again."

He walked away, suppressing a laugh lest Genzale see him. "Who knows?" he said. "Maybe it's exactly what they need."

It wasn't. That afternoon—after the fire marshals and police had inspected the trash can and, grinning, decided it must have been kids playing a prank—the Mariners got a superbly pitched game from rookie Dave Fleming. He took a 4–1 lead into the eighth inning before tiring. Russ Swan, the team's latest closer, came on after the Yankees closed to within 4–3 to strike out Danny Tartabull for the third out. In the ninth, after Roberto Kelly singled, Swan got the next two hitters out and only needed to retire backup catcher Mike Stanley to end the losing streak.

He didn't come close. Stanley singled to tie the game; Randy Velarde then hit a tenth-inning homer to win it, 5–4, for the Yanks. The losing streak was now 6, the overall record was 37-60, and the number on the blackboard was still 44. The next morning, the papers were speculating on how much longer Plummer would survive.

So was Plummer. Quiet and soft-spoken, he is not a fiery, rah-rah type of manager. He is, ironically, forty-four, a baseball junkie born and bred, someone who knew before high school that he wanted to play baseball and stay in baseball when he couldn't play it anymore.

"I never dreamed it would get this bad," he said, sitting in his office the afternoon after the Yankee debacle. "When I got the job last fall, I would have been very happy to take the team we had at that moment and play. But we lost some pitchers [through the Mitchell trade, free agency, and injury] and from the beginning of the season it's seemed like any bounce that can go wrong *does* go wrong. Hell, we were up eight–three with two outs in the eighth inning [against Texas] on Opening Day and gave up nine runs. *Nine!* I guess I should have seen that as an omen."

Plummer had waited a long time for this chance. Both his father and uncle had played in the old Pacific Coast League in the 1920s, and Plummer had grown up in Oakland dreaming of becoming a baseball player. He signed with the Cubs in 1967 and was in the majors a year later—getting a total of two at-bats as Randy Hundley's backup (Hundley played 160 games that season). That prepared him for his stint behind Bench. He played all or part of ten seasons in the majors and got to bat a total of 892 times.

In 1979, after spending a year with the Mariners' Triple-A farm team, he was offered the chance to manage in the instructional league. He enjoyed it so much that he decided to retire, on the spot, at thirty-two. "I realized that even if I made it back to the majors the next year I would enjoy managing more than I would enjoy being a backup catcher," he said. "It just seemed to fit me right away."

He was a successful minor league manager for two years, spent two years coaching with the Mariners when Rene Lachemann was the manager, then went back to the minors for five years before returning to Seattle as a coach in '89. When Lefebvre was fired, he was the popular choice. Now, he was watching helplessly as his chance of a lifetime slipped away.

"The tough thing about this organization is there's never been any stability," he said. "I remember when I was here with Lach in 1982. We had one of those seasons where everything broke right. Bill Caudill protected every lead, we made big plays, got big hits, and won seventy-six games, which for this franchise was outstanding. But instead of building on that, the owner [George Argyros] told us we should be able to take the same players and win ninety games the next year.

"Well, that wasn't going to happen. A lot of guys had career years in 'eighty-two. Lach had done a great job. So, the next year we start poorly and bang! Lach is gone. I know this is a small market, but if you want to win, there are times when you have to spend some money not just to get the team to .500 but to try and make it a winner."

Of course the Mitchell trade had been designed to make the team a winner. But it had been a dud. Mitchell's weight had been a problem, then he struggled with injuries. Mitchell was thirty, a man of fearsome strength who had led the majors in home runs with 109 during the previous three seasons. But Mitchell wasn't a leader. He would rather aid and abet Randy Johnson in a firecracker stunt than tell him he should worry about getting some outs (Johnson was 5-11 with a 4.05 ERA as July came to a close) instead of blowing up garbage cans. Terry Pendleton probably would have blown Johnson up himself if he had pulled the trash can stunt in Atlanta.

Plummer didn't have the stomach to jump on players either. On one of the rare occasions when he had, he ended up backing down. That had come down in May when Johnson, after being hit hard during the first two innings of a game against Baltimore, took himself out before the third inning. Plummer publicly accused him of quitting on the team, then apologized when Johnson complained. Johnson, who had as much pitching talent as anyone in the league, continued to be an enigma.

Then there was the case of Ken Griffey, Jr. With the sale of the team settled, the new big question in Seattle was whether the Mariners would come up with the money to keep Griffey with them when he became a free agent at the end of the 1994 season.

Griffey was already a .300 hitter and a wonder to watch in center field, finishing his fourth major league season at an age when most players are wondering if they can hit in Triple-A. His talent came as no surprise. Griffey had grown up around major league ballparks following his father, Ken Senior, through a nineteen-year career that ended in Seattle with the two of them becoming the first father-son combination to play together in the major leagues.

Unlike many young left-handed hitters, Griffey hit lefty pitching well. "I grew up hitting off my father," he said. "To me, lefties are what I'm used to."

Griffey often seemed to be two people. He could be very shy, sensitive enough to have been devastated by the death of his grandmother in spring training. He was depressed the entire spring as cancer ate away at the older woman; at one stage, he even talked about having contemplated suicide while in high school because of the pressures of being a young superstar.

Around children, however, Griffey was in his element. Suddenly he was the life of the party, outgoing and gregarious. "When I'm with kids, it's like I'm a kid again," he said. "Until I was a freshman [in high school] I was the class clown. Then I got serious about sports. When I'm with kids, I can be the clown again."

The same was true in the clubhouse. He was the focal point for much of the kidding that went on, whether it was over a new earring, a new car, or a new hairdo. "Did you *want* them to do that to your hair?" pitcher Dennis Powell asked one day when Griffey came in with his hair slicked back and greased up. Griffey and Mitchell, who lockered next to one another, became fast friends; given Mitchell's work habits, that might not have been what the Mariners had in mind.

"Mitch always gets mad at me because every day I say to him, 'Mitch, why is this game so easy?'" Griffey said, laughing. "Of course, I just say that to upset him."

Perhaps so. But the fact remained that what Griffey made look easy every day, his teammates managed to make look very, very hard.

"Can't let this game get you down," Mitchell said, the *44* still looming on the blackboard behind him. "It's a long season."

Especially in Seattle.

•

Nine hundred miles south of Seattle, another last-place team was drawing laughs almost every time it took the field. This was different, though. This wasn't the sad-sack Seattle Mariners. This was the Los Angeles Dodgers.

There is no prouder franchise in baseball than the Dodgers. After moving the team west from Brooklyn in 1958, the O'Malley family built the perfect ballpark in the Elysian Hills just outside downtown Los Angeles. For years, the rich and famous—and the not-so-rich and not-so-famous—flocked to Dodger Stadium. The Dodgers were contenders almost every year. If they didn't win, they came close. First Walter Alston, then Tommy Lasorda, produced consistent winners.

Dodger Stadium was the cleanest ballpark in the country—and often the quietest. The fans lived up to the jokes and really did arrive late and leave early, but they rarely left unsatisfied. In 1992, however, it all collapsed. Darryl Strawberry and Eric Davis, reunited to play the outfield, instead spent most of their time together in the training room. Strawberry struggled with a bad back that eventually needed surgery, and Davis was out with his usual assortment of injuries.

The pitching wasn't awful but the defense was. The symbol of the '92 Dodgers, fairly or unfairly, was twenty-three-year-old shortstop José Offerman. By the end of July, Offerman had made twenty-six errors and the joke around Los Angeles was: "How do you spell Offerman? O-F-F-E-E-E-E-E-E-E-E-E-E-E- . . .''

Rumors abounded that Lasorda would not be back in 1993. One story had him going to St. Petersburg if the Giants moved there. Another had him managing the expansion Florida Marlins. Lasorda's friend Sparky Anderson fueled that one by campaigning for it.

"It would be perfect for him," Anderson said. "He's sixty-five, he speaks Spanish, he can manage three or four years down there, be a hero and retire. Why should he beat himself up in L.A.?"

During spring training, Lasorda's contract had been extended through 1993 by team president Peter O'Malley. The extension had been a victory for the manager over general manager Fred Claire, who was widely reported to be ready to start fresh with a new manager after '92.

No one—not Claire, not Lasorda—could have envisioned the Dodgers' collapse in June that left them deep in last place. On July 30 they were a shocking 42-59. Claire, who insisted right through the All-Star break that he wasn't giving up on the season, finally threw in the towel that day, releasing veteran second baseman Juan Samuel and calling up rookie Eric Young to take his place. On that same afternoon, Strawberry, fighting tears, told the media that he had decided to have back surgery.

"I'm scared," he said. "I've never gone through this before and I don't want to do it. But they tell me it's the only way."

The crowd that night, for a game against the San Diego Padres, was 35,961, terrific by most standards, almost embarrassing for the Dodgers. This was a franchise that had drawn more than three million fans for eight of the past twelve seasons and hadn't been under 2.5 million for a season (except in strike-shortened 1981) since 1976. That string would end in 1992.

What's more, those fans who did come had learned to boo. When an Offerman error opened the gates for a three-run San Diego seventh inning, jeers rained down from the normally comatose stands. When the Dodgers rallied to win the game in ten innings, the place sounded more like a church. Many were already en route home. Those who had stayed clapped politely and headed for the freeway.

"It's funny, when I signed here, I thought I was coming to the promised land," said pitcher Tom Candiotti, who had spent almost six years pitching for terrible teams in Cleveland before going to Toronto for half a year in 1991. "But to be honest, there are days when I feel like I'm back in Cleveland. I say to myself, 'Wait a minute, I thought I left this behind.' "

One game may have summed up the Dodger season better than any other. In Atlanta, on June 16, the Braves battered L.A. pitching all night long, building a 7–3 lead going into the ninth. In the bottom of the eighth, Offerman and third baseman Lenny Harris collided on a Deion Sanders pop-up, letting it drop. The Braves were actually laughing in the dugout.

"We were almost to the point of feeling sorry for them," Charlie Leibrandt said later. "I mean, it was as if they couldn't do *anything* right. When the ninth inning started, we were giving Greg [Olson] a hard time because some friends of his from a restaurant were supposed to cater the postgame spread and they hadn't shown up yet. He kept saying, 'I need a couple more minutes.' Little did we know that we were going to give it to him."

As would happen all too often to the Braves before the end of the season, their bullpen gave Olson plenty of time. Four different pitchers combined to allow the Dodgers five runs in the ninth, a rally capped by a two-run homer by first baseman Eric Karros, the rookie of the year and the one Dodger bright spot throughout the season.

The Dodgers were up 8–7, Olson's spread was forgotten, and for once, there was joy in the Los Angeles dugout. It didn't last long. Four Dodger pitchers tried to protect the lead—and failed. The winning run scored on a base hit by the Braves' weakest hitter, shortstop Rafael Belliard. The final was 9–8. The inning had taken forty-seven minutes because there were seven pitching changes. It was baseball at its absolute ugliest.

Afterward, when someone pointed out to Braves reliever Kent Mercker that the game had taken just under four hours—3:50 to be precise—he shrugged and said, "That's not so bad. We've had *nine*-inning games that took almost that long."

Kent, it *was* a nine-inning game.

Win a game like that, no matter how long it takes, and you look to the sky, say thanks, and devour the postgame spread—which was almost cold by the time the game finally ended. Lose a game like that and you just sit in front of your locker and stare in disbelief, which most of the Dodgers did.

Except Lasorda. He got dressed and started walking back to the team hotel—three miles away—in spite of pleas from everyone around him not to do so. "I'm walking," he insisted. "I just can't ride the damn bus."

Halfway there, his foot began to hurt, but he still turned down rides when people pulled over. Finally, an ambulance driver stopped, insisted that Lasorda get in because he was hobbling so badly. Lasorda, exhausted and in pain, gave up and climbed in.

As the ambulance pulled up to the hotel, several of Lasorda's players were waiting for taxis to go out and get a late dinner. When they saw the ambulance, knowing their manager had been out walking the streets alone, they panicked.

When he climbed out of the front seat, they demanded to know what was going on. "Tommy, what the hell happened to you?" they all asked together.

"What happened to me?" Lasorda snapped. "This season, *that's* what."

With that he hobbled off to bed. Unfortunately for him, the season was still a long way from being over.

24

THE A'S

Tony LaRussa, as the commercial says, will never let you see him sweat. If his team has lost five straight, that just means it's due to *win* five straight. If another team in his division has won ten in a row, that means his team needs to figure out how to win eleven.

By the same token, he never relaxes, either. A four-run lead means you better not let them load the bases and bring the tying run to the plate. A five-game lead in July means nothing; check back in September—and he'll still be nervous, *unless* there are only four left to play.

During the first four months of the 1992 season, LaRussa spent a lot of time not showing anyone that he was sweating. But he was. His team was playing pretty good baseball, arriving at the All-Star break 51-36, just two games behind what had been a very hot Minnesota team. Still, LaRussa was worried. In 1991 the A's had been close at the All-Star break only to collapse in August and fall out of contention for the first time since 1987. Injuries had been a factor then; once again, in '92, injuries concerned LaRussa.

"You can only ask so much of guys," he said. "That's why 162 games always produces the best teams. There's no way to fake it.

Willie Wilson is thirty-seven, there are days when I just have to get him out of there. Carney [Lansford] will play on one leg if you ask him, but he's gonna wear down some in August. Eck [Dennis Eckersley], Stew [Dave Stewart], they'll give you heart and soul but they have to have the energy.''

LaRussa had first started to worry as far back as May about where his team might be when the dog days hit. On an eleven-game East Coast trip, the A's went into Toronto and lost twice; then, after winning a game in New York, they dropped two more there.

During that final game in Yankee Stadium, an uptight LaRussa almost got into a fight with Yankee manager Buck Showalter. LaRussa had been yelling at Yankee catcher Matt Nokes about throwing inside and Showalter screamed back at LaRussa to quit yelling at his player. The two men charged out of the dugouts at one another, only to be separated by home plate umpire Jim Evans, who then ejected them both.

Both managers were protecting their players. LaRussa thought that Nokes had been calling for pitches up and in, first on Willie Wilson, then on Scott Brosius. "I yelled at him [Nokes], 'Below the shoulders, asshole!' " LaRussa said. "I've always been clear on that. Throwing inside is part of baseball, but I've never told our guys they can throw above the shoulders and I don't expect other teams to do it to my guys. People can get hurt—*killed*—that way.''

Showalter, who, as a rookie manager, was trying to earn the respect from his team that LaRussa already had, wasn't going to let LaRussa scream at his catcher, regardless of the reason. Naturally, the incident was big news in New York and the media swarmed to both clubhouses when the game was over. Both managers played it close to the vest, although Showalter did say with a strong touch of sarcasm, "I think I helped my team by getting thrown out. After all, he's a much better manager than I am, so getting him out of there must have helped.''

LaRussa was still fuming when Arthur Richman, the Yankees' vice-president for public relations, came in to see him. The media had left by now. Richman told him that Showalter was upset about what had happened because he respected LaRussa and, even though he didn't feel bad about standing up for his player, he did feel bad that he'd gotten into a public shouting match with LaRussa.

When Richman left, LaRussa, who rarely makes snap decisions, made one. He picked up the phone and dialed the Yankee manager's office. Showalter answered.

"Hey Buck, you owe me one," he said.

"Owe you one?" Showalter said, baffled.

"Absolutely. I just made you a hero in this town for standing up for your guys.''

Showalter laughed. The two men talked for several minutes. They didn't exactly promise to get together for dinner the next time their teams played, but some of the tension was eased.

If not for the Showalter confrontation and all the hoopla surrounding it, LaRussa would have called a team meeting that night. Like Jim Leyland, he is not a big believer in a lot of meetings. But there are several times during the season, perhaps three or four at most, when a team needs to be reminded that a few losses are not the end of the world.

LaRussa waited until the next day in Baltimore, where things were quieter, to have his meeting. There was no fire and brimstone, just a reminder of some of the things he had said at the end of spring training: The focus had to be on *this* year for everyone, even the fourteen free agents who were wondering about their future. Play well and the future will take care of itself.

Like any good teacher, LaRussa is an excellent learner, someone who constantly picks things up from others. And so he brought up two concepts borrowed from two men he respected. He had read a quote in the New York papers that weekend from Pat Riley, the New York Knicks coach, about being willing to accept the burdens of being good. The A's had dealt with those burdens for a while now. LaRussa, paraphrasing Riley, told them how easy it would be for them to say, "What the heck, we've already won a lot, why work *so* hard to try to win again?" LaRussa's message was that work was what would make the winning feel so good.

Finally, the A's manager brought up something Leyland had told him about years earlier. Several times a season, when he brought his team to a visiting ballpark where he thought the going might be difficult, Leyland would tell his team to "go out and show off." In other words, leave the people in this town—wherever it might be—talking about what a good ballclub those guys had. This was the A's first trip to Camden Yards. LaRussa told his team to show off for the people in Baltimore.

Whether the meeting had anything to do with it or not—LaRussa would insist it didn't—the A's showed off for Baltimore for three straight nights. Mark McGwire hit a three-run home run—already his seventeenth—in the first inning of the first game and the A's never looked back.

They had survived their first crisis. But there were more coming. The injury toll continued. Dave Henderson hadn't played all year. Walt Weiss was hurt early and often. Dave Stewart's elbow tightened in June. And, of course, Rickey Henderson and José Canseco, Oakland's answer to the Blues Brothers (they couldn't sing but they always had the blues about something), were in and out of the lineup.

The injuries worried LaRussa. He had the sense that his team was barely hanging on. They would begin the second half with eleven games at home, but then go on the road for ten—beginning with three in Minnesota. The home stand did not start well. They split four games with the Tigers, then lost two of three to the Yankees, including a disturbing 1–0 loss to the less-than-masterful Shawn Hillegas, who would be waived by the Yankees a month later.

The Blue Jays came in next for four games. Then came the Minnesota trip. The Twins' lead was three and the A's were hurting. Both Canseco (back spasms) and Henderson (hamstring) said they were too sore to play, although neither was hurt badly enough to go on the DL. Jerry Browne, who had played just about every position during the season, strained a groin in the last game against the Yankees. Since LaRussa likes to carry twelve pitchers, that left him with a one-man bench—Jamie Quirk—going into the Toronto series.

When the Jays won the first game of the series easily, LaRussa was more than a little concerned. The team was now 3-5 since the break—*at home.* If the carnage continued against Toronto and if the A's had another bad series in the Metrodome . . .

"We could be out of the race, or close to it," LaRussa said. "But I can't worry that far down the road."

His worry on Friday night was Stewart, who came off the DL and pitched three good innings and one bad one. The bad one put the A's in a 4–1 hole. But the makeshift lineup somehow pieced together a run in the sixth and two in the seventh. The key hit was a double by Randy Ready, a thirty-two-year-old journeyman whose media guide picture showed him wearing a Milwaukee Brewers cap, even though he had last played for the Brewers six years—and four teams—ago. Ready was the prototype of what the A's had become. He was hitting .182 for the season and had been on the DL twice. The fact that he was important to the team at this juncture said a lot.

With the game still tied 4–4, LaRussa brought Eckersley in to pitch the ninth. He doesn't like to bring Eckersley in unless he has a lead, but he had already used four pitchers and, after the A's had scrambled back, this was now a game he desperately wanted. The Twins' victory over Boston had been hanging over them on the right-field scoreboard for almost three hours now.

This time, the infallible Eckersley failed. He had already saved thirty-five of the fifty-four games Oakland had won, but he was human on this night, giving up a long, two-out home run to Candy Maldonado. That put the Jays up 5–4 and brought Toronto's closer, Tom Henke, in to pitch the bottom of the ninth.

The game had already lasted well beyond three hours—most A's games do—and much of the tired and discouraged crowd of 39,206 headed for the parking lot after Maldonado's homer. After all, if Eck couldn't do it, who could?

How about Randy Ready? He had not had two hits in a game all season, but Ready led off the ninth with a solid single to center. LaRussa gave Walt Weiss one chance to swing away, then asked him to bunt. He did—foul. But, behind 0-2, he worked out a walk. That brought up Eric Fox, playing right field in Canseco's absence.

Fox was almost twenty-nine and had not played a single day in the major leagues until July 8, 1992. He had started the season in Tacoma and had played so poorly that he'd been sent back to the Double-A team in Huntsville. He was seriously considering giving the game up and going to look for a teaching job when the A's spate of injuries suddenly landed him in the major leagues. He had been in the majors for sixteen days now. LaRussa asked him to bunt. He failed, too, but didn't get as lucky as Weiss, striking out trying to bunt the third strike.

That brought up Mike Bordick, who, for half a season at least, had been the best story on the team. He had started the season at short-stop with Weiss out and had played so well that when Weiss came back, LaRussa moved Bordick to second base. He couldn't afford to take him out of the lineup. Bordick hit close to .340 for the first two months of the season, but had now come back to earth. When he'd grounded out in the seventh, he had dropped under .300 for the first time all season.

Bordick had turned twenty-seven three days earlier, but looks younger, even when he comes to the ballpark unshaven. When he had first come up to the team in 1990, he had lockered between Willie McGee and Canseco. Each night, as swarms of reporters would sur- round the two stars, Bordick would sit alone at his locker and say to the reporters' backs, "Sorry fellas, not tonight, maybe some other time."

He was the kind of player LaRussa loved: He was smart, tough, and would do *anything* to win. The A's needed something special from Bordick against the Jays, and, amazingly, he provided it. On Henke's first pitch, he turned on a fastball and drove it toward the left-field fence. Maldonado, shocked to see that the ball was going over his head, sprinted back, leaped, then watched it bounce off the fence. Ready and Weiss were flying to the plate and Bordick, stunned, was pulling into second. Weiss scored standing, the A's had won 6–5, and Mike Bordick was a big-time hero. The reporters swarmed all over *him* this time and he stood, grinning, and answered every question.

Drained, LaRussa sat behind his desk and shook his head. "That's why this is a beautiful game," he said. "You just never know. What just happened out there, that's why we're still in this thing. You get guys like Ready and Bordick, you've always got a chance."

He shook his head. "Tell you what, this one ranks right up there. It was really special."

He did not know yet just *how* special.

•

One reason this season meant so much to LaRussa was that he knew it was an ending, regardless of the outcome. Team owner Walter Haas, Jr., after taking a major financial hit in 1991, had decreed that the team's payroll for 1993 had to be cut by $5 million. That meant a number of players who had played key roles in the three championship seasons would not be back.

"It's almost like being on a college team that has a lot of seniors," pitcher Ron Darling said. "We know this team isn't going to be the same next year and we want the last memories to be good ones."

Even if they had won "only" one World Series during their run as a top team, the A's were easily the most compelling team in baseball. Theirs was a clubhouse full of character and characters. Rickey Henderson and José Canseco were the two prodigies, brilliant talents who would probably end up in the Hall of Fame someday. Yet they were wildly immature, prone to brooding, pouting, and—sometimes—not giving all they had.

Their tendency to cry "ouch" every time they stood up from a chair often caused tension; it made it difficult for their teammates to take them seriously, even when they really were hurt. LaRussa spent a lot of time coddling, prodding, and pushing his two superstars. Often, he covered up for them with the media.

Occasionally, he was pushed too far. In late June, Canseco told LaRussa that his back was killing him and he needed rest. He wanted to go on the DL to get himself healthy. LaRussa offered Canseco a deal: Stay in the lineup for a week with the Twins and Mariners, both of whom would be pitching a lot of lefties, coming up. Then, on July 1 he could go on the DL. That way he would only miss eleven games and could come back after the All-Star break.

Canseco agreed. He hit three home runs during the next six games and went on the DL, as planned, on July 1. With the A's on the road until the All-Star break, he was supposed to show up at the ballpark every day for rehab work. He didn't. When LaRussa heard that Canseco had twice missed rehab sessions, he was furious. To him, it was a sign that the outfielder really didn't care about the team—a team struggling to stay afloat without him.

Canseco's fellow Bash Brother, Mark McGwire, was as different from Canseco as was humanly possible. McGwire had to be pinned under a car to stay out of the lineup. He had played with injuries through most of 1991 and had ended up hitting a futile .201, a season so abysmal that some people speculated he might be through at age twenty-eight.

Sensitive and proud, McGwire was hurt by the boos he heard

during the season. He willingly took a pay cut during the offseason and worked out almost maniacally. He came to training camp nearly twenty pounds heavier—all of it muscle—began blasting home runs in April and never stopped. By mid-May he had been the subject of dozens of profiles about his comeback, his new batting stance, and his new outlook on life. McGwire found them, for the most part, amusing.

"Maybe I'm just stronger," he said one day. "I've hit a lot of shots this year that have gone out that might have been warning-track flies last year. I'm healthy, I feel confident again, and I'm happy. That all makes a difference."

McGwire had broken up with his girlfriend the previous season. What's more, his ex-wife and five-year-old son had moved to Los Angeles. He was still wounded by the treatment he'd received during his slump and he made no bones about it. "What I found out last year is that a lot of people I thought were my friends aren't," he said. "I think I have two real friends in the world—two. Everyone else, to tell you the truth, I couldn't care less about. Now, they're all calling me again, wanting to be pals. Where were they last year? They can keep on calling, but I'm not calling back."

McGwire was as respected by his teammates as Canseco and Henderson were often scorned. They knew he played hurt, they knew he was one of the game's best first basemen (and never got any credit for it), and they knew how much he hated to fail.

The same was true of third baseman Carney Lansford, who had come back from a 1991 knee injury suffered in a snowmobile accident. He was playing again after doctors had told him he was done. He was thirty-five, in his fifteenth season, and he and LaRussa knew it was probably going to be his last. If you told LaRussa he had one at-bat to win the World Series and could pick anyone on the team to hit, he might very well pick Lansford.

"Just look at how much ice he has to use on his body after a game," LaRussa said. "All the guy knows how to do on a baseball field is win."

There were others, like underrated catcher Terry Steinbach and backup Jamie Quirk. Quirk had been told by Whitey Herzog in 1978 that he might extend his career by five years if he learned to catch. Now, at thirty-seven, he'd extended it by fourteen years.

Willie Wilson, also thirty-seven, had come back from a drug conviction that had sent him to jail. He'd played for a world champion (Royals, 1985) and brought a quiet dignity to any clubhouse he stepped into. He never made excuses for what happened. He didn't blame anyone but himself.

"I'm proud that I came back and that I learned from my mistake," he said. "But I'm not proud of what I did. I might have had a great career in this game. I've had a good one, but it could have been great if I hadn't messed up."

They were all critical pieces of the puzzle, men the A's probably could not win without. But the heart and soul of the baseball team were the two aging pitchers, Dave Stewart and Dennis Eckersley. Each had seen great failures before their great successes. Each had an appreciation, not only for what he had accomplished, but for the game and what it had given him.

"Listen to them talk," LaRussa often said. "I'll guarantee you'll learn something."

Stewart had grown up in Oakland, the seventh of Dave and Nathalie Stewart's eight children. His father was a longshoreman who died of a stroke when Dave was thirteen. In high school, Stewart starred in football, basketball, and baseball. He was a catcher on the baseball team his sophomore year because he had a strong arm and because it was the only open spot on the varsity. The Dodgers drafted him on the sixteenth round after his senior year of high school, but Stewart's mother wanted him to go to college on a football scholarship. The Dodgers kept raising the ante until Stewart broke down at $21,500.

He was surprised and disappointed to learn that the Dodgers wanted to make him a pitcher. "I had pitched two games my senior year," he says. "One was a no-hitter that I lost one–nothing. They saw that game and decided I was a pitcher. I didn't like it. Catching was my thing."

For two years, he struggled so much that he asked if he couldn't try catching again. The man assigned to work with him, Bill Berrier, was firm. "You got two choices," he told Stewart. "You can pitch or go home."

Stewart pitched. After giving up seventy-six earned runs in 109 innings during his first two years, he went 18-4 in his third season and got promoted to Triple-A. In 1981, he made it to Los Angeles but found himself in a swing role. One week he was in middle relief, the next week he was closing, the week after that he was starting. Life was never easy for him in L.A. He was involved in an embarrassing incident with a hooker who turned out to be a transvestite—an incident he publicly apologized for after being voted the Dodgers' "Man of the Year" for his community and charity work. He pitched well for almost three years but he and Tommy Lasorda never hit it off; he was never one of Lasorda's boys.

"Tommy's just one of those guys who, when you're going well, you're his man," Stewart says. "If you're not, forget it. I could pitch fifteen times in seventeen days, have one bad game and then not pitch for two weeks. I would go in to Tommy and ask him to give me a role—any role—and he would say, 'Yeah, sure, Dave,' and never do anything about it. I finally got tired of it and told him so. That pretty much clinched my being traded.''

He was dealt to Texas in August 1983. Things quickly went from bad to worse there. Stewart became a starter and was ineffective. Everything he threw was hard, and he felt he needed something off-speed. He began experimenting with a forkball in 1984. ''It wasn't a very good pitch at the time,'' he says. ''I got hit with it, but I thought I had to keep working on it. They didn't want me to.''

Stewart hit bottom in 1985. His marriage, which had been in trouble for a while, broke up. Bobby Valentine, whom he did not like, replaced Doug Rader, whom he did like, as the Texas manager. His elbow began to give him trouble. He pitched poorly and was booed. One night, walking off the field, he heard a couple of racial slurs and responded by yelling profanities back. Valentine demanded a public apology.

''There was no way,'' Stewart says. ''I wasn't sorry. I don't care if I'm the worst pitcher in history, what those people had yelled at me was inexcusable. The fans in Texas were bad fans. They didn't know baseball at all, just football. I wasn't apologizing to them.''

Valentine told him if he didn't apologize, he couldn't play for him. Stewart said that was fine with him. Two weeks later, he was traded to Philadelphia. By now, his elbow was killing him. He had surgery during the offseason and was slowly getting his arm strength back when the Phillies released him on May 9, 1986. He was twenty-nine years old and had a major league record of 30-35. He had not won a game since 1984. Did he ever think it was over?

''No. I knew I could pitch. I knew once my elbow was a hundred percent I could help somebody.'' It took him two weeks to find a job. Pat Gillick of the Blue Jays was interested in him, but didn't have a spot open. He recommended calling the A's, who were struggling with their pitching. The A's weren't all that interested, but general manager Sandy Alderson told Stewart he was welcome to come to Oakland if he would throw for manager Jackie Moore and pitching coach Wes Stock. They were impressed enough to offer him a Triple-A contract, which Stewart took. He pitched one game in Tacoma and was called up to Oakland—as a relief pitcher.

A month later, Moore was fired and LaRussa hired to replace him. Before he joined the team, LaRussa called Stewart from his home in Florida. ''We play in Boston Monday and they're pitching Clemens,'' LaRussa said. ''I'd like you to be the starter.''

Stewart's heart jumped. For a split second he thought LaRussa was joking—but LaRussa rarely jokes about baseball. Stewart beat Clemens that night and went 9-5 the rest of the season. The next four years he was a 20-game winner, the game's most consistent and durable pitcher. In 1989, he had been the MVP of the World Series, but it gave him little joy. That was the earthquake Series and it was Stewart's hometown that was devastated.

"I don't even like thinking about that time," he says. "I drove around the city and all you could see were houses crushed and destroyed, lives battered beyond repair. The hurt was unbelievable. I still feel it, the city still feels it. We had seventy-one murders during the first three months of 1992. Imagine that, seventy-one!"

Stewart has worked hard to bring some happiness back to Oakland. He first worked in the Boys' Club there as a teenager. He set up programs for the underprivileged in both Los Angeles and Texas, long before he was a star. In Oakland, he has used his celebrity to raise money for programs for underprivileged kids and put in countless hours working with boys and girls who have lost one or both parents. "I know how much I missed my father when he died," he says. "I know how much I miss my two kids now. I want to feel like I'm helping someone's kids even if I can't be with my own. This is my way of doing it."

Now, at thirty-five, he was one of Oakland's many free-agents-to-be. Oakland was home and he wanted to finish his career there. But he was pragmatic enough to understand that it was not likely to work out. If he pitched well and the A's offered him a contract, he would be delighted. If not, that was okay too. If Dave Stewart was one thing, he was a man who knew exactly what he was about, exactly who he was, exactly what he had to give to people—and what he had given.

In his locker, framed, hung a Ralph Waldo Emerson poem that a fan had sent him at the end of his struggling 1991 season. The poem is called "Success":

> *To laugh often and much;*
> *To win the respect of intelligent people and affection of*
> *   children;*
> *To earn the appreciation of honest critics and endure the*
> *   betrayal of false friends;*
> *To appreciate beauty;*
> *To find the best in others;*
> *To leave the world a bit better, whether by a healthy child, a*
> *   garden patch or a redeemed social condition;*
> *To know even one life has breathed easier because you have*
> *   lived.*
> *This is to have succeeded.*

Dennis Eckersley isn't likely to quote Emerson or even read him. It isn't that he has anything against poetry, it just isn't direct enough for him.

Stewart and Eckersley are kindred spirits in the sense that both are gentle men who are transformed on the mound. But where Stewart is introspective, sensitive, and analytical, Eckersley prefers not to do too much thinking.

"I've always hidden my insecurities by being cocky," he says. "I don't even like to think back on things that have gone wrong because if I do I might start to focus on them. I just want to go forward. Take what comes today."

If Eckersley sounds a little bit like a recovering alcoholic, that's because he is one. He has gone from the fast lane to the slow lane without losing his desire to run the race.

Like Stewart, he was born in Oakland, although he grew up in nearby Fremont. He pitched and played quarterback as a kid because he liked the idea of having the ball in his hands. "That always fascinated me," he says. "The idea that everything started with you. And I had a hell of an arm."

He quit football as a senior to concentrate on baseball—"they wanted me to play defense in football and I never much liked the hitting"—and was drafted in the third round by the Cleveland Indians. His first thought was "Cleveland, are you *kidding?*" but it worked out just fine—less than three years later, he found himself in the major leagues.

He was a star from day one. He was twenty, had a wicked fastball, long black flowing locks, and a swashbuckling attitude that said, "No one can touch me." He won forty games in three seasons with very bad teams and was an All-Star at twenty-two. But what looked like the perfect life wasn't. His marriage to his high school sweetheart was falling apart. Even worse, he was losing his wife to a teammate, Rick Manning. "It was a love triangle thing," he said. "I was already drinking before it started. Afterwards, I was worse. I was totally devastated. I just wanted to bury everything. I was bad, very bad."

Eckersley didn't know how bad he was at the time. Traded to Boston in 1978, he won twenty games for the Red Sox that year. If there was a party, Eckersley was likely to turn up. He was single and he lived that life to the hilt.

"In a lot of ways, everything happened too quickly in my life," he said. "I never went through the maturation process most people go through. I didn't go to college, I didn't even spend much time in the minors. I was just kind of thrown out there. Everything went right for me *and* everything went wrong. That was a different time. You smoked marijuana, partied, drank, did wild things without even think-

ing about it. I look back now and think, 'What an idiot.' I can't say I
was robbed of anything, though. It was my choice."

He met Nancy O'Neill, the daughter of a Boston cop, while in
Boston, and he married her in 1980. She tried to settle him down but
it wasn't easy. He was still drinking. His pitching suffered. In 1984, the
Red Sox traded him to the Cubs. He had two decent years there but
had his worst season ever in 1986—6-11 with a 4.57 ERA.

That winter, Nancy convinced him to check into rehab after
showing him a video of what he looked like when he was drunk. Then,
at the end of spring training, the Cubs traded him to the A's as part
of a five-player deal. The four other men have long since been forgotten.

It was Dave Duncan, the A's pitching coach, who suggested he
try the bullpen.

"If I hadn't been sober, I don't think I could have handled it,"
Eckersley says. "But I was ready for anything after rehab. The trade
thrilled me. I was ready to go somewhere and start all over. The
bullpen was more of that. I didn't really like it at first but I grew into
it. I could always throw strikes. That's one reason I threw a lot of
dingers [homers] as a starter, 'cause I was always around the plate."

He saved sixteen games as a part-time closer that year and forty-
five the next, when he emerged as the game's preeminent reliever.
That was the year of the famous Kirk Gibson home run in the World
Series.

"It bothered me. How could it *not* bother me?" he says. "But you
know, at that point in my life, sobriety was all that worried me. Nobody
was going to fuck with that, nobody. What was important was that I
was *there* to throw that pitch, no matter how much it hurt.

"To me, the game itself isn't fun. Winning is fun. I get jacked up,
really jacked up when I pitch. I'm full of myself when I come running
in there. Part of it is fear. That's a big motivator. There's no room to
make a mistake. You throw a dinger as a starter, there's innings left.
You do it closing, that's it, you're done. I sit out in the bullpen and fight
negative waves every night. I don't want to think about what could
happen to me.

"When I blow a save, it kills me. I feel like the other guys have
worked three hours to get the ball to me and then I blow it. It's awful."

Eckersley doesn't blow many. He saved 169 games from 1988
through 1991. He has become one of baseball's numbers men, a player
who has so many numbers after his name that it is dizzying. He will
probably end up in the Hall of Fame. Like Stewart, he gives a lot of
credit to LaRussa.

"Tony knows people so well," he says. "People see the intensity
and they miss how sensitive he is. Last year, I blew a game on the road

and I was just miserable. We were falling out of the race and I made
it worse in a game we should have had. When we got to the hotel, I
picked up the envelope with my room key in it and when I opened it,
there was one of Tony's little index cards.

"He had written a note that just said, 'Eck, don't worry about it.
You're the best.' That was all. I read it sitting on my bed and it brought
tears to my eyes. He always knows when you need something."

Eckersley hadn't needed much in '92. He pitched so well during
the first half of the season that the A's had made him the exception
among their free-agents-to-be; they re-signed him for two more years
for almost $8 million. No one in the clubhouse was the least bit upset
about it.

"He deserves every nickel," said McGwire, another one of the free
agents. "Everyone talks about all the injuries we've had and how
we've hung in there. Well, we have. But the fact is, there's one guy on
this team who hasn't gotten hurt and he's the reason we're still in the
race. That's Eck."

•

Eck wasn't even needed during the last two games of the Toronto
series. After Bordick's miracle, the A's rolled. Ron Darling pitched a
brilliant two-hitter on Saturday, then the A's blasted Jack Morris en
route to a 9–1 win on Sunday. The Twins kept winning too. The
margin was three as the A's headed east.

In his office after the last Jays game, LaRussa could barely contain
his excitement as he dressed. Alderson, who wasn't making the trip,
sat in a chair and listened as he talked.

"I may be proven completely wrong," LaRussa said, "but I've got
a feeling about this team right now. Our pitching is set up perfectly
going to Minnesota. Eck is rested. Maybe they'll stick it up our ass, but
I just don't think so. These guys are really something right now."

LaRussa's instincts were right. In the opener, the A's bombed the
Twins 9–1 behind Bob Welch. The next night, they trailed 6–2 in the
fifth, rallied to lead 11–6, and hung on 12–10. It was as draining a game
as LaRussa could remember in years. The key hit was a two-run triple
by Eric Fox in the sixth inning. The lead was down to one. LaRussa's
fears of a week ago—dropping from the race—were now behind him.

The Twins took a 4–2 lead into the ninth inning of the finale. If
they won, they would be up by two games. The A's could live with
that. But they didn't have to. With one out, Jerry Browne on third, and
Harold Baines on second, Fox came up to face Twins closer Rick
Aguilera. LaRussa had no choice but to let him hit. The only man he
had left on the bench was Quirk, his backup catcher.

Fox had one career home run as he stepped in. A moment later, he had two. He crushed Aguilera's third pitch over the right-field wall and the A's led 5–4. Eck did the rest, retiring the Twins one-two-three in the ninth.

If there was one hit that defined the A's season, it was Fox's homer. Two months after seriously considering giving up baseball, Fox had produced the biggest hit of an improbable season.

As the A's left Minnesota, the American League West standings said that they were tied with the Twins for first place. In this case, the numbers lied. Everyone on both teams knew that, remarkably enough, the race was now for the A's to lose.

25

FATHERS, SONS, AND EXPOS

August is always the longest month in a baseball season. Almost everywhere, the weather is stifling and energy-sapping. Playing in a dome, while cooler, is depressing. Who wants to be indoors in August?

The bad teams have run out of excuses and second chances. Their hopes for a post–All-Star break reincarnation have gone unfulfilled. There is still a month to go before the September call-ups that can infuse some life into a dead clubhouse, give the fans something to look forward to and the media something to write about.

August is also tough on the contenders. They have already played more than one hundred games but there is still a long way to go. The games *are* crucial—but no one wants to admit as much and add to the building pressure. The fact remains that you can't play for a pennant in September if you don't play well in August.

By August, baseball has divided itself into two distinct groups: those looking to add a key player for a pennant race and those looking to trade that player for prospects (who can put them into a pennant race in the future). General managers work the phones harder. Scouts spend extra time on the road. Managers and pitching coaches must give honest assessments of how their players will perform when it matters most—in September. This is not a month for illusions.

In a literal sense, August is baseball's hottest period. In a figurative sense, August is the time when temperatures rise.

One clubhouse seemed devoid of all those feelings of building pressure. The Montreal Expos, the first team to fire a manager in 1992, had quietly made their move during July. They finished June at 35-38, leaving them almost exactly where they had been on May 22, when general manager Dan Duquette had fired Tom Runnells and replaced him with Felipe Alou. Their record under Alou at that point was 18-18 and they were in fifth place, eight games behind the Pirates.

But although things might have appeared the same from the outside, they were not. Alou was twenty years older than Runnells; twenty years more experienced; twenty years more relaxed. Runnells was like many of the other young managers in the game. He was a detail person, someone who believed in lots of meetings, lots of discipline, lots of rules. For some teams, this approach worked. Buck Showalter was very similar to Runnells and the Yankees loved him. LaRussa and Leyland weren't big on rules, but they were big on detail.

In the end, it came back to attitude. Showalter convinced his players they could win. Runnells, for whatever reason, had them thinking too much about losing. When Alou took over, he never told the players that the rules no longer existed. He just didn't talk about them anymore. The players got the message.

"We had gotten to the point where there was a fear of losing every night," said pitcher Mark Gardner. "We all respected Tom Runnells, but we weren't comfortable with him. Over the course of a long season, comfort is important."

Alou brought that comfort to the Expos. When people asked him if he felt pressure, managing with a contract that only ran until the end of the season, he laughed.

"You want to know what pressure is?" he said. "Pressure is leaving home when you're nineteen because your family needs the $175 a month you're gonna get paid. Pressure is managing winter ball and walking into your office and finding a lineup card on your desk that the owner has left there as a 'suggestion.' This isn't pressure, this is fun."

That approach seemed to get through to the Expos. Duquette had made the managing change because he saw potential in his team that wasn't being reached. The Expos had two excellent starters in Dennis Martinez and Ken Hill; two more with great potential, Gardner and Chris Nabholz; a rapidly improving closer in John Wetteland; and perhaps the best young lineup in baseball. Delino DeShields and Marquis Grissom at the top of the lineup were capable of running a team into the ground. RBI men Larry Walker and Moises Alou were hitting behind them. All they lacked was a legitimate power hitter and a consistent catcher.

In July, the young players began to find themselves. The team climbed to .500 just before the All-Star break, then went 9-3 immediately after, putting them at 53-47. That string coincided with a Pittsburgh slide and the continued mediocrity of the Mets, Cardinals, and Cubs. When the Expos beat the Cardinals for their fifth straight win on July 28, they were tied with the Pirates for first place.

The next afternoon, the Pirates lost again in Chicago, in eleven innings. That night, the Expos had a chance to go into first place all by themselves. But, playing in St. Louis and leading 1–0 in the seventh, they couldn't hang on. Martinez gave up a home run to ex-Expo Andres Galarraga to tie the game and Bernard Gilkey won it for the Cards in the ninth. Both teams won the next night, then a Pittsburgh win over St. Louis and a Montreal loss to Philadelphia put the Pirates back in first by a game.

It was the first of August and the Expos were in a pennant race. And loving every minute of it.

Much was made, naturally, of the father-son connection when Alou was named manager. Just as naturally, both Felipe and Moises played it down. "It's not going to be tough managing Moises," Alou said when he was hired. "Because he isn't going to play much. He's the fourth outfielder."

That didn't last long, though. Ivan Calderon was hurt shortly after Alou took over and Moises, who had missed all of 1991 because of shoulder surgery, quickly became one of the hottest bats in baseball. In early August, with Calderon almost ready to come back, Felipe Alou was insisting his son would have to go back to the bench.

"I didn't mind being the fourth guy early in the season because I hadn't proved anything," Moises said. "But if he benches me now, after I've hit the way I have, it's gonna piss me off. I have a feeling he'll figure something out, though. He usually does."

Felipe Alou had been part of the first and only all-brother outfield in major league history when he and brothers Matty and Jesus had all been starters for the San Francisco Giants in 1963.

"It didn't seem like a big thing at the time," he said. "We'd been playing the outfield together all our lives in the Dominican, so it didn't seem all that different. Of course now, almost thirty years later, it hasn't been done again, so I guess it was a big deal."

Alou had grown up outside Santo Domingo, the son of a carpenter. He was the second of six children and, although he played baseball growing up, he never thought of it as a profession. Back then, there was very little organized baseball in the Dominican Republic. In fact, Alou's clearest memory of baseball as a child is of the day he and his friends got caught cutting down a tree in a field so they could play ball.

He was a good athlete, running track, throwing the javelin, and playing baseball. In 1955, he made the Dominican Pan American team that went to Mexico City and beat the U.S. for the gold medal in baseball. That was when scouts first spotted him. Alou wasn't interested, though. He was enrolled at the University of Santo Domingo and planning to become a doctor.

But his coach there, Horacio Martinez, was also doing some scouting for the Giants. He offered Alou $175 a month plus a $300 bonus for signing. His mother wanted him to stay in school. His father, whose business was struggling, said to take the money. He did and headed to the U.S., knowing exactly one word of English: yes.

"But when I got to Miami, no one said 'yes,' " he remembers, laughing. "They all said 'yeah.' So my first lesson in English was that the one word I thought I knew, I didn't know."

He knew how to hit, however, and he made it to the Giants in two years. He ended up playing seventeen years in the major leagues and retired with 2,101 hits and 206 home runs, only the thirty-first player in history to have more than 2,000 hits and 200 home runs. When he retired, he went home to the Dominican for two years but found he missed baseball. So, he took a coaching job with the Expos in 1976.

He never finished spring training that year. On March 26, he received a phone call from his ex-wife, María. His oldest son, Felipe Junior, had been killed in a swimming pool accident. He was sixteen.

Felipe Alou left spring training and didn't come back. He spent that year in the Dominican, trying to deal with his grief and trying to help Felipe's younger brothers, José and Moises, twelve and nine at the time of the accident, deal with what had happened.

"It's been sixteen years now and I still have trouble talking about this," Alou said. "The pain of losing a child stays with you forever. For almost a year, I really wanted to do nothing, nothing at all."

Moises was just as traumatized by Felipe's death. "He was almost like a father to me," he said. "He was only sixteen, but he acted twenty-five. He would never let me leave the table until I had finished all my food. He was the one who really taught me how to play. I was seven years younger than he was, but I went everywhere with him. For me, growing up, he was the man of the house."

Felipe Alou returned to the Expos organization in 1977, managed in the minors, and had two stints coaching the major league team. In 1986, he asked to manage the Class-A team in West Palm Beach because he and his third wife (Alou has been married three times and now has a total of nine children, the most recent one born in May '92) were building a house nearby. He managed in West Palm Beach until

'92, when Dan Duquette asked him to come to Montreal as the team's bench coach.

"Your boss asks you to do something, you realize it's not a request, it's an order," Alou says. "If Dan wanted me in Montreal, that's where I went."

And so, on the night of May 21 when Dan said he wanted Alou to manage the team, that's what Alou did. "I wasn't happy about it," he says. "I told Dan that I thought things were going to come around for us. But he said no, he wanted to make a move. The funny thing was, I had been reading in the papers that if they fired Tom they were gonna try to hire [Earl] Weaver or [Don] Zimmer. Seems like every time a manager gets fired you read that the team is gonna hire Weaver or Zimmer. I was surprised when he told me I was first choice."

No more surprised than Moises. He figured something might be up when his father was called in from an offday fishing trip to meet with the general manager. But when he heard nothing from his father that night, he assumed it had been a false alarm.

"Next day I walk into the clubhouse and Mark Gardner says to me, 'Hey, Mo, you hear? Your dad's the manager.' I thought he was joking. But he wasn't."

Moises Alou had barely known his father growing up, since Felipe and María had split when he was two. For most of his childhood, he only saw him sporadically.

"The strange thing is, there are guys on this team who know my father better than I do because they played for him in the minor leagues," Moises said. "They've actually been around him more than I have."

The 1992 season marked the first year that father and son were ever in the same place—Pittsburgh—on Father's Day. Moises didn't want to make a big deal of it, so he slipped into the manager's office early and left his present sitting on the desk. Rich Griffin, the Expos' media relations director, caught him coming out of the office, checking to make sure no one had seen him go in.

When the Expos got hot in July, the Alous became a big story. Neither one really had much desire to focus on the father-son angle, but both understood it was going to happen whether they liked it or not.

"I've dealt with being an Alou all through the minor leagues," said Moises, who had originally been drafted by the Pirates in 1986 after two years of junior college ball in California. "I know what my father and my uncles did in the game and sometimes you get tired of hearing all about it. But then I look at someone like Pete Rose, Jr. [who had been an Orioles farmhand], and realize I've got it easy compared to him."

Alou was traded to the Expos in August of 1990 and ended up

playing in five different cities that season: Harrisburg, Buffalo, Indianapolis, Pittsburgh, and Montreal. The Expos were counting on him to make the team in 1991 but he hurt his shoulder playing winter ball. After that lost season, there was some question about whether he would ever make it in the major leagues. It was a happy twist that his blossoming coincided with his father's getting a chance to manage.

When his chance came, Felipe Alou had given up any hope that he would manage in the major leagues. Now that he had the chance, he had no idea how long it would last.

"My contract is just for this year, so who knows what will happen at the end of the season," he said. (The Expos signed him for three years at season's end.) "There's no doubt that people are hesitant to give Hispanics the chance to manage. Part of it is the language, I guess. I speak with an accent, but if I know baseball, so what? People tend to be judged in this world on where they come from, on what school they went to, things like that. I understand that. I've learned to deal with it.

"All I've tried to do as manager of this team is get the fear of losing the hell out of this clubhouse. We're gonna go out and play tonight and if we lose, we'll come in here and believe that we'll win tomorrow. That's all I can ask."

The Expos had a chance to compete every night. They usually got good pitching and they had speed throughout the lineup. Alou was actually the *oldest* member of the outfield; Grissom and Walker were twenty-five and Moses had turned twenty-six in July. DeShields, the second baseman, was only twenty-three and just starting to live up to his huge potential.

The team's versatility was never more evident than during an early August game in Philadelphia. DeShields, the leadoff hitter, hit two home runs. Grissom, the number-two hitter, also hit a home run and stole his fifty-fifth base of the season. Walker, the cleanup hitter, stole his tenth base. Ken Hill, picked up during the offseason from the Cardinals for first baseman Andres Galarraga, didn't have his best stuff, but still got his thirteenth win.

John Wetteland, who had begun his major league career as a starter for the Dodgers, picked up his twenty-sixth save. Wetteland, who would turn twenty-six later in August, had rescued his career a year earlier by doing something very few pitchers do: asking to go to the bullpen. Even though relief pitchers can make big money now, it is rare for a starter to decide he wants to give up a spot in the rotation.

After failing to make the Dodgers out of spring training, he struggled for four starts at Albuquerque. Frustrated, he asked for the chance to close—stamina had always been his biggest problem as a starter. He then went 20-for-20 in save chances. That was the reason the

Expos got him, even though he'd had only one major league save to his credit prior to 1992.

The Pirates reeled off eleven straight victories after the loss in Chicago that had left them tied with the Expos. But Montreal wasn't going away. Even after the Pirates' string, their lead was only two-and-a-half games.

No one was happier to see the Expos in a pennant race than Dan Duquette. When boy-wonder Dave Dombrowski left the Expos the previous September to become general manager of the Marlins, the team named boy-wonder-in-waiting Duquette to succeed him. Duquette was thirty-three at the time, but like Dombrowski had been working for a baseball team since the day he graduated from college.

Duquette had first run a baseball team at the age of eighteen, when he and his older brother Dennis put together a semipro team in their hometown of Dalton, Massachusetts. Duquette had been a decent high school catcher, but after going to a tryout camp at sixteen realized he wasn't going to make it to the major leagues as a player. So, like Dombrowski, he began focusing on being a general manager.

He and his brother ran the team every summer while Duquette was at Amherst College and did well, even if the catcher (Dan) didn't have the greatest arm anyone had ever seen. By the time he was a senior, Duquette was convinced he wanted to get a job in baseball and began working on getting an interview with Harry Dalton, the general manager of the Milwaukee Brewers.

"Harry had grown up in western Massachusetts, he had gone to Amherst, I knew people who knew him, I figured if I couldn't get in to see him, I wasn't going to get in to see anybody," Duquette said. "Finally, in April of my senior year, I got an interview."

He impressed Dalton enough that he was hired as an assistant administrator in the Brewers' scouting department. Five years later, at twenty-seven, he was the scouting director. During his time with the Brewers, Duquette got to know Dombrowski, then with the White Sox. "We would run into each other a lot at offseason banquets," he says. "We weren't close, but we got along."

Well enough that when Dombrowski, newly promoted to assistant general manager of the Expos, was looking for someone to be his successor as farm director, he called Duquette. "If my goal was to be a general manager, I needed to run a farm system," Duquette says. "This was my shot."

He joined the Expos before the '88 season and was promoted to assistant GM when Dombrowski got his promotion to GM. In 1990, he interviewed for the San Diego job that Joe McIlvaine ended up taking. A year later, after the Marlins were awarded one of the expansion franchises, Duquette began hearing the same rumors about his boss that everyone else was hearing.

"I finally walked in to him one day and said, 'Is Barger interested in you?' And Dave said, 'Yeah, it looks like it.' "

At the same time, the Colorado Rockies had expressed interest in Duquette. So, during the same week that Dombrowski was talking to the Marlins, he was talking to the Rockies. The Marlins offered the job to Dombrowski but the Rockies decided to go with Bob Gebhard. Duquette wondered if and hoped the Expos would turn to him.

"I thought I was ready," he says. "I didn't think my age should be a factor, especially since I was a year *older* than Dave was when he got the job. When Claude [Brochu] told me he wanted me to take over, it seemed like the logical thing."

Duquette was named as Dombrowski's replacement on September 19. Two days later, a huge chunk of the Olympic Stadium roof fell, forcing the Expos to finish the season on the road—twenty-three straight games. They finished last for the first time since 1976.

"I figured we had no place to go but up," Duquette says.

He hoped they would move up with Runnells as the manager, especially since he had been the one who recommended that Dombrowski hire him the previous year. But even before the end of April, he was beginning to think about making a change.

Symbolic of Duquette's concerns was a series in St. Louis in late April. Runnells dropped DeShields from leadoff to the eighth spot in the batting order one night, then benched him the next night. DeShields is a high-strung, often difficult young player—but very, very talented. Runnells felt he needed discipline. Duquette thought he needed to be put in the leadoff spot every night and left alone.

When he made the decision the following month to make the switch, it was not an easy one. He liked Runnells and he also knew that, after one year, Runnells probably hadn't been given a fair chance to prove himself. But his gut told him it was the right thing to do.

"It was certainly the toughest thing I've had to do in baseball," he said. "And when I called Felipe in and told him I wanted him to take the club, he really didn't want to do it. He thought Tom deserved more time. He probably did. But I was convinced we were going to be a better team with Felipe's approach."

That instinct proved correct. Still, Duquette wasn't gloating. The Expos are and will always be one of the more difficult franchises to have success with in baseball. They play in a ballpark that, even when the roof isn't falling in, is one of baseball's eyesores. Built in 1976 for the Montreal Olympics, it was supposed to be the first dome with a retractable roof. It was—but only when the roof worked, which wasn't often. The Expos now play with the roof closed at all times and the place is just about as dreary as the Kingdome. When the Braves came to Montreal in mid-August, a jackhammer blasted away behind the center-field fence every night throughout batting practice.

"How old is this goddamn place?" Braves manager Bobby Cox wanted to know. "I mean, are they ever going to be finished with it? Every time you come in here you go out with a headache."

Olympic Stadium *does* have one of the great scoreboard features in baseball, though. Whenever an opposing pitcher throws over to first base with a Montreal runner there, an animated chicken appears on the board, complete with clucking sound. Each additional throw over—which, with the Expos' speed, is frequent—adds a chicken to the board and the clucking grows louder.

When Tom Glavine threw over on Grissom eight times one night, the place sounded like a giant chicken coop—no doubt giving Cox an even bigger headache. The postscript: Grissom stole second anyway.

Attendance picked up as the team picked up, which was important, since the 1991 per-game average had been less than 15,000. That would have meant a total gate of about 1.2 million if the Expos had been able to play all eighty-one home games. In '92, the average would be closer to 21,000 and the total attendance a little more than 1.6 million. That represented progress.

Whether the Expos could take the step from young and talented to young winners was a question to be answered down the road. This is, after all, a franchise that came into being in 1969 and has produced only one Eastern Division title—in the 1981 strike year—since then. Keeping the young stars in Montreal is Duquette's next challenge.

"We have to make this an attractive place to play," he says. "I think we now have an atmosphere where our guys enjoy being a part of this team. The next thing we need to do is make them feel a part of the city."

Alou, whose wife is French-Canadian, is very aware of that fact. In August, he was asked if he would participate in a charity fashion show. He said yes. Then he was asked if he might be able to convince some of his players to show up.

"I told the guys it was an important thing to do," he says. "Almost the whole team showed up. I think that was a good sign. There were more than a thousand people there and they all noticed."

Maybe the players showed up so they could hoot at their manager as he walked down the runway in the winter coat he was asked to model. What matters, though, is that he asked and they came. In Montreal, the August dog days had become the fun days.

26

DOG DAYS IN THE DOME

When Baltimore Orioles manager Johnny Oates arrived in his office at Camden Yards on the morning of August 9, he was not in a good mood. Two nights earlier, with a chance to move to within two games of the Toronto Blue Jays, his team had squandered a ninth-inning lead and lost to the Cleveland Indians in thirteen innings. Twenty-four hours later, only a Glenn Davis infield hit prevented Charles Nagy from pitching a no-hitter for the Tribe.

"This is exactly what I was concerned about, coming into this weekend." Oates glanced pensively at a lineup card he had yet to fill out. "All the talk around here about the series in Toronto and the guys don't have their minds right here to play Cleveland. Last night, the way Nagy pitched, probably it would have made no difference. But Friday night we made mental mistakes that cost us the game. That frustrates me."

When Johnny Oates talks about being frustrated, he does so in a tone that is little different from his "happy" tone. He is as competitive as any man in baseball, but he has learned to enjoy the game, something he says he never did as a player.

"I was uptight my entire playing career, every single day," he said. "All I did was worry: Am I going to get cut, traded, released? Why don't I play more? Why am I not in the lineup today? What does it mean? Has the manager given up on me? I lived that way for ten years."

His attitude changed, Oates says, when he became a Christian. "I was missing something in my life and it turned out what I was missing was God. That isn't something I talk about a lot because I know a lot of people's eyes glaze over when you bring it up. I don't want to bore people with it or sound like I know something they don't. I'm bothered by people who do that. But the truth is, being a Christian did change my life."

It didn't change his competitiveness. Oates isn't a screamer and he isn't likely to kick things too often. But he does get snappish sometimes after losses, especially, he says, "if I know I screwed up. That will usually stay with me until I come to the ballpark the next day. Then I know I have to get rid of that feeling and start over again."

Oates and the Orioles had been one of baseball's most pleasant stories during the first half of the season. Their new ballpark was the talk of the game and sellouts had become the norm every night. The team was fun to watch because it knew how to play. The Orioles rarely made fundamental mistakes and they played excellent defense to back up pitching that, while greatly improved over 1991, still wasn't overwhelming. They were 49-38 at the break, four games behind the Blue Jays.

They began the second half on the road, winning three of four games in Texas. From there, they went to Chicago, where they won the opener but blew a 7–2 eighth-inning lead in the second game. That was aggravating. The last game in Chicago was an afternoon game. The Orioles would charter home afterward and open a home stand the next night against the Rangers.

Midway through the game, Orioles public relations assistant Bob Miller received a phone call in the press box. There had been an accident back home involving Tim Hulett's six-year-old son Sam. He had been taken to the emergency room at Johns Hopkins Hospital. Miller immediately got word to Hulett, the Orioles utility man in the infield, to call his wife Linda at the hospital.

A few minutes later, traveling secretary Phil Itzoe went down to the clubhouse to find out what was going on. Hulett was on the phone being switched maddeningly from one department of the hospital to another. When he finally found Linda, the news wasn't good. Sam had run out in front of a car. His condition was critical.

Itzoe immediately made arrangements to get Hulett on a flight home. His parents, who had driven up from Springfield for the game, went to the airport with him. By the time the game—another ag-gravating come-from-ahead loss—was over, everyone on the team had heard about Sam Hulett.

Tim Hulett is the kind of person every baseball team needs. At thirty-two, he was in his sixth year in the majors. His salary was a relatively modest $380,000, but he was invaluable to the team because he would play anywhere, anytime, and never complained about not playing. He is one of those rare baseball people whom *everyone* likes.

Sam Hulett was in a coma by the time his father reached the hospital that night. Early the next morning, the boy died.

On the day Sam died, the Orioles had to report to Camden Yards to play a baseball game. The entire city went into mourning and, as public figures, the Orioles were thrust into the strange position of being spokespeople—for Hulett, for the team, for all of Baltimore. Storm Davis, the team's player representative, who had spent the night at the hospital with the Huletts, was designated as spokesman; most of the players were too stunned to say anything. There was no music played during batting practice that night, no talk around the batting cage. The clubhouse was completely silent before the game. The Orioles lost to the Rangers 4–3. It was hard for anyone to care.

"I think we all went home that night and hugged our own kids," Oates said. "We all know that it can happen to any of us. You can't protect your children every single day of their lives. That's very scary."

Mike Flanagan, the forty-year-old left-hander who was usually responsible for the sharp-tongued one-liners that helped keep the team loose, was so numbed by Sam Hulett's death he could barely speak to anyone for two days. Earlier that week, he'd received a long letter from his father, who, like Flanagan's grandfather, had played professional baseball, although neither ever made it to the big leagues.

Flanagan still remembers playing catch as a little boy with his grandfather in the backyard. "He was already in his seventies by then and if I didn't throw the ball right where he was holding his glove, it went past him and I had to run it down," he said. "That's when I first learned the importance of control."

Flanagan's father never said much to him as his career progressed from high school to college to the minor leagues to the majors to the 1979 Cy Young Award to a career that had lasted seventeen big league seasons. Now, out of the blue, had come the letter.

"There's an old saying that says something like 'Pity the Irish because they cannot show their emotions,' " Flanagan said. "That's always been my dad. In this letter, he told me for the first time how he felt about what I'd accomplished. He said on the day I got called up to the majors my mother and sister were screaming at him to come and watch television because they were talking about it. Instead, he went upstairs. They were furious with him. The reason he went upstairs was because he didn't want them to see him crying. I read that and I almost started crying myself. It's taken him a long time to be able to say those things. I think being around his grandchildren has helped him. That, and being aware of time passing by."

Every time Flanagan thought about Sam Hulett, he thought not only about his own children, but about his father and the feelings that fathers and sons sometimes let go unspoken.

Cal Ripken, Jr., didn't have a son, he had a two-year-old daughter, but he felt many of the same emotions Flanagan felt. In a season that had turned into an emotional roller coaster—because of his ongoing contract negotiations and his struggles at the plate—Ripken was also dealing with the guilt he felt every time he left his daughter to go on a road trip.

"She's a real person now," he said softly one night after a game. "And she really gets angry at me when I have to go away. On this home stand, every time I go to put her to bed, she says she can't sleep unless Kelly comes in to see her because she knows Kelly isn't going to leave her like I do. This afternoon, when I put her down for a nap, I had a long talk with her about how much I loved her and how hard it was for me to go away. She finally went to sleep without asking for her mother."

Ripken smiled grimly. "Of course, tomorrow we leave again for ten days."

Every professional athlete grapples with these feelings. Ripken felt it so strongly before Sam Hulett's death that he talked about getting out of baseball completely as soon as he was through playing so he could get off the road and make up for lost time with his family.

Sam Hulett's death only made him feel more strongly about it. The day after the Orioles left for Toronto, Rachel Ripken turned to her mother and said, "It was very mean of Daddy to leave me again." When Kelly Ripken reported this to her husband, he had to fight the urge to get on a plane and fly home.

On the morning after Sam's death, Rick Vaughn, the Orioles public relations director, received a phone call from Tim Hulett. "I read the papers this morning," Hulett said to Vaughn. "It sounds like the guys are really hurting. Maybe I should come in and talk to them."

"Tim, you don't have to do that," Vaughn told him. "They understand."

"Rick, I want to come in," Tim Hulett insisted.

The next morning, he did. He and his family were flying to Illinois for Sam's funeral the next day. He talked to his teammates for a few minutes, telling them how much he appreciated their feelings and their support. He was clear-eyed and his voice never wavered.

"I have a message for you guys from Linda," he said finally. "She says if you guys are still four back when you come back from this road trip, she's going to be really pissed off at you."

With that, he left to go home and bury his son.

The Orioles finished that road trip with a three-game sweep in Boston, but it still left them three games behind the Blue Jays. Tim Hulett rejoined the team in Baltimore on August 3, taking batting practice that first night back. He had thought about taking the rest of the season off, but after talking it over with his wife, decided to return.

"We have to go on, all of us," he said. "The pain will be with us but we also believe that we'll see Sam again in Heaven. That keeps us going. I love to play baseball. Being back is therapeutic for me right now."

Hulett was activated four nights later and played in the thirteen-inning loss to Cleveland that left Oates and all the Orioles so frustrated. They could have closed the gap to two that night, but didn't. "We look up on the board and see that the Blue Jays have lost and we start to press," pitching coach Dick Bosman said. "We can't afford to do that. We can't start getting tight every time we think we have a real chance to catch these guys. Because the fact is, we *do* have a real chance to catch these guys."

They did finally close the margin to two games in the Sunday finale against Cleveland, beating the troublesome Indians 5–4 while the Blue Jays were losing their third straight game in Detroit. That set the stage for a four-game series in SkyDome. It was just another one of those noncrucial August series that everyone would insist was no big deal because it wasn't yet September.

But September was now less than three weeks away.

•

Since it opened in 1989, Toronto's SkyDome has become one of base-ball's showplaces. It is *the* state-of-the-art baseball playpen complete with hotel, Hard Rock Café, the very "in" Windows on SkyDome restaurant, and, of course, several McDonald's sprinkled around the ballpark.

When SkyDome (putting a "the" before SkyDome is generally frowned on in Toronto) opened, the Blue Jays had established them-selves as one of the better teams in the game, good enough to draw well in ancient Exhibition Stadium, an icicle disguised as an aging ballpark. The uniqueness of the new park, with all its space-age gadgetry, combined with the solidness of the ball club, made the Blue Jays the best draw in baseball. Night after night fifty thousand people pack the place. In 1991, the Blue Jays became the first team in baseball history to draw more than four million fans in a season. In 1992, they would repeat that feat.

The SkyDome story is not a perfect one, though. The projected cost, when the ballpark was first approved, was $225 million. The final cost was closer to $600 million and the debt—currently being picked up by the taxpayers of Ontario—grows daily because of the interest (that's bank interest as opposed to fan interest). The raking in the upper deck is almost frighteningly steep. Several people have had fatal heart attacks up there. The screen behind home plate is so thick that fans seated there sometimes have trouble following the ball.

And, while it is baseball's most spectacular setting when the roof is open—with the CN Tower standing majestically adjacent on the first-base side—it is just a dome when the roof is closed. It is a brighter, more attractive dome than any of the others, but it is still a dome.

"When we first opened, the idea was that we would play with the dome opened except when the weather was really bad," club president Paul Beeston said. "But the way things have evolved, we now play with the dome closed unless the weather is really good."

Which is really foolish. The point of a retractable roof is to play outdoors except when you can't. Since the roof can be closed in eighteen minutes, starting a game with it open represents very little risk even if rain is threatening.

The backward thinking of the Blue Jays was never more evident than on the first night of the series with the Orioles. The afternoon was warm and perfect but thunderstorms were in the evening forecast. And so, at four-fifteen, even before batting practice started, the dome was closed. It did rain later—but *much* later. The game should have at least started with the dome open.

The Blue Jays preferred playing with the dome closed because, for some reason, they had a much better record playing indoors at home than outdoors. That trend continued in the opener. Mike Mussina pitched his worst game of the season for the Orioles, giving up five runs in the first three innings, and Todd Stottlemyre, who had struggled all season, gave up just two runs in seven innings. The Jays won easily, 8–4.

"We can talk all we want about these games not being any different than any others, but we all know that's not true," said Dave Winfield. "You play a series like this, everything feels different. The pregame atmosphere is different, BP is different, the questions you get are different. We know it and they know it. This was a good start. Maybe it'll send them a message."

The message didn't get through very clearly, however. The Orioles came back the next two nights and won convincingly, 3–0 and 11–4. Suddenly, they were only one game back with one game left to play in the series. Panic began to set in around the city. The newspapers were full of "Jays Collapsing" headlines. There was even some talk that the team might just as well write this year off and begin preparing for next. Even the Jays appeared confused. After getting bombed in the 11–4 game, losing pitcher Jimmy Key tried to downplay the situation, saying "We're still only one game behind and there's a long way to go."

There *was* a long way to go, Jim, but the Blue Jays were one game *ahead.*

One person not likely to panic was Pat Gillick, the man who had pieced together the franchise from the very beginning. Gillick may be the most low-key man in baseball. He had decided during the offseason that he was going to retire at the end of the '94 season, even though he would only be fifty-seven. The reason? "It's just time," he said. "I want to do some other things. I've never really loved the game as much as I've loved the challenges of putting a team together. I don't sit in the ballpark every night and say, 'Isn't it great to be here?' There are other places I'd just as soon be."

One of those places was the theater. Gillick and his wife Doris both love going to theater and, when Gillick makes a rare foray out of SkyDome for lunch, he usually wanders a few blocks over to the theater district.

Gillick has the theater—or at least acting—in his blood. His mother, Thelma Daniels, was a silent-film star in the 1920s. She and Gillick's father, Larry Gillick, split four months after their only child was born. Gillick lived with his mother until she remarried. His stepfather was in the trucking business and that meant moving around a lot. Rather than take her young son on the road with her, Thelma Daniels left him in Los Angeles with her parents.

"My grandmother wasn't the easiest person in the world to live with," Gillick says, smiling at the memory. "She was tough, crusty. I had to toe the line all the time. She was a good person down deep, but living with her wasn't easy. My joy was playing ball."

Gillick played all sports as a kid, but always excelled in baseball. In junior high school, his grandmother sent him to military school but let him come home to L.A. as a high school junior to finish at Notre Dame High School. He was a good enough pitcher that the Giants (still in New York at the time) offered him $4,000 to sign when he graduated. But he wasn't quite seventeen and his grandmother didn't think pro baseball was the right route. So he went to college, graduating from the University of Southern California in 1959. By then, the Orioles were interested in him and offered him a contract—for $4,000. "Shows you how much I improved in college," he said.

He was in the Orioles system for five years but never made it to the majors. In 1960 he was sent to Fox Cities, where he played for Earl Weaver, who was just starting his managing career. "Earl was even wilder then than he was when he got to the big leagues," Gillick said. "I remember one night in Sioux City he got into this huge fight with our bus driver and fired him on the spot. Fortunately, he knew there was a backup driver available."

The backup driver was Cal Ripken, Sr., the team's catcher, who had learned to drive a bus in the lower minor leagues. Gillick still remembers the night in August of that year when Ripken announced to his teammates the birth of his first son, Calvin Junior—"my little ballplayer," he boasted proudly.

Gillick made it to the Orioles' major league camp in 1962 but never got to pitch above the Triple-A level. In 1963 he hurt his arm and decided it was time to get on with his life. He was getting ready to go back to USC as a graduate assistant under baseball coach Rod De- deaux. "I was going to get my master's and get into teaching or coaching," he said.

But before he could enroll in school, Eddie Robinson, who had been an Orioles hitting instructor, called him. Robinson was going to Houston, which had just completed its second year in the National League, and wanted to know if Gillick was interesting in a scouting job. He wasn't. "But Eddie kept after me and finally convinced me to give it a try. I figured I'd give it two years and see how I liked it."

He liked it enough to stay with the Astros for ten years before Tal Smith migrated from Houston to the Yankees and offered Gillick the job of farm director. Gillick was there three years before Smith, who had left the Yankees by then, recommended him to Peter Bavasi for the newly created Blue Jays job. Gillick took the job, although he says he would have been just as happy to have continued as a scout. "That's still the aspect of the business I enjoy the most," he said. "But the challenge, here was something I couldn't turn down."

He built the team around pitching and draft choices and by 1983, the Blue Jays were winners. Two years later they were in the play-offs. Every year since then, they have been in a pennant race. And yet, prior to 1992, they had never gotten to the World Series.

"I'm not at all unhappy with what we've done here," Gillick said. "In fact, I'm very happy with what we've created and the kind of team we put on the field every year. But you can't feel really satisfied until you've won the whole thing at least once."

The '92 season started as almost all seasons do now in Toronto: with high hopes and concerns about whether a talented team would perform under pressure. The Blue Jays won their first six games, caus- ing Johnny Oates to publicly wonder if they might go undefeated. But they came back to earth and now looked not only vulnerable, but fragile.

"Right now our pitching just isn't very good," Gillick said, munching on a piece of Italian bread on the afternoon of the 11–4 loss. "Our best pitcher [Juan Guzmán] is on the disabled list and we aren't sure when he'll be back. [Jack] Morris has pitched well, but he isn't what he used to be, and Key has struggled. Stottlemyre and Wells are both talented, but neither one of them has pitched the way he's capable."

Gillick had been trying for more than a month to convince the Angels' Whitey Herzog to trade Jim Abbott, but had gotten nowhere. He'd become convinced in early August that he wasn't going to be able to swing a deal for a pitcher, so he took the unusual step of going to his manager (Cito Gaston) and his pitching coach (Galen Cisco), seeking their approval to call Stottlemyre and Wells in to talk to them himself.

An an ex-pitcher, Gillick can tell quickly when a pitcher has lost confidence. That was what he believed had happened to Wells and Stottlemyre. "I told them to quit nibbling all the time, to work faster, to have confidence in themselves," he said. "Their numbers say that they're both very talented pitchers. But they haven't pitched that way most of the year.

"If we don't get Guzmán back, we aren't going to win. And if we do get him back, we still aren't going to win if some of these other guys don't pitch better."

A week after he talked to Stottlemyre and Wells, Gillick decided to intervene in the clubhouse again. This time it involved third baseman Kelly Gruber, who had gone from being a budding superstar in 1990 (118 RBI) to an oft-injured enigma in 1992. Gruber had played poorly all season, then injured his back just before the All-Star break and gone on the DL. During the break, there were reports in the Toronto newspapers that he had been seen waterskiing. Gruber denied that but there were strong suspicions in the clubhouse that he wasn't hurt as badly as he claimed. More likely, some Blue Jays thought, his feelings were hurt because he had become the target of boos due to his mediocre play.

With the Orioles coming to town, Gillick and Gaston thought it imperative that Gruber play in all four games, that his teammates know he was going to play, and that he understand that he was important to the team because of his work at third base, even if he wasn't hitting.

On the afternoon of the Orioles opener, Gillick and Gaston called Gruber into Gaston's office and told him they wanted him in the lineup that night. Gruber wasn't sure. He said his back was still bothering him. "If that's the case, Kelly, you should go on the DL," Gillick said. "We'll get someone in here who's healthy."

Gruber got the message: Play or go on the DL. "I can play tonight," he said. "But I'm not sure I'll be able to play tomorrow."

"Fine," Gaston said. "We'll worry about that tomorrow."

Gruber played in all four games of the series.

By the time the teams met in the final game, the momentum of the season seemed to have shifted to the Orioles. They had won two in a row, the Blue Jays were wounded and bickering, and Baltimore was pitching rookie Arthur Rhodes, who had pitched well in five of six starts since coming up from Rochester a month earlier. His opponent was Doug Linton, a twenty-seven-year-old lifetime minor leaguer who had been called up two weeks earlier from Syracuse. This was his first major league start. Linton would finish 1992 with one major league victory—and an ERA of 8.63—but on a rainy afternoon in August he pitched the game of his life. The Orioles got to him for only three hits in eight innings and he turned a 4–2 lead over to Tom Henke, who retired Baltimore in order in the ninth. The Blue Jays' first run scored on a Kelly Gruber triple.

The Blue Jay lead was back to two games. There were still forty-seven games to go but the Orioles had let a major chance get away. Not only could they have tied the Blue Jays for first, they could have sent them on the road reeling. Instead, they headed out of town thinking that the Orioles might be good, but if they couldn't beat Doug Linton when they had the team gasping, they probably weren't quite good enough.

After the Orioles won the third game of the series, Johnny Oates took his wife Gloria out to celebrate their twenty-fifth wedding anniversary. They had gotten married the same year that Oates signed with the Orioles. He had a clause put in his contract giving him a week off for his honeymoon, since the wedding date had already been set when he signed.

Now, in the middle of a pennant race, he was happy to have his wife along on the road trip. She reminded him that the games really weren't *that* important. The night before their anniversary, Oates had been ejected by Drew Coble when he had gone out to protect Ripken. The next day Oates was still disturbed about the incident, mostly because he suspected his mother had seen him lose his temper on television.

"I *had* to go out there," he said. "You have to defend your players. If you don't, why should they want to play for you? Still, I don't like losing my temper like that. I realize this isn't a church picnic, but I don't like to lose control, even for a minute."

He smiled. "It's over, though, and I'm not going to worry about it. In this game, you have to remind yourself to enjoy your accomplishments. I don't want the players to think for one second that I'm satisfied with where we are right now, but the fact is, I'm proud of them. I remember when I was managing Double-A a few years ago, we won the second-half title and the players were all fooling around on the bus.

I went back and screamed at them, 'You haven't done anything yet!' because I didn't want them to let down for the play-offs.

"I was wrong, though. They had done something and they were entitled to enjoy it. I want this team to enjoy what it's accomplished but understand there's more to do. There's almost always more to do."

It was time to go meet his wife. Oates wasn't satisfied, but he was happy.

27

TALE OF TWO
BOROUGHS

The New York Yankees had just come from behind for a satisfying road victory over the Seattle Mariners on a cool evening in July and manager Buck Showalter was conducting his postgame press conference.

On most days, trying to hear Showalter if you are standing more than six feet away from him is almost impossible. On this day, the ceiling was down to about two feet. About halfway through his analysis of the game, Showalter stopped suddenly. He started listing as if he might fall over, then he lunged for a towel, burying his face in it.

Buck Showalter was not well. He hadn't been healthy for a couple of weeks and he wasn't going to feel that much better for a while. No one—including Showalter—was surprised at this turn of events. Surprisingly, for a Yankee manager, his health had nothing to do with the team's play—the Yankees had played above expectations most of the season and were flirting with .500—or with the machinations of George Steinbrenner, still suspended from baseball (though lurking ominously in Showalter and the team's future).

Showalter was sick for one reason: He hadn't taken care of himself. Since the first day of spring training he had routinely kept ludicrous hours, rarely sleeping more than four or five hours a night, not eating well, and never exercising. In a profession that almost demanded one be obsessive, he took obsession to new levels.

"Sometimes, about the middle of the day I'll tell myself that I just have to get some exercise," he had said earlier in the season. "I'll go down to the weight room, get on the bike or something, and after about five minutes, I'll think of ten things I need to be doing that might not get done. So I just go back to work.

"I know it's not healthy. I know this isn't the best way to treat your body. But I can't help the way I feel. If we win a game, I enjoy it from the time I leave the dugout until the time I get to the clubhouse [perhaps a minute] and then I start worrying about tomorrow's lineup. If we lose, I know I'm not going to sleep much. There's no emotion quite like losing. I think that's what drives me, trying to avoid having that feeling as often as possible.

"Most managers get to a hotel and will be asked what they would like in their room. It's a courtesy kind of thing. I know most guys will ask for some wine or maybe a case of beer or a stationary bike. I ask for a VCR. I can't sleep at night until I've reviewed the entire game tape."

Clearly, this is Obsessive Personality Case 1A. But there is much more to Showalter than sleep-starvation and nocturnal sessions with a VCR clicker. Short, stocky, and blond, he has a dry sense of humor, a quick mind, and a sensitivity about things that often surprises people.

"I get really pissed off when I hear a white person say to a black person, 'I know how you feel,' " he said one day while talking about growing up in the South. "How can he know? He's never been black. You can be sympathetic, you can try to understand their experience, but you can't walk in their shoes.

"When I hear people say that we've made great progress in the South, I think, 'That's fine but let's not forget there's still a lot to do.' My father never let us go to private school when I was a kid because he thought private schools existed as a way to keep segregation alive. He always said that wasn't real life. In real life, you meet all people and live and work with them every day."

It was Showalter's father, William Nathaniel Showalter, Jr. (Buck is actually William Nathaniel III), who influenced his life and his career more than anyone. Growing up in the panhandle of northern Florida in the tiny town of De Funiak Springs, Showalter was always a good athlete. When he outgrew the local competition, his father, who had played football in college, drove him sixty miles to Pensacola so he could play in a higher-caliber league.

William Showalter was a teacher and a junior high school principal who had played a major role in helping desegregate local public schools. His son can still remember his sister using the word *nigger* at the dinner table one night—and also his father's reaction—angrily sending his daughter to bed without dinner and *with* a stern tongue lashing.

"She had picked the word up at school and he wanted to be certain she would never ever use it again," Showalter says. "I seriously doubt that she did."

Showalter wasn't recruited heavily coming out of high school so he went to junior college for two years. Every once in a while after a game a friend would tell him that his father had shown up—the school was three hours from home—watched the game and gone home as soon it was over. "He never wanted me to feel like I had to do well to please him," Showalter said. "He cared enough to make the drive, but he didn't want to add any pressure by letting me know he was there."

After junior college, Showalter went to Mississippi State. It was there, playing for Ron Polk, that he learned the importance of organization and detail. He hit .459 his junior year and was the Yankees' fifth-round draft pick. He signed in the spring of 1977 after promising his parents he would go back to school during the offseason to finish his degree (he did) and ended up playing in the Yankee system for seven years. Twice he made it as far as Columbus, but only got one hundred at-bats at the Triple-A level.

It was during his first minor league season, playing in Fort Lauderdale, that he acquired his nickname. Ed Napoleon, then the Fort Lauderdale manager, stuck it on him because of his penchant for sitting around the clubhouse (buck) naked. Showalter likes the nickname but doesn't like being reminded of how he got it. The Yankee media guide mentions that it was Napoleon who gave him the nickname but not the reason why. When Showalter appeared on Roy Firestone's show *Up Close* during the '92 season, Firestone asked him beforehand if he would tell the story of how he got the nickname on the show.

"Absolutely not," Showalter said. "And don't you dare bring it up."

By the end of 1983, it was apparent Showalter wasn't going to make it to the big leagues. Having spent six full years in the minors, he had the option of signing with another organization, re-signing with the Yankees, or accepting their offer to coach in Fort Lauderdale.

"I was twenty-seven and I had just gotten married," he said. "I knew I wasn't going to make it to the big leagues and this was a chance to start a new career. I decided to give coaching a shot."

He had met his wife, Angela McMahan, at the ballpark in Nashville. She was selling programs and, even though his name was *in* the program, made him pay for one. "That intrigued me," Showalter said. "That and her looks."

They were married just before the start of his last year as a player. Showalter ended up coaching one year in Fort Lauderdale, then managed in the Yankee system for five years—finishing first four times. In 1990, the Yankees brought him to New York as the "eye in the sky" (a coach who sits in the press box and talks to the dugout by walkie-talkie). That job only lasted until June. When Bucky Dent was fired as manager and replaced by Stump Merrill, Showalter became the third-base coach. He stayed there until the end of 1991 when Merrill was fired.

During the '91 season, as it became apparent that Merrill wasn't going to survive, Showalter was mentioned as a possible replacement. On several occasions, players came to him and told him they wanted him to get the job. Showalter was very uncomfortable with that since he had played for Merrill in the minor leagues and it had been Merrill who'd made him the third-base coach. Additionally, he thought his age—thirty-five—and his lack of major league experience would work against him with the image-conscious Yankees.

He was right. When the season ended, general manager Gene Michael called to tell him that Merrill was being dropped and that whoever was named manager would be allowed to put together his own coaching staff. "We'll recommend you," Michael said. "But I can't guarantee you anything."

That was hardly comforting to Showalter, who had been with the Yankee organization for sixteen seasons. He hadn't exactly been fired but he certainly couldn't afford to assume that he had a job for 1992. Showalter began looking for work and was gratified at the interest people had in him: Jeff Torborg, who had just been hired by the Mets, wanted him on his coaching staff; the Florida Marlins were interested in talking to him about their managing job.

Before Showalter got to the point of making any serious decisions, he got another phone call from Michael. It seemed that some of the people the Yankees had thought about to manage didn't want the job. Would Showalter want to talk about it?

Showalter wasn't certain. He had other opportunities elsewhere and he knew the Yankee situation was a mess. Steinbrenner was in limbo and no one even knew who the managing partner of the team was going to be in '92. If Michael hired him, would he even be around when Showalter managed his first game? And was it Michael who wanted him to have the job or someone pulling strings behind the scenes? Steinbrenner? Babe Ruth's ghost?

He talked it over with his wife. He knew the risks. The contract would only be for one year, and at $135,000, he would be the lowest-paid manager in the major leagues. The Mets had signed Torborg for four years to a deal worth more than $2 million. "In the end, though, I realized this was the chance I had always wanted," he said. "If I didn't take the shot after spending sixteen years in the organization, I would never forgive myself. The one-year contract wasn't reassuring but I had found out that there were other people in baseball who thought highly of me. I decided to go for it."

On October 29, two days after the seventh game of the World Series, he was introduced as the Yankees' thirtieth manager. Two weeks later, William Showalter, Jr., went into the hospital for heart surgery. He had undergone surgery three years earlier but wasn't doing very well. The doctors thought more surgery would help him feel stronger and better. "He told them, 'Let's go for it,' " Showalter said. "So they went back in. He never made it off the operating table."

William Showalter was seventy-two. His death left his son drained. "It leaves you feeling so vulnerable, so human, so *bare,*" he said. "The whole winter was a roller coaster for me. I get the job, then I lose my dad. Then, a few weeks after that, my son is born. At times, I lost track of myself."

In that sense, spring training was a relief; it allowed Showalter to bury himself in his work. The players seemed to take to him immediately and so did the New York media. They liked his dry sense of humor and figured that anyone who had seen all 249 episodes of *The Andy Griffith Show* had to have something going for him. But Showalter knew that the euphoria wouldn't last.

"Spring training is a false utopia," he said one morning. "I've had fun down here, but I think Stump and Bucky had fun down here too. The season is long and difficult. Any manager in New York who doesn't understand that is going to be in trouble."

Showalter's utopia lasted longer than most—the Yankees started 6-0. But their lack of pitching caught up with them and it was apparent by midseason that winning more games than last season (71) was a reasonable goal, while finishing at .500 was a difficult one.

Showalter wasn't about to admit that, however. He kept insisting he was trying to win the division; he was afraid his players might lose something if they thought that playing .500 ball was acceptable. He kept pushing them—and himself—until he was so sick by the end of July that he could barely stand up.

He didn't lose his sense of humor, though. One night, when Melido Perez had pitched brilliantly into the ninth inning in Yankee Stadium, it was apparent he was out of gas, even though he needed just one more out to finish the game. Showalter turned to pitching coach Mark Connor.

"I have to go get him, Mark," Showalter said.

"I know," Connor agreed. "They're ready in the bullpen."

"The fans are going to boo like crazy. They're going to hate seeing him come out this close to a complete game."

Connor nodded. "I know."

"It's going to be brutal, Mark."

Another nod. "I know."

"Okay then, go get him."

Connor hadn't removed a pitcher all season. He stared at Showalter in disbelief for a moment until Showalter burst into a huge grin and went out—showered by boos—to make the pitching change.

Through it all, Showalter kept winning people's respect. When he stood up to LaRussa in May, everyone in the game noticed. His players believed in him even when things weren't going well, and so, apparently, did the Yankees, who extended his contract by three years at midseason. The extension came in the midst of rumors that the Marlins—among others—were still interested in him.

The contract extension meant that the Yankees were committed to him for as long as their cross-borough counterparts, the Mets, were committed to Jeff Torborg. There was a fair amount of irony in that and in Showalter's rising star, because it was Torborg who had come to town as the anointed savior.

It wasn't turning out that way. The events of spring training—the rape incident and the ensuing media frenzy—had bothered Torborg, changing his relationship with the media. When he first arrived on the scene the previous fall, Torborg had come across as the perfect media-manager, something particularly important for New York. He loved to sit around and tell stories about his playing—or nonplaying—days with the Dodgers; about his old manager Walter Alston; about growing up in New Jersey as a Yankee fan; about getting into trouble as a kid "because I was a real red-ass."

The joke at the start of spring training was that if Torborg ever hid in his office the way Bud Harrelson had, he would probably take the media with him.

That changed after the rape charges and the players' boycott of the media. Torborg was extremely uncomfortable with the situation—understandably—especially since he is a man whose whole life is his family. Married to his high school sweetheart, he has three sons who are around the ballpark constantly; sometimes they even travel with the team. In fact, Torborg has a clause in his contract that requires that his wife, Suzy, be allowed to fly on the team's charters.

Under the gun, Torborg wasn't the same guy with the media that he had been when everything was fresh and new in the fall. He was evasive, and bridled at direct questions. When Steve Jacobson of *Newsday* asked one day in early April what Torborg really thought

about the rape incident—given that the 450-page report made it clear
that even if no rape had occurred the scene had not been G-rated—
Torborg said, "Ask me some day when I'm not managing here anymore."

"Isn't that a copout, Jeff?" Jacobson asked.

"No," Torborg said icily, "it's a right."

Torborg deserved the benefit of the doubt. He had just started a
brand new job and all of a sudden had been forced to face an ugly and
uncomfortable situation. But when the team began to struggle and he
refused to acknowledge that anything was wrong, the whispers
started—not only among the media but in the clubhouse.

"Jeff Torborg is a very good man," David Cone said late in the
season after he had been traded to Toronto. "But it seems that you
have to be a certain kind of guy to play for him. He doesn't want
individuals or leaders. He wants followers."

And he wanted the world to believe that all was well in the Mets
clubhouse even when it wasn't. It was that approach that cost Torborg
his credibility in New York.

The Mets were already having problems when they played the
Chicago Cubs on the afternoon of June 25 at Shea Stadium. Although
they had won the first three games of the series, their record was 35-36
and their play had been sporadic all season. Bobby Bonilla, the $29-
million man, hadn't hit much since his two homers on Opening Day;
he'd been particularly awful at home. Bret Saberhagen had been on
the DL since May 15. Torborg was doing so many radio shows on
WFAN, the city's all-sports radio station, that he had been derisively
nicknamed "Jeff from Flushing" as if he were a regular caller to the
station—which he was. Of the four newcomers who had been the
media guide cover boys, only Eddie Murray was flourishing, quietly
putting together another ninety-RBI season.

It was a sticky Thursday afternoon in New York and the press box
was more crowded than usual. Columnists love weekday afternoon
baseball games; they offer the chance to write something off a live
event and still be home in time for dinner with their families. So, in
addition to the beat writers, a number of the big-name local columnists were at the ball game.

What they saw was a seven-run Cub first inning that included an
error by Bonilla in right field that contributed to the onslaught. The
entire Met outfield had been under siege for a while. Vince Coleman
was chronically injured; when he did play his instincts in left field
weren't very good and his arm was weak. Howard Johnson was still
having trouble adjusting in center, often misjudging fly balls. And
Bonilla, who had shown up in Florida overweight and stayed that way,
played right field like a designated hitter.

When Bonilla got to the dugout after the Cubs had finally been retired in the first, he asked for the press box phone number. Then, to the amazement of his listening teammates, he called public relations director Jay Horwitz to complain about the fact that the scoreboard operator had left the "E-9" on the scoreboard longer than was—in Bonilla's opinion—necessary.

The TV cameras picked up the sight of Bonilla on the phone and beamed the picture not only to fans watching the game at home but reporters in the press box. It didn't take long to look around and figure out that it was Horwitz he was talking to. When he hung up, Horwitz wouldn't discuss what Bonilla had called about. In the dugout, Torborg, looking at a 7–0 deficit, was outraged when he heard Bonilla on the phone. And he told him so. Quite vehemently.

The rest of the game was routine, the Cubs winning easily. When it was over, everyone headed for Bonilla's locker. His story was that he had heard that Horwitz had been sick and was calling to see how he was feeling. No one was buying that. In the meantime, Torborg was claiming not to know what the conversation had been about. Yes, he said, he knew Bonilla had made the phone call, but no, he hadn't bothered to find out what it was about.

This also made little sense. A star player comes into the dugout after a seven-run inning, makes a phone call to the press box, and the manager doesn't bother finding out what the call is about?

Other players quickly shot holes in both stories. They had heard Bonilla complaining about the error on the scoreboard and they had heard Torborg ream him—properly, in their opinion—for the call. Quickly it became apparent that both Bonilla and Torborg were lying. With all the columnists in the ballpark, it quickly became the stuff of scandal. It isn't often that a manager is called a *liar*—no euphemisms inserted—in print, but that's exactly what Torborg faced the next day.

In less than three months he had gone from savior to swine in New York. So, too, had Bonilla. Torborg was shocked and hurt. At fifty, his life was, to quote a *Mets Magazine* cover, "Family, Team and Baseball." His whole notion of a baseball team as family had been shot full of holes. Rather than cover up for Bonilla, his teammates had willingly branded him a liar, and in so doing, had put the same label on their manager. Torborg had learned—the hard way—that keeping secrets in a baseball clubhouse in New York is impossible.

But he should already have known that. He had spent ten years with the Yankees as a coach. He had watched one manager after another—not to mention general managers, pitching coaches, and players—be publicly whipped by George Steinbrenner, who took some shots in return from angry, outspoken Yankees. Why Torborg would think that it would somehow be different in Queens from in the Bronx was a mystery.

His relationship with the media, which had already cooled before Bobbygate, was just this side of icy afterward. He continued his daily meetings with the press but he was guarded, defensive, and anything but the jovial storyteller of the winter and early spring. Frustrated, he ate late and he ate early and he put on twenty pounds. "In 1990, I got down to one ninety-five, which was my playing weight," he said. "Of course we won ninety-four games that year."

He did finally concede in early July that not all was well with the baseball team. After the team held a players-only meeting, he held a lengthy meeting of his own, during which some of the older players complained about all the pregame team meetings and the constant regimen Torborg was most comfortable with. Okay, Torborg said, if you think it will help, we'll meet less. Then, for the first time, he admitted to the media that the team had played poorly.

"I don't blame the fans for booing us," he said on the Fourth of July. "We've been awful."

The Mets and Houston Astros had been rained out the previous night, forcing a holiday twi-night doubleheader at Shea. They hadn't played a game since Wednesday afternoon in Chicago. Since then, the Pirates had dropped three straight games to the Reds.

Al Harazin, the general manager who had hired Torborg, signed Bonilla and Murray, and traded for Saberhagen, was in Torborg's office before the doubleheader.

"You realize Pittsburgh has lost three times since we last played a game?" he said to Torborg. "It isn't as if we aren't being given opportunities."

Torborg forced a smile. "Yeah, but I got a feeling we're going to have to go out here and play one ourselves here pretty soon," he said.

"Two," Harazin said. Neither man seemed cheered by the thought.

"I never dreamed that we wouldn't hit," Harazin said a few minutes later. "I knew we'd have adversity. That's part of the deal in New York. When I first talked to Bret Saberhagen and Bill Pecota about playing here I told them, 'You have to understand, in New York, baseball isn't life and death—it's more important than that.' But every night it seems like we get behind by a run and can't score again. Every morning I wake up and feel like I'm already one run down."

Bobbygate had hurt the entire team, he conceded, although he wasn't about to criticize his manager publicly for mishandling the situation. But he was clearly frustrated by Bonilla's thoughtlessness. "We tell the players all the time that when they're in the dugout they have to assume they're on camera at all times," he said. "That's why the league puts out all those directives about how to stand during the national anthem and about not smoking in the dugout. You have to assume the public is always watching."

Of course the fact that the public was watching had nothing to do with the larger issue: Bonilla. In every way he had not been what the Mets had thought they were getting. He was supposed to be an excellent hitter (and hadn't been), a standup guy with the media (wrong again), and a competitor who infused the clubhouse with an extra will to win (0-for-3).

What Harazin, Torborg, and his new teammates had learned was that Bonilla's smile masked a lot of insecurities. When Harazin or Torborg tried to talk to him about things, he nodded a lot, but clearly the message wasn't getting through. "Bobby talks a lot more than he listens," said one of the Mets. He was not only sensitive to criticism, he was hypersensitive to it. Bonds, his old running mate in Pittsburgh, brought that up later in the season one night while talking about whether he might play in New York in 1993.

"I can handle New York because I don't get my feelings hurt the way Bobby does," Bonds said. "I don't give a fuck what people write about me or say. Bobby does. He's too sensitive. I told him before he went there that he wasn't going to be able to deal with it but he didn't believe me. Now, he believes me."

Bonds wasn't the only one who felt that way about Bonilla. Jimmy Leyland never faulted him for seeking the big money when his chance came as a free agent but felt he had made the wrong choice by choosing New York. "I'm happy for Bobby that he was able to get the kind of money he got," Leyland said. "But all you ever hear from guys is they want to take care of their family. He was offered like twenty-five or twenty-six million bucks to play in California. Are you telling me you can't take care of your family for twenty-five million? Hell, you can take care of Guam for twenty-five million!"

The Mets continued to struggle in July. Only the Pirates' slide late in the month kept them in contention. It was looking more and more like Joe Torre's prediction—that no one in the division would be good enough to break away—would come true. On August 1, the Mets played another twi-nighter on a Saturday night. Their record was a moribund 49-52. Even so, they were only five games behind the Pirates. Saberhagen, finally back from the DL, pitched into the fifth inning when the finger that had bothered him in May began to feel sore again. He came out, gone again, as it turned out, until the last ten days of the season. The next afternoon, Bonilla hurt his knee trying to make a diving catch in the outfield. He joined Saberhagen on the DL.

The Mets left the following day on a six-game road trip. This was the time for players to step up and show the kind of scrappiness Torborg had been preaching about all season. The team went to Pittsburgh and lost two. Then to Chicago where they lost four more. They came home and managed to win one of three from the Pirates. They lost two more at home to the Phillies—aided only by a rainout—then flew to the West Coast and dropped two out of three to the Dodgers and two to the Padres. In twenty-one days they had gone 2-14 and dropped completely out of sight in the division race.

Throughout the Mets' swan dive, the Yankees puttered along, not playing all that well, but playing just a little better than their inter-borough rivals. They caught the Mets in their unofficial race on August 19 and, as it turned out, the not-so-scrappy Mets never got even with them again.

The injuries were devastating to the Mets but this had been a team going nowhere *before* the injuries. Things had gotten so bad in the clubhouse that by the end of the month, Jeff Innis, the thoughtful relief pitcher, summed up the atmosphere best: "I don't care about anyone giving me credit anymore. I just don't want the blame."

Innis needn't have worried. There was plenty of blame to go around, but it wasn't going to land in his locker. The smiling faces that had adorned the cover of the media guide in March were smiling no more.

28

HOLDING
THE
FORT

If the Mets hadn't come apart at the seams in early August, they still would not have been in a pennant race. The reason: the Pittsburgh Pirates. When they lost eight of ten in late July, the Pirates had let everyone in the National League East (except the Phillies) believe they had a chance to steal a championship. For a while, it looked like a weak year; eighty-five victories was starting to sound like a play-off number.

The last loss in that Pirate skein was a 6–4 eleven-inning killer to the Cubs that completed a three-game Wrigley Field sweep for Chicago and brought an end to a disastrous 2-7 road trip. On the flight home, manager Jim Leyland sat quietly thinking about his team, where it was and, most important, where it might be going. He was troubled and had been so for a while.

When he got home that night, Leyland did something he had never done before. He sat down at his desk and began making notes to himself. He was having a team meeting the next day, and it would be a delicate one. He wanted to be damn sure he knew exactly what he was going to say and how he was going to say it.

"When I meet with the team it's because something has been building inside me for a while," he said. "I'm a big believer that you don't hold a meeting unless you have to. But if I get to a point where something is really bothering me and I let it go, then that's bad. A manager has an *aroma* when he comes into the clubhouse every single day. Players can smell it—believe me. If you get to a point where you're holding something in, they can tell and it bothers them. What you have to do is hold the meeting before your aroma gets too negative."

Leyland had been walking a fine line all season with this team. He'd exploded at management in spring training after the John Smiley trade, then waited a week before calling the team together to say, "Okay, we were all pissed off, but it's over. Let's put it behind us and go from here."

The Pirates did. They got to the All-Star break at 49-39, comfortably in first place; now this dive had put them at 53-48, tied with Montreal, and the rest of the division was not far behind. August was two days away. If the Pirates continued to slide, Leyland believed a catastrophe was possible. That was what he wanted his players to understand.

He was up late that night, trying to get all his thoughts clear. The next day, before the players arrived, he was in his office studying what he had written. He would never call a team meeting and *read* something to his players; that just wouldn't fly. But he didn't want to forget anything.

Shortly before the team was scheduled to go on the field for batting practice, Leyland called them together. The Pirates clubhouse in Three Rivers Stadium is one of the smaller home clubhouses in baseball. It is rectangular with a basketball net hung from a stanchion in the middle of the room. Very intense, often physical Nerf-ball games are conducted on this net. Leyland stood in front of that stanchion as his players sat on chairs in front of their lockers or on the three couches in the middle of the room.

Later, he could remember his speech almost verbatim. "I said, 'Fellas, one of the things I like about managing you guys is that we all like each other and have fun together. If we want to stay together, then we have to start to pull together and roll again, because if we fall out of this race, there's no telling what an organization that's struggling financially will do. There's no telling what will happen and who will stay and who will go. Management in this game has a tendency to think that if they're out of the race, they might as well make a move with some players while they can.

" 'I've never asked you to win and I never will, but let's make sure this means enough to us every day. Let's make sure we want to play well because, to tell you the truth, I don't want to think about what might happen if we *don't* play well. I know you get tired of looking at my face and I know sometimes when you've been in one place for a while, other places start to look better. That's fine, if that's what you want—but be damn sure of it. Don't bullshit anybody and start ragging on each other because you're pissed off at me or because we've lost a few games or because you lost an arbitration case. Don't have that attitude unless you're ready to deal with the consequences. Because I promise you it will jump up and bite you—especially if you don't keep after things.

" 'I love this team and I love living in this city. That's why I signed on to stay here. Look around you and think about what we've got here. We're in first place. We're in contention for a third straight year. We like each other. Try looking at what we *do* have rather than what we don't. Think about it: *Is this so bad?* Let's weigh everything involved before we give up on it or walk away from it.' "

In all, Leyland talked for twenty minutes. For him, that's a long meeting. He never raised his voice but he repeated his points several times. Then, after the team had gone on the field, he went to players individually to make certain they understood what he had said and why he'd said it.

"I wasn't trying to threaten anyone," he explained. "But I wanted them to understand that economics in the game make things different than they were ten years ago or five years ago or even one year ago. I felt good about what I said and I was happy I'd done it. We might have gone out and lost the next eleven afterwards for all I knew. If that was the case, so be it. But I knew if I *didn't* say what was on my mind and the ship went down, that I would never forgive myself."

The Pirates didn't lose their next eleven. They swept four games from the Cardinals, two from the Mets, four more from the Cards in St. Louis, and opened a series at Shea Stadium with another victory. That put the winning streak at eleven before Mets rookie Eric Hillman finally shut them out. By then, the players were teasing Leyland about his powers as an orator. And, of all the other NL East teams, only the Expos—two-and-a-half games back—were still in the race.

"The thing about Jimmy is there isn't an ounce of bullshit in him," said Barry Bonds, who during the winning streak went on a tear that continued until the end of the regular season. "We all know we can count on anything he says. He's just not capable of dealing with people any way but straight ahead."

The same could not be said of Bonds. There was no better all-around player in the National League. At twenty-eight, he was on his way to a second MVP in three years and a multimillion-dollar contract with someone, since he would be the number-one free agent in the fall. He was handsome and articulate, the son of Bobby Bonds, a great major league player himself, and capable of being as charming as anyone in the game when the mood struck him.

The mood didn't strike him often. He could be rude, not only to outsiders, but to his teammates. They accepted him because he played hard and worked hard every day, but they were as mystified by him as everyone else was.

"You have to remember one thing at all times when you're dealing with Barry," said Pirates vice-president for public relations Rick Cerrone. "This is not an adult. This is a nine-year-old. He's a nine-year-old kid in the body of an extraordinary twenty-eight-year-old athlete. He's not a horrible guy, he's just a very immature person."

That didn't make Cerrone's job any easier. Sometimes, if ESPN or someone he deemed important wanted an interview, Bonds was an angel. At other times, he could be impossible. When the Pirates held their annual autograph day at the ballpark, hundreds of people lined up at the desk where Bonds was supposed to sit. Only he never arrived to sit there. The story the next day wasn't on the twenty-four other players who showed but on the one who hadn't.

When Bobby Bonilla was booed and had things thrown at him when he first returned to Pittsburgh with the Mets, Bonds said the fans had been motivated by race. His was a minority opinion of one. The fans were motivated by the fact that Bonilla had left town and deserted them. Whether he was black, white, green, or blue had little to do with it. But Bonds didn't see it that way and said so.

Bonds and Leyland had gotten into a shouting match during spring training in 1991; Bonds had shown up in camp with a huge chip on his shoulder after losing his arbitration case. In an era when a lot of managers are afraid to stand up to a superstar, Leyland had done exactly that. Partly as a result of his toughness, he and Bonds now got along well, although Leyland, like everyone else, had trouble figuring the player out at times.

"I think one thing I have going for me with Barry is that he's not quite sure whether or not I like him," Leyland said, smiling. "He's not used to that. He's used to people wanting to be his friend or wanting him to do things for them. I don't want him to do anything except come to play every day and he's going to do that no matter what. He knows I'll never ask him for anything beyond that. So we get along just fine."

Bonds had changed agents in July, signing on with Dennis Gilbert, the high-powered L.A. lawyer who had negotiated the huge free-agent deals for Bonilla and Danny Tartabull, among many others. Gilbert was a smart, clever operator who knew how important image was. As soon as he began working with Gilbert, Bonds's public image began to change.

If ESPN wanted him to do a Sunday night interview, he was happy to comply. *Sports Illustrated?* Sure. Local television? Happy to do it. Where once he had talked about the fact that he would never come back to Pittsburgh, now he called it home, talked about how much he loved his teammates and Leyland. Would he rule out playing in Los Angeles? Absolutely not. New York? Love the idea. Kansas City? If the offer is there, why not? How about Mars? Gilbert probably had contacts there, too.

Gilbert was the classic new-wave agent. He was always willing to talk to the media but was a master at saying nothing. The previous year, he'd done an interview with WFAN in New York when Bonilla was being shopped around. He spent his fifteen on-air minutes ducking every direct question he was asked. When the interview was over, Bob Gelb, the show's producer, picked up the phone to thank Gilbert for his time. "By the way," Gilbert said, "I heard you guys were giving away some T-shirts. Can you send me a few?"

By late summer, Bonds had mastered Gilbert-speak. Nothing mattered, he said, except getting a World Series ring. Money, he told ESPN, didn't matter to him at all. Awards, batting titles, MVPs were all meaningless. Barry Bonds smiled for the camera and said all he wanted was a ring. He would worry about the $43 million he *wasn't* thinking about later.

The Pirates' other star—if you didn't count Leyland—was Andy Van Slyke. The rest of their lineup consisted of role players, guys who worked hard, knew how to play the game, and rarely made mental errors. The pitching was decent but not overwhelming. Leyland had been casting around for a fourth and fifth starter all season and he didn't have a closer. The Pirates, it seemed, did just about everything by committee.

Bonds and Van Slyke dressed on opposite sides of the clubhouse and could not have been more different in their outlooks. Bonds was moody; Van Slyke almost always upbeat. Bonds was never really comfortable with the media; Van Slyke didn't feel a day was complete if he didn't give at least a half dozen interviews and come up with several memorable quotes.

Van Slyke had as sharp a wit as you were likely to find anywhere. He and the Orioles' Mike Flanagan were, without question, baseball's one-line kings. When the Astros left on their twenty-eight-day odyssey, Van Slyke said, "Are they giving those guys meal money or CD's?" Radically conservative in his political outlook, Van Slyke defended George Bush right to the end. "People get on him for saying, 'No new taxes,'" he said one night. "They misunderstood him. He actually said, 'No new *faxes.*' He's the environmental president. He's trying to stop the paper flow and save some trees."

Van Slyke was almost incapable of telling a story without making it funny. Ask most players their first memories of playing baseball and they will talk about playing catch with their dad or joining a Little League. Van Slyke's story is a little different.

"I was always a catcher as a kid," he said. "First day of practice, the coach comes up to me and asks if I want to catch. I figured that sounded good to me, lots of action, right? So I said that was fine. He hands me this thing and says I have to wear it if I wanted to catch. I had no idea what it was. I went into the locker room and said to my friends, 'What *is* this thing?' They told me it was a cup and where it was supposed to go. Well, I tried to put it on and I couldn't get it to fit. The whole day, the thing kept slipping down my leg. I spent the entire practice holding my hand in front of me, trying to get the cup to quit slipping all over the place."

Growing up in Utica, New York, Van Slyke starred in both baseball and basketball, although he liked basketball better. He never took baseball very seriously until his senior year. Naturally, there's a story attached to his turnaround as a baseball player.

"I was on my way to practice one day and I stopped to talk to this girl," he said. "I was taking my time, just kind of goofing off and Mike Callan, my coach, comes up, grabs me and tells me to go wait in his office until he gets there. He leaves me sitting in there the whole practice. Finally, he comes into the office with a fungo bat in his hands. He snaps it in half and then smacks me on the head. I had no idea what he was so mad about and I was trying not to laugh because he was so wild.

"Finally, he starts screaming at me. 'You've got more potential than any player I've ever coached. You should be drafted and you should go to the major leagues and I'm not going to let you ruin it and make *me* look bad as a coach. From now on, you're carrying all the equipment just like a freshman and you're going to be the first one on the field every day and the last one off. And don't think I'm doing this for *you,* I'm doing this for *me*! Now get the hell out of here!' "

Years later, Callan, now a good friend, told Van Slyke that after throwing him out of the office, he called Van Slyke's father, who was the school's principal, and asked to see him.

"I was trying to make a point to Andy and I went too far," he told Jim Van Slyke. "I hit him."

"Did you hurt him?" Jim Van Slyke asked.

"I don't think so," Callan said.

"Too bad," the father answered. "He's a real wiseass."

Van Slyke cracks up as he finishes the story, clearly relishing the idea of the two men trying to get him to push himself. He responded after Callan's speech and was the Cardinals' first-round pick that

June—the sixth player chosen overall. The day after he was drafted, Van Slyke was playing first base in a state play-off game and collided with a base runner while reaching for a wide throw. He broke his right wrist and missed the entire summer.

A year later, he was in the Cardinals' camp as a bonus ($50,000) baby, a hotshot first-round draft pick. "I acted the part every day," he said. "I loved it. I was very arrogant. But it was a persona. I didn't like myself back then."

His first two years in the minor leagues were ordinary. In 1981 he became a born-again Christian and says it changed his outlook as a player: "I've heard a lot about guys losing their competitiveness when they become Christians, but it doesn't have to be true. When I became a Christian, for the first time I realized I didn't *have* to make it as a baseball player to be a success in life.

"Before, my whole self-worth was tied to being a baseball player, to being a number-one draft pick, to getting to the big leagues, to going out and partying with the boys. But I wasn't satisfied or happy. I didn't like myself very much.

"There was a lot of Christian-bashing in baseball in the eighties. The notion was that if you became a Christian you were through as a player. If a Christian has the right perspective, and not all of us do, then knowing that God will accept your performance, good or bad, frees you. That's what it did for me anyway."

Van Slyke made it to the majors in 1983 but was never comfortable in St. Louis. He played the infield and the outfield and never established himself anywhere as a regular. When he was traded to the Pirates during spring training in 1987, he was relieved—but also disappointed.

"I figured God was proving that he had a sense of humor by sending me to Pittsburgh," he said. "I wanted a chance to play but when Whitey [Herzog] called me in and told me they had traded me, I remember saying, 'That's great Whitey, just tell me it's anyplace but Cleveland or Pittsburgh.' He said, 'Well, it's not Cleveland.' I couldn't believe it."

Leyland had just finished his first year managing in Pittsburgh, having lived through a miserable 64-98 season. Seventeen of the 98 losses had come at the hands of the Mets, who won 108 that season as well as the World Series.

"I remember right before the Series that year, someone asked me if I thought the Mets were really that good," Leyland said. "I said no I didn't. The guy looked at me kind of funny and said, 'How can you say that when they beat you seventeen out of eighteen?' I told him if they were any damn good they never would have lost that one time."

Van Slyke immediately became his everyday center fielder and

Mike LaValliere, who also came over in the trade, became the catcher. The Pirates improved rapidly, finishing 80-82 that year. The next year they stayed with the Mets until the end of August and ended up winning 85 games. That sent them into 1989 as contenders, but injuries devastated them early. That year was one Leyland would like to forget. "I don't think I managed very well that year," he said. "I really got down because of all the injuries and my aroma coming to the park was definitely negative."

There were no negatives the next year. Bonds, after three ordinary years, exploded into stardom, the pitching stayed healthy, Doug Drabek was 21-6, and the Pirates held off the Mets to win their first division title since 1979. But they lost a six-game NLCS to the Reds, at least in part because Bonds never hit. The next season, after all the Bonds-created turbulence of the spring, they ran away with the East and led the Braves 3–2 in the LCS going home to Pittsburgh. But they never scored another run, losing 1–0 to Steve Avery in a brilliant sixth game, then losing the seventh, 4–0, to John Smoltz. Adding insult to injury, there were more than seven thousand empty seats in Three Rivers Stadium for the finale.

Those empty seats, the departure of Bonilla, and the impending free agency of Bonds and Drabek made a lot of people wonder if Leyland, who by now was one of baseball's most respected managers, might not jump ship for a lucrative offer elsewhere. The hot rumor was that he would head for Miami to join his ex-boss, Carl Barger, and his old friend from Chicago days, Dave Dombrowski.

"Carl Barger's one of my best friends in the world and I think Dave Dombrowski is a tremendous guy," Leyland said. "But I've always believed in that old cliché that if it ain't broke don't fix it. Pittsburgh has been good to me and, the way I look at it, *most* teams in baseball are in the same financial fix we're in. How many teams really have big money to throw around? Five? Six?

"Was it tough to lose those two games to Atlanta? Hell, yes. But sometimes in this game the other guy is just better than you. It's like [Notre Dame football coach] Lou Holtz says, 'The other team gives scholarships too.' Avery pitched the two games of his life against us in that series. It hurt, but it wasn't the end of the world either."

Leyland's resiliency was once again evident throughout 1992. It was a strange season, not only because of all the talk about the certain changes to come in '93, but because the Pittsburgh newspapers went on strike in May and were still on strike when the season ended. That meant the team's main writers were only around at home games—and they weren't writing.

Some of the suburban papers expanded their coverage of the team, but a city without a major morning newspaper has a strange, empty feel to it during baseball season. The fans knew the games were happening because of TV and radio, but unless they bought *USA Today,* there were no box scores to peruse in the morning. And *USA Today* didn't replace the kind of saturation coverage baseball fans crave.

Even with the Pirates in first place for most of the season, attendance was down. Weeknight crowds in early September hovered around seven thousand, embarrassing numbers for a team that had been so consistently good for three years. Granted, Three Rivers was another artificial-turf donut park. When the original plans had been drawn up in 1968, they didn't include the upper deck in the outfield. The park was *supposed* to be open beyond the outfield fences so that downtown Pittsburgh would provide a backdrop. It was similar to the plan used more than twenty years later in Baltimore for Camden Yards. Unfortunately, football ruled in Pittsburgh, and the outfield was closed in to provide more seats for the Steelers.

"The strike has hurt us," Cerrone said during a game against the Cubs that had drawn 7,720. "But that's not the only thing. There's an assumption in this town that we're going to win, even though the Expos are breathing down our necks. We've already got ticket orders pouring in for the play-offs. Those games will sell out. In the meantime, most people don't even really think of this as a pennant race."

Leyland certainly did. He respected the Expos. He also knew his team had played over its head to get the lead and hold it. "If we do go on and win this time, it will be the most satisfying one of all for me," he said. "This team is not as talented as the teams we've had the last two years but it's figured out how to win and how to stay ahead. I know how hard they've worked, because I know how hard the coaches and I have worked."

Leyland always seems to look tired. At forty-seven, he is completely gray and always seems in search of a cup of coffee and a cigarette. He is, without question, baseball's most notorious smoker. Time and again, National League President Bill White has asked him to try not to smoke in the dugout during games. Time and again, the TV cameras have caught him with smoke coming out of his mouth (even though he keeps the cigarette hidden, cupped in his hand). Earlier in the season, Leyland tried wearing a smoker's patch for a month. When someone asked him how he was progressing, he answered, "Great. Only a few more days and I can take this thing off and have a fucking cigarette."

Leyland had become far more conscious about his health in the last year. The previous October, after two miscarriages, his wife Kate gave birth to their first child, Patrick. Leyland stopped smoking inside the house, walking onto the porch when he *had* to have a cigarette.

He'd tried the patch at Kate's urging, but during the season, under the pressure of a pennant race, he couldn't stop himself.

"There's a part of me that's really bothered by the fact that these little sticks of nicotine have so much power over me," he said. "I'm not ashamed of it and I know I'm not the only one who has the problem, but it does bother me. My wife tells me sometimes that she worries I'm not going to be around to watch Patrick grow up, and I do think about that. Having a child changes your outlook on life, especially when it comes at a time when you'd stopped thinking that it was going to happen to you."

Patrick's presence in Leyland's life made him look even more tired than usual. He'd gotten into the habit of lying awake in bed waiting for his son to cry, knowing that the brunt of the boy's care fell on Kate when Leyland was on the road. "I'm always tired late in the season," he said. "I've always said if you show me a manager who isn't tired in September, I'll show you a manager who has probably done a horseshit job. Other managers may get upset when I say that, but I think it's true.

"This year I'm even more tired because of Patrick, but it's worth it. Picking your son up and having him stop crying and go to sleep is the greatest feeling in the whole world."

Leyland was tired but satisfied as September approached. He was proud of the way his team had played, he was pleased with how hard his coaches had worked. And deep down he was satisfied, maybe even *very* satisfied, with Jim Leyland.

He was entitled.

29

WEEKEND
IN CHICAGO

There are only two cities in the country where, on occasion, you can see two major league baseball games in two different stadiums on the same day. West Coast people might make the case that you can make the trip between Oakland and San Francisco or Los Angeles and Anaheim, but given the distance and traffic involved, you would have to be extremely lucky and patient to see the last pitch in one park and the first pitch in the other. In the Bay Area, where the teams do play at twelve-fifteen on some days, you might have a chance to make a night game on the other side of the bridge. But in 1992, there were only two dates that fit that description.

To go a step farther, trying to do the Queens-Bronx thing in New York is no picnic either. The distance between Shea Stadium and Yankee Stadium is only about ten miles, but traffic can make these ten seem like a hundred. The best route between the two ballparks is by subway, which involves going into Manhattan and changing lines. *That* is easier said than done, especially during the early evening rush hour.

The best place to try to see two games in two parks in one day is, without question, Chicago. For one thing, the Cubs still play more day games than anyone—sixty-three in 1992—meaning there are more chances to do the day-night routine in Chicago than anyplace else. What's more, the ten-mile distance between Wrigley and Comiskey Park is usually negotiable, even in traffic, in under an hour.

On the third weekend in August, both the Cubs and White Sox were home. The Cubs were playing a Thursday night game followed by three afternoon games against the Houston Astros; the White Sox were hosting the Yankees in three straight night games beginning on Friday. A little piece of baseball heaven.

The weekend brought a lot of scouts to town, including the two expansion general managers, Dave Dombrowski and Bob Gebhard. It also brought quite a few members of the national media who were trailing the Astros through all or—in most cases—part of their bizarre twenty-eight-day odyssey.

The Astros' road trip had been created by owner John McMullen's decision to rent the Astrodome to the Republican National Committee for its convention. Although the convention did not begin until August 17, the RNC required control of the building for two weeks prior to the opening night to build platforms and to set up massive security for all the various right-wing luminaries, led by George Bush.

The trip had been the subject of a great deal of national attention since first announced almost a year earlier. The players' union filed a grievance against the Astros because of the twenty-six straight road games; the Astros agreed to fly the players' wives or girlfriends to Chicago—first class—for the weekend; and the team would get to go home for an offday at the end of that weekend.

"People have made much too big a deal of it," relief pitcher Doug Jones said before the opener in Wrigley Field. "We make two-week road trips all the time. On this one, we're staying away for a third week before we go home. Then we go back on the road for another week. Hell, most of us live out of a suitcase at home and on the road during the season anyway. It isn't that big a change."

The national media didn't quite see it that way. This was billed as perhaps the greatest journey taken since the *Eagle* had landed in 1969. *Sports Illustrated* had a writer and a photographer trailing the Astros. ESPN tracked their every move. Virtually everyone in America—okay, not quite *everyone*—knew that the Astros would fly exactly 9,186 miles before the trip was over.

Art Howe didn't really mind the trip. If the Astros had been in the middle of a pennant race, he might have felt different. But they were an extremely young team that had won 65 games in 1991 and, when they began the trip on August 3, their record was 44-54. What did concern Howe was a road record of 13-27 as their travels began. That meant the trip had the potential to really bury the team.

"I've tried to look at the trip as something we can use," Howe said. "If we can play respectably, well, we aren't going to face a trip as tough as this one next year. Maybe we can build on this."

Uphill battles in baseball were nothing new to Howe. His twelve-year major league career was as unlikely a story as there was in a sport filled with unlikely stories.

Howe grew up in Pittsburgh, the youngest of six children. Always a good athlete, he was more into football than baseball. But back problems forced him to give up football during his freshman year (on a football scholarship) at the University of Wyoming. He ended up playing baseball for four years but needed back surgery at the end of his senior season. "If any team was interested in me, the surgery pretty much took care of that," he said.

He graduated with a degree in business administration and went home to a job at Westinghouse in Pittsburgh. On weekends, just for the heck of it, he played in a semipro league that he had first played in back in high school. "My boss, a guy named Bill Howser, was a big baseball fan and he would come out to watch our games. I was hitting about .500 and he said to me, 'You ought to go to a tryout camp somewhere.' I was twenty-three years old and I figured those days were behind me. I had been to a couple of tryout camps in high school. It was stuff for sixteen- or seventeen-year-olds, not for an adult."

But Howser kept pushing. He called all the major league teams and found out that there was one tryout camp left that season—in Pittsburgh. "I guess there was some kind of karma there," Howe says, laughing. "He finally talked me into going. I guess, in the back of my mind, I was still trying to keep my dream alive. I guess we all do that to some extent."

When the long afternoon was over and most of the teenagers had been sent home, Howe was one of three players asked to stay for extra drills, to play some infield, to be timed going to first and second base. When the scouts were finished, they thanked him for his time and sent him home. "I figured, 'Oh well, I took my shot,' " he says. "It was one of those 'don't call us, we'll call you' type things."

Only this time, they *did* call. The next day, Pirates farm director Murray Cook asked Howe to come into the team's office. There, he offered him a free-agent contract. "This was 1970, when 'free agent' had a very different meaning than it does now." Howe smiles. "Back then, *free* agent meant you were *free*. All they offered me was a plane ticket to Bradenton [round trip] for spring training and the chance to try to make one of their minor league clubs. If I made a club, I would make five hundred dollars a month."

Howe was making almost three times that much as a young executive at Westinghouse. But the dream kept pushing him. He convinced his wife to go along with the scheme and headed off to spring training in 1971. He not only made a team, Class-A Salem, but he led the league in hitting at .348. A year later, he was in Triple-A, one step from the majors. But by the time the 1974 season started, he was still one step from the majors and just about ready to give up.

"By that point we had two little children and had long ago used up all our savings," he says. "My salary had soared to six-fifty a month. I told my wife that 'seventy-four was it. If I couldn't make it to the majors by then, it was time to go home. After all, I was already twenty-seven."

He did make it to the major leagues that year but it was another three years before he made it to stay. By then, he was with the Astros. "The turning point for me was at the end of the 'seventy-six season. I'd been called up late and hadn't played at all. The last week of the season [manager] Bill Virdon said to me, 'You've played second base before, haven't you?' I said, 'Absolutely.' So he put me in the lineup at second. I had never played second in my life but I hit enough that I spent most of the next two years playing there."

Howe ended up spending seven seasons in Houston, before finishing his career in St. Louis. He retired early in the 1985 season. "To be accurate, Vince Coleman retired me," he said. "Willie McGee started the season on the DL and they brought Coleman up, even though they didn't think he was quite ready. Turns out, he was. He started stealing three bases a game and I knew I was in trouble. As soon as Willie came back, I was gone."

Howe wasn't out of the game for very long, though. Less than a month after he was released, Bobby Valentine was named to manage the Texas Rangers. The two men knew one another through third base—Howe had played it for the Astros, Valentine had coached it for the Mets. Often, during games, they would talk. When Valentine came through Houston in late April, amid rumors he was going to get the Texas job, Phil Garner, who was with the Astros, recommended that he consider Howe for a coaching job.

He did. Four years later, when the Houston managing job opened up, Howe took the unusual step of calling the Astros himself to ask for an interview. "I had been sitting around waiting for people to call me," he said. "That was the way I thought you were supposed to do it. But after a while, I figured if I didn't do something myself, I might never get a call."

Howe is not flashy or colorful or Van Slyke/Flanagan funny. He looks like what he might have been: a bald, forty-five-year-old Westinghouse executive who comes to work every day, puts in his time, and goes home. But he is a man of great patience, who suffered quietly when John McMullen, in an effort to save money, dismantled the team that finished 86-76 in Howe's first season. By 1991, the cheaply put together Astros looked like a Triple-A club and their record reflected the look.

But there was good young talent on the team. Jeff Bagwell, acquired in a late-August prospect-for-a-pitcher deal (the Astros sent Larry Andersen to Boston) in 1990, was Rookie of the Year in '91. Craig Biggio was an All-Star as a catcher and was being asked to make the almost unique switch to second base to preserve his legs, which had stolen sixty-five bases in three seasons. Center fielder Steve Finley and pitcher Pete Harnisch, acquired from the Orioles in the Glenn Davis trade following the '90 season, were also budding stars. In his first full major league season, Luis Gonzalez had shown both speed and power.

"We still make mental mistakes because we're so young," Howe said. "But I understand that's part of the deal. We're learning on the job. That's tough to do in the majors, but I've really enjoyed the way this team has progressed.

"The funny thing is, I think the players have kind of enjoyed this trip. Look, we're the Houston Astros. We never get any media attention. Most people around the country have no idea who any of our guys are. Now, we're starting to get some attention and we're not playing badly either."

The Astros arrived at Wrigley Field 6-10 on the road trip. They had played well, except in San Diego, where they lost four straight to the Padres. The Cubs had just dropped a three-game series to the Expos, putting them below .500, at 55-58, once again. Their entire season had been a battle to get to .500. Like the Boston Red Sox, they were a team known for hitting that wasn't hitting. But they *were* pitching well.

Wrigley Field, like Fenway Park, is a hitter's park. Also like Fenway, it's one of the last of the true neighborhood parks. There is no parking to speak of, and the presence of so many homes in the surrounding neighborhood was the main reason there were so many objections to the eventual installation of lights in the park (which finally took place in 1989).

With its ivy-covered outfield walls, the fans hanging out on the rooftops across the street, the hand-operated scoreboard, and the intimacy of a 35,000-seat park, Wrigley is the National League's answer to Fenway. And, much like the Red Sox, the Cubs have given their fans far more heartache than joy over the years. Only the Cubs can compete with the Red Sox when it comes to literary teeth-gnashing (you know: that frigid winter wind sweeping over Lake Michigan, reminding the Northsiders of the glory denied the denizens of Wrigley while the warmth of another spring of hope is still months away) over their years of woe and lost opportunities.

Their last World Series title, as anyone in Chicago can tell you, came in 1908, ten years *earlier* than the Red Sox' last championship.

In fact, the Cubs have *never* won a World Series in Wrigley; it didn't open until 1914. They have won one National League pennant—1945—and two Eastern Division titles (1984 and 1989). Cub fans everywhere remember 1984, when they led the San Diego Padres two games to none before collapsing to lose the NLCS in five games.

The Cubs aren't the cute, cuddly bears they were when the Wrigley family owned them. They are now a wholly owned subsidiary of The Tribune Company, the media giant that owns not only the *Chicago Tribune,* but superstation WGN and several other television stations around the country. The Cubs and Harry Caray are beamed into millions of homes every day; along with the Braves and Mets, they get more national exposure than anyone.

Caray, something of a national treasure himself, adds to the Cub mystique. During the seventh-inning stretch at Wrigley, the honchos at WGN are smart enough to delay their cutaway to commercial so America can see and hear Harry as he sings "Take Me Out to the Ball Game."

"The thing I love most about it," Caray says, "is looking down into the stands and seeing the love in all those faces looking back."

Caray is a man of no small ego. But if you look around Wrigley when he's singing, you'll see that the fans *are* looking up to Caray with love in their eyes. Harry's singing is, without question, the highlight of any game at Wrigley Field, even if he does substitute "the Cubbies" for "the home team."

The unfortunate thing about the '92 Cubs was that they weren't much fun to watch. They had three bona fide major league hitters in their lineup: Hall-of-Famer-to-be Ryne Sandberg; first baseman Mark Grace; and another possible Hall of Famer, thirty-eight-year-old creaky-kneed right fielder Andre Dawson. This was not a bad threesome to build around, especially on a team that had starting pitchers Greg Maddux and Mike Morgan. But the second-line players weren't good enough to make the Cubs a consistent team, no matter how strong their nucleus might be.

Jim Lefebvre knew all this, but it didn't stop him from coming to the ballpark every day eager and excited about managing. Lefebvre would be eager and excited if he got the job as captain of the *Titanic* right *after* it hit the iceberg.

"We'll just have to work a little harder," he would probably say as he bailed water.

There had been a lot of skepticism about Lefebvre's enthusiasm early in the season—his constant team meetings, his motivational talks, the self-help tapes he showed the players on rainy days in spring training. The same kind of whining had been heard in Seattle, where Lefebvre produced the city's only winning record in 1991. The Cubs were not a very good team but they played respectable baseball for most of the season.

Lefebvre was fifty, a man who loved what he was doing every minute he was doing it. He played in the major leagues for nine years with the Dodgers, then went to Japan for five years. He managed successfully in the minor leagues before joining Tony LaRussa's staff in Oakland. That's where he was in 1989 when the chance came in Seattle. Lefebvre bridled when people asked him if he was too intense—"What does that *mean* exactly? What is too intense?"—but there was no doubting how he felt about the game.

"The hardest thing about playing baseball is knowing that there's an ending out there," he said one day. "I think a lot of players are bothered by that throughout their careers. We all know, no matter how great a player someone might be, that there's going to come a day when someone is going to come into the locker room, and in one form or another say, 'Get the hell out of here.' It might be the team president coming in to tell you they want to give you a day and retire your number, but the message is the same: Your time is up.

"For me to still be able to come to the ballpark every day is the best thing that's ever happened to me. I love the idea of spending an entire day sitting in a ballpark. You get there early, hours before the gates open, and it's quiet. This huge empty place and all you can hear are maybe a few concessionaries getting ready. You sit there and wait and you start to hear the sounds of ballplayers coming onto the field. They talk, they play catch, they stretch. Then they start to hit and there's that crack of the bat, over and over. If you close your eyes you can almost always tell the difference between a ball that's hit well and one that's been fouled into the net.

"Then the fans start to come in and you hear them calling for autographs or looking for their seats or trying to get a hot dog. The noise builds until the umpires come out and they play the national anthem and the game starts. And then, for about three hours the noise rises and falls, the tension mounts, the decisions are made. Pitchers leave, pinch-hitters bat, managers make choices. Finally, it's the ninth inning and there are two out and the bases loaded and the count is three-and-two and the pitcher throws and the batter swings and the center fielder takes off . . ."

Lefebvre paused and smiled for a moment. "And it doesn't really matter if he catches the ball or not. Because either way, the park empties, the custodians come out to clean up, and a couple of hours later, there's silence again, but you can look around you and see and hear everything that happened that day. Then, the next day you come back and the whole cycle begins again."

If it all sounds hopelessly romantic, there's a reason for that. In a business where cynicism and realism are considered necessities for success, Lefebvre is a romantic. He really believes that the old college try can succeed, even if the other team has more talent. "You can't accept losing," he said. "That was my big problem in Seattle, so many people were willing to accept losing. I know there's been a lot of losing here too, but it isn't the same. The Cubs have won and have been competitive and I don't see any reason why we can't be again soon."

The Cubs' best player for the last ten years has been Sandberg, the stoic second baseman who is so quiet he was described by one member of the organization as having a personality that was "about as interesting as a blue spot on a blue wall."

It isn't that Sandberg is unpleasant, it's just that he doesn't have very much to say. He's the son of a mortician who grew up in Spokane, Washington, figuring he would go to college on a football scholarship. He was a highly recruited quarterback who'd planned to go to Washington State. That's why he wasn't drafted until the twentieth round—by the Phillies—in the baseball draft in 1978. He changed his mind about baseball when the Phillies upped their offer to $90,000. He was a shortstop all through high school and in the minor leagues, but the Cubs asked him to play third base after they acquired him, along with Larry Bowa, for Ivan DeJesus, in a trade prior to the 1982 season. He stayed at third for a year before being moved to second. He won the Gold Glove there in 1983 and has won it every year since.

It was in 1984 that Sandberg exploded into stardom. He hit .314, and, after hitting fifteen home runs his first two seasons, hit nineteen and led the league in fielding percentage. Since then, Sandberg has grown as a power hitter—he hit forty home runs in 1990—while continuing to be a flawless defensive player. He went one entire season without making a throwing error and had one errorless streak that lasted 123 games.

Just prior to the start of spring training, the Cubs signed Sandberg to a new contract that would pay him approximately $7.1 million a year for four years beginning in 1993. General managers were aghast when the Sandberg numbers came out. Bonilla had established a new standard for annual pay when he signed his five-year deal with the Mets for $5.8 million a year. Now, the Cubs had rushed past the $6 million barrier without even pausing to catch their breath before crashing past $7 million.

Some general managers, most notably the Twins' Andy MacPhail, ripped the Cubs for caving in to Sandberg's demand that the contract be signed by March 1. The fact that Cubs chairman Stanton Cook had stepped in and done the deal himself, with little apparent regard for how it would affect other salaries, also upset people. And, the question was asked, if Ryne Sandberg is worth $7.1 million, how much will Barry Bonds be asking? Kirby Puckett? Cal Ripken?

Of course, later in the summer Stanton Cook would be one of the owners pushing to dump Fay Vincent on the grounds that he had led major league baseball into an untenable economic situation.

None of this mattered to Ryne Sandberg—and why should it? He would turn thirty-three during the season and this was his last chance to get a huge contract that would set him up for life. He had simply taken advantage of his situation. None of the other players begrudged him that; in fact most were happy for him. In baseball, if Ryne Sandberg's salary goes up at the top of the scale, most other salaries farther down the scale go up with it.

"I'm happy about the contract, but I can honestly say I don't play baseball for the money," Sandberg said one day in spring training. "I've always played because it's something I love doing and that hasn't changed since I was in high school."

He almost smiled. "Of course, I'm not complaining about the money, either."

It was sad, though, that in their rush to pay Sandberg, the Cubs had decided to ignore Andre Dawson. There were sound economic reasons for this: Dawson would turn thirty-nine during the 1993 season; there were serious questions about how much longer his knees would hold up; and with Greg Maddux coming up for free agency at the end of the '92 season, the Cubs had to make hard decisions on whom they could (or would) pay and whom they couldn't (or wouldn't).

Dawson had come to the club in 1987—in the midst of owners' collusion—for what amounted to a pittance: $500,000. He won the MVP that season, and while Sandberg had been the team's most solid and consistent player, Dawson had been its heart. There was no questioning who the Cubs' leader was, who it was that everyone in the clubhouse looked up to.

Dawson wanted to finish his career in Chicago. He felt he'd given the team and the city everything he had to give for six years and at least deserved a contract offer—*any* offer—from the team. It wasn't forthcoming. If baseball owners wonder why they're viewed by many as cold and heartless, they need only examine what happened to Dawson in Chicago in 1992.

After watching the Cubs put more than $28 million on the table for Sandberg, he had to endure a season in which the club said it just couldn't come up with *anything* for him. It was Jim Lefebvre's version of every ballplayer's nightmare: What Dawson had done in the past didn't matter; the Cubs were telling him to get the hell out of the clubhouse. He finally did—signing with the Red Sox during the off-season.

They were *not* telling Maddux to get out. Maddux, who at twenty-six was emerging as one of the game's premier pitchers, had been ready to sign a long-term contract prior to the season, but Cook, once again overstepping the authority of general manager Larry Hines, pulled the deal off the table. When he had a change of heart at midseason and authorized a five-year, $27.5-million offer, Maddux, who was on his way to winning the Cy Young Award (and leaving for Atlanta) said thanks, but no thanks, talk to me in November. By then, it was too late.

This was a Cub team full of dichotomies. They played hard because Lefebvre, by the force of his personality, insisted they do so. Sandberg was having a good, though not overwhelming, year, and the pitching had been solid. Dawson had also played well. But Gary Scott, who was awarded the third-base job two years running in the spring, had failed two years running.

George Bell, after one less-than-great season, was traded crosstown to the White Sox for Sammy Sosa, a lightning-fast center fielder who proceeded to spend most of the season on the DL. Shawon Dunston, the shortstop, missed almost the entire season. Dave Smith, signed two years earlier as the closer, had been miserable in 1991 and had elbow and shoulder troubles in 1992. At thirty-seven, he looked finished.

Like the Mets and Cardinals, the Cubs were able to make it look as if they were in the pennant race until the Pirates' eleven-game winning streak of early August. The fans knew earlier, however, that this was not a very good team. When the Cubs left base runner after base runner on in close games, they let the entire team hear about it.

The opening game against the Astros was typical. Frank Castillo pitched well for the Cubs but Jimmy Jones pitched better for Houston. Jones hadn't won a game in six weeks but he matched zeros with Castillo until the Astros came up with four runs in the seventh. That was enough, though just barely. Dawson homered in the seventh, Sandberg homered in the eighth, and the Cubs came up with another run off Doug Jones in the ninth.

They might have tied the game if catcher Rick Wilkins hadn't missed a sign and failed to bunt the runners on first and second over with no one out. The game ended when Jones got Joe Girardi to ground out with the tying run on third and the winning run on first. Cubs lose 4–3; 32,340 leave Wrigley having seen a perfect summer night ruined.

For the Astros, the victory made them 7-10 on the trip, and the save for Doug Jones was his twenty-sixth of the season. That number was remarkable: Jones had been sent to the minors by the Indians just a year earlier and was thought by many to be washed up at thirty-four.

"My game is control and confidence," he said. "Always has been. I never threw hard, even when I was a kid. That's probably why I wasn't considered a prospect coming out of high school."

Jones had graduated from high school in Lebanon, Indiana, and gone from there to play for one year down the road in Indianapolis at Butler University. He found the academics tough and money—he was not on a full scholarship—hard to come by. He quit school and, looking for warm weather, moved to Tucson. He got work there in a copper mine and was asked by some of the other miners to join their city league baseball team.

"I started on a level where you played in T-shirts and blue jeans," he said. "During the play-offs, the lower divisions played first, then the higher ones. If one of the higher-division teams liked someone on a team below, they could ask him to play. I kept moving up, until by the end of the season, I was wearing a full uniform—sanitary socks and all."

At that level, a number of college scouts were watching. One of them was Ken Richardson, then the coach at Central Arizona Junior College. He liked what he saw of Jones and called him to ask if he wanted to come down, throw for him, and, if all went well, enroll in school. Richardson was enthused about Jones's pitching ability, so much so that he honestly believed he was a pro prospect.

"Doug," he said, "I really think if you come to school here, you might get drafted in a year or two."

"Drafted?" Jones answered, aghast and ready to end the conversation. "Why in the world would I want to be drafted? I have absolutely no interest in going into the military at all!"

Richardson had never gotten that response from a prospect before. He explained to Jones that he meant the *baseball* draft—and, within a few hours, Jones was on campus.

"I was completely serious when I said it," Jones recalled. "I had never even thought about professional baseball. To me, that was Hollywood, something totally different and apart from the baseball I had played all my life. The thought that I might be a pro never once occurred to me."

A year later, he was in Hollywood—or at least Newark—having been drafted by the Milwaukee Brewers on the third round of, yes, the baseball draft. It took Jones a long time to get any closer to Hollywood. He kicked around the Brewers organization for seven years, missing one season with a shoulder injury before being released after the 1984 season. He signed a minor league contract with the Indians and shuttled between Triple-A and the majors for three years before finally making it to Cleveland in 1988.

For the next three years, he was one of the game's best closers, saving 112 games. He grew one of those dark, bushy mustaches that Rollie Fingers had made fashionable for closers during his career, and with his dark, curly hair, Jones came charging into games in the ninth inning looking fierce and ready to throw smoke.

Only he didn't throw smoke. His fastball topped out at eighty-six miles per hour and Jones had discovered in the minors that when he threw that hard, he didn't have very good control. If he took something off his fastball, though, it moved and became that much more effective. Control, the ability to change speeds off that fastball, and, most important, being able to spot the ball exactly where he wanted it made Jones effective. All of that seemed gone in '91 when he lost the closer's job early in the season, went to the minors, then came back to Cleveland as a starter.

"I needed to go someplace where I knew exactly what my role was going to be," he said. "When the Indians lost confidence in me last year, I lost confidence too. Here, I felt I had a chance to close if I could throw strikes."

He had done exactly that in 1992 and had become the anchor of a Houston bullpen that was used more than any in baseball (largely because the Astros' starting pitching was so mediocre). If Howe could get his starter into the sixth inning still in the game, he felt he had a chance to win. Jones was a big reason for that.

•

Across town, the White Sox returned home from a successful West Coast trip that had ended with them winning two of three in Oakland. Unfortunately, that hadn't been good enough. "We needed to sweep," manager Gene Lamont said. "That would have gotten us to within eight and a half. Instead, it's ten and a half. I have a feeling that's too much."

If Lamont felt a bit like Sisyphus by this stage of the season, he was entitled. Since the first day of spring training, when it had been apparent that Bo Jackson wasn't going to be able to play, the White Sox had been pushing the rock uphill with little to show for their effort.

Carlton Fisk's foot had continued to trouble him all through spring training and it was June before he'd been able to get back in the lineup. By then, shortstop Ozzie Guillen, the infield's glue, was gone for the year because of a knee injury. Guillen's backup, Craig Grebeck, also landed on the DL, forcing the White Sox to use Phillies castoff Dale Sveum at shortstop. Steve Sax, picked up from the Yankees to add punch at the top of the lineup, struggled all season.

"This is the most frustrating season I've ever had in my entire life," Sax said. "It started bad and it's stayed bad."

The same could be said for the Chicago pitching. With the exception of Jack McDowell, the starters had been ineffective. Alex Fernandez, who had been expected to step in as the number-two man, wound up going back to the minors. Charlie Hough wasn't terrible, but he was beginning to look his age—forty-four. Greg Hibbard and Kirk McCaskill both had ERAs of well over four. Worst of all, Bobby Thigpen, who'd saved a record fifty-seven games for Jeff Torborg's ninety-four-victory team in 1990, wasn't even a shadow of that pitcher. His ERA was also well over four and Lamont, while never publicly acknowledging it, had gone to a bullpen-by-committee after the All-Star break.

Through it all, the White Sox didn't roll over and die. They did have the best young power hitter in the game in Frank Thomas, who was quietly having another remarkable season. At twenty-three, Thomas was as mature as any young power hitter to come along in years. He was on his way to walking over one hundred times for the second year in a row and, although his youthful ego was sometimes big enough to fill the entire clubhouse, he never seemed to get so carried away that he forgot what the job was. His shower slippers summed up his approach perfectly. They said "DBTH"—Don't Believe The Hype.

For Lamont, the year had been a learning experience. He talked on the phone often to his old boss Leyland, who reminded him about their first year in Pittsburgh (64-98). Leyland told him not to worry about the expectations that had been placed on the White Sox before the season.

"You can't do anything about the expectations," Lamont says. "I knew that was part of the deal when I came here. It has been frustrating at times but I honestly feel the players have never stopped playing hard. That's why we've played a little better here of late. They haven't given up on themselves."

One of the tougher parts of the job for Lamont had been dealing with Fisk. The two men had gotten off to a bad start in the winter; Fisk had felt that Lamont was playing the role of mouthpiece for team president Jerry Reinsdorf and general manager Ron Schueler. The foot injury made things worse; then, when Fisk was finally healthy, playing time had been an issue. Fisk wanted to play—period. He felt he deserved to be in the lineup as long as he was hitting, *and,* by the end of the season, he wanted to break Bob Boone's all-time record for games played at catcher. But Lamont wanted Ron Karkovice to play, too—period.

Things came to a head on July 22 when Lamont pinch-hit for Karkovice in the eighth inning, then put Nelson Santovenia in to catch the ninth instead of Fisk (who had been the starter the night before and was being given the afternoon off). Fisk thought he should have finished the game—and said so publicly. The next day, in Milwaukee, the two men sat down to talk about Fisk's role.

Lamont was firm. He told Fisk he would continue to do what was best for the team and if that included Fisk, he would play. If it didn't, he wouldn't play. And if Fisk couldn't live with that, he didn't have to hang around.

Fisk walked out of the office wondering if his career might be over. "I came out of there with the impression that he was thinking about releasing me," he said later. "I was a little hurt, a little angry, a little confused. Instead, he starts playing me more."

Lamont smiled when the subject of that meeting came up. "Pudge really won me over this season," he said. "In spring training, I just wasn't sure about a forty-four-year-old guy trying to catch, especially when he lost so much time with the injury. But you know what, the guy can still really hit. When he's in the lineup he really gives us a boost. I'm not sure I've ever seen anyone who comes to the park more mentally ready to play. We had it out that day in Milwaukee but there's no doubt about how much I respect him. If I have anything to say about it, he'll be back here next year."

That was fine with Fisk, who had come around to a grudging respect for Lamont. Fisk is a man with very simple desires: He wants to play baseball for as long as he can play it well. He still believes firmly that he can catch and hit effectively in the major leagues. All he asks is a chance to prove that. Lamont was willing to give him that chance.

And, perhaps by coincidence, perhaps not, the White Sox won 13 of their next 19 games with Fisk playing almost every day. That streak brought them from below .500 to the fringes of contention. But, after winning the opening game of a series against the Yankees, they ran into a rookie pitcher named Sam Militello. With the Yanks hopelessly out of the pennant race (they arrived in Chicago 52-62), the organization wanted to take a look at some of their young pitching prospects who'd been tearing up the minor leagues. Militello was twenty-two and a comer. A year earlier, he'd spent most of the season pitching in Class-A. He finished up at Double-A, then had started '92 in Triple-A.

Five days prior to his start in Chicago, he had made his major league debut in Yankee Stadium against the Red Sox and had pitched seven shutout innings. He was almost as good against the White Sox, giving up two runs in eight innings before Steve Farr pitched the ninth in a 4-2 Yankee victory. Afterward, the New York media was all over Militello, who seemed to have "star" written across his uniform.

On the other side of the clubhouse, Don Mattingly sipped a beer and watched the scene with a wry grin on his face. "It's just so tough to keep things on an even keel on this team, in this city," he said. "I've seen so many guys come in here and have a few good games and get that savior label. It's tough to understand it when you're going through it. The thing they all have to remember is that you can't believe everything—or maybe anything—you hear. That's not easy."

Mattingly made a mental note to try to talk to Militello about what he would face if he continued pitching well. He remembered when he had first come up to what was a still-strong Yankee team and older players like Rich Gossage, Graig Nettles, Willie Randolph, and Dave

Righetti had made a point of showing him the ropes that were unique to New York and the Yankees.

"I know I've been criticized in the past for not being loud enough as a leader on this team," he said. "But that's just not my style. It doesn't mean I don't try to help the younger guys out."

In fact, if you talked to anyone on the Yankees, there was no doubt about who the leader and role model on this team was. Mattingly was thirty-one and had been with the Yankees for eleven years. His career batting average at the start of the season was .314 and the numbers he had put up for most of his career—on offense and defense—were enough to make him the unquestioned centerpiece of the team, even coming off a frustrating 1991 season.

But there was more to it than that. For four years, the Yankees had been a bad team. George Steinbrenner kept the revolving door extraordinarily busy, moving general managers, managers, pitching coaches, and players in and out as if they were pinballs, pinging their way around the New York clubhouse. Through it all, the one constant had been Mattingly.

From 1987 through 1990 he had been on the disabled list three times, due to a chronic back problem that wasn't likely to go away as long as he continued to play baseball. In '91, he played in 152 games, but to those who had watched him over the years it was clear the back was still bothering him. He hit .288 but only had 9 home runs and only drove in 68 runs, a far cry from his last healthy year (1989) when he hit 23 homers and drove in 113 runs.

Mattingly would not use the back as an excuse, however. "If I couldn't play, that's a different story," he said. "But I only missed ten games. If you're in the lineup every day you can't use an injury as an excuse."

There were other reasons for him to hate the '91 season: The Yankees were awful, winning just seventy-one games, and most of the team quit on manager Stump Merrill during the last two months. In August, Mattingly was actually benched one day for refusing to get a haircut. Gene Michael, the general manager, said it was his decision to sit Mattingly, whose long black hair has always flopped a little bit beneath his helmet. But the incident smacked of Steinbrenner and had everyone wondering if King George was invisibly pulling strings, in spite of Fay Vincent's edict that he not be involved with the club in any way, shape, or form. Whoever made the decision, it was a joke on a baseball team that had turned into a sad, unfunny laughingstock. For Mattingly, it was another surreal moment in a career that's had as many frustrations as remarkable accomplishments.

"When I was a kid, the idea of getting to travel and play baseball was kind of a dream," he said. "I think that's why I turned pro instead of going to college. It's not like the money was that huge or anything, I just liked the idea of playing."

Growing up in Evansville, Indiana, Mattingly, the youngest of four brothers, was also a good basketball player. In fact, if God had come down from Heaven one day and told young Don that he could be brilliant in one sport, Mattingly, Hoosier that he was, would no doubt have chosen hoops. To this day, if a friend of his isn't playing or if one of the players he enjoys watching—Kirby Puckett, Roberto Alomar, or someone on that level—isn't involved, Mattingly will often choose to watch an NBA game over a baseball game.

But his greatest talent was in baseball. He can remember, in an American Legion game, getting two hits as a high school freshman against a pitcher who had just been drafted by the Reds—in the first round. "I got two hits and hit the ball hard all four times," he says, smiling. "After that I started getting letters from scouts and recruiters. I was fourteen. But that was when I started thinking I might have a chance to play professionally."

He wasn't taken until the nineteenth round of the draft in 1979, partly because many teams thought he'd decided to go to college. Bill and Mary Mattingly thought that was the best idea for their youngest son; the chances of anyone making it to the major leagues were so slim.

But Don had the notion of playing etched into his brain, and when the Yankees upped the offer to $22,500 (with another $7,500 worth of incentives if he made it to the majors), he decided to take his shot.

A little more than three years later, he did make it to the majors, albeit briefly, getting a seven-game September call-up that produced twelve at-bats. The next year, he spent two months in Columbus before coming back to the Yankees for good in June. A year later, he was a batting champion who'd hit twenty-three home runs, putting to rest the notion that he couldn't hit for power. In 1985, he was the game's best run-producer with thirty-five homers and 145 RBIs.

Early in 1984, Steinbrenner told reporters that Mattingly was going to be a better ballplayer and a bigger star than the Mets' Darryl Strawberry, the National League's Rookie of the Year in 1983. Everyone laughed, as people often do when Steinbrenner makes one of his definitive statements. By the end of 1985, no one was laughing. Mattingly was the game's most feared hitter.

For Mattingly, all the attention that came with stardom in New York was a bit much. He was always polite and usually willing to talk, but he wasn't willing to lay his life out on the clubhouse floor the way some stars—like Strawberry—often did. When the veterans he had come up with began to disappear from the team, he was looked to more and more as a spokesman and leader. He wasn't always comfortable with the mantle but understood it came with the territory.

"You have to learn how to give the media what it needs without letting it get in the way of what *you* need," he said. "That's not easy if you're considered a star in any city, but it's even harder in New York. Especially with this team. I mean, let's face it, I could stand around and analyze what's going on and what's gone wrong and why this or that has happened all day. But I can't afford to do that. I have to keep focusing on what I need to do every single day to become a better player."

One evening in Seattle, in the ninth inning of a tie game, the Mariners had the winning run on first with no one out. They put on a bunt play which Mattingly promptly and brilliantly turned into a double play. After the game, he was glowing.

"For years I could never make that play," he said. "I would get to the ball in time, but by the time I picked it up, checked to see where the runner was, and then threw, I would be too late. Or, I would realize I couldn't get the guy and have to go to first.

"What frustrated me was that whenever I watched the Mets on TV I saw Keith Hernandez make the play every time. I mean he made it every single time! A couple of years ago I ran into him at a banquet and I asked him about it, how he could make it every time. He said the whole key was *not* checking the runner. 'Most guys field the ball, check, and then throw,' he told me. 'You have to field it and come up throwing. You read the play while you're in your throwing motion. If you see you can't get the guy, you don't follow through. You stop and you still have time to throw to first. But if you read before you start to throw you have no chance.' Now, I make the play that way—start to throw and then read—and now I make it more often than not."

The sheer joy of making such plays is what keeps Mattingly coming back to the ballpark. Early in the season, he had been so baffled by his problems hitting that he almost called his ex-teammate, hitting coach, manager, and friend Lou Piniella, seeking advice. In the end, after getting Piniella's phone number in Cincinnati, he decided not to pursue it.

"I almost did," he said. "But now, I'm kind of glad I didn't. I think I've been able to figure some things out on my own. I've had to make adjustments because I'm thirty-one and I've had back problems. I don't take extra batting practice as much as I used to, and even if I'd like to take a ton of ground balls, I know that's not the best thing for me. I do what I have to do to be ready to play and I think things have started to come around for me."

He didn't become the Mattingly of 1985 in 1992, but he came a long way back. By the end of the season he had fourteen home runs and eighty-six RBIs. He also had forty doubles; the line-drive double had been his calling card when he was at his best. And, as he watched the young pitchers like Militello come up, he hoped they would provide some stability in the years to come.

"I'd like to play in the play-offs before I'm through," he said. "The last few years have been difficult here. I've gotten to the point where I don't even really like to watch the World Series. I like playing for Buck [Showalter]; he's really given us some direction. If some of these young pitchers work out, well, at least there's some hope here for the future."

And when those young pitchers need some direction from someone who has seen about all there is to see in New York, they know just where to go seeking it. The kid from Evansville may not be very loud, but when he talks, listening to him is a very sound idea.

30

VOICES . . . AGAIN

O n the night of July 23, Bob Rathbun and Rick Rizzs were in the visiting radio booth at Anaheim Stadium when, midway through the game, they had a visitor: Ernie Harwell.

Harwell was also broadcasting the game, working a few yards away from Rathbun and Rizzs in the Angels booth. Early in the season, the Angels had asked Harwell if he'd be interested in adding fourteen of their games to the twenty-six he was doing on weekends for CBS Radio and he'd said yes.

Not surprisingly, several of the games the Angels wanted Harwell to do were against the Tigers. And so, when his old club came to Anaheim, Harwell was there to greet them—and the two men who had succeeded him in Detroit.

For Rathbun and Rizzs, the relative anonymity they had hoped for once the season got under way never materialized. On Opening Day, local newspapers, TV and radio stations took polls asking people what they thought of the new announcing team. The reviews were mixed. If Harwell himself had succeeded Harwell, a large chunk of the populace probably would have said, "Well, he sure isn't Ernie."

That was expected. What wasn't expected was Tom Monaghan's announcement that he was planning to sell the team. Monaghan, the man who built Domino's Pizza, was in serious financial trouble and had decided to unload the Tigers to pay off some of his debts. As soon as word got out that Monaghan was planning to sell, the rumors and questions began. Would the new owners bring Ernie back?

"You would think," Rathbun grumbled one night in June, "that the guy could win twenty-five games *and* hit fifty home runs for us."

Rathbun and Rizzs tried very hard to stay away from any Ernie-inspired controversy. Both respected what he had accomplished and both were smart enough to know that for the new kids in town to come out against Ernie would be a little bit like saying that Al Kaline really wasn't such a hot right fielder. Harwell had also been saying all the politically correct things. He said he liked both his successors and thought they would do fine work.

But underneath the smiles and warm words, there was tension. After all, Harwell had not left on his own terms; he felt—correctly—that he was still a pretty good broadcaster. On the other side, Rathbun and Rizzs didn't think it was fair to make them out to be the bad guys—they weren't the ones who had fired Ernie—and both got tired of hearing how awful it was that Ernie had been fired. To them, it was in the past. All they wanted to do was deal with the present and the future. But Monaghan's planned sale meant that the past might become a big part of the future.

"We had the impression that Ernie had put the whole thing behind him," Rizzs said one night as the rumors grew stronger. "Remember, he came to me and told me to apply for the job."

Making the decision to apply for the jobs and then accepting them when offered meant huge changes of life for both men. Rizzs had lived in Seattle for nine years and had two young children. Rathbun had never lived anywhere but in the Southeast. Both had willingly made the move, but both had assumed that once spring training and the early part of the season had come and gone, so would all the Ernie talk.

Now, the All-Star break had come and gone and Erniemania was hotter than ever. Almost every night in Tiger Stadium, someone would hang a sign just below the center-field scoreboard that said BRING BACK ERNIE. And, when Harwell was asked by reporters if he would come back should the new owner ask him to, he made it clear that he would seriously consider it.

"I'm not sure what I would do," he said just before the All-Star break. "But I'm not going to say I wouldn't do it. I've enjoyed doing CBS this year and traveling less, but I miss being with one ball club. That's what made the job fun. If they asked me back, I'd have to think about it."

Comments like that shook up both Rizzs and Rathbun—especially Rathbun. Rizzs had a clause in his contract requiring that he do six innings of play-by-play on every Tiger game. Rathbun, as the number-two man, had no such protection. If Harwell was brought back, that would leave Rathbun as a play-by-play man with no play-by-play to do.

Harwell's intention in visiting the Tigers booth in Anaheim was to calm the waters. He walked in during a break, shook hands with Rathbun and Rizzs, and said, "Now boys, you shouldn't be nervous about what you may be reading back home. Don't let the newspapers bother you."

Rathbun's instinct upon hearing that was to fake a laugh, say something like "Ernie, we aren't worried," and go back to the broadcast. He is, by nature, a gentle soul, not given to confrontation. Rizzs is less placid. He took off his headset, turned to face Harwell, and said, "To tell you the truth, Ernie, we're very concerned about what we've been reading. Exactly what are your intentions concerning the future?"

Harwell wasn't going to lie. "Well, if you really want to know, I think I have to keep my options open," he told them. "I don't know if I'll be asked, but if I am, I have to consider it."

It was time to go back on the air, so neither Rizzs nor Rathbun had a chance to respond. But as Harwell left the booth, Rathbun felt sick to his stomach. "If he'd walked in there and said, 'I've burned your house to the ground and taken everything you own and you'll never see any of it again,' I couldn't have felt worse," he said. "He basically looked me in the eye and said, 'I want your job.' Deep down, I knew if he wanted it, he was going to get it."

Rathbun's concern wasn't financial. Like Rizzs, he had a three-year contract with an option for a fourth year, which team president Bo Schembechler picked up just before he was fired. What sickened Rathbun was the thought of waiting so long to get his crack at a major league play-by-play job and then finding himself, for all intents and purposes, kicked out for reasons that had nothing to do with the quality of his work.

"My feeling was that Ernie was acting as if there was a *vacancy*, which there was when we came on," Rathbun said. "Now, there was no vacancy. There were two guys hired to do the job and he was saying he just might like to do it too. I felt so damn helpless. What was I going to do, come out and say Ernie Harwell was being unfair to me? That wasn't about to fly in Detroit."

By this time, Monaghan had a buyer. Ironically, it was another pizza baron, Mike Ilitch, the owner of the Little Caesar's pizza chain. Ilitch, who also owns the Detroit Red Wings, offered Monaghan $82 million for the team and Monaghan accepted. The sale was expected to be approved in August. In the meantime, Ilitch, without saying anything publicly, was sending out vibes that he wanted to bring Ernie back.

The vibes got worse on August 3 when Monaghan fired president Schembechler and executive VP Jim Campbell. The Tigers were in Baltimore when Dan Ewald, the vice-president for public relations, received a fax telling him what had happened. Clearly, the firings were part of the sale. Ilitch, who planned to make wholesale changes when he took over, wanted Monaghan to take care of the initial bloodletting.

It had been Schembechler who'd made the final decision not to bring Harwell back. Schembechler had also made the final decision to hire Rizzs and Rathbun and extend their contracts to protect them. Now he was gone. In a cruel twist, he learned of his firing by fax. His wife Millie had died in July after a long bout with cancer and Schembechler was at home the day Monaghan made his move—so Monaghan simply sent a fax to his house.

Rizzs and Rathbun were standing on the field during batting practice when Jeff Rimer, who did the Orioles pregame show for WBAL in Baltimore, began shouting to them from the press box. "Someone just called from your station," he said. "They want you to call them right away. Something big is up."

Rathbun and Rizzs charged into the clubhouse to find a phone and instead found Ewald, looking pale and shaken, holding the fax copy in his hand. Sparky Anderson came out of his office, looked at the fax, and shook his head. Campbell had brought him to the Tigers and the two were close friends.

"Fellas," he announced, "this is only the beginning."

Anderson knew what he was talking about. On August 26, the owners formally approved the sale of the team to Ilitch, who had been a Tiger farmhand for three years before making his fortune in dough and tomato sauce. The next day, twenty-one members of the front office, including several longtime employees, were told their services were no longer required. Ilitch would do things his way; Rathbun and Rizzs suspected that Harwell would be part of that way.

"He'll bring him back as sure as we're sitting here," Rathbun said two days after the sale was finalized. "I think he's convinced he has to. Everyone in this town believes that Ernie is the savior."

Rathbun and Rizzs had become close as the season unfolded. Rizzs had told Rathbun that he would give up two of his innings, if necessary, to keep his partner in the play-by-play mix. Neither man was happy about what was happening. On the morning of August 28, the day of the Tigers' first home game under the new ownership, they went to see Ilitch without an appointment. "We just thought we should make the first move," Rathbun said later. Ilitch couldn't—or wouldn't—see them. Moves would be made when the owner was ready to make them.

That night, with the Kansas City Royals as the opposition, the new regime began. It was a strange night in Tiger Stadium. The temperature was in the fifties, the winds were swirling, and scudding black rain clouds circled overhead all night. Everyone in the crowd of 24,715 came bundled up. The evening felt more like early April than late August.

Tiger Stadium is known in Detroit as "The Corner" because it sits on the corner of Michigan and Trumbull streets. It is one of baseball's intimate, ancient gems, a creaky old park full of poles, seats nearly on top of the field, obstructed views, and dank underground runways, complete with water dripping on players' heads as they walk from dugout to clubhouse.

The neighborhood around the ballpark is not exactly Beverly Hills. Signs in the parking lots inform drivers that security people will be stationed there until thirty minutes after the game. On a sunny afternoon, Tiger Stadium is as nice a place to be as there is in baseball. On a frigid, blustery night, it is dreary and forbidding.

"Been this way all summer," Anderson said, sitting in his tiny office before the game. "I think we've had five hot days total. It's as if summer never made it to Detroit this year."

Certainly the pennant race never passed through. The Tigers, after their awful 3-11 start, flirted with .500 a couple of times without ever getting there. They were now 61-67, and, since July, Anderson had been going with all the young players he had. The sale (and all the ensuing talk about who would and would not be back) had been a major distraction.

For a month now, Anderson had been at war with one of the local columnists, Jerry Green, because Green had written that as long as the new owners were cleaning house they might as well go all out and change managers too. Every time Green went after Anderson in his column, Anderson fired right back on his pregame radio show. Like a lot of people, Anderson felt bad for Rathbun and Rizzs.

"They're caught in the middle," he said. "They came here thinking everything was new and they could go from there. Now, this has been hanging over their heads all year. They deserve better."

The Ilitch era began with a 4–2 Tiger victory. Before the game, some of the players wondered if the presence of new ownership would boost the crowd, which it did by six thousand over the season average. Beyond that, there was little talk about how the new ownership would affect the team.

For baseball players, like everyone else, a change of bosses matters only if it affects their work (the players were not part of any of the immediate changes) or their pay. Ilitch clearly had more money to spend than Monaghan. That meant that someone like Cecil Fielder, a free agent after 1993, would be in a better position to re-sign with the Tigers (which he did for $36 million). To the middle-class player, Ilitch's presence made little difference.

"If it's good for the team then we're happy," pitcher Mark Leiter said. "For someone like me, being in the major leagues is what it's all about. Period."

Leiter had good reason to feel that way. He had been released four years earlier by the Baltimore Orioles after having had elbow surgery. He'd gone home to New Jersey and spent some time working as a prison guard before scouts spotted him pitching in a semipro league. His brother Al, then a Yankee phenom, had convinced the Yankees to bring him to spring training and he had made it to the majors for the first time at the age of twenty-seven.

The following year, after being traded to the Tigers during spring training, he made the ball club only to be sent down on Opening Day after the Tigers signed Pete Incaviglia as a free agent. "I was putting my uniform on for my first Opening Day in the majors when Sparky called me in and told me," Leiter said. "It was awful."

He made it back a month later and had been a spot starter and long reliever ever since. To Leiter, $82-million sales weren't part of his world. When he would pitch next was what mattered.

Anderson, as always, managed to sum up better than anyone what the sale meant. "This is a very good thing for me," he said, puffing on his pipe. "My grandchildren like Little Caesar's better than Domino's. Now we can order Little Caesar's and not feel guilty."

Of course, none of it was simple or easy for Rathbun and Rizzs. They did get their meeting with Ilitch the week after the sale and he promised that they would not be hurt if he brought Ernie back. But they left the meeting knowing that Harwell was going to return. Two weeks later, Ilitch made it official: Harwell would come back in 1993 for what amounted to a farewell tour. He would do three innings a night.

"It's just for one year," Harwell said. "That's all I want. I'm going to be seventy-five next year and I really don't want to do the travel full-time anymore. But it's exciting for me to be asked back."

He admitted that he was concerned about his relationship with Rathbun and Rizzs. Both had made it clear in the Detroit papers that they were not happy about his return. With the Tigers' season down to nothing more than trying to finish fourth, the "Ernie Returns" story was huge in Detroit. "I need to sit down with Bob and Rick and talk all of this out," Harwell acknowledged. "I know they're upset about what's happening, but I'm sure we can work things out. Heck, it's only for a year."

That it was only a year did provide consolation for Rathbun and

Rizzs. "If they hadn't committed to us that it was just a year, I would have walked," Rathbun said. "At least this way, there's light at the end of the tunnel."

The two broadcasters were not happy campers, though. They had arrived at spring training, like everyone else, with high hopes that the season would go well. Instead, it had turned into a nightmare that wouldn't end. Now, that nightmare was going to be extended for another year. No matter how the innings were divided, no matter how the men were billed, Harwell was going to be the star. He would be back as the conquering hero. There was nothing that anyone, not Rathbun, not Rizzs, not Harwell, could do about that.

Ernie was back in the booth. Rathbun and Rizzs, like it or not, would be there with him. That meant that 1993 might be a lot like 1992 on the Corner: Cecil Fielder would no doubt hit a lot of home runs, but most of the fireworks would take place above the field, not on it.

31

RUNAWAY?

Shortly before eight o'clock on the morning of August 4, the Cincinnati Reds boarded Delta Flight #351 en route to Atlanta. They had beaten the Houston Astros the previous afternoon in Riverfront Stadium to up their record to 61-43 and were now about to begin a critical three-game series with the Braves, who held a half-game lead over them in the National League West.

Flying commercial, especially out of Cincinnati, was not unusual for the Reds. Team owner Marge Schott was not a big believer in charters, even in an era when most major league teams *only* use charters for their extensive travels.

What disturbed some of the Reds was not so much flying Delta as *when* they were flying Delta. Even if Schott had not wanted to spring for a private plane, the team could easily have made a commercial flight the previous night. That way, they would have reached their hotel at a reasonable hour and been able to get a good night's sleep, waking up whenever they pleased, then making their way to the ballpark at their leisure for the 7:40 game.

Instead, most of them had been awake before sunrise in order to get to the Cincinnati airport—which is actually across the Ohio River in Kentucky—in morning rush-hour traffic. Even Tom Balton, who was to be the starting pitcher that night, was on that flight. Frequently, major league teams will send a starting pitcher to a city one day ahead of time if the rest of the team has to travel on game day; it ensures that he's rested. But Schott didn't want to spring for Balton either.

It was an important series. Neither the Reds nor the Braves had been playing all that well of late. Although the Braves had won the last three games they'd played in San Francisco over the weekend, they'd lost five of seven prior to that. The Reds had won the last two games of their series with the Astros, but prior to that had been only 8-8 since the All-Star break.

The teams would play again in September, but only five times. The Reds had dominated the Braves in Cincinnati, winning all six games. The Braves had won three of four in their first series in Atlanta. If the Reds could win two of three—and move back into first place in the Braves' ballpark—it might be important psychologically.

The Reds knew how other teams traveled. That's what made this so difficult for them to handle. Schott, who inherited her millions when her husband Charles, a wealthy automobile dealer, died in 1968, had bought the team in 1984 and turned the Reds into something of a circus. Stories about her frugality were legendary among team employees.

"People like to think Marge is eccentric," said one employee. "We all wish that was it. She's not eccentric, she's really mean-spirited. She has no qualms about humiliating people if she's unhappy. And when she drinks, it's worse."

Schott's drinking was one of the most whispered-about secrets in baseball. Fay Vincent was absolutely convinced she'd been drinking on that World Series night in 1990 when he tried to get her off the stadium microphone.

After the 1992 season was over, a lawsuit filed against her in 1991 by a former employee revealed that Schott used the word "nigger," had owned a swastika for years and couldn't understand why that would offend someone who was Jewish, and had referred to some of her ballplayers as "million-dollar niggers." Those who worked for her were hardly shocked. They had heard her talk that way in the past; a lot of the time they believed such talk was after she'd been drinking.

The players knew all the Marge stories and really didn't care about them very much. The dog running around on the field before games was a nuisance, and they would certainly care when it came time to negotiate a contract, but if Marge was a bitch for people in the front office to deal with, that wasn't their problem. Their problem—other than lack of sleep—was the Braves.

They started well that night, leading 5–2 in the sixth inning. But with the Atlanta crowd tomahawk-chopping throughout the humid night, the Braves came back. They tied things up at 5–5, then won it in the bottom of the ninth when Terry Pendleton hit a two-out, two-run homer off Norm Charlton.

It was an emotional, deflating loss for the Reds. Would they have won the game if they had been just a little bit fresher? Who knows? The only knowable thing was that the loss hurt. It hurt even more when the Braves held them to four runs over the next two nights and swept the series. The Reds limped out of Atlanta with their egos bruised and the deficit larger than it had been all season: three-and-a-half games.

The Braves, given a huge lift, promptly went on a binge that lasted through August 20. During that period, they won fifteen of eighteen games and opened their lead to six-and-a-half games. By the time they cooled off, the Reds were swooning. Manager Lou Piniella was talking about getting out of Cincinnati and rumors were flying that Schott was going to fire general manager Bob Quinn. All the rumors eventually proved true.

The biggest surprise in Atlanta—and perhaps in the game—had been Deion Sanders. The only reason he'd been in the lineup at the start of the season was Otis Nixon's drug suspension, which still had sixteen games left when the season began. To almost everyone in baseball, Sanders was a football player picking up some extra publicity by moonlighting. There was some truth to that, but when the Braves signed him to a minor league contract in January of 1991, it had not been as a publicity stunt.

"Remember, I'm the guy who drafted him out of high school when I was with the Royals," general manager John Schuerholz said, referring to his 1985 fourth-round choice. "He would have been drafted higher, by me or someone else, if not for the fact that everyone knew he wanted to play football."

Sanders had good reason to play football. He was an extraordinary defensive back and kick returner, blessed not only with great speed but with superb instincts. At Florida State he became a megastar, and was the Atlanta Falcons' first-round draft pick in 1989. By then, he was known in the college game as "Neion Deion," and was wearing so much gold that being able to stand up straight was proof of his athletic ability. In college, he played some baseball and ran some track, but his one and only focus was football.

"That was the sport that was going to make me rich," he says. "I liked baseball, especially when I was a kid, but in college, it just took up a lot of time when I could have been relaxing. In fact, if it hadn't been for the Yankees' drafting me, I would have given up on baseball completely."

The Yankees drafted him, for the heck of it, in June of 1988 on the thirtieth round. He played briefly for them in the minor leagues that summer and showed potential. His speed alone could help a team, but there was serious doubt about whether he would ever hit major league pitching.

The next two summers he again had flings with the Yankees. Each year, he was briefly called up to the majors and had his moments. When he hit his first major league home run in Milwaukee, he stopped when he reached home plate, bent over with his back to the pitcher, and tied his shoes.

That kind of attitude did not make him the most popular man in the game. In 1989, he arrived for his first spring training with the Yanks and asked for a single-digit uniform number. The Yankees only have two single-digit numbers (2 and 6) that haven't been retired and both were taken. So, grudgingly, Sanders took number 30. When his new teammates saw him jogging out for the first day of practice, they went crazy—30 had been Willie Randolph's number during his thirteen years with the team. When he left the club at the end of 1988 there had been talk of retiring it. Now, before a single game had been played in the next season, here was this football-playing rookie punk wearing it.

That incident certainly wasn't Sanders's fault. But others were. At one point, when he was playing in Columbus, he refused to ride the bus with the rest of the team. In Richmond one night, he refused to talk to the local media because "I don't talk to minor league writers." After he hit a home run one day while with the Yankees, Marty Noble of *Newsday* walked over to ask him a couple of questions about it. "Hey man, I don't do one-on-ones," Sanders told him.

"That's fine," replied Noble, a man rarely intimidated by athletes, "because I don't do groups."

The Yankees released Sanders at the end of the 1990 season. His mind, for good reason, was on football, and he had yet to show any evidence that he would ever hit in the big leagues: In 180 at-bats with the Yankees, he batted .178. And he was a pain in the ass.

That winter, Schuerholz and Bobby Cox decided to take a chance on him. Cox, like Schuerholz, thought Sanders had huge potential. "I had this memory of going over one day during spring training when I was still general manager to watch [Yankee farmhand] Bernie Williams take batting practice," Cox said. "Deion was hitting too and he couldn't hit the ball at all. Two weeks later, I saw him again and he had improved about one hundred percent. I remember thinking if he ever wanted to work at the game, he could really be something."

Schuerholz and Cox suspected that if Sanders could play baseball in the same city where he played football, he might hang around long enough to develop some of that potential. Skip Caray, the Braves' longtime broadcaster, remembers being in the ballpark the day the announcement was made that Sanders had been signed.

"I didn't really give it any thought," he said. "But I was down in the clubhouse and I ran into a couple of the players who had come in to do some preseason conditioning. They all said the same thing: 'Why in the world do we need that asshole?' "

They changed their tune quickly that spring, and not because Sanders hit .400. Knowing only his reputation, they were surprised by the person. No one worked any harder. Sure, he wore lots of gold, and rarely was he seen without a cellular phone in his hands. But he enjoyed the camaraderie of the clubhouse as much as anyone and had no problem taking part in the give-and-take put-down wars that are an essential part of any baseball team. In short, to everyone's surprise, he fit in.

"There was never any of the 'I'm better than you' stuff that people think is part of him," said pitcher Kent Mercker, who often fished with Sanders. "From the beginning, it was obvious that he liked us and we liked him."

Even though Sanders fit in with his teammates in '91, he was still little more than a flashy sideshow. He spent part of the year in Richmond, and, when he was with the Braves, hit .191 in 110 at-bats. He did get a lot of attention when he rejoined the team for a few games in September to serve as a pinch-runner during the pennant drive. No one had ever played two sports simultaneously. That made headlines.

What the '91 season did do was pique Sanders's interest in baseball. He had the notion, for the first time really, that if he worked at the game, he could do more than pinch-run. He put in a batting cage and pitching machine in the backyard of his house in suburban Atlanta. He worked out almost every day during his brief offseason. Even so, as spring training ended, most of the Braves thought of him as a fill-in until Nixon was ready.

Not Sanders. "I had decided that this was going to be the year that I found out about baseball," he said. "When I had come up to the Yankees before, it was too soon. I wasn't ready for the majors. Here I come, big name and all, to the New York Yankees—a bad team—and I'm not ready. Who are they going to rip in New York? Don Mattingly? No way. Now I'm with a good team with a lot of other good players. This was my chance and I wanted to take it."

He took it from day one, leading the league in hitting well into May. When Nixon came back, there was no way Cox could take Sanders out of the lineup. When he finally did cool down, Cox was faced with the happy dilemma of having four very good outfielders—Sanders, Nixon, Ron Gant, and David Justice. Sanders wanted to play all the time, which wasn't possible. By July, the biggest question in Atlanta was "What Sport Will Deion Play?" The Falcons offered him a $1-million bonus if he reported to camp on August 1. The Braves were renegotiating his contract because they wanted him to stay with them for the entire season.

Sanders seemed to be loving every second of it, basking in all the attention. But the football-baseball question had one negative side effect: It virtually ended his relationship with the Atlanta media. During the first half of the season, Sanders and most of the Atlanta writers had gotten along famously. He was, after all, playing remarkable baseball. He'd also been accommodating and enjoyable to deal with. But, as football season drew closer, the tone of the questions changed, as did the tone of the stories. Some writers speculated that Sanders was just playing the Braves and Falcons off against one another, trying to squeeze each of them as hard as he could.

The Atlanta writer Sanders had the most trouble with was Terence Moore, a black columnist for the *Atlanta Journal-Constitution.* Moore had been tough on Sanders at times and Sanders resented it. He didn't like criticism on any level, but it bothered him more when it came from someone who was black. This was not the first time Sanders had publicly clashed with another black over the issue of sticking together. Two years earlier, film producer Spike Lee had criticized Sanders for fostering stereotypes of young, rich blacks. Sanders had been furious then; he was furious now.

"That brother [Lee] had no right to say the things he said," Sanders fumed. "He's never been an athlete and he has no idea what the pressures are like or what we go through to get where we are.

"You see, what he should understand is that any successful black man is going to be threatening to a lot of white folks, especially if he speaks his mind and says things he's not supposed to say. The way it is in this country, if you're rich and black, you're supposed to be humble, just happy you're as lucky as you are. Well, I'm not that way. I walk into a room, people know I'm a success and I like it that way. I've never shied away from that and I never will. You speak up on issues, you're going to get criticized. But it shouldn't come from someone like him.

"Now, with all this stuff about the football, it pisses me off that I have to read all this crap in the paper again. You know, if a white dude holds out, you never hear anything about it. They hold out a few weeks, they get their money. A brother has to cry, has to threaten to do anything in the world to get some damn money in sports.

"Everyone knows this is a white man's world. I was in jail three times as a kid, each time because a white dude told a lie on me. Every time, the charges were dropped when they found out the white dude was lying. My teammates have seen that crap happen to me. They understand. But now, I've got this brother [Moore] writing all this crap about me that just ain't the truth."

Sanders confronted Moore in the clubhouse earlier in the season, screaming angrily at him. When Moore didn't back down, Sanders actually had to be held back by teammates from going after the reporter. In August, he told all Atlanta writers—regardless of race, creed, or newspaper—that he would no longer speak to them. "They had a privilege," he said. "They abused the privilege. They lost the privilege."

Not everyone in the Atlanta media viewed not talking to Sanders as a huge loss of privilege. One writer who did try to keep Sanders talking was Bill Zack of the Gwinnett papers. When he pointed out to Sanders that he hadn't written anything Sanders considered offensive, Sanders shook his head and said, "Doesn't matter. On the Falcons, one guy screws up, we all run."

"But Deion," Zack said. "*We're* not on the same team."

"Still doesn't matter," Sanders told him.

What was a shame in all this was that Sanders's stubbornness overshadowed the fact that he is not at all like the stereotype he's been made out to be—or has made himself out to be with his behavior. As Gary Sheffield pointed out in talking about his situation in Milwaukee, there is a tendency to slap easy stereotypes on blacks who talk in street lingo, which Sanders frequently did, especially when he was excited or upset.

Sanders is bright and often thoughtful. Asked about growing up poor, he said, "No, that's not right. My mother worked two jobs when I was a kid so I could have anything I wanted. It's not fair for me to say I was poor. I wasn't."

Asked if he was close to his degree at Florida State, he shook his head again. "I got a ways to go. It wasn't that I didn't ever try. At times I did. But for me to say I'm close, that would be a lie. Anyway, I'll probably never go back, to tell the truth. You go to college to become a success. To me, being a success was buying my mother a house and making sure she never had to work again. I've done that. I'm a success."

He was also an enigma. As the season wore on, even his teammates, much as they liked him, found him confusing. Early on, he had become close to Steve Avery, even taking $6,000 of Avery's money (at the pitcher's request) to buy him a new wardrobe. "He needed help," Sanders said, laughing. "*Serious* help."

But as the season progressed, Sanders hung less with Avery, less even with Nixon, who had been a mentor to him, and in the eyes of the other players, a steadying influence. Nixon was one of the most standup people in baseball. He had taken full responsibility for his drug suspension, blaming no one but himself. He seemed to have helped Sanders understand the notion of taking responsibility for his actions early in the season.

Now, as the pennant drive approached, Sanders was spending

more and more time with David Justice, who was as bright as anyone in the game (he had skipped seventh and eighth grades as a kid) but was also one of the league leaders in blaming the media for anything he did wrong. It may have been coincidence, but the more time he spent with Justice, the more negative Sanders became on the media.

His play faltered only slightly, though. He wasn't going to hit .340 all season, but although he was frustrated by nagging injuries that were limiting his playing time, he was still hitting .307 at the end of August.

"What separates me from other athletes is that I've never wanted to be *one* of the best," he said. "That's not good enough for me. I want to be *the* best. I want it all, every bit of it, because I honestly think I have that kind of ability. It would be very easy for me to settle back now and say I've done enough. I'm making a lot of money and I have two sports to choose from. But that's *not* enough. Never has been, never will be."

Wanting more, wanting it all, was something Sanders would come face-to-face with in October. The results would not be pretty.

•

For the moment, all the Braves wanted from Sanders was that he get healthy and promise to remain with them the rest of the season. After their hot streak ended, they lost seven of their next nine, giving the Reds a chance to climb back into the race.

But the Reds couldn't take advantage. On the final weekend in August, they went into New York for a series with the hapless Mets. They dropped a doubleheader on Friday and lost again on Saturday. Even so, they went into the Sunday night game that would close the series with a chance to move to within four of the Braves.

Tim Belcher pitched brilliantly for the Reds. After giving up a run in the first inning, he retired twenty-three straight Mets through eight innings. The Reds built a 3–1 lead that looked rock-solid.

But Lou Piniella then made the kind of move managers make in the nineties. Because Belcher had thrown 125 pitches, Piniella brought in his closer, Rob Dibble. With that one move, Piniella gave the world a clinic on how managers overmanage.

Belcher is not a young flamethrower whose arm must be protected. The weather was comfortable and his lead was two runs—not one, where one bad pitch would tie the game. At the very least, he should have started the ninth and stayed in until the Mets figured out a way to get someone on base. But the book said bring in the closer, so Piniella—as so many managers do these days—brought in the closer.

Tony LaRussa, who almost always brings in Dennis Eckersley in the ninth, pointed out later in the season that, for him, the easy way out is to do exactly that. "I'm never going to get criticized for bringing Eck in. But if my gut tells me it's not the right move and I give in and do it the easy way, then I've screwed up. Most of the time the right move *is* to bring Eck in, but if it isn't, I hope I have the guts to know it and not do it."

Bringing Dibble in was the easy way out for Piniella. He could cite Dibble's record, his fastball, and Belcher's pitch count. But on this night, it was the wrong move. Easy second-guess? Perhaps. But in the Shea Stadium press box, a number of people who had watched Belcher all night were screaming before Dibble threw a pitch.

He struck out Daryl Boston to start the inning, but only after going 3-2. Then, he walked Chris Donnels on another 3-2 pitch. That alone should have told Piniella he had problems. Jeff Kent struck out. Dibble walked Eddie Murray on four pitches, clearly afraid to throw a strike to him. That brought up Bobby Bonilla. Pitching coach Larry Roth-schild went to the mound, no doubt to suggest to Dibble that he consider not falling behind Bonilla.

He didn't. His first pitch was a strike and Bonilla turned on it and hit it into the right-field bullpen. Game over. Mets win, 5–4. Dibble was so enraged he ripped his uniform shirt off before he even got to the dugout, then tried to break a soda machine in the clubhouse. Piniella went after a water cooler (later in the year he would go after Dibble following a *win*), then retreated to his office where he shut the door. For the first and last time all season, he refused to speak to the media. The feeling in the Reds clubhouse was total despair. And fury. A couple of players talked briefly about what the loss meant. Belcher, in one of the class acts of the year, backed his manager's decision to take him out.

Two days later, when Piniella had cooled off, he sat down back home in Cincinnati with the local media and discussed his decision. When he was through, he shook his head, looked at the writers, and said softly, "I fucked up."

He had. The Reds were five games back. It might as well have been twenty-five. The moment Bonilla's shot landed in the bullpen, the National League West race was over.

PART V

SEPTEMBER... FINALLY

32

WHEELING
AND DEALING II

Every August, as the month winds down, general managers begin playing their games. There is an intensity to the GM games of August that doesn't exist at other times of the year. A trading deadline, a real one that can't be skirted, looms, and the phone lines between the twenty-six major league cities are usually scorched by the time midnight (Eastern Daylight Time) arrives on August 31.

Once upon a time, baseball had all sorts of trading deadlines. There was an interleague trading deadline during the offseason, there was the June 15 deadline during the regular season, and there were various times when waiver deals could or could not be made.

The rules have been simplified in recent years. Now, the only date that really has any meaning is August 31. There is still a July 31 trading deadline, but that's an artificial barrier, easily worked around. Once that date is passed, no player can be traded without first clearing waivers. Most general managers routinely put their entire roster on waivers during the first week in August. The process takes four days since no more than seven players can be put on waivers during any twenty-four-hour period.

If a general manager sees a player on the waiver wire who he thinks may be traded to someone he's in a pennant race with, he *might* go ahead and claim him. If he does so, the team that has waived him must withdraw him from waivers or lose him. That means the player cannot be traded for the rest of the month.

This tactic is known as "blocking" and is generally frowned upon in the fraternity. "You block too many times and you get everyone pissed off at you," one GM said. "If a guy blocks me, I'll get even with him sometime, sooner or later. That's the way it works. It takes an extreme situation for someone to block."

And great prescience. During that first week in August, no one really knows what kind of dealing is going to be done during the last week in August. As the names come tumbling through the waiver wire, most general managers pay little attention. After all, even if a superstar shows up—as almost all of them do—you know his name will be withdrawn if you make a claim. All you will accomplish is upsetting your fraternity brothers.

During that first week in August, virtually every player in the game clears waivers. Once that's done, the trading deadline has, for all intents and purposes, been extended thirty-one days. It's during the last week that all hell often breaks loose.

By the last week in August, the Mets' season, so promising in March, had turned to dust. From the fringes of contention in early August, they had completely fallen apart and were now in the frustrating role of seeking prospects for the future rather than players for the present.

On the morning of August 25, general manager Al Harazin made a "maintenance call"—as in "maintaining contact"—to Blue Jays general manager Pat Gillick. This was part of the routine. General managers of noncontending clubs put in calls to general managers in contention to see if one of them, seeking to fill a hole for the pennant race, might be willing to part with a couple of young players.

Gillick was still concerned about his pitching. Although Juan Guzmán had come back from the disabled list, he was still on a tight pitch count and didn't look anything like the pitcher he'd been before his injury. The rest of his staff still looked shaky, too, and now the Brewers had joined the Orioles in close pursuit of his team.

The Brewers were coming to Toronto that weekend for what was now a key series. Gillick had been in touch with several teams, looking for starting pitching. He had talked to the Mariners about Randy Johnson and to the Tigers about Bill Gullickson. He had even tried one more time to pry Jim Abbott loose from the Angels. So far, he'd gotten absolutely nowhere.

"Have I got anyone you're interested in?" Harazin said.

"Sure," Gillick replied. "David Cone."

Both men had a small laugh over that one. Any general manager with money to spend would be interested in Cone. Sandy Alderson of the A's had called a few days earlier to ask Harazin about Cone and had been turned down flat. Cone was twenty-nine, hadn't missed a start in five years, and generally was thought to have the best pure "stuff" in baseball. Not only did he throw hard, he had a variety of breaking pitches that could make any batter look foolish. He was well on his way to a third consecutive National League strikeout title, and although he had struggled somewhat in August, there was no questioning his talent.

Cone would be a free agent at the end of the season, having earlier in the year rejected a four-year, $17-million offer from the Mets. Harazin had been asked two weeks earlier, as the Mets were in the midst of their freefall, if he would consider trading Cone before the end of the month rather than lose him at the end of the season and get nothing in return.

"Absolutely not," he said then. "Even if I didn't think our chances of signing him were very good, I wouldn't trade him. I would wait until the end of the season and then see what might happen."

Harazin repeated that statement to Gillick, who wasn't surprised. He had thrown Cone's name out, as general managers often do, just to hear Harazin's reaction. "Well, if you change your mind, let me know soon," he said. "We have the Brewers here this weekend and if we did do something, I'd love to have him here for that."

Gillick's words stuck with Harazin. If getting Cone quickly—the trading deadline was still six days away—was that important to Gillick, maybe he could pry something loose from him that he might not normally be willing to part with.

Other factors were at work here. In July, Greg Maddux had turned down the Cubs' offer of $27.5 million for five years. Although Cone was three years older than Maddux, the two were generally rated in the same class as pitchers. In fact, Cone had twice used Maddux's salary in arbitration cases against the Mets as evidence that he should be paid the same kind of money. Both times, he had won.

Harazin already knew that team co-owners Fred Wilpon and Nelson Doubleday, burned by injuries and inconsistencies from starting pitchers making big money, would never go for a five-year deal for a pitcher, even though Cone was the one member of the staff who *had* been both healthy and relatively consistent.

"The Maddux thing really spooked me," Harazin said. "Before that, I thought signing David would not be easy, but that it was something we could get done. But when Maddux *turned down* those numbers, knowing how David felt about how he matched up with

Maddux, my stomach really began churning. I began to think it was really going to be uphill to get him back. That's why I began to think that if I could get Pat to give me two guys who could play for us every day next year, I had to at least consider doing it, even though I knew trading David would be very traumatic for him, for the team, and for me."

Harazin began making calls to his scouts. What young players did Toronto have, either in the big leagues or at Triple-A Syracuse, whom the Mets might have a chance to get, who could provide help in 1993? He needed to know quickly.

By the next morning, Harazin had his answers. Two names stood out: Jeff Kent, a twenty-four-year-old infielder who had played a fair amount in Toronto during the season because of Kelly Gruber's injury problems; and Ryan Thompson, also twenty-four, a center fielder with speed and lots of potential as a hitter. Thompson wasn't likely to get a chance in Toronto anytime soon, not with Devon White ensconced in center field.

Both players were young, both had enough experience to be big leaguers next year. Kent, who the scouts thought had fifteen-home-run power, was already there. Thompson might have farther to go as a hitter—his long, looping swing was something of a concern—but there was no doubt he could give the Mets something they had lacked since they traded Len Dykstra in 1989: a center fielder who could run, catch, and throw.

Harazin called Gillick back. He was very direct. "I'm willing to trade David Cone," he said. "But there are two guys I want in return and I don't want to negotiate."

He threw out the names of Kent and Thompson. Gillick was stunned. He had never expected to hear Harazin say he'd be willing to trade Cone, especially for a price he thought reasonable. He probably would have been less surprised if Harazin had called back and said he would trade Cone but wanted Roberto Alomar and Devon White in return.

"I'll have to get back to you, Al," Gillick said.

"Fine," Harazin told him. "But remember, you said you wanted Cone with your club for the weekend. I'm not going to put him up for bid with other teams. If you say yes, fine, if not, we'll keep him."

Gillick knew if he said no, that scenario might change. The Orioles were also trying to pick up a pitcher for September, although they were less likely to pay Cone's salary—he would cost slightly less than $1 million for five weeks of regular season work—than the Blue Jays.

As soon as he hung up with Harazin, Gillick began phoning his scouts. He also called manager Cito Gaston in Chicago to tell him that a trade might be made that would bring Cone to the Blue Jays and that it would probably involve Kent. Then he began setting up a conference call so he could find out what his scouts thought about losing Thompson and Kent. He already knew all about Cone. "Flaky, great stuff, competitor, that's the book on David Cone," he said later.

While Gillick was rounding up his scouts, Harazin was on the phone to San Francisco, where the Mets were playing. Frank Cashen was traveling with the team, which was playing an afternoon game with the Giants, then flying home afterward. After sounding Cashen out on the deal, Harazin asked him to tell Jeff Torborg what was going on.

"What do you think I should tell David?" Cashen asked.

"For now, nothing," Harazin said. "Gillick may come back and say no."

"Try to let me know something before we get on the plane," Cashen said.

Harazin promised to reach him immediately if he had word—one way or the other.

It took Gillick a while to put together a conference call with his staff and scouts that morning; when he did, there was a serious split. Scouts hate to give up on prospects. This was a trade that would gamble the future against the present. Since Cone was a free agent, the trade would really be a "rental," a relatively new phrase in baseball. It was very likely that Cone would not pitch for the Jays again after 1992.

A year earlier, Toronto had made a similar deal with the Cleveland Indians, acquiring Tom Candiotti in June, then losing him through free agency to the Dodgers in the offseason.

Gillick likes to lead by consensus. He wanted to hear what the scouts had to say in case someone raised an issue he hadn't thought about. But in his mind, this was a trade that had to be made. He was convinced his team needed another pitcher if it was going to hold off the Orioles and Brewers. If the Jays made the play-offs, Cone would give them another starter with postseason experience to go with Jack Morris.

"The player there was concern about was Thompson," he said. "Kent is an offensive player, not someone we thought would develop into a top-flight all-around player. But Thompson we felt had a chance to do that."

Gillick's assistant, Al LaMacchia, suggested trying to substitute another player, José De La Rosa, who was playing at Double-A Knoxville, in Thompson's place. Everyone agreed *that* deal should be made. Gillick called Harazin and offered De La Rosa instead of Thompson. Harazin was adamant: Kent and Thompson or no deal. Gillick rounded up the scouts again.

"The thing in my mind was that the game has changed to the point where you can't always follow your game plan," Gillick said. "There's no way for us to know in August of 1992 where we're going to be in August of 1993. Joe Carter was going to be a free agent at the end of the year and so were Jimmy Key and Tom Henke. Sitting there that day, we felt we knew what we needed to win right now, this year, and that it might very well be Cone. So I decided we had to call an audible."

Gillick explained how he felt to his staff. Some agreed; others still weren't happy about losing Thompson. He tried to call Harazin back but Harazin had left the office and was in transit to his home in Westchester.

Just before he left, Harazin talked to Cashen again and updated him. The Mets had beaten the Giants and were leaving for the airport for the long flight home. It would be well after midnight before they arrived at LaGuardia Airport. Cashen wanted to say something to Cone on the plane. Harazin was against it.

"Right now I'd say it's fifty-fifty at best that we're going to make this deal," he told Cashen. "If we don't make it and David knows we were thinking about it, what does that do to his psyche?"

Cashen understood, but was concerned. "I just don't think it's fair if we do make the deal to have him get a call tomorrow out of the blue."

Harazin understood. "Do what you think is best," he said. "If anything happens in the next hour, I'll try to reach you at the airport."

Driving home, he listened to radio reports on Hurricane Andrew, which was about to slam into south Florida. He walked in the door of his house to find his wife on the phone. "It's Pat Gillick," she said.

"We want to make the deal," Gillick said.

"Kent and Thompson?" Harazin asked, wanting to be sure.

"Kent and Thompson," Gillick said.

Harazin hung up the phone and turned to his wife. "I think there's another hurricane about to hit," he said. Then he told her what he'd just done.

It would take several hours to go through the formalities of closing the deal, but Harazin tried to call the airport in San Francisco to reach Cashen. Too late. The plane had just left.

Not knowing what the status of the trade was, Cashen was left with a dilemma. Halfway through the trip, he walked from the first-class cabin to the back of the plane and sat down with Cone.

"I was surprised when I saw him because he almost never came in the back," Cone said later. "I wondered for a second if something was up. But then he sat down with me and just started talking about Scottish and Irish golf courses. We had a real nice talk, then he got up and went back up front."

It was almost 2 A.M. when the plane landed. As the players wearily deplaned, Cashen took Cone by the arm and pulled him aside. He looked him right in the eye and said, "Stay by your phone in the morning."

Cone understood exactly what that meant. He was stunned. "Later on I really appreciated Frank doing that," he said. "I mean, it was really classy of him to alert me that way. But when he did, I was dazed. I went into Manhattan and went looking for a bar. Fortunately, there's always someplace open in New York. It was probably five or six o'clock by the time I got back to my apartment."

Analyzing the situation, Cone was convinced he was going to be traded to Oakland. He knew that Bob Welch had just gone on the disabled list and the A's desperately needed a starter. He tossed and turned in bed, telling himself that being reunited with Ron Darling would be fun, and finally dropped off to sleep.

At 11 A.M. the phone rang. "I think I'd been sleeping five minutes," Cone said. He reached for the phone, certain it was Harazin telling him he was going to Oakland. He was half right.

"David, this is very, very hard to do," Harazin said. "But I think I've just traded you into the World Series." Then he told him it was Toronto.

Even with the warning from Cashen, Cone was stunned. He had been with the Mets for almost six years and thought of New York as home. A few minutes after Harazin hung up, the phone rang again. It was Gillick and Gaston welcoming him to the Blue Jays.

Harazin's Hurricane began almost as soon as the trade had been announced. No one in New York had ever *heard* of Jeff Kent or Ryan Thompson. When reporters began contacting other Mets, all of them were aghast that Cone had been traded for what sounded like so little. The following morning, the *New York Post* ran a front-page picture of Harazin—wearing a dunce cap.

In February, still basking in the glow of his offseason deals, Harazin had cautioned against getting too carried away with positive publicity. "You never know in this game," he said. "Before this is all over, I could end up looking like a dunce."

Now he had a picture to prove it. But Harazin didn't lose his sense of humor, even as he took one hit after another during the next few days. He had the dunce picture framed for his office; he even talked about marching in the annual Banner Day Parade wearing a Cone-head.

"It might be my last act as general manager," he said, sitting in the dugout that night. "But it would be a hell of a way to go out."

He shrugged and forced a laugh. "I was a genius in February, I'm a dunce now. Who knows, a year from now, when Jeff Kent and Ryan Thompson have had great years, I might be a genius again."

A banner went by that made Harazin wince slightly. The Mets'

slogan for 1992 had been "Hardball is back." The banner was succinct: "Hardball," it said, "Ain't Back."

•

Sandy Alderson's call to Harazin about Cone was one of a series of calls
he had made as the trading deadline began to draw near.

The A's had taken control of the American League West race after
their sweep of the Twins in the Metrodome, but Alderson, Tony
LaRussa, and team president Wally Haas, the troika that ran the team,
were concerned about their ability to make it to the finish line.

"We had overachieved to get the lead," Alderson says. "But there
were signs that we were falling apart. Especially the pitching staff."

The A's had been unable to find a consistent fifth starter all season. Bob Welch had been on and off the disabled list. The bullpen,
which had held the team together through much of the season, was
showing serious signs of fatigue. Jeff Parrett, who served as the bridge
between the starters and Dennis Eckersley, was no longer the same
pitcher he'd been during the first half of the year. More and more often,
LaRussa had been forced to bring Eck in before the ninth. He *hated*
doing that. Eck would be thirty-eight in October. Even he was human.
On August 25, in Boston, he came into a game in the eighth inning,
and for the first time all year ended up with a loss.

So Alderson had started making phone calls. He inquired about
Cone in New York; Gullickson in Detroit; Lee Smith in St. Louis; Greg
Harris in Boston; Bobby Thigpen in Chicago; Jeff Russell in Texas; and
Steve Farr, also in New York, but in the other borough. In most cases,
there was interest—but no one had come up with an offer worth taking
seriously.

The Cone trade on August 26 intensified Alderson's search. If the
A's did make the play-offs, their likely opponent had just become that
much more formidable. That weekend, the Cleveland Indians, a team
that had given the A's considerable trouble during the past two seasons, came into Oakland. In fact, on their first trip back in May, they
had swept.

Not this time. The A's won the opener 7–6, then came back on
Saturday afternoon and won 4–1. The team was in a real groove. "It
was one of those situations where everyone on the team was playing
great," LaRussa said. "Except for one guy."

That guy was José Canseco. "Every time up, he was trying to hit
the ball five hundred feet," LaRussa said.

Sitting upstairs, watching the Saturday game together, Alderson
and Wally Haas had the same feeling LaRussa had. Alderson had been
through another round of talks with GM's that morning and was no
closer to a deal for a pitcher. Alderson doesn't remember the exact

moment when he first thought about bringing Canseco's name up in a trade, but he does remember him swinging wildly at a pitch and popping up.

"I looked at Wally and said something like 'What if we did *this*?'" Alderson said. "His answer, as I recall, was 'Why not go for it?'"

That answer hardly surprised Alderson. This was not the first time that Canseco's name had been discussed as a candidate for a trade. The previous winter, frustrated by Canseco's attitude, Alderson had tested the waters to see if there was interest. He'd talked to the Mariners, Yankees, and Red Sox, but had gotten little response.

During the season, the troika's frustration with Canseco had grown. LaRussa lectured him constantly about trying to hit the ball to all fields rather than trying to pull every pitch out of the ballpark. "I often told him that if he would hit the ball to all fields, he could hit .330," LaRussa said. "I really believe he's capable of it. I can remember telling him, 'You know José, you may find this hard to believe, but I think I actually believe you're more talented than you do.' And he would look at me and say, 'That's not possible.' It was a joke, but it *wasn't* a joke. I was serious."

What disturbed the troika most of all was Canseco's approach to injuries. They felt he never worked hard at rehabbing, an indication he didn't care that much about helping the ball club. The injuries almost became a crutch. The incident in July—when he didn't show up for rehab after asking to go on the DL—had stuck in everyone's mind.

Of the three, Haas was the one most inclined to want to move Canseco. But he has always left the final decisions on personnel moves up to Alderson and LaRussa and this was no exception.

Haas is forty-two, the son of Walter A. Haas, Jr., whose father founded Levi-Strauss. It was Haas Junior who bought the A's from Charles O. Finley in 1980 when the franchise was on the verge of going under; he turned it around both financially and on the field. His son, Wally (who is not Walter A. Haas III but *did* name *his* son Walter A. Haas III), was a musician who played keyboards growing up and had worked as the business manager for a rock group, Sons of Champlin, for several years before joining the family business. When his father bought the A's, Wally Haas served as executive vice-president for seven years before becoming the chief operating officer and then team president.

Wally Haas was anything but the stereotypical rich kid. He was funny and self-deprecating. He often joked that when people asked him what his qualifications were to run a baseball team, he answered, "I have a rich father."

Rich father or not, Haas worked hard at running the team. He was not a meddler, but he was very definitely a factor in all major decisions.

He had been bothered by Canseco's attitude for a long time and both Alderson and LaRussa knew it. "He had become the villain wrestler," Haas said. "That may be popular but I don't think it's very positive. And his approach didn't help the ball club, even though his talent was extraordinary."

Even though it had been discussed before, trading Canseco was not something anyone took lightly. After all, this was a player who had just turned twenty-eight, and, injuries and all, already had 231 career home runs. He was Oakland's most recognizable player, the first name most people brought up when talking about the A's franchise. He was a potential Hall of Famer.

Alderson had not given any thought to making him part of a deal until that Saturday afternoon. Once the idea surfaced, he went into action. He left Haas in the box while the game was still going on and went back to his office. He called Tom Grieve, the Texas general manager, and proposed a three-for-one deal: Russell, starting pitcher José Guzmán, and right fielder Ruben Sierra for Canseco. Grieve swallowed hard. "I'm going to have to get back to you on that one," he said.

Alderson wasn't surprised by that reaction. He followed his call to Grieve with a similar call to Red Sox general manager Lou Gorman. Again, he suggested a three-for-one swap: Canseco for Greg Harris, Frank Viola, and Tom Brunansky. Gorman's reaction was the same as Grieve's: "I'll get back to you."

As soon as the game was over, Alderson went to LaRussa's office and told him what he'd done. LaRussa's first reaction was a double-take. "Then I thought about the names he was throwing out and I thought, 'This could make the club better.' "

Canseco was still a long way from being traded. The next morning, Gorman called back and wanted to add players—A's players—to the deal. That wasn't workable as far as Alderson was concerned. The focus shifted to Texas. Alderson and Grieve talked several times on Sunday. The Rangers didn't want to trade Guzmán, who was a free agent at the end of the season, because they thought they could re-sign him. Grieve offered Bobby Witt instead. That didn't thrill Alderson.

"We liked the idea that all three guys we were talking about [Guzmán, Russell, and Sierra] were free agents at the end of the season," he said. "That was consistent with the approach we had been taking. We had twelve guys already who were going to be free agents and if we added three more, that meant we had flexibility with all of them. Plus, bringing in three guys who were in the same boat with a lot of our players worked in terms of the chemistry in the clubhouse. Witt had a big-money contract for 1993. We weren't so sure if we wanted to add that."

Alderson kept hammering on Grieve about Guzmán. Grieve wasn't moving. But they did keep talking. At one point, Grieve said, "You know I'm really looking forward to your next call. Maybe we'll just trade your whole team for my whole team before this is over."

There was another sticking point: Sierra's health. Saturday, Grieve mentioned that it was possible Sierra had chicken pox. Sunday he confirmed it. It would be at least a week to ten days before Sierra could play. That would leave the A's very vulnerable offensively for several games if they traded away Canseco. When LaRussa came off the field Sunday—after another victory over the Indians—Alderson gave him the news about Sierra. They talked it through. The lead at that moment was seven-and-a-half games.

"It was one of those things where, when you first hear about it [the chicken pox], you think, 'Someone up there's trying to tell us not to make this deal,' " LaRussa said. "But then you have to put that aside because, let's face it, there's no one upstairs paying any attention to the race in the American League West. My feeling right then was, if Sierra was healthy, we should make the deal. Only he wasn't."

That night, the Red Sox traded Jeff Reardon to the Braves. Alderson had felt all along that Gorman wanted to move Reardon rather than Harris; this confirmed it. The trade meant the Sox definitely wouldn't part with Harris. But it also meant that the Braves, who had really wanted the Mets' John Franco (his elbow had suddenly tightened on him again on the day he heard he might be traded), were now out of the picture in terms of Russell. They had also been talking to the Rangers about him.

Armed with that knowledge, Alderson called Grieve again on Monday morning—the 31st. "I just don't think we can make the big deal because of this chicken pox thing," he said. "But I'd still like to make a deal for Russell."

Grieve said he would think about it and call back. Alderson wasn't optimistic. He told his staff and scouts, all of whom he'd brought into town for the weekend so they could be around to make evaluations on any names that came up, that it looked like there would be no deal.

Shortly after Alderson's last conversation with Grieve, a group of staff and scouts, led by Walt Jocketty and Karl Kuehl, Alderson's two closest advisors, went to lunch. The group sat around the dining room of the Airport Hilton, about a mile from the ballpark, discussing the trade. When they returned, Jocketty went straight to Alderson's office. "Sandy," he said. "We all agree. you have to try to make this trade, chicken pox or no chicken pox."

The trading deadline was midnight on the East Coast, 9 P.M. in California. It was now two o'clock in the afternoon in Oakland. Alderson called Grieve. "Tell me again about this chicken pox thing," he said.

Grieve did better than that. He had Sierra's doctor call the A's doctors. It was almost four o'clock by the time everyone was straight on the chicken pox issue. Alderson, after briefing Haas again, convened a meeting in LaRussa's office. He and Haas, along with Jocketty, Kuehl, special assistant Bill Rigney, and several of the team's top scouts, went downstairs. There they were joined by LaRussa and all his coaches.

As he usually does when he's in the manager's office, Alderson sat in a chair by the door that sits next to LaRussa's desk. Wally Haas was in the far corner next to the refrigerator. Everyone else either sat on the two benches from old Comiskey Park that LaRussa has in the office or stood. The room was extremely crowded.

Alderson spelled out the trade one more time. Without telling anyone about the Jocketty lunch-bunch, he asked each of the coaches what they felt. "I wanted them to answer before Tony said anything," he said. "If he answered first, they would probably go along with whatever he said. This way, even if they were anticipating what he might say, they would probably be more exact about what they thought. They knew we might or might not go along with them, but that we respected their thinking. That's why we asked."

Pitching coach Dave Duncan was particularly enthusiastic about getting Russell because he could take pressure off Eckersley. The coaches were unanimous: They liked the deal.

Alderson adjourned the meeting. Everyone left except Haas, LaRussa, Jocketty, and Alderson. They talked for a few more minutes about the players involved, the public's reaction to trading Canseco, and the notion of making this kind of deal with a seven-and-a-half-game lead. Finally, Alderson asked Haas and Jocketty to leave so he could have a few minutes alone with LaRussa.

"The notion of asking your boss to leave may sound funny, but I thought it was appropriate at the time," Alderson said. "Tony and I are paid to make these decisions and I thought we should go over it one more time by ourselves. Of course, Wally would have had a perfect right to overrule us, but that's not his style."

Haas had no problem with Alderson's request. "In the end, it had to be their decision," he said. "That's the way it's always been around here. I may get emotional about things sometimes but I know Sandy and Tony will always do what they're convinced is right for the club. They take emotion out of it, which is the way it should be.

"This was a huge decision. If we made the deal, whatever we might think about José, it would be the end of an era for us. And Sandy and Tony were the ones who were going to take the heat."

That was what Alderson wanted to talk to LaRussa about. He wanted to be certain they agreed this was not an emotional decision, that it was being made strictly because they believed the club would be better. The trade would be distracting and in some ways traumatic.

"Are you sure about this?" Alderson asked one more time.

"I'm sure," LaRussa answered.

That made the decision final. Alderson went back upstairs and told Haas, who authorized the trade. Alderson called Grieve and told him the A's would take Witt, Russell, and Sierra. Now it was Grieve who needed time. He had to find *his* owner, George W. Bush, to get authorization.

It was less than two hours before that night's game against the Orioles. LaRussa wrote Canseco's name on the lineup card. If he hadn't, the media would have descended with a million questions. "If we didn't put him in the lineup and then we didn't make the trade, people would wonder what we had been up to," Alderson says. "This way, if the trade didn't happen, there would be no questions."

LaRussa kept checking with Alderson as game time approached. At six-fifty, fifteen minutes before the first pitch, he called again. Still no deal. At seven, just before he walked the lineup out to the umpires, he called from the dugout. Still nothing.

Shortly after the A's, including Canseco, took the field, Grieve called back. The deal was on. Both teams then had to call the American League office to confirm that the four players had indeed been traded. At seven-fifteen, just after the A's retired the Orioles in the top of the first, Alderson called the dugout.

"First time in my life I've ever called the dugout during a game," he said.

LaRussa answered on the first ring. "It's done," Alderson said. "Get José out of the game."

Canseco was standing just outside the dugout at that moment, leaning on a railing. He had a bat in his hand, since he would be on-deck as soon as Rickey Henderson was finished leading off the inning. Canseco was *not*—as has been reported—in the on-deck circle. Close, but not quite there.

LaRussa walked over to Canseco and said softly, "José, I need to see you in the runway."

In Oakland, the runways leading to the clubhouses are located about ten yards from the dugouts. From the press box, several writers noticed LaRussa and Canseco walking there and wondered if something was going on.

Once they reached the runway, LaRussa was direct. "José, we just traded you to the Rangers," he said. He told him who he'd been traded for and shook hands with him. Canseco went directly up the ramp to the clubhouse. He was in shock.

"It wasn't an easy thing to do, because José had meant a lot to the club," LaRussa said. "But it wasn't the hardest thing I ever had to do either, although I'm sure José wouldn't understand that. Releasing someone is harder than telling a player he's traded. I know to *José* it was traumatic and huge. Once I told him, I had to tell the club."

LaRussa walked back into the dugout—without Canseco—and told the players, "We just traded José for Ruben Sierra, Jeff Russell, and Bobby Witt." Then he turned to Lance Blankenship and said, "You hit for José."

The players stared at one another in disbelief. "For a split second we thought it was a joke," Mike Bordick said. "I even thought to myself, 'Hey, this isn't April Fools', is it?' But then we all realized that Tony doesn't joke during a game. And there was Lance going to get a bat."

As soon as LaRussa walked back to the dugout without Canseco, all hell broke loose in the press box. Something big was clearly up. When Blankenship walked to the on-deck circle, it was obvious. Then came the announcement: press conference at eight o'clock. The writers all knew what it was about: José Canseco was no longer an Oakland Athletic.

"In the end, it was a different kind of trade than the ones you usually make going into a stretch drive," Alderson said. "Usually, when a contender does a deal like that, you're trading part of your future to help your present [the Cone trade being an example]. In this case, we went the other way. We traded part of our *past* to help our present."

With Canseco gone and Sierra sick, the A's promptly dropped their next six games. It looked like in trading their past, they'd *damaged* their present. There was even talk about a "Curse of Canseco." But on the night Sierra returned, the A's pulled out a 2–1 ten-inning win over the Red Sox. Bobby Witt pitched seven strong innings. The winning run was scored by Sierra. The lead went back to five and a half. And Alderson, Haas, and LaRussa all smiled for the first time in almost a week.

•

Almost no one caught Cal Ripken smiling throughout July and deep into August. His slump kept getting worse and he was beginning to think that his contract negotiations might never end.

Ripken's agent, Ron Shapiro, and Orioles president Larry Lucchino had held their first meeting to discuss a new contract on September 26, 1991, even before Ripken's MVP season had concluded. Both men knew that this would not be an easy or a brief negotiation.

They were right. In all, it would take 333 days to produce a signed contract.

Shapiro and Lucchino were an odd and interesting couple. Lucchino was forty-four, a lawyer who had gotten involved with the Orioles through his friendship and business partnership with Edward Bennett Williams. It was Lucchino who had convinced Eli Jacobs to buy the team from Williams's widow after Williams's death, and the Orioles had become the most important thing in his life. He had beaten cancer several years earlier. One of his closest friends during that trying period in his life was Ron Shapiro.

Shapiro was forty-nine, a onetime boy wonder who had been the secretary of Maryland's Securities and Exchange Commission when he was twenty-nine. A graduate of Harvard Law School, he'd been brought into the business of representing athletes in 1976 when the Orioles asked him to take over Brooks Robinson's failing finances. Once Shapiro had gotten Robinson on his feet, he started to represent other Orioles. By the early 1980s he was representing almost the entire team.

He never had a client list larger than thirty or so players, but most of his clients did very well. In 1992, he would negotiate a new deal not only for Ripken, but for Kirby Puckett. Shapiro felt strongly that both men should stay where they were since each was an icon in the city where he played. But he also knew that to get them top dollar he had to convince their teams that they were willing to go elsewhere if the money put on the table wasn't acceptable.

Lucchino's first offer was a long way from acceptable: two years for $10 million. Shapiro's counter was fairly predictable: He wanted five years at $39 million. The two men began only three years and $29 million apart.

"You have to understand where we were coming from at the beginning," Shapiro said. "Cal was coming off an MVP year and it wasn't unreasonable to think that the market at the end of the 1992 season for someone at that level would be in the neighborhood I was in."

Lucchino didn't see it quite that way. He wanted to talk not about what MVPs were making but about what shortstops were making. On February 6, he upped his offer to four years at $20 million, double the original numbers but well shy of what Shapiro and Ripken were thinking.

Two weeks later, Lucchino made his first unusual move. He wrote a letter directly to Ripken and his wife Kelly—three pages, single-spaced—pointing out not only how much the Orioles wanted to keep him with the team but that the offer on the table would make him the highest-paid shortstop in baseball. Shapiro, after seeing the letter, came down to $38 million.

Ripken went to spring training confused. Where did he stand with the Orioles? Did they really want to sign him? Were they willing to gamble on him becoming a free agent? Were they secretly hoping that his numbers would come down in 1992, thus allowing them to sign him for less money? He wanted to stay in Baltimore, but he wanted to feel as if the Orioles wanted him to stay.

On March 6, as the Orioles were playing their first exhibition game, Lucchino entered the financial reality of the nineties. He began a letter to Shapiro by saying he found it "puzzling and surprising that our first offer was inadequate." But, he added, the Orioles were now prepared "to make Cal the first $6 million man in the game." (Many clubs consider Ryne Sandberg's contract to be worth only $5.8 million a year.) The offer on the table was up to $30 million for five years.

"Now," said Shapiro, "we were beginning to come together."

But they were a long way from signing anything. Shapiro came down in his counter to $36 million, but made it clear that neither he nor Ripken would move very far off that figure for a while. In the meantime, Shapiro had opened negotiations with the Twins for Puckett. He was both impressed and somewhat amused at their first meeting when general manager Andy MacPhail handed him a booklet with a picture of Pickett on the cover along with the caption "The Best in the Game." Inside was an analysis of Puckett's career and his value to the Twins.

"They conceded right off the bat that Kirby was the best," Shapiro said. "What was amusing was that in their statistical analysis, Cal actually was better than Kirby. But the Twins still said Kirby was the best while the Orioles, from the start, were trying to tell me that Cal wasn't as good as I was saying he was. It was an interesting contrast."

Shapiro thought he had the Puckett deal wrapped up in May when MacPhail put a $27.5-million, five-year deal on the table. Puckett, knowing that the Twins were a small-market team, was willing to accept that figure. Shapiro had one concern: that the union would be upset with his willingness to take less than what the market appeared ready to bear. He and Puckett called Don Fehr to explain what was going on.

"Kirby, are you happy with this deal?" Fehr asked. "Do you think it's the best thing for you and your family?"

"I really do," Puckett answered.

"Then how can I ask you not to do it?" Fehr said.

But Puckett didn't sign. Twins owner Carl Pohlad pulled the deal off the table at the last second. Pohlad was the head of baseball's small-market committee and apparently didn't want to deal with the wrath of other small-market owners over a deal this big—even if it made perfect sense to his team. When Pohlad pulled out, Puckett said that was the end of all negotiations until the season was over. He would test the free-agent market.

Ripken thought about cutting off negotiations at the end of spring training. But he knew he didn't want to talk to other teams; he was hoping to get the deal done and behind him. He told Shapiro to keep talking to Lucchino. The two sides remained about $6 million apart.

While this was going on, the Baltimore *Sun* was blasting Jacobs and Lucchino for not having signed Ripken already. Columnist Mike Littwin called Jacobs "cheap" and derided the Orioles for leaving Ripken blowing in the wind. Jacobs, who hates seeing his name in print, and Lucchino, who reads everything written about him and about the team and takes it all *very* seriously, decided the *Sun* had to be punished.

So they leaked the $30-million offer to Mark Maske of *The Washington Post*. On May 25, Maske reported that the Orioles had put the offer on the table in March. The leak had two purposes: to prove to people in Baltimore that the Orioles were serious about signing Ripken and to embarrass the *Sun* by having the first major story on the negotiations break in the *Post*.

Shapiro was furious about the leak. He and Lucchino had agreed at the outset that neither would engage in such tactics. Lucchino was not the leak in this case—Jacobs was. But the agreement had been broken. "It was a potential deal-breaker," Shapiro said. "For a few days, I was actually tempted to counterleak. But I calmed down before I did anything I would regret."

Seven weeks later, Lucchino wrote another letter directly to Ripken. This one was dated July 11 and was delivered to him at his locker by traveling secretary Phil Itzoe. Shapiro found out about the letter before it was delivered and tried to get Lucchino to stop Itzoe. Too late.

"Cal was struggling a little bit and I was worried that he might get his hopes up too high if he read the letter," Shapiro said. "He was already on the roller coaster and this was going to push the volume up."

Mixed metaphor or not, it did exactly that. In the letter, Lucchino, after again laying out the deal, wrote, "The Orioles want to sign you now and get this matter behind us without further distraction and delay." At the end of the letter, Lucchino concluded by saying, "We look forward to reaching agreement now."

To Ripken, *now* meant today. Or at the latest tomorrow. He was excited and convinced the bargaining was about to end when he flew to San Diego two days later for the All-Star Game. "To me, the letter said, 'Enough with the bargaining, let's make a deal,'" Ripken said. "I talked to Ron afterwards and we put together a package that I thought was going to be it. I was convinced we were just a couple of days away from making an announcement."

But they weren't. Ten days after the letter, Shapiro wrote Lucchino laying out what it would take to sign his client. The money was now in the $33 million range with an escape clause after three years in case the market went crazy.

Lucchino said no.

When Ripken heard that the Orioles rejected the deal, he went into a funk. He was already struggling at the plate; things immediately got worse. He started avoiding his teammates in the clubhouse. "Even they were asking me what was going on by then," he said. "I just didn't want to deal with it anymore.

"I don't like to make excuses for the fact that I wasn't hitting. But I was distracted. It's easy to say why worry about whether you're going to make five million or six million. Either way, I'm set for life. That's true, but that wasn't what it was about at that point. I just felt like the Orioles were somehow playing mind games with me. Whether that was right or wrong it was bothering me."

Ripken began trying too hard at the plate. His mechanics were all messed up. He was pressing, trying to hit a home run every time he got a 2-0 or 3-1 pitch. He hadn't hit one since June 23. He was even getting booed at Camden Yards.

By the middle of August, Shapiro was convinced that if he didn't get a deal made with the Orioles, Ripken might never hit another home run. Or, at the very least, the shortstop would be distracted throughout the pennant race, which wouldn't be good for anybody. One more conversation produced one more offer: Ripken would accept $30.5 million for five years, plus a four-year $500,000-a-year contract with the team whenever he stopped playing—at his option. Total package: $32.5 million.

There were details that had to be finalized, but Lucchino accepted. On the night of August 24—Ripken's thirty-second birthday—the contract was signed. Moments before the Orioles started their game with the California Angels, Orioles PA announcer Rex Barney announced that the deal was done. Ripken walked to home plate with Lucchino and general manager Roland Hemond. They shook hands and everyone smiled.

"I hated that part," Ripken said. "I just didn't think it was the right thing to do. But everyone else said it was, so I did it."

He then went 0 for 4 and made an error that night. He was booed again. Such are the vagaries of life in the big leagues as a $6-million man. "Hindsight is twenty-twenty," Ripken said later in the season. "But if I had it to do over again, I wouldn't have negotiated during the season. Kirby did the right thing cutting it off. I was too up-and-down thinking about the whole thing. I analyzed every little thing that happened. I need to be completely focused to play well and for a couple of months there, I wasn't."

As it turned out, it was more than three months later before Puckett signed. His contract was very similar to Ripken's—$30 million for five years—but it came only after an all-night session between Shapiro, Puckett, and his wife, Tonya. During that session, Puckett decided to make one last counteroffer to the Twins, rather than call the Red Sox, who were willing to pay substantially more. Shapiro called Andy MacPhail at four o'clock in the morning and told him what Puckett would sign for. Six hours later, MacPhail called back and said it was a deal.

Two more icons had stayed home. But it hadn't been easy for either one.

33

CALIFORNIA DREAMING . . . OR SCREAMING

They talk often about the weather in San Diego because it is almost always a pleasant subject. On an average day, the temperature is usually around 75 degrees with a mild breeze. On a below-average day, the temperature may dip all the way to 65. Every once in a while, it will rain. But not very often and not for very long.

The 13th of September was an average San Diego day. The temperature would reach 79, the breeze was comfortable, and there was a baseball game at one o'clock involving two good teams: the Cincinnati Reds and the San Diego Padres. The Reds entered the game second in the National League West with a 77-65 record; the Padres were right behind them at 75-66. San Diego's Gary Sheffield still had a chance to become baseball's first Triple Crown winner since 1967. The Padres' ticket prices are the third lowest in baseball.

The paid attendance at San Diego–Jack Murphy Stadium was 12,895. The night before on a similarly beautiful evening, it was 15,879.

"I don't have any answers," said Joe McIlvaine, the Padres' general manager, sitting in his office on that Sunday morning. "Granted, we're not in the pennant race anymore but when we were we weren't putting forty thousand a night in here either. We aren't even going to draw two million people [1,722,102 to be exact] and I think it's fair to say we've put a pretty exciting team on the field this year."

The Padres had certainly done that. McIlvaine's spring training trade that brought Sheffield from the Milwaukee Brewers had turned out to be the game's trade of the year. Sheffield had been dropped into the lineup in the third spot between four-time batting champion Tony Gwynn and cleanup hitter Fred McGriff and had thrived from day one.

"The day we made the trade for him, he arrived after our game [against the Indians] had started and I asked him to come sit with me outside the dugout," manager Greg Riddoch said. "I told him about the club, what we wanted, what we hoped for from him, and why we were happy to have him. The whole time I was talking to him, he looked me right in the eye. Never blinked. It gave me a good feeling from the start."

Riddoch deserved some of the credit for Sheffield's success. So did Gwynn and so did McGriff. It was Gwynn who came up with the idea of batting Sheffield third. When the Padres first started hearing rumors that Sheffield might be acquired, the assumption among the players—correctly—was that the plan was for him to bat fifth.

"I was sitting around with Fred one day and I said, 'What if he batted in between us—a righty between two lefties?' " Gwynn said. "It would guarantee he would see a lot of good pitches. That might help him get a good start and build his confidence."

Gwynn took his idea to Riddoch, whose initial response was something along the lines of "Why don't you let me manage the team and you win the batting titles." But the next day he walked into the clubhouse and told Gwynn, "I think you're right about Sheffield." A couple of days later, the trade was consummated and Sheffield became the number-three hitter, courtesy of Gwynn.

He also became McGriff's shadow. Although Fred McGriff, at twenty-eight, was five years older than Sheffield, the two men knew each other well. Both are from Tampa. They had worked out together during the offseason. McGriff is a class act; he works hard every day, always shows up ready to play, and runs out every ground ball and pop-up. He had long talks with Sheffield: about taking care of the little things, about making sure he was ready to play every single day.

Eventually, Sheffield developed a pregame routine that included several minutes alone in the weight room before batting practice. There, he would talk to himself about the opponent's pitcher that night, what he needed to do to hit him and how he could be better that day than he had been the day before. If it sounded corny, that didn't bother Sheffield. The results certainly weren't anything to laugh at.

With shortstop Tony Fernández leading off, followed by Gwynn, Sheffield, and McGriff (who would finish with a league-leading thirty-five home runs, his fifth straight season with at least thirty homers), the Padres had the most dangerous top of the order in baseball. They even acquired a cute nickname: The Four Tops.

Unfortunately, there wasn't quite enough bottom to go with them. Even so, the Padres stayed within striking distance of the Braves right through August. On August 31, they were only seven games out. There was at least some reason to think the Padres had a chance to win the division. It was a long shot, but a shot nonetheless.

And yet, instead of trading to add to his team in those final hours, McIlvaine traded to detract from it, sending pitcher Craig Lefferts to the Orioles. The reason for the deal was simple: money. Lefferts was making $1.8 million in 1992 and would be eligible for arbitration in 1993. McIlvaine had been under pressure from ownership to slice his payroll all season. Now, with the team still on the fringes of contention, he was forced to make a move.

It did not make him happy. "I can't begin to tell you how frustrating the whole season has been," he said two weeks after making the Lefferts deal. "I might as well be a graduate of Wharton Business School right now as anything else. We never ever talk anymore about how to improve the team. All we talk about is what has to be done to get the team to break even. It's very unsettling. I didn't get into this business to be a financial guy, I got into it to try to build winning teams.

"I made the Lefferts trade to take some heat off and because I didn't think it would hurt us that much on the field. I knew it would hurt in the clubhouse, though. There was bound to be some backlash. You work hard all season to get into contention and then management comes in and says, 'You aren't *really* in contention.' It's bound to be upsetting. One thing I've learned in this business is you can't fool players. They know what's going on.

"I don't think we're that far from being a serious contender with the team we have now. But I'm not being told to go out this winter and get the players we need to take the next step. I'm being told to go out and gut the team and go back to square one."

The Padres' payroll in 1992 was approximately $28 million. If the same players came back in 1993, that figure would rise, McIlvaine guessed, to nearly $34 million. Principal owner Tom Werner told him the payroll had to be about ten times the paid attendance for the season. By that measure, McIlvaine would have to slash his total salaries to less than $18 million. That meant some very good players would have to go.

The first thing McIlvaine wanted to do was change managers. He and Riddoch had never gotten along, but McIlvaine hadn't wanted to dump him without giving him a fair chance. He felt that two years was enough, however, and after the season was planning to promote his Triple-A manager, Jim Riggleman, to replace Riddoch.

But he wasn't even certain he could make *that* move. Riddoch is articulate and bright and was well liked by the ownership group. McIlvaine felt the veteran players on the team didn't respect Riddoch as a baseball man, thus a change had to be made. But he had yet to convince the owners that he was right about that.

Even if he did get his managing change, there was no telling what kind of team Riggleman would be managing, not if the owners stuck to their plan to overhaul the team and move out as many high salaries as possible. The player payroll wasn't the only place where cutbacks were planned. McIlvaine had been told he was going to have to fire a large chunk of his front office staff too.

After dealing Lefferts, he talked to Werner to try again to get him and his partners to reconsider their position. "I said to Tom that he needed to look at it from my point of view," McIlvaine said. "To him, the baseball team is just one of a number of businesses. If he decides to sell the team, that's no big deal, he's got other things to do. But this is my life, all of it. I like to think of myself as an architect, someone who builds things. We've all gone through blood, sweat, and tears to get this thing to the point where we aren't that far away. Now we're being asked to tear the whole thing down. Frankly, I just don't know if I can do it."

What kept McIlvaine from jumping ship too quickly was the knowledge that while the situation in San Diego might seem extreme, things weren't much better throughout the rest of the game. He knew he had been spoiled by his experience in New York, where the Mets had, generally speaking, been an open-checkbook club. But he had never thought things would turn sour so quickly in San Diego. "If I had known, I doubt I would have come," he said.

McIlvaine's notion that the players know when a ship has been abandoned by management was accurate. The Padres were 69-60 when they dealt Lefferts. They would limp home the rest of the way with a 13-20 record. With a week to go in the season, McIlvaine did win one battle—he was allowed to fire Riddoch. It wasn't a pretty scene. The Padres were getting ready to go on the road for the last week of the season and Riddoch had gone to McIlvaine to ask him for a definitive answer on his status. If he was being fired, he said, he would rather just leave from San Diego that week and drive home to Colorado with his family.

McIlvaine told Riddoch he was fired. On the final Monday of the season, he introduced Riggleman as the new manager. The Padres then lost five of their first six for him. Only a victory on the last day of the season enabled them to finish above .500 (82-80) and hold off the fast-closing Houston Astros for third place.

The real bright spot at the end of what had once been a season with great hope was Sheffield, who, despite missing the last five games, hit .330 with 33 home runs and 100 RBIs. McGriff had 104 RBIs to go with his 35 homers, and Gwynn, who missed most of the last month with a groin injury, hit .317.

The gutting that McIlvaine was hoping to avoid began soon after the World Series. Tony Fernández was traded to the Mets for two journeyman—and low-salaried—pitchers. Benito Santiago, the starting catcher, would not be offered arbitration, even though he'd made it clear he had no intention of returning. If the Padres offered Santiago arbitration and he signed elsewhere, they would be entitled to two draft picks. But if he accepted their arbitration offer, the team could be obligated to pay him an arbitration-decided salary in 1993. The owners did not want to take that risk. Santiago signed with the Florida Marlins.

"Almost every winter you hear that everyone in baseball is going to cut way back on their salary structure," McIlvaine said. "This is not something new. In the end, most teams decide they're going to pay the money to keep their teams together. I don't want to get stuck being the one guy out there gutting his team because of finances."

The shame of it all is the great potential the Padres have as a franchise. Although their stadium—the only one in sports named for a sportswriter, the late San Diego columnist Jack Murphy—is a football/baseball facility, it is not a donut with no character. At sunset, with the San Diego hills in the background, it can be a spectacular baseball setting. And, as McIlvaine notes, the '92 Padres were a team that was fun to watch and not far from being very good.

"We had more All-Stars this year than any team in baseball," he said. "Next year when we get to the All-Star break, who knows where any of them will be playing."

He sighed. "This just hasn't turned out the way I pictured it."

•

Six hundred miles to the north, the San Diego situation looked like Shangri-la compared to what was unfolding in San Francisco. On the other side of the Bay Bridge, the Athletics were on their way to a fourth division title in five years. Although attendance was down slightly, it would still fall just shy of 2.5 million.

In San Francisco, they would draw almost one million less. Bob Lurie, the owner of the Giants, had correctly declared Candlestick Park unplayable. When he couldn't get a new ballpark built, he followed through on his threat to sell to *anyone*—and sold the team to an ownership group in St. Petersburg, Florida. Slowly, the city was realizing that the Giants' September 27 home finale might truly be *the* finale. Mayor Frank Jordan was appealing to local businessmen to ride to the city's rescue.

Candlestick Park is every bit as bad a place to play baseball as has been reported over the years. It sits on a hill overlooking San Francisco Bay and, in the morning and early afternoon, appears to be a tranquil, lovely place.

It was on one of those tranquil early afternoons that Horace Stoneham, then the Giants' owner, viewed the site after he had moved his team west from New York. It was scenic and not too far from downtown. It was perfect.

Wrong. By mid-afternoon, the winds whip up from the bay, and even though the stadium was turned from a horseshoe into a circle years ago to accommodate football, those winds come swirling into the stadium. At night, it is worse. Much worse. Often, fog joins the wind. Since San Francisco's warmest weather is in October, fans and players frequently have to bundle up in winter clothes for games in July and August.

Lurie, who bought the Giants in 1975 to keep them from leaving San Francisco, tried for years to get the city—or any Bay Area city—to build a new ballpark. The June 2 "no" vote in San Jose was his fourth and, he said, final defeat. He threw his hands up and went in search of a buyer. Less than ten weeks later, he had a $115-million offer in hand from the St. Petersburg group.

That city had built a $135-million white elephant of a dome downtown—basically on spec as an inducement for a team on the move to head their way—but had lost out in bids to move the Twins, the White Sox, and the Mariners. It had also lost in the expansion derby to Miami. Now, at last, it appeared to have found itself a ball club. In San Francisco, there was some distress over the impending departure of the team, but the city was hardly beside itself with grief. Across the bridge, the Athletics quietly began preparing to be the Bay Area's only team, a position they were certain, as one of baseball's brightest organizations, to take full advantage of.

The two men who had resurrected the Giants in the mid-eighties, general manager Al Rosen and manager Roger Craig, assumed (correctly) that new ownership, whether it be from San Francisco or Florida, would want to clean house and bring in their own people. That and a team that would finish the season with a 72-90 record had turned things rather melancholy around Candlestick.

"I really don't want to manage in Florida, wouldn't want to do it even if they asked me to," Craig said one morning. "Funny thing is,

I've thought all along that I was ready to retire any day. I already did it once after we won in Detroit in 'eighty-four [Craig had been the Tigers' pitching coach and had gone home to his ranch outside San Diego before Rosen lured him back to manage the Giants at the end of '85], but now, when I think about it, I know I'll miss the game a lot.

"Last night, we win the game in the bottom of the ninth. We're not even in the pennant race. But I was so excited driving home I almost went off the road. I just had that feeling you can only get after you win a game like that."

The Giants were not without talented players. Will Clark, their first baseman, was one of the best pure hitters in the game. Matt Williams, the third baseman, was in the midst of an off year, but was still one of baseball's better power hitters. Cory Snyder, given up on by three teams, had come to the Giants, and after working with Dusty Baker had put together a solid season. But teams rise or fall with pitching and the Giants just didn't have enough to stay competitive, especially after Bill Swift, who had started the season 6-0, went on the DL.

The season fell apart with shocking quickness. It grew steadily worse after the August 7 announcement that Lurie had sold the team. During the last eight weeks, the Giants were 21-32, a dazed team merely going through the motions.

"God, it's been a long season for everyone," said relief pitcher Dave Righetti, whose personal travails mirrored the struggles of the team. "The whole feeling has been nothing but frustration."

Righetti was thirty-three and had signed a four-year $12-million contract with the Giants before the 1991 season. After ten years with the Yankees, during which he established himself as one of the best relief pitchers in the game, he struggled in '91, but still finished with twenty-four saves. In '92, he pitched poorly from the start and lost his job as the closer. He tried starting for a while, found that didn't work either, and eventually was reduced to the role of mop-up man. It was a humiliating comedown for someone who six years earlier saved a then-record forty-six games.

Righetti was secure financially, but if anything, that made pitching poorly tougher to take. He felt he was letting people down. "It's an awful, helpless feeling," he said. "It's especially tough when you know you've pitched better and still feel like you can pitch better. You search and search for the answer and you keep coming up empty."

That summed up the Giants' season pretty accurately. The team was searching for answers—and not finding them. Lurie had searched for a stadium—and had failed. Baseball was searching for a way to keep the team in San Francisco—and would find one, but still without a new ballpark.

The Giants would play at Candlestick again in 1993. They would have new owners, a new general manager (Bob Quinn over from the Reds), and a new manager, Dusty Baker. They would also have the most expensive player ever to play baseball, Barry Bonds (they were "rescued" for San Francisco when Lurie's cronies—the owners—forced him to accept a $100-million offer—$15 million less than St. Petersburg had offered—from a Bay Area ownership group). The Giants had a new beginning.

But, sadly, they would still have the same old problems.

34

THREE
THOUSAND HITS—
AND ONE RACE

If you picked up a newspaper on the morning of August 1 and studied the major league standings closely, you would almost surely reach the conclusion that baseball was heading for a spectacular September.

The Reds led the National League West by a half-game over the Braves. The San Diego Padres were only four and a half back. In the East, the Pirates had a one-game lead on the Expos with the Cubs (four and a half) and Mets (five) lurking. Even the Cardinals (six and a half) still had a shot if they got hot.

The American League West was clearly going to be an excellent two-team race. The Twins were clinging to a half-game lead over the Athletics. Only in the East did it appear possible that the race might not go down to the final week. There, the Jays had pulled out to a four-and-a-half-game lead on the Orioles with the Brewers barely hanging in, six-and-a-half games back.

So what happened? During the next six weeks the Reds and Padres fell apart, leaving the Braves in command of their division; the Pirates put together a 27-11 burst that left the Expos gamely pursuing them but still four games back; and the Twins self-destructed, going 19-24. Shortly after surviving their Curse of Canseco scare, the A's went on an eight-game binge that culminated with a three-game sweep of the Twins in Oakland. That put them nine games up with sixteen to play and the only question was when they would clinch.

At that stage, the Blue Jays still looked like comfortable winners in the East. The Orioles had made a big run in early September, closing to within a half-game on the morning of September 6. They won seven straight games on a West Coast swing and appeared poised to overtake Toronto. Instead, they dropped their final game in California—in Craig Lefferts's first start for them—and then were rocked when the Yankees came to Camden Yards and swept three.

By the time the Brewers followed the Yankees into Baltimore for the weekend, it looked like the two teams were playing for second place.

For most of August and early September, virtually all of the attention in Milwaukee had centered not on the pennant race—since there didn't really appear to be one—but on Robin Yount's pursuit of his three-thousandth hit. Yount had been facing questions about the milestone—only sixteen players in history had been there before—all season and had not been too thrilled about the attention.

Yount is one of those athletes who would be happy to play the games in an empty stadium, collect his hits, make his fielding plays, and go out with the boys for a couple of beers. No cameras, no reporters, no fans. That would be just fine with Yount.

But in Milwaukee, his pursuit of the magic three thousand was a huge story. Even though the city is only a little more than an hour's drive from Chicago, it seems to get skipped over in the national psyche. It is a city made famous by beer rather than ballplayers.

Because of his taciturn nature, Yount had largely remained Milwaukee's secret over the years, in spite of all his numbers and his two MVP Awards. He was the complete opposite of George Brett, who also played in a relatively small midwestern city, but was a national figure. In part that was because Brett had hit .390 one year, the last player to make a serious run at .400; in part it was because, during the 1980 World Series, he'd had history's most famous case of hemorrhoids. Mostly Brett was famous because he was as outgoing and easy to talk to as Yount was introverted and quiet.

Brett, at thirty-nine, two years older than Yount, was also pursuing 3,000 hits. Both men had found the season difficult. Neither was the player he'd once been and the hits had come more slowly than they had hoped, stretching out the melodrama of the chase. In Brett's case it was particularly agonizing; getting to the 3,000 mark wasn't a certainty for him. For him, the question was *if;* for Yount, who only needed 121 hits starting the season (Brett needed 164), the question was *when.*

During the spring, it looked as if Brett might not even stick around long enough to get to 3,000. He and the Royals got off to horrific starts, the team going 1-16 to begin the season while Brett's batting average slipped to as low as .130. He was so discouraged that he actually considered retiring on the spot.

"I didn't handle things very well in April," he said. "I wasn't a leader in any sense of the word when the team needed one and I was so down on myself I really was ready to quit. Instead of trying to pick the other guys up, I let myself get dragged down by what was going on. I can remember seeing [general manager] Herk [Robinson] one day and saying to him, 'Herk, old buddy, I may be about ready to save you a lot of money.'"

Brett was being paid $3.1 million to play for the Royals in 1992. He also has a personal services contract to work for the team when he retires, but that's for considerably less money. When Brett told manager Hal McRae he was thinking of quitting, McRae, his old friend and teammate, told him to be patient with himself.

"You've been in slumps before and you've always come out of them," McRae counseled. "Give yourself until the All-Star break."

Brett wasn't sure if he was in a slump or if he was simply old, but he decided to hang in for a while. He also knew, deep down, that he was having trouble keeping his mind on baseball, and that almost certainly was affecting hitting.

On the night of May 1, he'd gotten a call in Boston from his father. Jack Brett didn't call his youngest son often; George sensed something was wrong as soon as he heard his father's voice. He was right. Jack Brett had cancer.

"They told him two to six months," Brett says. "The funny thing was, he'd spent about ten days with me in spring training and, I guess this is the way it always is, he seemed fine. He always coughed a lot because he was a smoker, so you didn't pay any attention to it. But when he got home from that trip, he was doing some expenses and all of a sudden he realized he was having trouble adding and subtracting. Well, he had been an accountant until he retired, so he wondered what that was about. Then he began sleeping for long periods of time. Finally, he went to the doctor. They ran tests and told him."

It was brain cancer and Brett had the sense that two months might be optimistic, especially after he talked to the Royals' team doctor. McRae told him to go home and take as much time as he needed there. After consulting with his three older brothers, Brett called his father and told him he was coming out to California to see him.

"What the hell for?" Jack Brett said.

"To see you, spend time with you," George Brett answered.

"I just spent ten fucking days with you in March," Jack Brett said. "You can't make me better. You have a job to do. Keep playing."

Brett followed orders. He knew how important his success was to his father. Jack Brett had always been the Brett brothers' biggest supporter. Three of them—John, Ken, and George—had played baseball professionally. Ken, who was now a broadcaster for the Angels, had been on the Red Sox 1967 World Series team at the age of eighteen and had spent twelve years in the majors.

"Kemmer was the one with the most talent," Brett says. "He could do everything. There are still some people I know in baseball who say he would have had a better career if he'd been an outfielder instead of a pitcher. I always had to be pushed to do things. My father was always the one doing that. He never ever told me I was doing well. The year I hit .390 I'd give him a call and he'd say, 'What are you hitting right now?' And I'd say, '.402.' And he'd say, 'Yeah, well I saw you on TV the other night when you had two hits and if you'd been concentrating it would have been four.' That was just his way. He thought it helped me and I think it did. If I went four-for-four he was happy all day no matter what. If I was oh-for-four, he was pissed off."

When his father told him not to come home, George asked him to keep in touch and let him know if his health grew any worse. "But that was tough too," he says. "I mean, how do you say to your father, 'Look, when you feel like you're about to die, give me a call.' So, I just called him every day. Before, if I called once a week, that was a lot. Now, it was just about every day."

On the afternoon of May 23, Brett was with the Royals in Texas, spending the afternoon at a PGA golf tournament outside Dallas. He was following John Cook, a neighbor in California, when a stranger walked up to him and said, "Are you Mr. Brett?"

"I figured the guy was going to ask for an autograph," Brett says. "Instead, he said, 'You need to call your wife at home right away.' I really hadn't thought it was going to be so quick. As I'm heading into the clubhouse I'm wondering if something is wrong with Leslie or if maybe our house got robbed. By the time I got there I was convinced these two new kittens we'd just bought had gotten outside and run away. That's what I was thinking as I dialed the phone, that we'd lost our kitties."

The cats were fine. Jack Brett wasn't. He had been in New York earlier in the week, having requested a last tour of the old neighborhood where he grew up in Brooklyn. Ken, traveling with the Angels (on the same trip that later included the bus crash), had made arrangements through Arthur Richman, the Yankees vice-president for public relations, to have George Steinbrenner's driver take them on their tour.

Two days after he returned home, Jack Brett went to the hospital. "It was as if he went back to see Brooklyn once more and then said, 'Okay, I'm done,' " George says.

Brett flew from Dallas to Los Angeles that Saturday afternoon and went straight to the hospital. His father had been sleeping and was extremely doped up, but he opened his eyes when he heard his son's voice.

"He looked at me and the first thing the son of a bitch said was 'Did you guys win last night?' I swear to God, that's what he said. I said, 'No, we lost.'

"He looked at me and said, 'How did you do?'

"I said, 'Dad, I was oh-for-four.' He said, 'Shit,' and closed his eyes."

Several hours later, Jack Brett died. Every day, for the rest of the season, George Brett thought about his father as he chased the three thousandth hit he knew would have meant so much. But on the days when he didn't hit, when he was shut out, he was comforted by one thought: "I didn't ruin my dad's day by going oh-for-four."

As the weather turned hot, so did Brett. His average picked up steadily; when September arrived, he was closing in on his goal. "I'm not the player I was ten years ago," he said. "Or even two years ago for that matter. But I should still be able to hit. I know I can't do it like I used to, but after twenty years in the game I should have learned something."

Yount felt the same way. He hadn't hit the lows on or off the field that Brett had, but the hits came at an almost agonizingly slow pace. His average hovered around .250 for most of the season. But by the first week in September, the goal was clearly in sight. With the Indians in town, County Stadium was sold out each night in anticipation of The Hit.

He got number 2,999 in his first at-bat on September 8, but with the crowd screaming on every pitch, he couldn't come up with another one that night. By now, every move Yount made was drawing a standing ovation. "If he walked to the end of the bench to get a drink of water, everyone stood up and cheered him," Phil Garner said.

On some teams, the Yount Watch might have been a distraction. The Brewers were a rising young team with a lot of healthy egos that might have resented all the attention the old man was receiving—but none of them seemed to mind.

"Robin has been the franchise around here for so long and he's so low-key about it that no one is going to be bothered by him getting all this attention—except maybe him," said Paul Molitor, who had been with the Brewers since 1978 and was on his way to a .320 season. "The funny thing is, Robin has never been a numbers guy. What makes him great is the attitude he brings to the park every night, not any number.''

If anyone on the Brewers was qualified to know about dealing with a media crush, it was Molitor. As a rookie, he had been handed the starting shortstop's job when Yount retired briefly from the game to consider a fling on the pro golf tour. By his own admission, he wasn't ready for the notoriety that came with sudden stardom (he was Rookie of the Year), and ended up involved with drugs and dealing with the public embarrassment of having his name linked with local drug dealers in the Milwaukee newspapers.

"I was immature,'' Molitor said. "I was thrown into Robin's spot in a year when I expected to be in the minors. It was all too much for me. I liked the life-style, the parties, and all the people—unfortunately I had to learn about growing up and getting away from that sort of thing the hard way.''

He did that, and although injuries have dogged him his entire career, he has produced more than two thousand hits himself, including a memorable thirty-nine-game hitting streak in 1987. During that streak, he was exposed to the kind of media crush Yount was now dealing with. For Molitor, it was easy. For Yount, a major burden.

The burden was finally lifted on the night of September 9, when Yount singled to right-center in his first trip to the plate. County Stadium was so jam-packed that the start of the game was delayed for twenty minutes to let the crowd get into the ballpark.

For at least one night, the drama of the moment and what it meant to the people he had played in front of for so many years seemed to affect Yount. He was clearly moved by the fans' reaction to The Hit, and even expressed surprise afterward that he felt the way he did.

"I never thought it would be such a big thing,'' he confessed. "But when I realized it meant so much to so many people, it really did hit me. It was kind of fun to share it with the other guys and with everyone here. I'm glad I got it tonight since I wanted to get it at home and I didn't want to wait until the end of this road trip [thirteen games] to get it either. It worked out just right.''

Baseball being baseball, the Brewers lost that night. The last out of the game was made by—you guessed it—Robin Yount.

Even the ending couldn't detract from the magic of the evening. Garner had told Yount that he was enjoying every second of the countdown, "because this is as close to three thousand hits as I'm ever going to get in my life.'' The whole team seemed to be on a high, basking in the extra attention that Yount brought to Milwaukee. Garner even joked that his wife found him more attractive on the night Yount got The Hit.

Why was that? he was asked.

"I turned out the lights and told her I was Robin," he said.

Not surprisingly, Yount began to hit better than he had all season once he had three thousand out of the way. The Brewers had picked up momentum and adrenaline during the last days of the countdown and it seemed to carry over.

After his brief emotional outburst on the night of The Hit, Yount was his old self two days later when the Brewers arrived in Baltimore to begin their series with the Orioles. When someone asked if he'd enjoyed everything that had surrounded the chase for three thousand, he laughed.

"I enjoyed getting the hit and the way people reacted to it," he said. "This, though"—he waved his arm at the notebooks and cameras surrounding his locker—"I could certainly do without."

The Orioles would gladly have done without the Brewers that weekend and the following one in Milwaukee. The Brewers took five of seven in all, and, as it turned out, passed the Orioles for good. Garner was a long way from satisfied, however.

"The Blue Jays have to play three with the Orioles now," he said, waving his ever-present cigar. "Let's just see what happens there because I guarantee you we aren't going to go away."

The Orioles hadn't given up yet either. Their plan was simple: Sweep the Jays, cut the margin to two, and make Toronto start wondering if it could hold on. The Brewers were now a factor too, but the Orioles couldn't afford to worry about that. Johnny Oates adjusted his rotation so Rick Sutcliffe could open the Toronto series. Oates had been through enough pennant races to understand that winning two of three this late would be virtually meaningless. "To have a chance we have to sweep," he said. "We all understand that."

The weather on the night of the opener was atrocious. It was hot, humid, and rainy. Once upon a time, the game would have been called off by nine o'clock and the teams would have come back the next night to play a twi-night doubleheader. But there were forty-five thousand people in the ballpark, and with the remaining six home games also sellouts (the Orioles would finish the season with fifty-nine straight sellouts), greed dictated that there was no way the crowd was being sent home until and unless someone spotted Noah rounding up animals two-by-two.

The first pitch was finally thrown at 10:17—two hours and forty-two minutes late. Amazingly, most of the crowd had stayed. They knew what was at stake. If the Blue Jays were intimidated by the circumstances or by Sutcliffe's presence on the mound, they didn't show it. Devon White hit the fourth pitch of the night over the right-field fence for a 1–0 lead. By the fourth inning the lead was 4–1 and Sutcliffe was gone.

The Orioles bullpen dug in and held the Blue Jays right there, though, and Baltimore crept back. Toronto's starter, Todd Stottlemyre, had pitched much better since Pat Gillick's session with him in August. Ironically, though, he credited his improvement to an incident in Boston that had been his low moment of the season.

Stottlemyre was ejected from a game there on August 5 after arguing a call at third base with umpire Jim Joyce. During the argument he bumped Joyce, leading to a five-game suspension. "About thirty seconds after the argument was over, I realized he was completely right and I was wrong. I just forgot a rule and went crazy and I was wrong. It was embarrassing."

Stottlemyre had a long talk after the incident with his father, Mel, who had been an outstanding pitcher for the Yankees in the sixties and seventies and was now the Mets' pitching coach. At the same time, Tom Henke, the Blue Jays' wise old head, took him under his wing. "My dad and Tom both talked to me a lot about growing up," he said. "It's one thing to be immature and hot-tempered when you're young but I'm twenty-seven now. The time had come. I was really hurting myself. Since then, I've really tried to take things more in stride."

On this night, he took the Blue Jays into the eighth inning with a 4–3 lead, then gave the ball to Duane Ward and Henke. The Orioles had one last chance in the ninth; with one out, they got Tim Hulett, the tying run, to third base. Mark McLemore hit a fly ball to medium-range center field. It was now well after one o'clock in the morning but a lot of people had hung in until the bitter end. Virtually all of them had their eyes on Devon White, knowing the play at the plate would be close as Hulett tagged up.

There is no one in the game better at chasing down a fly ball than White. His arm, however, is considered average. He lined up the ball, took a step in, made the catch, and hurled the ball toward the plate. With the ball in the air, everyone now looked to see where Hulett was. Would he be able to beat the throw?

No. He couldn't beat the throw because he never left third base. As the throw came in, slightly up the line, Cal Ripken, Sr., was standing between the plate and third base with his arms in the air, giving Hulett the stop sign. He had made the split-second decision that all third-base coaches must make and had concluded that Hulett would be out at the plate.

There was certainly some logic in his thinking. Hulett was not a speed demon by any stretch of the imagination, and the Orioles' two best clutch hitters, Brady Anderson and Mike Devereaux, were coming up. Ripken didn't want the game to end with Hulett thrown out at the plate. On the other hand, it was going to take a near-perfect throw from White to get Hulett. Baseball odds say that Hulett had a better chance of scoring that way than on a hit off Henke, who had not blown a save since Mike Bordick's double in Oakland back in July.

"The only way Senior can win in that situation is if he sends the runner and he's safe," Oates said later. "If he sends him and he's out, he's wrong. If he holds him up, he's wrong."

With two men now out, Anderson walked to load the bases. But Devereaux popped out to end the game and Ripken was wrong forever—at least to almost everyone in the ballpark.

"I gave us a chance to win the game," he said, standing in front of his locker, tucked in the far corner of the Orioles clubhouse. "The man's going to be out if he goes and the game will be over. White's arm is no slouch. I guess you guys sitting nine hundred and fifty feet up in the air in the press box saw it differently."

Regardless of how anyone saw it, the loss sealed the Orioles' fate. Sadly, it also sealed Ripken's fate. He had been taking heat all year for some of his decisions at third base. Two weeks before the Toronto game, he sent his son to the plate on a play in which Junior had been thrown out by twenty feet. Sitting in the back of the press box, team president Larry Lucchino writhed in agony and screamed, "That was coaching malpractice!" Ripken would probably have been fired if the Hulett play hadn't happened. When it did, he might as well have started cleaning out his locker. The Orioles waited until the World Series was under way to make it official. Ripken was offered a job in the minor leagues. He turned it down, and, after thirty-six years, he was no longer an Oriole employee. (It was a bad offseason for the Ripken family. The Orioles also released Cal's brother Billy.)

On that rainy night in September, Senior was, as always, the first one out of the clubhouse. Most of the Orioles lingered in spite of the late hour. Oates was certainly in no rush to leave. He knew he wasn't going to sleep anyway.

"Ninety-nine point nine percent of the time when I leave the ballpark, I leave the game behind," he said. "But this one was a little different. There were so many chances to win the game and we didn't get it done. And I knew exactly what the loss meant. You work for something for seven months, then see it fly out the window, you don't just shake it off."

Oates was living in a downtown hotel for September. His wife and two younger children had gone home to Richmond so the kids could start school at the beginning of the month. Gloria Oates had driven up for the game that night and Oates was happy she was there, even though he had absolutely no desire to talk.

While Gloria watched television, Oates stared at the ceiling, trying to purge his memory of the game that had just ended. "Every once in a while she would look at me and say, 'Want to talk?' " he said later. "I just said, '*You* talk.' I couldn't think of anything to say. I was down, really down. It was one of the few nights I didn't have the feeling that I have a great job. It was just a yucky feeling. I felt physically sick. I'd forgotten to eat and I hadn't slept much the night before, since we got home from Milwaukee so late. And I just couldn't help but think that we'd given up the chance to win."

Gloria Oates finally drifted off to sleep. Shortly before 5 A.M., Oates heard a thud outside the door. He knew it was *USA Today.* He walked outside, picked it up, and glumly read it. Fortunately, the game had ended so late it hadn't made the paper. Oates didn't have to read the gory details.

He glanced at his sleeping wife and remembered a billboard he had seen two days earlier in Milwaukee after another discouraging loss. It said, "A word of encouragement at a time of failure is worth a novel of praise at a time of success." Oates had memorized the words. His wife had been there to give him the few words he needed. Finally, just before the sun came up, he slept.

•

The Orioles' chase ended with that loss to Toronto. The next evening was clear and crisp, the temperature twenty degrees cooler than the night before. Fall was in the air and a lot of the pregame questions now switched their focus to what the Orioles needed for '93. It was as if the summer had ended with Devereaux's pop-up at one-twenty that morning.

In Milwaukee, the weather was even colder, but there was no talk of next year. The Brewers were still nipping at Toronto's heels. They were in the process of sweeping three games from the Angels, raising their September record to 17-6. It was not as if the Blue Jays were collapsing. After they split the last two games in Baltimore, they were 15-8 for the month, and their lead was still three-and-a-half games. They only had eight more to play, none against contenders. The Brewers had three home games left against Oakland, then finished the season on the West Coast. The Toronto lead looked quite comfortable.

Garner still wasn't hearing any of that, however. After his team beat the A's 4-1 on another wet, cold Friday night, he sat behind his desk, feet up, and smiled.

"I got the whole thing figured out," Garner said. "We aren't gonna catch 'em until the last day of the season. We'll end up tied, then go up there and win the [one-game] play-off in Toronto. How's that for drama?"

The city of Milwaukee was only just now beginning to catch on to the fact that its team had played itself into a semidramatic situation.

The A's arrived in town needing one victory to clinch the West—but the Brewers wanted nothing to do with a clinching party unless it was their own.

"You try never to pay too much attention to what the other club is doing except in terms of preparation," Tony LaRussa said. "But right now, you can't help but notice that these guys are playing their asses off."

LaRussa and the A's desperately wanted to beat the Brewers on Saturday to clinch the title themselves. If they lost, they would have to wait around in a restaurant that night, watching TV to find out if the Twins lost in Kansas City. "We're a baseball team, not a fraternity," LaRussa said. "We should do our celebrating on the field, not in a bar."

There was no lack of effort from his team that afternoon. The day was dreary and rainy. For most of the morning, it looked as if the game wouldn't even be played. But the rain stopped thirty minutes before game time. Both starting pitchers, Bill Wegman for the Brewers and Ron Darling for the A's, were outstanding.

The atmosphere, from the first pitch, was that of a postseason game. In the top of the second, with two out and the bases loaded, Bordick hit a ground ball deep in the hole at shortstop. Pat Listach, a serious contender for Rookie of the Year, tracked the ball down and made an excellent throw to first. Bordick beat it by a half-step but umpire Greg Kosc, never an A's favorite, called him out.

The A's screamed—to no avail, of course. In the press box, Sandy Alderson marched in, watched a replay that showed Bordick clearly safe, and shook his head. "Greg Kosc blows another one out his ass," he muttered, and stalked out.

It was 1–1 in the sixth when Darling made his one mistake of the day—a hanging forkball that Greg Vaughn crushed deep into the left-field bleachers. A huge sign hangs out there, dubbing that section "Vaughn's Valley." Vaughn had struggled to hit .200 most of the season and hadn't been anywhere near his valley in a while. Now, he was closing with a rush.

His home run was enough. The Brewers escaped with a scorching 2–1 win. The Yankees had beaten the Blue Jays earlier, so the lead was down to two and a half.

"One-game play-off," Garner said, the cigar waggling as always. "Just remember I told you that."

One of the local writers wanted to know what it meant to the team to be playing so well, "even if you fall short."

"Fall short!" Garner roared. "Don't even *say* those words!"

The A's retreated to wait on the outcome of the Twins game. They were not too disappointed when the Twins won, leaving the magic number to clinch at one. LaRussa liked the idea of the team eating together, regardless of the outcome of the Minnesota game.

"When I was playing in Denver in 'seventy-five we started the season with thirteen straight road games," he said. "We lost the first two in Evansville and Jim Burruss, who was the general manager, decided to take the whole team out to dinner. I think we won ten of the next eleven. After that, he made a deal with us: Any time we had a winning road trip, he'd buy the whole team dinner.

"My first year managing, in 'seventy-eight, I was in Knoxville. I always thought, when I played, that teams that spent time together on the road were teams that played better on the road. So on our first two trips, I took the team out to eat. I was only making twelve thousand dollars that year, so I took them to Red Lobster once and to an all-you-can-eat Pizza Hut the next time. For me, that was still a lot to spend. The team played well. When the owner found out what I'd done, he reimbursed me, which was nice. But the point was, I thought it helped. Ever since then, I've tried to get the team out together a few times a year."

And it still worked: The A's went out together on Labor Day, just before they started the winning streak that put them in command of the West race.

Sunday was the home finale for the Brewers. Cars filled the stadium parking lots hours before game time. As they had done on the night of Yount's Hit, the Brewers delayed the start of the game for twenty minutes to give the people trying to jam into the ballpark a chance to get in. By the time everyone was there, the attendance was 54,985, the fourth-largest crowd in the team's history.

The game they saw had none of the crispness of the Saturday game. Oakland starter Bobby Witt faced ten batters and went to a three-ball count on seven of them. He was gone before the second inning was over. The game dragged on—it would end up lasting three hours and forty-nine minutes—with the Brewers, after briefly trailing 2–1 in the third, building a 5–2 lead in the eighth.

The A's put together one last rally in the eighth. With two outs, men on first and third, and the score 5–3, LaRussa sent Rickey Henderson up to pinch-hit.

Henderson had been out of the lineup with another of the minor injuries that always afflicted him at strange times. Every member of the A's media contingent was convinced that Rickey's latest injury was directly related to his being one hit shy of two thousand.

The A's would be home on Tuesday, thus Rickey could get number two thousand in front of the home crowd and—most important—his mother.

Henderson could have blown that theory out of the water with a hit. But he never really had a chance to do so. Jesse Orosco's first pitch came in high. Henderson watched it. Greg Kosc, working the plate, called strike one. Henderson's head swiveled back toward the umpire and several words were exchanged, none about the weather.

Orosco threw again. This pitch was closer, but looked outside. Not to Kosc. He called strike two. This time, Henderson threw his bat down and turned to go jaw-to-jaw with Kosc. Within seconds, Kosc's arm was in the air, signaling that Henderson had been ejected.

"Man says 'fuck you' to me, he's going to get ejected," said Kosc. "First he called me a fucking liar, then he said 'fuck you.' I'm not out there to be denigrated like that."

LaRussa charged out of the dugout as soon as he saw Henderson in Kosc's face. He arrived too late to save Rickey, but he took up the argument anyway. He and Kosc went at it for a couple of minutes—with the crowd screaming in delight—before Kosc finally said, "Get a hitter up here, Tony."

LaRussa nodded. "You want a hitter, I'll give you one," he said. He turned to Weiss, waiting patiently in the on-deck circle through all this, and said, "Give me your bat." Weiss complied and LaRussa, bat in hand, walked into the batter's box and gestured to Orosco to throw him a pitch. He was showing Kosc up, demanding ejection. Kosc granted his wish, then tossed Bob Welch, too. With most of the A's screaming at Kosc from the dugout, Welch had crossed the line with an obscene gesture.

When the dust finally cleared, it was Randy Ready who had to go up and finish Henderson's at-bat. Everyone in the press box was convinced that Kosc would call strike three even if Orosco *rolled* the ball to the plate. Instead, he called two balls before Ready went down swinging.

The A's went quietly in the ninth. As the Brewers congratulated each other on the victory—and the sweep of the A's—almost no one in the crowd made any move to leave. They were all standing at their seats, applauding their team's effort.

The Brewers disappeared into the dugout, but the crowd stayed, demanding a curtain call. Finally, they came back—all of them: Molitor, Listach, Vaughn, Darryl Hamilton, seventeen-game winner Jaime Navarro, rookie pitcher Cal Eldred, who had come up in July and won ten straight games. Even Yount and Garner. Most of them were no-names nationally, but to this crowd they were heroes. Big-time heroes.

The crowd cheered their Brewers, and as they stood facing the fans, tipping their caps, the Brewers cheered back.

The Jays crushed the Yankees 12–2 earlier that day, sending a clear message that they weren't going to cave in. Their lead was two-and-a-half games. Three nights later, in Seattle, the Brewers got a chance to close to within one game, but they failed. Then they just ran out of days. With forty-eight hours left in the season, the Jays finally clinched—the last of the four division winners to do so.

Garner's dream of catching them on the last day of the season had gone up in cigar smoke, one day short.

But although the Brewers had failed to win a pennant, what they did win was worth at least as much: their fans and their town. These days in baseball, that is no small feat.

RETURN
TO CLEVELAND

As it turned out, the Athletics did clinch in a bar. The night after they returned from Milwaukee, they gathered again at a local restaurant to wait and see how the Twins would do against the White Sox. The answer came early in the evening. Chicago built a quick lead and cruised to a 9–4 victory.

LaRussa hadn't gotten his celebration in the ballpark, but neither he nor any of the A's were likely to complain. It was their fourth Western Division title in five years, and, without doubt, the most gratifying.

"When we won in 'eighty-nine, we overcame a lot of major injuries the second half to do it," LaRussa said. "But nothing like this. Watching these guys celebrate, knowing what they went through to pull this off, is a memory I'll cherish a long time."

The day before, the Pirates had become the first team to clinch, holding off the Expos' charge. The Pirates pulled away, wrapping up their third straight division championship on a Sunday afternoon against—appropriately enough—the Mets.

The team that was supposed to run away with the National

League East was now holding on, trying not to finish last. The Pirates had embarrassed them on Saturday with a 19–2 victory, prompting LaRussa to plead with Leyland, via phone, to send some runs to Milwaukee. Leyland had to settle for four on Sunday, but that was plenty as the Pirates won 4–2.

Leyland got a ride to the clubhouse on the shoulders of his players. During those few seconds, he was as happy and satisfied as he had ever been as a manager. Then he started worrying about the play-offs.

His opposition there, for the second straight season, would be the Braves. Two days after the Pirates wrapped up their division, the Braves beat the Giants 5–0, behind Charlie Leibrandt's second straight shutout, to clinch their title. The Braves had struggled down the stretch, letting the Reds get to within four for a brief moment, before righting themselves when they had to.

Three of the '91 play-off teams—everyone but the world champion Twins—would be returning. The one new team, the A's, had certainly been in this neighborhood before.

While the division winners were lining up their pitching and making final decisions on their postseason rosters, everyone else was playing out the string. Some did so with more gusto than others.

The Dodgers wound up with the game's worst record, 63-99, finishing last for the first time since 1905. Their record was one game worse than that of the Mariners, who finished last for the first time since 1989. The Red Sox were the cellar dwellers in the American League East with a 73-89 record, while the Phillies, after making a final-week run at the Mets, finished 70-92—two games behind New York's staggering 72-90. The Mets, Dodgers, and Red Sox were so embarrassed by their seasons that they took out full-page ads in their local newspapers, apologizing to the fans for their play.

There was one other race going on during that ultimate weekend, one that wasn't receiving a lot of national attention. The Indians, the Yankees, and the Tigers were going right to the wire to decide who would finish fourth in the American League East. All three teams wanted to finish as high as possible, but the Tribe really and truly were looking at fourth as an important accomplishment.

And with good reason. This was a team that had won fifty-seven games in 1991. And the Indians had started '92 as if it might be a repeat, only with younger players.

In late April, Rick Bay, who'd become the team's president during the offseason, was in a hotel room, preparing to give a speech the next day. He turned on his TV, looking for his new team's game. The movie *Major League,* in which the Indians miraculously come from nowhere to win the pennant, was on. "It was the beginning of the movie, when the Indians are really bad," Bay said. "After a while, I was having trouble telling the difference between the game and the movie. They looked almost alike."

The next day, Bay predicted in his speech that the Indians would win seventy games. When he was finished, an elderly woman walked up to him and said, "I'll bet you ten dollars on those seventy wins." Bay took the bet—but not eagerly.

By the time they reached Oakland on Memorial Day, the Indians were 14-30, coming off two losses in Seattle that had manager Mike Hargrove ready to jump off the top of the Kingdome.

In both games, the Indians led late, made foolish plays and ended up losing. They weren't getting shut down by great pitching. And it wasn't as if they didn't have the talent to compete. They did.

"It had gotten to the point where we were using our inexperience as a copout," Hargrove said. "We would make a mistake and the attitude was, 'That's okay, we're still learning.' Well, that wasn't good enough anymore. If we kept thinking that way, we were going to get buried the way we were buried last year. I thought we were better than that."

Before the first game in Oakland, Hargrove called a team meeting. The visitors' clubhouse in the Coliseum is long and narrow; players are forced to crowd close together. Hargrove pulled a chair into the middle of the room, put his feet up on another chair, and started talking. He didn't raise his voice. He talked about the kind of attitude winning players brought with them to the ballpark. He talked about the notion that players had to be responsible for their actions. "We've used being young as a crutch," he said. "If we go on like this much longer, it's going to become an obstacle."

He talked for twenty minutes, then asked Brook Jacoby, a long-time Cleveland veteran who'd spent most of '91 with the A's, returning to the Indians in the spring, to say a few words. Jacoby spoke about the difference in approach he'd found in Oakland, the notion that you go into every game knowing there's some way to win. "Here, it's always been the opposite," he said. "We always think there's a way to lose."

After Jacoby was finished, some of the younger players talked about successes they'd had in the minor leagues. The consensus was that it was time to stop being the Cleveland Indians and start being the talented young team that was assembled in that room. "We always talked about getting other people to stop looking down at us," Hargrove said. "Well, the first thing we had to learn to do was stop looking down at ourselves."

The Indians swept the A's in that series. From that point on, they were a different team. Going into their final four-game series with the Orioles, they had a record of 61-53 since Hargrove's Oakland meeting.

People in baseball were noticing. With a payroll of a little more than $8 million, they were going to finish with more victories than the Mets, Red Sox, and Dodgers, each of whom had a payroll over $40 million.

"That's a good baseball team right now," Johnny Oates said in August after the Indians won two of three from his team. "They're going to be a handful for teams to play down the stretch."

General manager John Hart's signing of younger players to long-term contracts—before their arbitration seasons—was suddenly being looked to by other franchises as a model for the future. Charles Nagy had emerged as one of the best young pitchers in the game. Kenny Lofton, the superb young center fielder, would steal sixty-six bases and finish behind only Listach in the Rookie of the Year balloting. Albert Belle finished with thirty-four home runs and 112 RBIs. And Carlos Baerga would do something no second baseman had done since Rogers Hornsby: hit over .300 (.312), get 200 hits (205), hit twenty home runs, and drive in more than 100 runs (105). At twenty-three, he was one of baseball's rising superstars.

"All of a sudden I'm very popular with my colleagues," Hart joked. "Everyone's calling me wanting to know if I'm interested in dealing. It's a lot different than a year ago."

The feeling in the city was upbeat for the first time in forever. Although attendance didn't skyrocket, it did go up by more than 200,000 to 1,224,274. That included a crowd of 30,187 on closing day, a windy, blustery October afternoon in cavernous Cleveland Stadium. It was the largest crowd at a home finale since 1948. That was the last year the Indians won the World Series.

There was still a long way to go. The team would finish below .500, twenty games out of first place. But for the first time in years, there was hope in Cleveland. "You have to walk before you run and crawl before you walk," Hargrove said. "We're walking now, but we haven't even broken into a slow jog yet. There's still a lot to do."

Hargrove and Hart were hoping that team owner Richard Jacobs would be willing to spend some money on at least one free-agent pitcher in the offseason. They had a couple of pitchers in the minors who might—or might not—be ready in '93, and another experienced arm to go with Nagy and José Mesa, a mid-season pickup from the Orioles, would make them feel more comfortable. The rest of the starters were still question marks but the bullpen, led by Steve Olin and Derek Lilliquist, looked solid, as did the lineup.

"It doesn't feel as if it's that far away," said Bay. "The feeling around here the last couple of months has really been positive. Finishing fourth would really be a boost. Give us a starting point for next season." Bay felt so strongly about that, he asked Hargrove for permission to speak to the team for the first time since he'd been introduced to the players. He wanted to remind them how important it would be to finish fourth. For Bay, though, there would be no 1993: In an ominous austerity move, Jacoby fired him during the winter, saying he thought Hart should report directly to him.

If there was one man in the organization equipped to analyze the ups and downs, it was Bob DiBiaso, the public relations vice-president who had spent almost his entire life watching bad Indians teams.

"The test is going to come in 'ninety-four," he said. "Remember, when we signed our first big free agent, Wayne Garland, to a ten-year contract in 1978, he tore a rotator cuff and never pitched again. When we hosted the All-Star Game in 1981, the season was just about destroyed by a strike. Now, we have a state-of-the-art eighteen-million-dollar spring training facility just completed in Homestead, Florida, and Hurricane Andrew comes through and completely destroys it.

"That's what this franchise has been like. In 1994, we're scheduled to finally open a brand new ballpark. That should give us a huge boost. We should have a talented young team in place. If that turns out to be the year that baseball is wiped out by a lockout or a strike, then you know we're jinxed, truly jinxed."

The last weekend, sadly, brought back memories of the bad old days. In the opener, on Thursday night, the Tribe led 2–0 in the ninth. Eric Plunk was pitching to Mike Devereaux with two out and one runner on. "The first two pitches were fastballs that just blew Devereaux away," Hargrove said. "Then he goes and throws him a curve."

A hanging curve, which Devereaux hit about nine miles to tie the game at 2–2. The O's won the game in the tenth on a Glenn Davis homer, giving Mike Mussina, the incredibly intense twenty-three-year-old, his eighteenth victory of the season. With all the attention that had been heaped on Ben McDonald, it was Mussina who'd become a star in '92. He would end up fourth in the Cy Young voting— and no doubt would be angry with himself for finishing behind three other pitchers. He is that kind of competitor.

Hargrove didn't sleep that night. "Worst loss of the season," he said. "The game was over. But how they bounce back will be interesting to watch. I really believe these kids are winners. This is the kind of game that tests you."

The Indians passed one more test in that second game, beating the Orioles, 8–5. Baerga got his milestone two hundredth hit and a long standing ovation. It was the Indians' seventy-sixth victory of the season and left them tied for fourth with the Yankees.

The loss meant the Orioles would fall short of their final goal— ninety victories. Nevertheless, they bounced back the next day with an easy 7–1 win. The Yankees lost too, so they and the Indians went into the final day holding at seventy-six wins.

Both managers held team meetings after Saturday's game. Oates knew this would be the last night his players would be together for a while and their inclination would be to throw themselves a serious party. "Have a good time tonight," he told them. "But remember, we still have one public appearance to make. We've accomplished too much this season to end up by embarrassing ourselves."

If there is an *i* to be dotted or a *t* to be crossed, Johnny Oates will make certain they are.

Hargrove was angry. He felt his team had let down after Friday night, that it somehow felt it had done enough. He let the players know he expected them to play until the last out—whenever it came. The next morning, sitting in his office, Hargrove heard rap music blasting from the middle of the clubhouse. He walked out, turned it down, and looked around the room. There was silence for a moment. Then Hargrove smiled. "Put on some country and you can play it as loud as you want." The tension broke.

Closing day is rarely one of mixed emotions in baseball. The players, coaches, and managers (and media) have been together almost nonstop for seven-and-a-half months; they don't have any real desire to spend as much as ten minutes more together. It isn't that they don't, in most cases, like one another; it's just that the baseball season is an exhausting marathon.

Even the Orioles and Indians, who would finish with the two most improved records in baseball (the Orioles adding twenty-two victories to their '91 total, the Indians nineteen), were ready to pack up for the winter. Their adrenaline would get them to the finish line, then they would head for their homes to collapse and watch the four survivors go at it in the play-offs.

The Orioles really had nothing left to play for. A victory would give them eighty-nine victories, not ninety. Oates planned to pull Cal Ripken, who was finishing with a rush, after he had batted twice. He wanted to give Manny Alexander, the young shortstop, a chance to play a few innings. Ben McDonald, who had been up and down all season, would pitch, hoping to go out on a good note.

For the Indians, though, this was a huge game. Not only would they be playing in front of their biggest home crowd since Opening Day, not only would they be trying to clinch at least a tie for fourth, but Nagy would be going for his eighteenth victory. In a season that had started with so little hope, this was a day that could send the Indians into the winter on a real high.

For eight innings it looked like it would happen. Nagy was brilliant, shutting the Orioles out on four hits going into the ninth. McDonald also pitched well, allowing two runs in the fourth because of some uncharacteristically shoddy fielding, but stopping the Indians from that point on.

The crowd gave Nagy a standing ovation as he walked to the

mound for the ninth. By now, most of them were standing, as much to keep warm as to support the team. The temperature had been 61 degrees at game time, but it had dropped at least 10 degrees since then. The swirling winds off the lake made it seem much colder than that.

Nagy never got an out in the ninth. He gave up singles to Joe Orsulak and Alexander—the latter's first major league hit—and Hargrove decided that was enough. Nagy had thrown 115 pitches on the day and 252 innings on the season. He'd earned a long rest.

Derek Lilliquist was summoned to try to finish the Orioles off. He had been brilliant all year. But not today. Tim Hulett punched a double into the right-field corner; both runners scored, tying the game at 2–2. Now, Nagy couldn't win. A moment later, after two perfect bunts, Hulett scored too, and it was 3–2, Baltimore.

The discouraged fans stared at one another, reminded that this was *still* the Tribe they were watching. Many headed for the warmth of their cars. But the game was far from over. McDonald couldn't hold the lead. The Indians tied the game on a walk, a stolen base, a ground ball, and a wild pitch.

Tied at 3–3, they battled on. Both teams wanted the season over, but neither could end it. Bay walked out of his box in the top of the twelfth and shook his head. Remembering the nineteen-inning epic on Opening Day, he said, "The fans can't say we haven't held their interest from start to finish this season."

The ending, though, was just like the beginning—a maddening loss. The Orioles broke through in the thirteenth. Again, there were no hits involved in the run, just two walks, a wild pitch, and a sacrifice fly—and the season finally ended in the bottom of the inning.

Being Cleveland, however, the ending wasn't routine. With two outs, Baerga smacked his 205th hit to right-center and decided to try to get into scoring position. Orsulak, in what turned out to be his final act as an Oriole, came up throwing, Alexander applied the tag at second, and four hours and one minute after the finale had started, it ended: Baltimore 4, Cleveland 3.

The Yankees had already lost by the time the game was over, so the Indians did finish tied for fourth. Even so, it was a tough loss to take.

Hargrove sat behind his desk one last time and talked about what had been accomplished, rather than what had been lost. "Last weekend, we were getting blown out thirteen–one by the Tigers and I went out late in the game to make a couple of lineup changes," he said. "Jim Joyce was the home plate umpire. As I gave him the changes, he asked me how I was doing. I probably looked real tired. I told him, 'Struggling.'

"He said, 'Well, you shouldn't be. You guys are doing okay. You're one of the best teams in the league right now. No one wants to play you. You've earned everyone's respect.'

"Remembering back to early in the season when I had umpires telling me we were no good or we had no right to yell about calls, that really meant a lot to me. Heck, I remember when I *played* here and [former umpire] Bill Deegan called me out on strikes one night on a pitch that wasn't even close. I said to him, 'Bill, that's not a *strike*.' He followed me back to the dugout and said, 'So what if it wasn't a strike? You guys are playing over your heads, anyway.' That's why Jim saying that really meant something. I'll take that memory home with me this winter."

There was one other thing Hargrove was going to take home with him for the winter. It was a note Tony LaRussa had sent him after the Indians' last game against the A's. It said, "Grover: It really looks like you guys have got things going in the right direction. Keep it up. Good Luck . . . Tony."

The Indians did have it going in the right direction. The question now was simple: Could they keep it up? Their next opener was 184 days away.

PART VI

OCTOBER

36

THE PLAY-OFFS

I n 1969, when Major League Baseball expanded from twenty to twenty-four teams, it was decided that the time had come to also expand postseason play, from two teams to four teams. The two ten-team leagues, grown now to twelve teams apiece, were divided into four six-team divisions.

Some of the geography, as Fay Vincent would point out twenty-three years later, made little sense. Regardless, the creation of the divisions led to the pre–World Series play-offs, known officially as the League Championship Series.

Although the LCS were created for television, they did make sense. To have twenty-four teams play for two postseason spots would eliminate too many teams too quickly each season. But the creation of the LCS did more than just add TV games and September contenders. They put teams that had worked 162 games to become winners under a white-hot, best-of-five (until 1985 when they became best-of-seven) play-off spotlight.

Win one hundred games in the regular season, then lose three in the LCS and it was as if the hundred victories never happened. In the past, winning the regular season meant you were in the World Series. Even if you lost, you were *still* the league champion—and you had at least *been* in the World Series.

Now, two teams that won their regular season races never made it to the Series. "Division champions" doesn't have the same ring as "league champions." And as the play-offs evolved over the years, everyone agreed that there was more pressure—far more pressure— there than in the World Series.

"As a baseball player, you grow up wanting to play in the World Series," says John Smoltz, who would open the 1992 play-offs for the Braves. "No one says to you, 'Hey, someday you're going to pitch in the play-offs.' They say *World Series*. But to get there, you have to win the play-offs. And that's not easy."

The Blue Jays and Pirates could certainly attest to that. Three times in seven years (1985, 1989, 1991) the Jays won the American League East only to come up short in the play-offs. The Pirates had been in two World Series since the start of divisional play (1971 and 1979) and had won both times. But they had been play-off losers six times, including the last two years in a row under Jimmy Leyland.

Their opponents, by contrast, had done quite well in the play-offs. Overall, the A's had been in the play-offs nine times, winning six pennants. Under Tony LaRussa, they were 3-for-3. The Braves were only 1-for-3, but under the current regime they were a perfect 1-for-1, having beaten the Pirates in '91.

There was a bit of extra pressure on the Blue Jays and Pirates as postseason began. Fairly or unfairly, they had been tagged as losers, chokers, teams unable to win the big ones—because of their recent inability to reach the World Series.

"The most unfair thing about the play-offs is that they can wipe out the fact that you've done the hardest thing there is to do in baseball, and that's win over the 162 [games]," LaRussa says. "Best-of-seven, you get a pitcher hot or a batter cold, it can change the whole thing. But over 162, the best team always wins."

That was the nature of sports, however. The A's were still convinced that if they had been in the same division as the Cincinnati Reds in 1990, they would have finished ahead of them in a 162-game season. But that didn't matter. In the best-of-seven World Series, the Reds swept them. They were the better team at that time and that was all that mattered. They were the champs.

Some years, one team comes into the play-offs as a clear favorite, based on their regular-season record. That only adds to the pressure on that team. The best example of this was in 1973 when the Reds, having won 99 games in the regular season, had to play the Mets, who had won the worst division race in history, taking the National League

East with an 82-79 record. Didn't matter. The Mets had better pitching for a short series and won a decisive fifth game to advance to the World Series.

In 1992, there were no overwhelming play-off favorites. Three of the teams had identical records: 96-66. The Braves were two games better at 98-64. It could be argued that in twenty-four years of LCS play, never before had four teams come in so evenly matched and with the pressure on them so evenly divided: The Pirates and Blue Jays were trying to make up for past play-off failures; the Braves made it clear that the only way for their season to be a success was to get back to the World Series and win; and the A's, with all their free agents, knew this was a last go-round. Ron Darling's theory about the A's being like a college team full of seniors rang quite true now.

The play-offs are staggered nowadays so that CBS can show every game nationally—and sell advertising for up to fourteen games. This means that one league will have completed two games before the other one has thrown a pitch. In 1992, the National League began play with the first two games in Atlanta.

By now, most of the Braves were convinced that winning the World Series was their destiny. Their torrid streak in August had put them in command of the National League West race, and even though they were less than impressive during most of September, it was apparent that this was a team that knew how to turn itself on when it needed to.

Manager Bobby Cox was not a man given to lengthy philosophical speeches on the meaning of postseason play or the intangible rewards of playing the game well. His message to his team before Game One with the Pirates was simple: We started in February with a goal—winning the World Series—and the only way to reach that goal is to beat the Pirates. "There wasn't a lot of rah-rah to it," said Tommy Glavine. "It's not like we don't all know what the deal is here."

Normally, Glavine would have pitched the first game. He was the team's twenty-game winner—for a second straight year—and probably would have won a second straight Cy Young Award if a rib injury in August hadn't ruined his last month, turning a 19-3 record into a final 20-8 mark.

Since Glavine had not pitched often or well down the stretch, Cox decided to start Smoltz, then come back with Steve Avery in Game Two before giving the ball to Glavine. His thinking was simple: Smoltz was his strongest pitcher and, if the series went seven games, he was the best person to pitch three times. Avery would pitch the second game because he had totally dominated the Pirates in the '91 play-offs.

In going with a three-man rotation, Cox was passing up the two men who had pitched the best baseball for the Braves during the last six weeks of the season, Charlie Leibrandt and Pete Smith. Smith had gone 7-0 after being recalled from Triple-A in July. Still, Cox felt he had to go with his three studs. If any of them showed weakness, he had now deepened a questionable bullpen by adding his fourth and fifth starters.

Jim Leyland had no such dilemma. He knew only one thing for sure: Doug Drabek would start Game One, Game Four, and Game Seven. The rest of his pitching was a crapshoot. He had decided to give Danny Jackson, the moody, inconsistent lefty, the start in Game Two, then come back with knuckleballer Tim Wakefield in Game Three. Wakefield had been Leyland's savior in August and September, going 8-1. Leyland didn't want to start him in Game Two for two reasons: He was worried that the knuckleball might be tough to catch in the lengthening shadows of late afternoon (the game would start at 3:07) and he thought it better to give him his first postseason start at home.

•

Just as Pittsburgh fans had seen winning the National League East as a given, Atlanta fans saw their team's second straight pennant as a virtual lock. As the play-offs began, none of the wild, joyous fever that had taken over the town in 1991 was evident.

The spontaneous tomahawk-chopping that had been both re- markable and controversial a year earlier was now a tired part of the act. Five minutes before the first pitch, PA announcer Marshall Mann urged the fans to join in doing the chop while the organist played the Seminole War Chant that accompanied it. Dutifully, the fans followed instructions.

What was gone in Atlanta was the innocence. The '91 pennant race, the play-offs, the spine-tingling World Series, had been totally unexpected. The fans had embraced the team unabashedly, loving every second of the unforeseen joyride. Now, inevitably, it was all sort of ho-hum. "Of course the Braves won the division. Of course they'll handle the Pirates. Wake me when the World Series starts" was the prevailing attitude in town.

"It's definitely not the same as it was last year," Pirates vice- president Rick Cerrone said during batting practice. "They're taking it all for granted."

For two games, there was no reason for anyone not to. Drabek was gone in less than five innings in the opener, allowing four runs. Smoltz was as overpowering as Cox had hoped he would be and the Braves cruised, 5–1. The only good news for the Pirates was José Lind's eighth-inning home run, which broke a twenty-nine-inning play-off drought for them against Braves pitching.

By then, most of the crowd was heading for the parking lot. Since CBS did not authorize Smoltz to throw the first pitch until 8:42 Eastern Time it was closing in on midnight by the time Mike Stanton threw the last one, even though the game was not exceptionally long for postseason—three hours.

Throughout the play-offs and the World Series, the lateness of the Eastern starting times would be hotly discussed. Much of America didn't seem all that interested in waiting until midnight for the games to get exciting. As for the next generation of baseball fans, their World Series memories would be limited to player introductions.

The easy victory reconfirmed the Braves' notion that this was not going to be a difficult series. "We're better when we have to win," Glavine said. "That's just the kind of team we are. When we got that big lead, we lost our edge. Now, we're back."

And they were facing Danny Jackson in Game Two. "We can rattle him," Kent Mercker said. "Drabek, you go out a little nervous because he could shut you down. Not Jackson. We can be up like four–nothing after two on him."

That is *exactly* what they were up and Jackson was long gone. The Pirates did finally score some runs but they all came after the Braves built an 8–0 lead. The good news for the Pirates was that Barry Bonds, after another miserable postseason start, did finally get a hit in the second game. By then, however, he was in the middle of another controversy.

Bonds had gone 0-for-3 in the opener, hardly significant unless his play-off history (.156 batting average, zero home runs, and one RBI in forty-five at-bats) was taken into account. This was a man who had disappeared in two straight postseasons. After Game One, Bill Conlin of the *Philadelphia News* referred to Bonds in his column as "Missed October."

On the morning of Game Two, Bonds pulled up at the players' entrance to the ballpark and found Jim Gray and a CBS camera crew waiting for him. Normally, CBS likes to shoot the players and managers as they arrive at the ballpark. They'll ask the visiting team when their bus is scheduled to arrive and post their crews at the players' entrance early (since, nowadays, most players skip the bus and arrive on their own).

What's more, CBS has the right to request any player on either team for a one-on-one interview either before or during batting practice. The unwritten rule, though, is that the network doesn't interview players *before* they're in uniform.

Note the word "unwritten." As soon as Bonds got out of his cab, the TV lights went on. Bonds was caught off guard. Gray asked him

if he was concerned about his postseason slump. "What slump?"
Bonds said angrily. "I'm oh-for-three. That's not a slump."

As he stalked away, Bonds turned back to Gray and said, "You
better not put that shit on the air. I'm warning you."

When Gray reported what had happened to his producer, Ric
LaCivita, the Pirates were contacted and Bonds was offered the
chance to redo the interview on the field. He refused, saying he didn't
want to talk to Gray again. He spent a good portion of batting practice
talking to a horde of print reporters. He then uncorked a throw to the
plate in the second inning that would have embarrassed most Little
Leaguers.

Leyland and the Pirates were upset—by CBS, by Bonds, by their
pitching, by the first two games. Feet up on his desk, cigarette in one
hand, coffee in the other, Leyland was the last man out of the Pittsburgh clubhouse.

"The way we've hit the ball, all three years now, you put too much
pressure on yourself," he said. "The pitchers go out every inning
thinking they have to shut the other guys down or they're in big
trouble. The hitters are tight because they think if they don't drive in
the run right now, there might not be another chance. Even the games
we've won, we've been tight."

He shook his head. "What bothers me about these two games is
we haven't played like the Pirates can play. I'm not saying we beat
Atlanta if we play our best because they've got a hell of a club, but
we're better than this. That crap today with Barry didn't help anything, but the whole two days was discouraging."

The following day, back in Pittsburgh, Cerrone met with LaCivita
about the Bonds incident. The next day a memo was issued to all CBS
personnel to use the Atlanta dugout to get to and from the field while
in Pittsburgh. Before the weekend was over, that wouldn't be very
friendly territory for some of the CBS people either.

•

In Toronto, the big question before Game One was why American
League President Bobby Brown ordered the dome closed. The weather
was perfect, with temperatures in the sixties, and if there was ever a
night to play outdoors, this was it. Brown didn't care. The dome, he
said, would remain closed for any and all home games the Blue Jays
played. So much for atmosphere.

If the fans in Atlanta were taking their team's trip to the World
Series as a given, the fans in Toronto took nothing—except perhaps
impending disaster—as a certainty. But if there was one person they
were pinning their hopes on, it was Jack Morris.

Morris, who was thirty-seven, had signed a contract with the Blue

Jays during the offseason that guaranteed him $12 million—$5.5 million a year for two years and a $1-million buyout if the Blue Jays opted not to keep him around for a third. Pat Gillick signed him for one purpose: to have him around as his centerpiece pitcher in postseason. In all likelihood, Toronto would have won the American League East without Morris.

His 21-6 record was deceiving since his ERA had been well over four. The prevailing wisdom was that old Jack the Gunslinger pitched just well enough to win during the regular season but would turn it up in postseason, just as he'd done a year earlier, when he helped the Twins beat the Blue Jays, then was nothing less than amazing in the World Series.

As Morris left the dugout before Game One to walk to the bullpen to warm up, the entire crowd came to its feet. The ovation grew and grew until Morris finally acknowledged the fans with a wave of his arm. *This* was the game he had been paid all that money to pitch. The fans wanted there to be no doubt in his mind that they were counting on him.

Morris's mystique lasted one inning. In the second, it took the A's three batters to produce three runs. Harold Baines singled, Mark McGwire homered, and Terry Steinbach blasted a hanging 0-2 forkball on a pitch so bad that Morris could do nothing but stand on the mound and grin in amazement as the ball flew out.

SkyDome was silent. The fans were so stunned they didn't even boo. They just sat and looked at each other as if to say, "Will this torture never end?"

Morris settled down after that and the question for the rest of the evening was how long Dave Stewart could hold off the Jays. For Stewart, this start was a form of redemption. All year, as he had struggled, dealt with injuries, and answered questions about whether he would be back in Oakland, he'd said he had one goal: "I want Tony to give me the ball for the first game of the play-offs, not because of what I've done in the past but because I've convinced him I deserve the start."

LaRussa was convinced by Stewart's performance in September, and now his decision was being justified. Inning after inning, he pitched in and out of trouble, staring down the Toronto hitters in every key situation.

He had help on a couple of occasions from his defense, specifically Mike Bordick. All season long, people had doubted Bordick's performance, waiting for him to fold. He never did, finishing the year hitting .300. (LaRussa pulled him from the penultimate game of the season against the Brewers after two straight hits put him right at the .300 mark.)

"I wanted to make sure he finished there," said LaRussa, who hit

.199 during his major league career. "I remember one year I missed hitting .300 in the minors on my last at-bat of the year and it ruined my whole winter."

Bordick wasn't concerned with the winter right now. He was far more concerned with the play-offs. Unlike most ballplayers, who try to convince outsiders that postseason is no big deal, Bordick willingly admitted he was nervous. "My stomach's been churning all day," he said, sitting in the dugout before the game. "Tony told me during the workout yesterday that he was thinking of starting me at shortstop and since then I've had butterflies. I was sure I wouldn't sleep last night but I've got such a bad head cold that I kind of hacked and coughed myself into complete exhaustion.

"I asked Lance [Blankenship] if something was wrong with me because I felt so nervous. He said something would be wrong if I *didn't* feel nervous. That made me feel better."

In the first inning, Bordick and Blankenship turned a double play. In the second, they turned another. In the third, Bordick made a running catch on a Pat Borders pop-up. Finally, in the ninth, he went deep in the hole on a Kelly Gruber ground ball and robbed him with a remarkable play. Blankenship had been right—the butterflies had been a good sign.

By the time Bordick made his play in the ninth, both starting pitchers were gone. Stewart had given up solo homers to Borders and Dave Winfield, but was still clinging to a 3–2 lead in the eighth. But when Winfield doubled with two out, LaRussa went for Jeff Russell to pitch to John Olerud. Russell got to 2-2, watched Olerud foul off two good pitches, then gave up a single to tie the game. Now, SkyDome was a madhouse.

That lasted all of five minutes. Baines hit Morris's second pitch of the ninth into the right-field bullpen and Eckersley came on to finish. The final was 4–3, A's.

Play-off baseball games didn't get much better than this one. Second-guesses abounded: Had Gaston gone too long with Morris? Should LaRussa have brought Eckersley in to face Olerud?

The answer to the latter question wasn't so simple. LaRussa had used Eckersley in the eighth at times during the season; asking him to get four outs rather than three didn't seem that unreasonable. There were easy reasons LaRussa could give for going to Russell—Olerud was 3-for-7 lifetime against Eckersley, for one—but none of them would have been the truth.

LaRussa was worried about Eckersley. He knew the long season had worn him down; he'd seen signs in the final week that Eck was tired. There had been a blown save against Milwaukee the previous Friday—a concern, but not *that* big a deal since the Brewers were fighting for their lives. Two days earlier, though, in a game against Texas, Eck gave up a game-winning single to a twenty-six-year-old journeyman infielder named Jeff Frye.

To LaRussa that was a danger sign. It wasn't that Frye was a terrible player—"Actually the kid is a decent hitter," LaRussa said—it was just that he was the kind of player Eck *always* got out in the clutch. Not *almost* always. *Always*. And this time he hadn't.

LaRussa knew that if Oakland was to win the series, Eckersley would have to pitch the ninth virtually any time his team had the lead. He hadn't wanted to ask for even one extra out from him in the opener. After all, that was one of the reasons the trade had been made for Russell.

The victory was gratifying for the A's, especially for Stewart, who'd spent the better part of two days getting himself angry reading all the stories about Jack Morris, the Master of Postseason. The A's had never lost a play-off game Stewart had started (seven), but all he'd heard about was the indomitable Jack Morris.

"Jack's a fine pitcher," Stewart said, grinning, his high-pitched voice just a little bit higher than usual. "I can see why they thought he would whip me, though. After all, I didn't win twenty-one games this year—with an ERA of four."

Zap! Take that, Jack Morris. LaRussa had no desire to zap anyone, but he was relieved that his team had been as intense as it had been. He had been concerned beforehand that because so much had gone into winning the division, the players might feel satisfied. He'd sent his coaches on a scouting mission Monday to find out what the players were thinking. They came back and told him the intensity was there.

"All I want is for us to go out and give every single thing we've got," he said. "I put it to them in simple terms: no regrets. Walk away when it's over with no regrets and we can live with whatever happens."

He paused for a moment to cough (like Bordick, he had a bad head cold). "You know what I want," he said, finally. "I want to be like [Nick] Faldo and [Andre] Agassi. I want to work so hard to win that when it's done, we all break down and cry."

As it turned out, the next three games would make LaRussa want to cry. The A's could have won all three; they probably should have won two and had an absolute lock on one. They lost them all. In Game Two, trying to take David Cone out of his rhythm, they kept running themselves out of innings. Cone was superb, pitching the way Morris had been expected to. He took a 3–0 lead into the ninth before weakening. Tom Henke finished. The final was 3–1. The A's had chances against Cone, but couldn't break through. A 2–0 lead going to Oakland might have broken the Jays. Instead, Cone and Kelly Gruber were the heroes. Gruber, who had been booed on a regular basis during the last two months of the season, quieted the fans for one night with a two-run homer in the fifth. Ironically, on the night when he should have had the most to say, Gruber had no voice. He stood in front of his locker, sipping orange juice and talking in a whisper about how tough the season had been for him.

Across the way, Morris expressed the feeling about Gruber in the clubhouse better than anyone. "Were we glad to see him hit the homer? Hell yes. We were glad to see him get a *hit.*"

The only person in Toronto who didn't seem uptight was Pat Gillick. He spent most of the afternoon test-driving a Mercedes he was planning to surprise his wife with. Doris Gillick was turning forty-eight and had talked about wanting a Mercedes for years. She had been so nervous about the play-offs that she'd been having trouble sleeping. Her husband, who never lost sleep over the outcome of a baseball game, thought the gift might take her mind off the pressures of post-season.

He was right. Gillick arranged to have the new car parked in his spot. He also arranged to have the scoreboard congratulate her on her *55th* birthday. "That will get her attention," he said, laughing. For Gillick it was a gratifying night: David Cone had come through, Kelly Gruber had finally hit, and, most important, his wife *loved* her present.

Still, the Blue Jays now had to go to Oakland for three games, a daunting notion. When they won a sloppy, error-filled third game 7–6 on Saturday afternoon, to go up 2–1, they breathed a huge sigh of relief. The last two times they had been in the play-offs they had split the first two games and then lost the next three. Now, at the very least, they would take the series back to Toronto. They had counted on winning Game Four with Morris pitching. That meant they had a chance to go up 3–1.

But the next afternoon, Morris was rocked again. He didn't pitch nearly as well as he had in Game One. He was gone early and the A's built a comfortable 6–2 lead behind Bob Welch. But when Welch tired in the eighth and Russell couldn't get anybody out, LaRussa, reluctantly, went to Eckersley. He couldn't afford to wait for the ninth this time around. Gingerly, Eckersley got out of the eighth with the lead down to 6–4. He ended the inning by striking out Ed Sprague.

Eckersley was wound so tight by that point that when he got Sprague, he punched his fist into the air and pointed at Sprague, as if to say, "Gotcha!" This was not unusual for Eckersley, who brings to the mound all sorts of fears and insecurities about failure. The Jays took it personally, though, and said so after the game.

And despite Eck's tough-guy gesture, the game wasn't over.

Devon White opened the ninth with a slicing line drive to left that Rickey Henderson played from a single into a triple. That brought up Roberto Alomar, who was in the process of proving definitively that he is as good as any player in the American League. He took one pitch from Eckersley, then crushed a fastball way over the right-field fence. Amazingly, the game was tied 6–6. The team with no heart had shown as much heart, guts, and will as anyone could ever hope to see.

As soon as the ball came off the bat, Alomar's arms were in the air and everyone in the ballpark was thinking the same thing: Kirk Gibson, 1988. It didn't end the game the way Gibson's home run had, but like Gibson's shot, it was the defining moment of an entire series. For the first time all season, LaRussa had to go get Eckersley during an inning, and there was a sense that Alomar had removed any doubt about the outcome—of the game and the play-off.

The Blue Jays won it in the twelfth and crowed over shooting Eckersley down. Angry words were exchanged between Morris, Eckersley, and LaRussa but they really didn't matter. Eckersley spent an hour answering questions after the game, shouldering all the blame. Almost, it seemed, *wanting* the blame. Eckersley is the ultimate believer in the notion that if the closer accepts the glory he must accept the blame.

The next day, Stewart proved one more time why he is *the* big-game pitcher of his time, tossing a 139-pitch, complete-game masterpiece. Although everyone knew the odds were that Stewart's performance could not, ultimately, save his team, it was extraordinary to watch anyway. Inning after inning he went back to the mound, the green and gold cap tugged low on his head as always, staring his intimidating stare, refusing to give in to what was now a confident, high-riding team.

For six years, Stewart had asked for—demanded—the ball in every big game the A's had faced. Clearly, he was not the same pitcher he'd been during his twenty-win seasons, but his pride in competing hadn't dimmed one bit. If Stewart was never going to pitch another game in an Oakland uniform (he signed with the Blue Jays in December), he was going to leave the fans and his teammates with a memory they could savor for a long time.

"I can't remember a game that was more emotional for *me*," LaRussa said. "We all knew what was involved, what was happening. For Stew to say beforehand, 'I will carry you today,' and then go out and do it, was a remarkable thing to watch."

The A's 6–2 victory sent the series back to Toronto with the Blue Jays leading 3–2. It may have made the folks back in Canada a little nervous, too, given past history. Mike Moore was bombed early in Game Six and Juan Guzmán shut the A's down right from the start. It was 6–0 before the third inning was over and the noise in SkyDome kept building as each inning passed. When it was over, and the Jays had won 9–2, even Gaston shed a few tears. The rest of the evening was like a giant catharsis for the players, the fans, for, it can be argued, an entire country. The Blue Jays were in the World Series—at last. The choker label had been emphatically removed. The indomitable A's had, in the end, been dominated.

For the A's, the pain in defeat was palpable. They had known from the beginning that this was the last hurrah, but they had never thought the finish would come so soon. They had not expected to lose one game because of sloppiness and another because Eck turned human at the worst possible moment. And they certainly had not expected to get blown out when they were playing for their lives.

Moments after the game ended, LaRussa talked to his team one last time. He told them it had been a privilege to work with them all year and reminded them about his spring training request—that they make a total commitment to trying to win. They had done that, he said, and more. As he started to talk about different players and what they had meant to the team, he felt himself fighting not to lose his composure.

The players weren't doing quite as well. A lot of eyes were wet as LaRussa spoke, but no one was having a tougher time than Eckersley. He hadn't pitched again after Game Four, and now the frustration kicked in on him and he broke down.

When he did, a wonderful thing happened. One by one, his team-mates went to him, comforted him, and told him how much he had meant to them—not just the way he won, but the way he competed. They knew that LaRussa was right when he said they wouldn't have been here without him and they wanted to make damn sure he knew that they knew.

Baseball is a big, brawling, often ugly business. The antipathy many fans now feel toward the people in the game is more than justified. But if you wanted to find a team worth caring about in 1992, you could end your search in Oakland. The loss to the Blue Jays was disappointing because the series was winnable. But the A's had done what LaRussa had asked of them all season: They had given every ounce of energy they had.

In doing so, they had accomplished their manager's goal. Every one of them could walk away from the season with no regrets. None.

•

While the Blue Jays were finally getting the A's under control, the Braves seemed to be on their way to an easy victory over the Pirates.

The Pirates did bounce back after their embarrassing performance in Atlanta to win Game Three behind the knuckleballing phenom Tim Wakefield, and Wakefield became an instant national celebrity. The story was irresistible: A journeyman infielder going nowhere begins fooling around with a knuckleball at the age of twenty-five and ends up in the big leagues less than two years later.

Not only does he become the key man in the pitching rotation at the height of the pennant race, he picks the team up in the play-offs just when it looks as if it may get swept. It would have made a great movie script, only no one would believe it. Neither Leyland nor pitching coach Ray Miller had ever seen Wakefield pitch when he came up to the team in late July because he hadn't been invited to their training camp in March.

"You could see right away he had the whole package," Miller said. "First thing you do with a knuckleballer is you try to run him out of the game, send every base runner you get. But this kid is so quick to the plate, they can't run on him."

They couldn't hit him, either. Tommy Glavine pitched well for the Braves, but Wakefield was better. The Pirates won 4–3. "We're still pushing the car to try to get it started," Leyland said. "Our next goal is to get into the backseat."

They lost their footing the next night and the reason was John Smoltz. Only this time, it wasn't Smoltz's pitching as much as his hitting that beat the Pirates. He singled in a run in the second. Then, with the score tied at 3–3 in the sixth, he singled again with two out. He then *stole second* and scored the go-ahead run moments later. The Braves went on to win, 6–4.

The other Atlanta pitchers were thrilled that the team won, but not so thrilled with the method. "He's going to be absolutely impossible," Leibrandt said. "We're going to hear about this forever. We can handle him talking about the pitching, but now we'll have to hear about the hitting."

"Please," Glavine pleaded, "don't even bring it up to him."

The Braves now had a commanding 3–1 lead and appeared poised to move into their second World Series. But there was a bit of a distraction. His name was Deion.

Throughout the latter part of the season, Sanders had negotiated with both the Braves and Falcons about his role with the baseball team should it reach postseason play. During September, he spent his Sundays with the Falcons, which the Braves didn't mind. They were in control of the pennant race and Sanders was only playing a part-time role anyway. But if they were going to use one of their twenty-five postseason roster spots on him, they wanted assurances that he would be there when they needed him. Sanders said he wouldn't miss a game.

"The deal that John [Schuerholz] made was that Deion would be with the team full-time," Stan Kasten said. "To me, full-time means all the time, as in 'there isn't any more time left.' "

Deion didn't quite see it that way. Initially, he had planned to miss the Falcons game in Miami on October 11 because Game Four in Pittsburgh was scheduled to start at four-thirty. But then CBS entered the picture. Because the National League traditionally drew higher ratings than the American League, the network wanted to flip-flop the games, play the American League game in the afternoon and the National League game at night. Major League Baseball, knowing who its lord and master was, agreed to the switch.

That's when the trouble started. Sanders now had a one o'clock football game in Miami and an eight-thirty baseball game in Pittsburgh. If he could charter a plane right after the game Saturday, he could make the Falcons game, fly back to Pittsburgh, and probably make the start of the play-off game.

Of course, he would be exhausted. Of course, if Bobby Cox wanted him in the starting lineup there was no way he could just show up at eight-fifteen for an eight-thirty game. Of course, he was pulling a publicity stunt. And, of course, his shoe company, Nike, and CBS were right there to help him do it.

Nike agreed to put up the money (about $8,000) to charter the plane. CBS added to the hype (as if the stunt *needed* hype with the entire national media focused on the play-offs) by sending Pat O'Brien and a camera crew on the plane with Sanders.

All week, the question of where Sanders would or would not be on Sunday hung in the air. Deion certainly wasn't telling the media (either because he wasn't speaking to them or merely to heighten the suspense). More important, though, he hadn't told the Braves. When Kasten arrived in Pittsburgh on Friday, having missed the first two games because of Yom Kippur ("When my wife heard that Yom Kippur fell during the first two play-off games, she said to me, 'You're the team president, change the schedule,' " Kasten said. "I told her, 'Dear, I probably have less control over that than I do over when Yom Kippur falls.' "), he called Schuerholz and asked him what Deion's status for Sunday was. "I don't know," Schuerholz said. "I can't get an answer out of him."

By two-thirty the next afternoon, the Braves still didn't have an answer. Angrily, Kasten called Sanders's room at the hotel and demanded to know what he was going to do.

"I'm going to Miami," Sanders finally told him.

Kasten exploded, telling Sanders exactly what he thought of that decision. When Sanders told his teammates a little later, most of them just shrugged. He wasn't in the starting lineup and they knew what kind of publicity it would generate. Privately, some expressed disappointment that he would risk not being on the bench for the start of a play-off game after all they had gone through together. But publicly they supported him.

Kasten, Schuerholz, and Cox did not. All three were steaming when they arrived at the ballpark, although they did their best not to blow up in public. "Remember one thing," Kasten said. "We've worked years to get to where we are. This is a team that might be wearing World Series rings right now if not for a baserunning [Lonnie Smith, Game Seven, 1991] mistake. Even if he just pinch-runs in a game, that can be crucial. This isn't fantasy stuff we're talking here, this is reality. John *never* would have made this deal if he thought for a second this kind of thing would happen."

It happened, though. Sanders, the TV lights shining in his eyes, left the ballpark after the Braves' victory and headed straight for the airport. He was in a bad mood, having learned after the game ended that Tim McCarver had blasted him on CBS for his decision to go through with his stunt. Actually, both McCarver and play-by-play man Sean McDonough had been critical of him, but Sanders focused on McCarver.

Ex-players shouldn't be dissing players. Or so Deion thought. Sanders, it should be noted, did not think of TV people as "media." During his many media blackouts, he was almost always available to talk for a camera. He almost made an exception to that rule in his anger at McCarver, threatening briefly not to take O'Brien and crew on their ride to Miami. He rethought that idea quickly, however. Deion was too smart to blow off three or four minutes of free network publicity.

He landed in Miami around 5 A.M., slept a few hours, played the football game, had to have fluids intravenously injected into him afterward, then flew back to Pittsburgh. He arrived on the bench, carrying a cup of coffee, in the bottom of the first inning.

By then, the game was over. The Pirates had bombed Steve Avery for four runs in a third of an inning. Even Bonds finally hit, getting a double in the middle of the rally. Standing on second base, Bonds could be seen screaming, "It's over, it's over."

His slump, that is. Perhaps it had been inevitable that he would hit at some point. Perhaps his late-night session with Leyland the night before had lifted some kind of weight from his shoulders.

While Sanders was heading for the airport, Bonds had gone looking for his manager. Both men knew that the end of their baseball relationship might be less than twenty-four hours away. One more Braves victory and Bonds's Pittsburgh career was over, even though Bonds was now telling people he might take less money to remain in Pittsburgh. Leyland and Bonds knew that wasn't true, that it was just more example of (agent Dennis) Gilbert-speak. Bonds had, so far, refused to acknowledge his play-off slump—not after the first game to Jim Gray, not after the fourth game to anyone else.

But he knew he'd been awful. He was 1-for-11 in the series with all sorts of men left on base. He knew he'd let his teammates down. And, most of all, he knew he'd let Leyland down. Leyland would never put that kind of guilt trip on a player. As LaRussa had done with Eckersley, he would focus on what Bonds had done to get the team to where it was. But Bonds simply had not done the job under pressure, and now, finally, he admitted it. He cried on Leyland's shoulder, a lonely and unhappy young man who perhaps for the first time in a long time had looked around at a room of men he had worked with and lived with and realized he didn't have a single close friend among them.

"I think he's really a little bit scared of what's ahead," Leyland said softly the next night. "He kept saying over and over that he had let everyone down. I told him not to think it. I mean, my heart really went out to the guy. He sees the end here and there's part of him that doesn't want to leave. But he knows he has to and he's hurting because he doesn't want to go out feeling like he didn't do the job."

Leyland and Bonds had never been close. They respected one another but Leyland was as baffled by Bonds's approach to life as everyone else in the clubhouse was. But what Leyland saw in his office that night wasn't the smooth, cocky, kiss-my-butt superstar with more money than he would ever know what to do with, but rather a twenty-eight-year-old kid who was going to have to leave home soon and was frightened by it. Worst of all, the realization was hitting him that, as talented as he was, there would be few tears shed when he said his goodbyes. *That* bothered him more than anything.

After his talk with Bonds, Leyland knew he had to speak to his team before Game Five. "Everything going on around Barry had to affect them," he said. "It started with the CBS thing and never let up. Plus, we were looking at a three–one deficit."

Leyland was short and to the point. "Guys, we're in a deep, deep hole," he said. "But I'll tell you what, there's no group in the world I'd rather be in a hole with."

The Pirates knew he meant that. Leyland isn't capable of saying anything he doesn't mean. They went out and battered Avery, got a brilliant three-hit pitching performance from thirty-five-year-old Bob Walk, and sent the series back to Atlanta. Then they did almost the exact same thing to Glavine—shelling him for eight runs in the second inning, the rally starting with a Bonds home run—and cruising to a 13–4 victory behind Wakefield.

All of a sudden the cocky, stunt-happy Braves found themselves looking at Game Seven against a team that honestly believed it was now destined, some way, somehow, to win the series.

Momentum shifts very quickly in a short series and the Braves, for the first time, were uptight going into the game. Cox took the unusual step of calling a pregame meeting to try to calm everyone down. In the end, it was the often-silent Justice who made the most telling comment: "Just remember no matter what happens that the game is nine innings," he said to his teammates. "Make sure we play until the very last out."

The evening was perfect, the temperature 74, the breeze light and comfortable. But there was little comfort in the stands when the Pirates pushed a run across in the first against Smoltz. In the second, the game was delayed for eleven minutes when plate umpire John McSherry had to leave the game after feeling dizzy and woozy. There was fear for a short while that McSherry, who weighs well over three hundred pounds, might be having a heart attack. Fortunately, that wasn't the case.

While McSherry was taken to the hospital, first-base umpire Randy Marsh went into the locker room to put on his chest protector so he could move behind the plate. Since six umpires are used in postseason, McSherry's absence did not cause a big problem. It just meant there was no umpire down the right-field line. But before the evening was over, Marsh would play a significant role.

In the meantime, Drabek, who'd lost two straight, wasn't overpowering anyone, though he was in control from the start. Through five innings he had a one-hit shutout; the early run was standing up. In the sixth, a double by Jay Bell and a Van Slyke single extended the margin to 2–0.

Finally, in the bottom of the inning, with the cheers of the Atlanta fans beginning to sound like pleas, the Braves rallied. Singles by Mark Lemke, Jeff Treadway (pinch-hitting for Smoltz), and Otis Nixon (a bunt) loaded the bases with no one out. The chop was back in vogue— loudly in vogue.

But Jeff Blauser crushed a line drive right at third baseman Jeff King, who caught the ball and in one step doubled Lemke off the bag. Drabek then got Pendleton on a liner to left. He was out of the inning, the lead was still 2–0, and the fans sat back in stunned silence.

The Pirates had chances to pad the lead in the seventh and eighth. In the seventh, Van Slyke smacked a bases-loaded line drive off Avery, but the ball was hit right at Nixon in center field. In the eighth, Bonds singled leading off and was forced at second by Orlando Merced. Then came a crucial play: King slammed a double into the right-field corner. Third-base coach Rich Donnelly, desperately wanting the third run, waved Merced in. Justice's arm is strong, but often erratic. This time it was strong and accurate and Merced was out by ten feet. The margin was still 2–0. Drabek got the side in order in the eighth and the Pirates didn't score in the ninth.

By now, Drabek's pitch count was approaching 120 but Leyland wasn't about to take him out with one inning left. If he had a closer like Eckersley, it might have been different. But what he had was a bullpen full of question marks. So Drabek went out for the ninth with everyone in the Pittsburgh dugout holding their breath.

Their breath got shorter when Pendleton, who had slumped throughout the series, opened the inning with a double into the right-field corner. Leyland had the bullpen working now, but he wasn't ready to go and get Drabek yet. His faith was justified when Justice hit a ground ball to second baseman José (Chico) Lind. It was a backhand play, not routine, but certainly not something Lind, who would win the National League Gold Glove, should have had trouble with.

This time, though, he did. The ball glanced off his glove and everyone was safe. It was only Lind's sixth error of the season. Now, Drabek really was done. He threw four pitches to Sid Bream, none of them close. The walk loaded the bases with no one out. Drabek had thrown 129 pitches. Leyland had no choice now. He waved Stan Belinda into the game.

Belinda was the closest thing Leyland had to a closer. Born and raised in Pennsylvania, he was twenty-six, right-handed, and had spent his entire professional career in the Pittsburgh organization. He had saved eighteen games during the season but had also blown six saves. At his best, he was about as good as anyone in the game. But often as not, he wasn't at his best. That was why Leyland wasn't always certain about using him.

It didn't take Belinda long to justify Leyland's fears. Ron Gant, who had done little throughout the series, crushed a fastball that looked as if it were going out of the ballpark for a game-ending grand slam. But the ball died on the warning track and Bonds caught it with his back against the fence. Pendleton tagged up and scored to make it 2–1. Justice, taking no chances with Bonds's arm, stayed at second.

One out. Damon Berryhill, who became the Braves' starting catcher in late September, when Greg Olson had his leg broken in a home plate collision, came up. Belinda's first pitch was either just on or just off the outside corner. Randy Marsh called it a ball.

"When you come into a game as a relief pitcher you have to figure out an umpire's strike zone pretty quick," Belinda said later. "You can't afford to not know what a strike is and end up walking a guy. When Randy called that first pitch a ball, it made me uncomfortable. It meant he wasn't giving me any margin for error."

Belinda, still nibbling, fell behind Berryhill 3–1. Almost certain Berryhill would be taking, he threw a fastball that was unquestionably strike two. Marsh called it ball four. The bases were loaded again.

Cox, with no left-handed hitters left on the bench, sent Brian

Hunter up to pinch-hit for Lemke. Francisco Cabrera, the second-string catcher, who had not yet been to bat in the series, came out on deck. Hunter, a power hitter with a big swing, took a huge cut at a Belinda slider and popped it up toward right field. The crowd screeched, thinking the ball might drop, but Lind took a couple of quick steps back and caught it.

Two out. Cabrera walked to the plate. Some fans actually headed for the exits. In their defense, Hunter had, realistically, been the team's last, best chance. Cabrera was four days past his twenty-sixth birthday and had spent the last three seasons shuttling between Triple-A Richmond and Atlanta. He'd been recalled to the Braves on August 31, the last day players could be added to the roster and still be eligible for postseason. Schuerholz and Cox brought him back for two reasons: They wanted a third catcher and Cabrera's was a bat worth having on the bench. The book on him was simple. He was a dead fastball hitter. You got him out with breaking pitches.

Belinda started by throwing him two sliders. The first one was close. Marsh, consistent on the borderline pitches, called it a ball. The second one was way outside. Belinda was now behind 2-0. "You can't walk in the tying run," he said. "You have to make a guy beat you."

With the crowd alive again, Belinda came in with a fastball. Cabrera took a wicked cut and hit the ball hard—but it was foul down the left-field line. In the Pittsburgh dugout everyone sighed with relief. The swing had been a good one. Scary good.

It was 2-1. The scoreboard clock read 11:52 P.M.. A lot of people around the country had gone to bed thinking the Pirates had the game won. Belinda looked in at catcher Mike LaValliere who, somewhat reluctantly, called for another fastball. The pitch headed toward the inside corner but never got there. Cabrera put another good swing on the ball and this time he hit it fair, a screaming line drive to left-center.

There was no doubt it was a hit as soon as it left the bat. Justice scored easily to tie the game. Bream, who hadn't been fast even before his knee surgery, turned third and chugged for the plate, which looked to him as if it was a million miles away. Bonds raced over, scooped the ball, and in one motion uncorked an almost perfect throw to the plate.

Almost perfect.

"I'm five foot eight," LaValliere said later. "I'd say the throw was five feet eight-and-a-half inches off the plate because that's how much I missed him by—a half inch."

LaValliere took the throw, spun and dove at Bream. He did tag him, but not until a split second after Bream's toe hit the plate. Marsh gave the safe signal and, as the stadium exploded, everyone in an Atlanta uniform tried to pile on top of Bream, who was lying flat on his back screaming, "Thank you, God!" at the top of his lungs.

Slowly, not really believing that the game—and their season—was over, the Pirates began leaving the field. Except for Bonds and Van Slyke. The two of them sat frozen on the outfield grass, staring at, but not seeing, the Braves' celebration. With one swing, Cabrera had turned the Braves from certain losers to delirious winners. He made himself a part not only of baseball history but of the presidential election. For weeks after Cabrera's hit, George Bush kept telling supporters to remember that "the game's not over until Cabrera hits." Unfortunately for him, he had Dan Quayle on his bench instead of Francisco Cabrera.

After perhaps five minutes, first Bonds, then Van Slyke walked slowly off the field. Bonds spent almost an hour sitting in the doorway leading to the showers, staring into space. For perhaps the first and only time in his life, Van Slyke was speechless. "Season's over," he said as reporters approached. "I've got nothing left to say."

Although baseball rules say that both clubhouses are to be open immediately after the conclusion of the final game, Leyland asked for some extra time. No one argued.

"I needed a few minutes to be alone with them and tell them to hold their heads up," he said later. "A lot of people thought after two games we were just token participants. I think we proved that wasn't the case. There were a lot of things I wanted to tell the guys, but I knew it was pointless. They weren't going to hear anything anyone said to them for a couple of days."

It took Leyland almost twenty minutes to regain enough composure to walk down the hallway to the interview room. En route, he encountered Cox. The two men hugged. "I can't remember ever feeling so awful for another manager," Cox said. "They didn't deserve what happened. They deserved better."

In the madhouse that was the Braves clubhouse, Stan Kasten, who sat down to watch the ninth inning only because he had given up hope, hugged John Schuerholz.

"Is there any way to feel better than this?" Kasten screamed above the din.

Schuerholz thought about that one for a second. "No," he finally answered. "There's *no* way to feel better than this."

Or to feel worse. Leyland's voice broke a couple of times in the interview room, but he answered all the questions. Then he walked back to his office, slumped in his chair, and dealt with wave after wave of cameras, tape recorders, and notebooks. Every so often his head would drop into his hands and his voice would waver. He would take a deep breath, compose himself, and look up, eyes glistening.

Once, when a couple of reporters walked in and saw Leyland with his head down, they paused, thinking perhaps they should leave.

"Come on in, fellas," Leyland told them with a wave of his hand. "I'm a big boy. Tell me what you need."

It was after one o'clock in the morning by the time Leyland finished answering questions. "It's a long flight home," he said. "Maybe I can do some work on our expansion list." He tried a smile. "You have to turn the page in life, right?" he said. "The thing we have to do now is try to be good again next year."

He looked at his coaches, who were now dressed. "I just wish," he said softly, "it didn't have to hurt quite so much."

·

The A's boarded their charter back to Oakland just as the Pirates and Braves were beginning their seventh game. LaRussa knew that he and Leyland would have to wait at least another year for their fantasy—managing against one another in the World Series—to become reality.

Almost no one sat still during the flight. People were up in the aisles, talking, saying their goodbyes, reminiscing throughout the five-hour trip. "I was glad we had the trip home together," LaRussa said. "To just leave the ballpark and go our separate ways wouldn't have felt right."

LaRussa was up a lot himself, not simply talking to people, but checking with Carl Young, one of the team's television producers, on the progress of the National League game. Young had a tiny Watchman sitting on his lap.

"The picture kept going in and out," said LaRussa, who was hoping Leyland would make it to the Series even without him. "But we knew what was going on, that the Pirates were ahead. When it got to be the ninth, we went back to watch."

LaRussa and his coaches were looking over Young's shoulder as Pendleton doubled to lead off. Then they lost the picture again. LaRussa paced. The picture came back. The bases were loaded. Oh no, LaRussa thought, this can't happen. The picture flickered out again. More pacing. Then Young thought he heard Sean McDonough say there were two out and the Pirates were still up 2–1. Two out, LaRussa thought. One out left for Leyland. The picture was gone again. LaRussa wondered who was pitching, who was hitting for the Braves. He tried to picture Leyland in the dugout and his stomach began to knot up as if he were managing the game himself.

Young had more news: The Braves had tied it on a sacrifice fly. But that was impossible. There had been two out. Young couldn't hear well enough to be certain what was going on. LaRussa went back and sat down. His mind raced. If the Braves had tied it, the stadium would be going wild. Winning in extra innings on the road was always tough, but the Braves' one real weakness was their bullpen. Maybe the Pirates could scratch out a run and hang on. Fifteen minutes passed. LaRussa got up again. Five more minutes went by. Finally, Young got just enough of a picture to figure out who had won the game.

"Tony, I don't know exactly what happened," he said finally. "But the Braves won."

LaRussa felt a little bit sick. He sat down again. Had there really been two out? Had Leyland been that close to the World Series and not gotten there?

It was after midnight when the plane finally landed. Everyone said their goodbyes. The airport was closed down so LaRussa got in his car, still not knowing what had taken place in Atlanta. He pulled into a Shell station, hoping he would find an early newspaper with the details. The first editions had just arrived. LaRussa grabbed one off the stack and opened it. He read the description of the ninth inning and finally walked back to his car. He almost felt worse for his friend than he had for himself a few hours earlier in Toronto.

"Reading it, I put myself in Jim's place," he said. "And it broke my heart. If anyone has ever deserved to manage in the World Series, it's Jim. Players win the games, we all know that, but no one does a better job than Jim. He did everything he could to get there and then it doesn't quite happen. The killer, to me anyway, was that they *get* Hunter, the guy you're really scared of, and then *Cabrera* beats them."

Normally, LaRussa would have called Leyland the next morning to commiserate. But he waited five days. "There was nothing I could say and I knew it. There was nothing that was going to comfort him."

When he did call, he still didn't have anything brilliant to say. But it was okay. Leyland talked. LaRussa asked questions. And then, after a while, the two friends began wondering about what their teams would be like in 1993.

37

THE WORLD SERIES

Whenever the play-offs end dramatically, there is always a feeling of anticlimax as the World Series begins. Regardless of how they got there, the two teams have now reached a stage where no one could or would tag them with a loser label, no matter what the outcome. In the case of the Braves, who had looked right down the barrel at their mortality and survived, there was a strong sense that no one was going to come between them and a world championship. The city of Atlanta spent most of two days partying in the aftermath of Cabrera's hit, the overwhelming feeling of relief and joy sullied only by one person: Deion Sanders.

While the rest of his teammates hugged and wept and doused each other in celebration, Sanders was busy seeking revenge. He was still angry at Tim McCarver over McCarver's on-air comments about Sanders's two-games-in-one-day stunt. Deion was also upset with Terence Moore, who had once again been critical of him in print. During batting practice before Game Seven, Sanders had actually lobbed a baseball at Moore, who stood with his back turned talking to Brian Hunter. The ball narrowly missed conking Moore on the head and also just missed several other people standing in the vicinity. Sanders was about to take a second shot at nailing Moore when Justice dragged him away.

With the Braves having just pulled one of the most dramatic comebacks in history, Sanders was thinking not about the sweetness of the moment, but about being dissed by McCarver. So he found a bucket, filled it to the top with ice water, and while McCarver was still standing on the CBS platform finishing postgame interviews, Sanders doused him. Then, he doused him again. Finally, after McCarver walked off the platform and strode toward Sanders to confront him, Sanders nailed him one more time, hurling the water in his face.

"You're a real man, Deion," McCarver shouted as Sanders scooted away.

The scene was yet another embarrassment for the Braves in the continuing Sanders saga. CBS asked National League President Bill White to look into the incident, which he did. White eventually announced that Sanders would be fined the huge sum of one thousand dollars. If Sanders had gotten a gun and shot McCarver, who knows what White would have done. He might have fined him *two* thousand dollars.

While everyone in Atlanta was watching the tape of the McCarver dousing over and over on Thursday and Friday, the big question in town was the left arm of Tommy Glavine. Cox had announced that Glavine would start Game One of the World Series. Smoltz and Avery had both pitched on Wednesday and Glavine had only thrown thirty-six pitches in his brief stint on Tuesday. Nonetheless, there were some who wondered if Cox shouldn't bring Avery back—he'd only pitched two innings in relief in Game Seven—or perhaps use Leibrandt or Pete Smith.

Glavine heard all the talk and smoldered. He wondered if everyone in Atlanta had forgotten the forty games he'd won in the last two seasons. Yes, he had pitched poorly in Game Six. There were no excuses for that performance—Glavine is not an excuse-maker.

"If you accept the glory that comes with success," he said, "you have to accept the criticism that comes with failure. You can't hide from it."

History said that Glavine would not only not hide, he would come back and pitch well. "He's as tough and competitive a kid as I've ever dealt with," pitching coach Leo Mazzone said. "With Tommy Glavine, payback is a bitch."

Mazzone spent an hour with Glavine on Friday, showing him tapes of his mechanics when he was going well and tapes of his mechanics the previous Tuesday when he'd been shelled. There looked to be no difference. Then Mazzone spent a long time talking to Glavine about being himself, not overthrowing.

Glavine went home Friday, spent most of the evening playing Nintendo with his nine-year-old nephew, and woke up on Saturday feeling good. He sat down to read the papers but his sister grabbed them out of his hands. "Don't waste your time," she said. "You'll only make yourself angry."

Glavine didn't argue. He got to the ballpark early and sat quietly watching his teammates go through their pregame rituals. At one point, Terry Pendleton, the captain and leader of the team, walked over to say something to him. "I was going to tell him we all knew he was going to go out and pitch well," Pendleton said. "But I took one look at him and realized I didn't need to say anything."

Jack Morris would pitch the opener for the Blue Jays, just as he had pitched Game One for the Twins a year ago. The Braves expected him to bounce back from his poor performance in the play-offs and give them a tough time.

Before the first game of the Series, there are always logistical problems. These are usually caused by the minor differences that exist in structure between the two leagues. This time, the person with the biggest headache was John Holland, the visiting clubhouse manager in Atlanta.

In the National League, when teams go on the road, they take their own pine tar and their own lineup cards with them. In the American League, pine tar and lineup cards are provided by the visiting clubhouse man. The Blue Jays had never been in the World Series before. They arrived expecting to find both pine tar and lineup cards waiting for them.

They weren't. Holland was able to scramble around and find some extra pine tar. The lineup cards, which had to carry the club's official logo, were another problem altogether. Finally, somewhere in the bottom of a desk, Holland found some yellowing lineup cards marked "Toronto Blue Jays 1978" on them.

"How they got there or why they were there I have no idea," he said. He crossed out the 1978 and presented them to Cito Gaston. The first crisis of the World Series had been averted.

The first run of the Series came shortly thereafter when Joe Carter led off the fourth inning with a home run deep to left field off Glavine. Morris, meanwhile, continued his mastery over the Braves for five innings. But in the sixth, he weakened. Justice walked, Bream singled, then Morris hung a forkball to Damon Berryhill, who hit it over the right-field fence.

Glavine was never in trouble after that. After Carter's home run, the Jays had only one more base runner—Pat Borders, on an eighth-inning single—and he was quickly wiped out by a double play. Glavine ended up with a complete-game, 126-pitch four-hitter. He had silenced the doubters.

"We were all pretty pissed off by what people were saying and writing about Tommy," Smoltz said. "We give each other a hard time, but when you get down to it, you mess with one of us, you're messing with all of us."

Glavine, who rarely admits publicly that anything bothers him, admitted he had been upset by all the talk. "You would have thought these last couple of days that the only game I'd ever pitched was the one on Tuesday," he said. "It was aggravating. One bad game and you stink."

At the other end of the hall, the Blue Jays were calmly talking about their one bad game. They had lost Game One—at home—to the A's, so this loss was hardly going to panic them. If there was concern it was over Morris's continuing struggles. Now, it would again be up to Cone to come up big.

The ex-Met didn't appear up to the task. From the beginning of Game Two, he was in trouble. The Braves had figured out that Pat Borders couldn't throw their base runners out and they were running amok on the basepaths. They stole four bases in the first five innings. Two of the steals were by Sanders, given a start by Cox because he'd hit Cone well in the past. The hunch proved correct. Sanders walked and stole second in the third, then singled and scored in the fifth. By the end of that inning, Cone was gone and Smoltz had a 4–2 lead. The Blue Jays got a run in the eighth to make it 4–3, but Cox brought Jeff Reardon in with men on first and second and two out and he struck out Kelly Gruber looking.

Reardon was not the pitcher Schuerholz and Cox had wanted at the end of August, but he'd pitched well in September and the play-offs. Four outs from a 2–0 lead, he was the man Cox wanted in the game. When he struck Gruber out, Reardon got a standing ovation from the crowd.

In the ninth, Cito Gaston did something he very rarely did: He went to his bench. Gaston had used pinch-hitters less than any manager in the game during the season—a total of fifty-five times. Now, he had no choice. With one out, he sent rookie Derek Bell up for shortstop Manuel Lee. On 2-2, Reardon looked like he had Bell struck out, but home plate umpire Mike Reilly called the pitch a ball. On the next pitch, Bell walked.

That brought up another pinch-hitter, Ed Sprague, hitting for pitcher Duane Ward. Sprague was a twenty-five-year-old rookie catcher who had two claims to fame at that moment: He was married to Kristen Babb-Sprague, who had won an Olympic gold medal in synchronized swimming in July; and it had been his strikeout in Game Four of the ALCS that caused the Eckersley "gotcha" controversy.

In the clubhouse, Smoltz shook his head nervously when he saw

Sprague coming up. The two of them had played Junior Olympic baseball together and Smoltz remembered how strong Sprague had been. "He was just about as big then [six feet two, 215 pounds] as he is now," Smoltz said later. "I was talking to him around the batting cage before the game and I remember telling myself that if I had to pitch to him I better not throw him a fastball. He always crushed fastballs. I was hoping that Jeff wouldn't try to sneak one by him to get ahead."

That is exactly what Reardon did. And, as Smoltz feared, Sprague made himself considerably more famous. He turned on the ball, getting every bit of his 215 pounds into it, and it was gone from the moment it came off the bat. Reardon stood stockstill, completely shocked. The Jays led for the first time in the Series, 5–4.

Now it was Gaston's turn to go to his closer, Tom Henke. In a harbinger of things to come, Henke struggled through the ninth. He walked Lonnie Smith with one out and—naturally—pinch-runner Ron Gant stole second. Then, with two gone, Henke walked Sanders. The crowd sensed another Cabrera-comeback as Pendleton came up. They all stood, led by Mrs. Ted Turner—a.k.a. Jane Fonda—who also prayed to the heavens for a hit.

Maybe God doesn't approve of exercise videos. Pendleton popped the first pitch to Gruber, who did his own version of the chop after making the catch as the Blue Jays put the second game in their pocket.

•

Game Two had the first real controversy of the Series—the bungling of the colors presentation during the national anthem by a U.S. Marine Corps detachment from nearby Fort McPherson. Somehow, the marine assigned to carry the Canadian flag got it upside down.

It was a silly, careless mistake but it certainly wasn't anyone's intention, least of all the young marine's, to insult Canada. But as soon as Major League Baseball realized what had happened and what the reaction was bound to be in Canada, damage control began. Rich Levin, baseball's spokesperson, read a release over the press box PA in the second inning in which baseball apologized to the people of Canada for the gaffe. Two innings later, another announcement had to be made. The release had blamed the U.S. Army for the foulup. The Army had called to make certain everyone knew it was the Marine Corps that had caused the problem, not them.

Baseball's most immediate concern was how the incident might affect the crowd in SkyDome for Game Three on Tuesday night. There was already a feeling among Canadians that they were unwelcome guests at the premier event of the national game of the United States.

They knew that CBS was unhappy with the Blue Jays' presence and assumed that most Americans didn't want a Canadian team in the World Series, even if not a single Blue Jay was Canadian-born.

Most Americans had no problem with the notion. The Blue Jays had earned their victory, had an outstanding organization, and played in one of the game's best facilities. Why shouldn't they be in the World Series? Even so, there were some signs of the silly jingoism that has afflicted sports in this country ever since the U.S. hockey team's upset of the Soviets in Lake Placid in 1980. There are some people who want to turn every sports event into Us vs. Them.

Before the first two games in Atlanta, there were a few bozos handing out miniature American flags to people walking into the stadium. The *Atlanta Journal-Constitution* had an embarrassing headline the morning of the first game that read: IT'S OUR GAME. And a few jerks tried to start a "USA" chant during the game. Most of the crowd ignored them.

But the flag flap brought all of these simmering feelings to the surface. By the time the teams arrived in Toronto, T-shirts with up-side-down American flags were on sale. The papers were full of commentary about what had happened. And Major League Baseball officials were genuinely concerned that "The Star Spangled Banner" would be booed when it was played before the start of Game Three.

It was Rich Levin who came up with the idea to give the marines another shot at carrying the flag. A Marine Corps contingent from Buffalo was scheduled to carry the American flag before Game Three. A group of Royal Canadian Mounted Police would carry the Canadian flag. What if, Levin wondered, they could switch flags? A call was made to the Marine Commandant Gen. Carl E. Mundy, Jr. His initial reaction was straightforward: absolutely not. But the baseball people kept pushing Mundy, explaining that this might be the one way to put the embarrassment the marines had suffered behind them. By mid-afternoon Mundy was convinced that *he* had come up with this wonderful idea.

There were still logistical problems: Clearance had to be obtained to allow members of a foreign country's armed forces to carry the Canadian flag on Canadian soil. An entire day's worth of phone calls and meetings finally paid off before the game when, as the crowd was preparing to stand for the national anthems, public address announcer Murray Eldon asked for everyone's attention.

Eldon made reference to the incident prior to Game Two and then said, "The commandant of the United States Marine Corps has apologized for this incident and the marines have requested the privilege of once again carrying the flag of Canada. We ask your courtesy while the anthems of both these great countries are played."

Just like that, the whole thing had been defused. The key phrase was "The marines have requested the *privilege* of once again carrying the flag of Canada." As soon as those words were spoken, the entire crowd roared. They reacted warmly as "The Star Spangled Banner" was played; when Anne Murray, who had been the anthem singer at the Blue Jays' first home game in 1977, sang "O Canada," everyone in the building sang it with her.

As a bonus, everyone got to watch an extraordinary baseball game. This time, no one argued with the dome's being closed. It was 36 degrees, windy and rainy outside when Juan Guzmán threw the first pitch. Guzmán and Avery proceeded to hook up in a classic pitchers' duel, backed by some remarkable defense.

The play of the night—of the Series, the year, perhaps the decade—took place in the fourth inning with the game still scoreless. Sanders and Pendleton started the inning with singles. Justice then slammed a drive deep toward left-center. Devon White, as quick off the mark as any outfielder in the game, turned his back on the plate and raced full-speed at the wall as if he intended to run through it. At the last possible second, White launched himself at the ball, stretched his glove as far as he could, and just as he slammed into the padded wall, made the catch.

He bounced off the wall, whirled, and threw the ball back to the infield. Pendleton, as smart a base runner as there is in the game, was so certain the ball was going to drop for extra bases that he was running with his head down in order to make sure he scored. It wasn't until he had run *past* Sanders that he realized his mistake.

Shocked, he spun around and headed back to first—he was already well past second—but it was too late. Once he passed Sanders, he was automatically out. Taking the throw from White, Robby Alomar turned and threw to first, not knowing that Pendleton was already out. Seeing the unnecessary throw, Sanders, who by now had gone back to second and tagged up, took off for third. John Olerud grabbed the throw from Alomar and threw quickly to Kelly Gruber. Sanders was caught in a rundown. Gruber finally chased him back to second, dove and tagged him on the back of his foot.

A *triple play*! It was the first one in the World Series since 1920 when Bill Wambsganss of the Cleveland Indians pulled one off unassisted.

There was only one problem: Second-base umpire Bob Davidson missed the call. He didn't see Gruber's tag and he called Sanders safe.

The blown call didn't affect the outcome of the game—Guzmán struck out Lonnie Smith to end the inning—and fortunately it didn't alter the fact that White had made a catch that was immediately compared to Willie Mays's brilliant catch off Vic Wertz in the 1954 World Series.

Davidson's missed call, though, once again raised the issue of umpire selection during postseason. Technically, umpires were supposed to be selected based on merit. But that never happened. The umpiring supervisors made certain that every umpire got his shot at the extra pay and prestige every few years; that meant the crew working the World Series did not consist, by any stretch of the imagination, of the best six umpires in the game.

"If you had the same guys working every year you'd have morale problems," American League supervisor Marty Springstead said.

Perhaps. But you'd also have better games and you might give the weaker umpires more incentive to improve. As it was, umpires considered it more a right than a privilege to be selected.

To his credit, Davidson conceded his mistake the next day after looking at replays and a front-page picture in the *Toronto Sun* that showed Gruber making the tag. To his *dis*credit, Mike Reilly, who in Game Two blatantly blew a call on Alomar at the plate, continued to insist that Alomar had been out. Without question, Alomar was as safe as Sanders was out.

Guzmán and Avery battled into the eighth, tied at 1–1. Gruber made an error on a Nixon grounder in the top of the inning that allowed the Braves to go up by a run, but just as the boo-birds were warming up, he led off the bottom of the inning with a game-tying homer. That set up the bottom of the ninth. Alomar led off with a single, then stole second. Bobby Cox had Joe Carter walked intentionally, then Cito Gaston made a bold move, ordering Dave Winfield to bunt.

Any time you ask a man with more than four hundred career homers to bunt, you set yourself up to be second-guessed. As a rule, most power hitters are terrible bunters (mostly because they're never asked to put one down in a real game). But Winfield is not most players. One of the reasons he became the first forty-year-old to drive in a hundred runs was his work ethic. In the batting cage before a game, he is all business on every swing. Joking around is for later; BP is work time. When it's time to lay down his BP bunt, Winfield concentrates and makes sure he lays it down.

"Every time I do it, I turn around and say, 'This isn't what they're paying me for,' " he says. "I'm not paid to bunt or take. But I make sure I get my bunt down every night."

So when Gaston walked over to him in the dugout and told him he wanted him to bunt if Carter was walked, Winfield wasn't shocked or insulted or frightened. He laid down a perfect bunt and Alomar moved to third with the winning run, Carter to second.

Cox now brought in lefty Mike Stanton to face Olerud. Gaston immediately countered with Sunday's hero, Ed Sprague. Cox had expected that move. He had Stanton walk Sprague to load the bases, then brought in the right-handed Reardon to face the right-handed Candy Maldonado.

As soon as Reardon popped through the door in the right-field fence, the crowd was on its feet, giving him a mock ovation for throwing the home-run pitch to Sprague on Sunday. For Reardon, a proud man who had become the all-time save leader in baseball history earlier in the year, this was a tough time and an even tougher situation. He had to get a strikeout, a pop-up, or a double-play ground ball from Maldonado to keep his team in the game.

Quickly, he threw two good sliders to get ahead 0-2. Then he made a mistake. Trying to throw a third slider, he got the ball too far inside. Maldonado, looking breaking pitch, poked the ball to center over the drawn-in outfield. Alomar scored. The game was over.

"He had made me look bad on two straight sliders, I figured he'd throw another one," Maldonado said. "I was surprised he let the ball get that close to the plate."

After the melodrama of the third game, the next two games were almost anticlimactic. The Blue Jays won a taut fourth game, 2–1, as Jimmy Key outpitched Glavine. The game brought back memories of the blissful old days—it only took two hours and twenty-one minutes.

The Jays led the Series 3–1 and the Braves were sniping at one another. Justice, after refusing to talk to anyone after Game Four, went on an Atlanta radio station the next morning and ripped his teammates, accusing the bench of having been "as dead as during a spring training game" the previous night. Cox called a team meeting to calm the waters but the Braves certainly looked like they were done.

And they might have been, if not for Jack Morris. Given one last chance to redeem himself and be a postseason hero, *again,* Morris was blitzed one more time. He and an exhausted Smoltz wheezed into the fifth inning tied at 2–2. SkyDome was rocking on every pitch in anticipation of the celebration that was to come. The parade route for the next day had already been announced publicly.

But Morris never made it through the fifth. He got the first two men out, then Nixon singled and stole second. Sanders drove him in with a single to make it 3–2. Pendleton doubled for the second time in the game and Justice was walked intentionally to load the bases. Gaston had his bullpen ready, a bullpen that hadn't given up a run throughout the Series. But he stuck with Morris. That proved to be a fatal mistake. Lonnie Smith, the baserunning goat of 1991's Game Seven, redeemed himself to some degree by hitting a 1-2 pitch over the right-field fence for a grand slam. The Braves led 7–2.

Forget the parade route. The only ride the Jays would be taking on Friday would be a plane ride back to Atlanta.

"We had Smoltz on the ropes," Pat Gillick said with a sigh. "If we could have stayed in the game, I'm sure we would have gotten to him."

They didn't, though. Jack Morris's postseason was done. He had

started four games and pitched to an ERA of 8.26. The Blue Jays still
led 3–2. But history was against them. The last five teams leading 3–2
that had gone back to the other team's park ended up losing the Series
in seven games. Back in Atlanta, the choppers were warming up for
one last raucous weekend. And, most ominously for the Blue Jays,
through five games of the Series, Francisco Cabrera still hadn't hit.

•

As the Blue Jays took batting practice before Game Six, the PA system
pumped out all sorts of slow love songs and opera selections. This was
in response to the Muzak that the Braves were forced to listen to
during their BP sessions in Toronto. Braves PR assistant Glen Serra
had suggested bagging the usual upbeat rock-and-roll while the Jays
were hitting and John Schuerholz had gone along with the suggestion.

One person who didn't seem to mind was Pat Gillick. "I think this
is great," he said. "Isn't that Pavarotti?" It was Pavarotti, who had
been preceded by Mario Lanza's version of "Over the Rainbow."

Gillick, an opera buff, approved of the new selections. Most of the
Blue Jays laughed it off. David Cone was too busy hitting home runs
and pointing them out to people to notice the music.

"Did you see where that one landed?" Cone said to *Newsday*'s
Tom Verducci, an old friend from New York, after pumping one over
the right-field fence. "I think I may take one deep tonight."

The Blue Jays were far more concerned about Cone *not* being
taken deep than any hitting he might do himself. In the eight weeks
since he'd been acquired from the Mets, Cone had pitched very well.
After a horrid first outing against the Brewers, he had won four games
during the stretch drive, including two 1–0 gems. He pitched superbly
in his first outing in the play-offs against the A's, but had been
knocked out early in play-off Game Five, then again in Game Two of
the Series. Now, he was being asked to close things out in a hostile
ballpark.

"I love the idea of pitching this game," he said. "I still remember
Al Harazin saying to me the morning of the trade, 'I think I just traded
you into the World Series.' I want to make the most of this."

For Cone, the eight weeks since the trade had been fairly rocky.
Once the initial shock wore off, he found himself in Toronto surrounded by a group of people in strange uniforms, most of whom he
didn't know. He'd left his Manhattan apartment behind and lived in
the SkyDome Hotel. His room was not one of those overlooking the
field. Instead, he found himself staring at railroad tracks each night.

"It was very lonely and depressing," he said. "I really felt all alone
in the world for quite a while. It wasn't that the guys on the team
weren't good guys, they were, and they really made me feel a part of

things right from the beginning. But I spent a lot of time staring at those railroad tracks feeling like I was some kind of drifter. It was as if my roots had been cut out from under me.

"There were moments when I cried, moments when I was sad to a point beyond crying. The only thing that kept me going was the baseball."

Cone was trying to end the baseball and move on with his life. (And, as it turned out, go back to Kansas City, his hometown, for 1993.) He knew he was a hired gun in Toronto and he wanted to do the job he was being paid to do. The home runs in batting practice, at least according to longtime Cone-watcher Verducci, were a good sign. "It means he's loose," he said. "With David, it's all mental."

His teammates helped loosen Cone a little more when they scored a run in the top of the first. The Braves did tie the game in the third, but Candy Maldonado hit Avery's second pitch in the fourth inning over the left-field fence to make it 2–1. Cone worked in and out of trouble after that, most notably in the fifth, when the Braves put men on second and third with two down and Pendleton at the plate.

A base hit would put them in front. Cone was tired; he'd thrown a lot of pitches and traveled a lot of miles in the eight months since spring training had begun. But he had just enough left. He took a deep breath and threw his favorite pitch—a backdoor slider—which breaks down and away from a left-handed hitter. Thrown correctly, the pitch is almost unhittable. Pendleton didn't hit this one. He swung and missed and the Jays still led.

"That might be the best pitch I threw all season," Cone said later. "For me, it was the most important pitch I threw all year."

Cone got the Braves out in the sixth, then Gaston decided to turn the game over to the bullpen. Cone had thrown 103 pitches and Gaston didn't want to make the same mistake with him that he'd made with Morris in Toronto.

Todd Stottlemyre, who had been superb out of the bullpen throughout postseason, came on in the seventh and retired the first two hitters before Otis Nixon singled. Gaston, who would prove once and for all before the night was over that he could maneuver as well as anybody in the game, brought in lefty David Wells. He did this for two reasons: He thought Cox would pinch-hit for Deion Sanders, who had been the Braves' hottest hitter in the Series, and he thought Wells might hold Nixon a little closer to first than Stottlemyre would.

Gaston was right twice. Ron Gant pinch-hit for Sanders and when Nixon tried to steal second, Borders, sided by that extra step, finally threw out a base runner. The Jays were now six outs away.

An insurance run might have been nice at that point, but, like the Pirates, the Blue Jays couldn't build a cushion. So it was left to the closing tandem of Duane Ward and Tom Henke to protect the one-run lead. Ward did his part in the eighth, helped by a sliding catch on Gant by Old Man Winfield in right field. Henke now had the responsibility of getting the final three outs.

At thirty-four, Tom Henke was one of the wise old heads on the team. He had been the Blue Jays' closer since 1985, the year of their first division title, and like Key and Winfield was destined to move on after the season. A licensed bricklayer, he had been a voice of reason in the Toronto clubhouse for a long time. Stottlemyre was one of many younger players who regularly went to him for advice and counsel,

The Braves, as they had proven many times before, are not a team that dies easily or quickly. Jeff Blauser led off the inning by slapping an 0-2 forkball to left for a base hit. Berryhill laid down a perfect bunt to move him to second, then Henke walked pinch-hitter Lonnie Smith.

Cox looked back into his dugout and signaled for Francisco Cabrera, who had spent most of the Series until this moment warming up pitchers in the bullpen. But the hour was late and the Braves were two outs (rather than one) away from extinction and it was time for Cabrera to hit.

Amazingly, as he settled into the batter's box, the scoreboard clock said it was 11:52 P.M. That was the *exact* same time it had been ten days earlier when Cabrera got his hit against the Pirates.

Henke wasn't going to make the same mistake Belinda had. He worked the count to 2-2 and threw nothing but forkballs. Cabrera kept fouling them off. One, two, then three pitches. Finally, Henke threw one more forkball and Cabrera hit a screaming line drive to left field. Maldonado froze for a split second, then took a step *in*. Finally, he realized his mistake, raced back a couple of quick steps, and threw his glove up just before the ball cleared his head.

Two more inches and the ball would have been rolling to the wall and Cabrera would have been the hero again. Both runs would have scored easily. Instead, there were two out, the runners were still on first and second, and midnight was fast approaching for the Braves.

Up came Otis Nixon. A year earlier, Nixon had watched the World Series on television from a drug-rehabilitation clinic. No one appreciated being able to play more than he did. Batting left-handed against the right-handed Henke, he calmly slapped a soft line drive between Gruber and shortstop Manuel Lee.

As Blauser raced for the plate with the tying run, Maldonado, who has one of the game's stronger arms, charged the ball and came up throwing. But he was so pumped up that he uncorked a wild throw. It sailed way over Borders's head, slamming into the screen behind the plate on a fly. If it had been six inches further to the right, it would have gone into the stands and Lonnie Smith, running behind Blauser with the winning run, would have scored and the game would have been

over. For a split second, Henke, backing Borders up, thought his team
was done.

"When I saw it was going over my head, I held my breath for a
second because I thought it might be in the seats," Henke said.
"Then, when it did hit the screen, I was so flustered that I kicked it.
Fortunately, when I picked it up, Lonnie was holding up at third."

Few people noticed, but Lonnie Smith may have made one more
World Series baserunning error. If he'd been watching Henke and seen
him kick the ball, he might very well have scored. Instead, he held at
third and the game was tied at 2–2.

The ballpark was complete bedlam. Clearly, the Braves simply
wouldn't lose. Twice now they had been one out from elimination and
twice they had gotten the hit they had to have. Henke somehow
regained his composure and got Gant to fly to center field. The game
went into extra innings.

It was well past midnight but no one was leaving. Both managers
were deep into their bullpens. Cox brought in Leibrandt for the tenth,
Gaston let Henke pitch to one batter—Terry Pendleton—in the bottom
of the inning before bringing in Jimmy Key.

No one scored in the tenth. Then came the eleventh and Charlie
Leibrandt's memorable confrontation with Dave Winfield. "It was one
little hit, that's all," Winfield said later. "But it was the one little hit I've
waited for all my life."

His two-run double put the Blue Jays up 4–2, but even that almost
wasn't enough. Blauser led off the bottom of the eleventh against Key
with another base hit. Berryhill hit a bouncer to shortstop that looked
like a double-play ball until it took a funny hop and bounced off the
glove of Alfredo Griffin, who had come in an inning earlier after Manuel
Lee had been pinch-hit for.

"That was the one moment when I wondered if maybe we just
weren't meant to win the thing," Gillick said. "I mean, after all we had
gone through to get the lead, you see a hop like that and you begin to
think maybe it just isn't meant to be."

A sacrifice moved both runners up. Brian Hunter's twisting
ground ball to first scored Blauser and moved pinch-runner John
Smoltz to third with two out. The most frightened man in the park on
Hunter's grounder was first baseman Joe Carter.

"When the ball came off the bat the first thing I thought was
'Buckner,' " Carter said, referring to another memorable Game Six—
the one in 1986 when Billy Buckner booted Mookie Wilson's ground
ball to lose the game. But Carter didn't boot this one, and for the
second time, the Jays were one out away from a championship. Also
for the second time, Otis Nixon was coming up.

Gaston made one last move. The Blue Jays' scouting reports
showed that Nixon was a little better hitter righty than lefty, even

though his ninth-inning hit had come lefty. So he waved in one more pitcher, righty Mike Timlin. This was, most assuredly, a calculated risk. Timlin had been up and down between Triple-A and the Jays during the season; he'd only pitched one mop-up inning, in Game Five thus far in the Series. But Gaston was convinced he could jam Nixon and give him trouble.

Timlin did just that on the first pitch for strike one. Nixon felt uncomfortable on that pitch, so he decided to gamble and try to surprise the Blue Jays with a bunt. But he didn't surprise them. Gaston and Carter had both warned Timlin to be alert for a possible bunt and he pounced off the mound as soon as Nixon put the ball down.

It still wasn't an easy play. Nixon runs as well as anyone in the game and Timlin had to loft the ball over the outfielder's head as he went down the baseline. But he did it, the ball hitting Carter's glove one step before Nixon crossed the bag. It had taken four hours and seven minutes. The scoreboard clock said it was 12:50 A.M.

The Blue Jays didn't care how long it had taken or what time it was. They were finally champions. They jumped all over one another as the Atlanta fans did the classy thing and applauded them. Then, they gave their team one last chant of "Braves!" before going home to wait for Next Year.

In the clubhouse, the Blue Jays stood around singing their version of the Seminole War Chant. Timlin and Ward jumped on the TV platform and danced with one another. Winfield, eyes wet from champagne and tears, shook his head and said, "Of the ten thousand days I've played the game, this is the most satisfying. I was beginning to think the Braves would just never go away. Holding them back was like trying to hold water back with your hands."

Down the hall, the Braves quietly said their goodbyes to one another, offering words of encouragement to Leibrandt and one another. Little did any of them know that Leibrandt had just pitched his last game as a Brave. He would be traded to Texas in December after the team signed Cy Young Award winner Greg Maddux as a free agent. Maddux would give the Braves a pitching version of Murderer's Row, but it was unlikely Glavine, Smoltz, and Avery would ever feel about him the way they felt about Leibrandt. The club had been broken up. That was baseball in the nineties.

It was just after two o'clock in the morning when Bobby Cox finally walked out of the clubhouse. He paused at the door for a moment and looked around.

"I'm so tired right now, I'm not sure I can even think straight," he said. "It's such a long season when you get this far." He forced a smile. "But I sure would have liked to see it last one more day."

He walked out the door, leaving a completely empty clubhouse behind him. Opening Day was 163 days away.

EPILOGUE: DECEMBER 6, 1992... 7:30 P.M.... LOUISVILLE, KENTUCKY

Everything was in place. The room was jammed with reporters, television cameras, and baseball officials. This was the official coronation of Barry Bonds as the richest player in the history of baseball.

The deal had been leaked two days earlier so everyone knew it was coming. The new ownership of the San Francisco Giants, which had come up with $100 million to keep the team in San Francisco, was going to give Bonds a contract that would pay him $43.75 million over six years. Even in an era of huge salary escalation, this was a staggering sum.

There was more. As part of the deal, the Giants, after consulting with Willie Mays, agreed to let Bonds wear Mays's retired number 24. Mays, who'd been a teammate of Bonds's father, Bobby, was also Barry's godfather. And the Giants' new batting coach would be Bobby Bonds.

The press conference to make it all official had been called for seven-thirty. Everything else at baseball's winter meetings came to a halt as the hour approached. At exactly seven-thirty, Barry Bonds and his entourage swept into the back of the room. Bonds wore a pin-striped gray suit that easily cost a couple of thousand dollars. To him, of course, a couple thousand dollars *was* easy.

Behind him came his agent, Dennis Gilbert, wearing an equally expensive-looking suit, and his henchmen, each of them dressed to the nines for the TV cameras. Someone who worked for a company that sold sunglasses broke through all the various suits and henchmen and handed Bonds a pair of sunglasses. He tried them on, mugged for the cameras that surrounded him, then took them off. "Can't see anything, man," he said.

Bonds glanced around the room, which was filled with desks where the print reporters worked. "Lots of phones in here, huh?" he said to nobody in particular.

Slowly, the entourage moved to the front of the room. Reporters who tried to get close to sneak in a pre–press conference question were fended off by security people and the Gilbert henchmen. Everyone waited. The entourage chatted with one another.

Five minutes went by; then ten. There was no sign of anyone from the new Giants ownership group. Reporters wondered what the hell was going on. Perhaps the group was awaiting a cue from ESPN, which had planned to cut into their regular programming to show the press conference live. No, that wasn't it. ESPN was ready to go.

After fifteen minutes, Jim Small, the public relations director for Major League Baseball, slipped out of the room and called upstairs to the Giants suite. Matt Fischer, his counterpart with the Giants, answered.

"Matt, you've got a room full of people waiting for an announcement," Small said. "Including Barry Bonds."

"Tell them we never called a press conference," Fischer said, hastily. "There's nothing to announce."

Small was stunned. Something had gone very wrong here. He walked back into the room and told Gilbert what Fischer had said. Gilbert asked if there was any way to get out of the room without going all the way back the way they came.

There was—through a kitchen. And so, twenty minutes after strolling into a room to officially become $43.75 million richer, Barry Bonds walked out of that room—through a kitchen—without a cent. He didn't even stop to eat anything.

Small then went back into the room and announced that there would be no announcement. "The Giants say they never called a press conference," he said. "There's nothing to announce."

A roar went up from the room. What in the world had happened? The answer came several hours later. It went something like this:

Although the National League's owners had voted 10–4 against the sale of the Giants to the St. Petersburg group that wanted to pay owner Bob Lurie $115 million in order to move the team to Florida, the official sale to the San Francisco group—for only $100 million—had not yet been approved.

A number of owners, upon hearing how much the new group was planning to pay Bonds, had gone to Lurie and told him how much they disapproved of the contract. They disapproved so much, in fact, that they might vote down *this* sale of the team, too. That could leave Lurie stuck with the Giants *and* Bonds's $43.75 million contract. At the last possible second, he told the new ownership group that it could not announce the deal since he—Lurie—still technically owned the team. But no one had gotten word to Bonds and entourage in time.

At eleven o'clock that night, Gilbert came back to the media room and told several reporters the deal had now been worked out and the group would be down shortly to formally announce it. At 1 A.M. Gilbert and Larry Baer, the Giants' new executive vice-president, came back one more time and said, uh, well, the deal wasn't quite done yet.

That was where it ended that night. The game's best player had been humiliated in public at what should have been his grandest moment. The owner of the Giants, who had been *forced* by his fellow owners to undersell his team by $15 million, was now being told they might not allow him to make a deal *they* had arranged because the owners-to-be had pulled a fast one on them by giving Bonds so much money. Nothing defined the chaos that was baseball quite so well.

Two days later, after new team president Peter Magowan had promised that he, not Lurie, would be liable for Bonds's contract if the sale somehow didn't go through, the Giants at last announced the signing of Barry Bonds. Bonds then announced that, on second thought, he would wear his father's number, 25, rather than Mays's 24.

By then, Bonds had become old news. That was because there was now serious doubt about when he would get to wear his new uniform, regardless of number. Almost twenty-four hours after the fiasco of a non–press conference, Bud Selig, the game's acting commissioner, and Richard Ravitch, the owners' labor negotiator, who was, for all intents and purposes, the real commissioner, walked into the same room.

The owners had met for four hours that afternoon. The discussion centered around whether they should reopen the labor contract with the players now or let the contract run its course through the 1993 season. Baseball's public profile had never been worse. The sport needed a commissioner the public would respect; it needed to get Ravitch and Players Association leader Donald Fehr together to begin a negotiation that would produce a contract before the 1994 season. It needed the owners not to confront the players, but to confront themselves and realize that revenue sharing was an absolute necessity.

It did not need the contract to be reopened. It did not need the

specter of a lockout hanging over the game as it tried to negotiate a
new TV contract. It did not need Ravitch's defensive rhetoric about
how he had been miscast as a union-buster by the media.

But that is exactly what it got. By a vote of 15–13, the owners
voted to reopen the contract. "We need to get started on this," Ravitch
claimed. What he failed to mention was that he could have gotten
started on any day he chose *without* reopening the contract.

"I am not in favor of an employer-initiated work stoppage," Ravitch said, using the code words that meant *lockout*. "We are not
looking for a confrontation with the players."

That isn't what most people believed. "History," Fehr said, "certainly isn't on our side."

He was certainly right about that. The last seven labor negotiations in baseball had resulted in work stoppages. But the owners of
baseball felt they had to reopen. They knew the history. They knew
their TV ratings were down. They knew the consequences of a lockout. They knew that they had tried to break the union before and had
never succeeded. They knew that public opinion had run strongly
against them since they had tossed Vincent out of office in September—at Ravitch's urging—to clear the way for a confrontation with the
players.

"A lot of these guys went home to their country clubs and
churches and were shocked to find that people thought they were nuts
to fire Fay and to be doing what they were doing," Fehr said. "I think
that made a lot of them at least rethink what they're considering. No
battle that is fought just for the sake of winning is worth fighting. But
that's what they're looking at creating here."

Some of the owners had rethought the situation. Their second
thoughts forced the hard-liners to amend their constitution to require
twenty-one votes, rather than fifteen, in order to impose a lockout.
That gave the public some hope, but it did not remove the possible
specter of a spring without baseball.

But that was where baseball stood in anticipation of the '93 season. As players jumped from team to team so fast that even rotisserie-
league nerds had trouble keeping up, while owners who weren't even
owners yet agreed to pay a player $43.75 million, while everyone
agreed that a confrontation that could lead to a lockout would be a
disaster for the entire game, the owners decided to reopen. They
decided to add a black cloud to an already dark sky.

That sky became even darker on February 3, when the owners,
cowed by her high-powered lawyer, let Marge Schott off with a minor
wrist-slap in the wake of her racist, anti-Semitic comments. The owners proudly announced a one-year suspension and a twenty-five-
thousand-dollar fine. But all the suspension really amounted to was a

different seat at the ballpark for Schott—upstairs rather than at field level. Presumably, Schottzie 02 will still have the run of the field—pretty much just like her mistress.

These are the most difficult times baseball has ever faced. Once upon a time, only bad teams were broken up. Now, championship teams split up—routinely. Dave Winfield was a hero in Toronto in October; he will play in Minneapolis in April. A year ago, it was just the opposite: Jack Morris, the hero of Minnesota in '91, migrating to Toronto in '92.

But that is now commonplace. In 1993, Wade Boggs will be a *Yankee*. So will Jimmy Key. Tom Henke will be in Texas. David Cone, who wanted so much to return to New York, will not—he couldn't resist a $9 million signing bonus (that's right, $9 million on the spot for signing his name) offered by the Royals.

But as the millions were tossed around all winter (amid continuing claims of poverty by the owners) and as players switched teams on what seemed like an hourly basis, one signing stood out as a symbol of all that is wrong with the game:

Dave Stewart signed with the Blue Jays.

Dave Stewart, born and raised in Oakland. Dave Stewart, who resurrected his career in Oakland and then helped resurrect the city after the earthquake of 1989. Dave Stewart, who pitched the game of his life to keep his team alive for one more day last October—against the Toronto Blue Jays.

Now, Dave Stewart is a Blue Jay. Something is rotten in Denmark. And in the national pastime.

At least, though, the game's owners did do one thing right. Ravitch and Selig did show up for their press conference right on time. No one was going to catch *them* leaving through a kitchen.

ABOUT THE AUTHOR

Play Ball: The Life and Troubled Times of Major League Baseball is JOHN FEINSTEIN's sixth book and his fifth nonfiction look at the world of sports.

His first book, *A Season on the Brink*, is the best-selling sports book of all time. He is the author of two other college basketball books, *A Season Inside* and *Forever's Team*. His book examining the world of professional tennis, *Hard Courts*, was selected as one of the best sports books of 1991 by *The New York Times* after reaching number four on the newspaper's best-seller list. His first novel, *Running Mates*, a political mystery, was published in 1992.

Mr. Feinstein was born in New York City and graduated from Duke University in 1977. He spent eleven years on staff at *The Washington Post* before working at *Sports Illustrated* and *The National*. Currently he is a regular contributor to *The Washington Post, Inside Sports, The Sporting News, Tennis* magazine, and *Basketball Times*. He is a commentator for National Public Radio and appears on ESPN's *The Sports Reporters*. He also teaches journalism at Duke.

Mr. Feinstein is a past president of the U.S. Basketball Writers Association and the U.S. Tennis Writers Association. He has won twenty U.S. Basketball Writers Awards and has been chosen three times as D.C. sportswriter of the year by the National Sportswriters and Sportscasters Association. He has also won a Golden Gavel Award from the American Bar Association and the Ron Bookman Award from the U.S. Tennis Writers for service to the game.

He and his wife, Mary, live in Bethesda, Maryland, and Shelter Island, New York.